All J

All Joking Aside

American Humor and Its Discontents

REBECCA KREFTING

Johns Hopkins University Press
Baltimore

Johns Hopkins University Press
2715 North Charles Street
Baltimore, Maryland 21218-4363
www.press.jhu.edu

Library of Congress Cataloging-in-Publication Data

Krefting, Rebecca, 1978-
    All joking aside : American humor and its discontents / Rebecca Krefting.
        pages cm
    Includes bibliographical references and index.
    ISBN-13: 978-1-4214-1429-4 (hardcover : alk. paper)
    ISBN-13: 978-1-4214-1430-0 (pbk. : alk. paper)
    ISBN-13: 978-1-4214-1431-7 (electronic)
    ISBN-10: 1-4214-1429-5 (hardcover : alk. paper)
    ISBN-10: 1-4214-1430-9 (pbk. : alk. paper)
    ISBN-10: 1-4214-1431-7 (electronic)
    1. Stand-up comedy—United States.   2. Comedy—History and criticism.
3. Participatory theater.   I. Title.
    PN1969.C65.K74 2014
    792.7'60973—dc23   2013045490

A catalog record for this book is available from the British Library.

*Special discounts are available for bulk purchases of this book. For more information,
please contact Special Sales at 410-516-6936 or specialsales@press.jhu.edu.*

Johns Hopkins University Press uses environmentally friendly book materials,
including recycled text paper that is composed of at least 30 percent post-consumer
waste, whenever possible.

To all the comics that do

CONTENTS

ACKNOWLEDGMENTS

Thanks to the comics and folks in the industry who graciously volunteered hours of their time, enduring interviews, e-mails, and phone calls for years. Special thanks to the comics serving as case studies: Micia Mosely, Robin Tyler, and Hari Kondabolu. You have been exceedingly patient over the past several years as I continued to pepper you with follow-up questions and revisions. A good manuscript only becomes an excellent one under the watchful eyes of a phenomenal editor. I was more than lucky to have landed in the competent hands of Robert J. Brugger, senior editor at Johns Hopkins University Press. Among many other things, you gave me much-needed encouragement and explication throughout the process, not to mention a kick-ass title. This process was made smoother with the assistance of Melissa Solarz, part acquisitions assistant and part magician, who kindly guided me through the valley of the shadow of death. An additional note of thanks goes out to Dr. Helen Myers— fearless copyeditor and kind supporter of the manuscript in its latter stages.

Mary Corbin Sies, my dissertation chair, friend, and adviser, your incisive feedback and comments throughout this process have been invaluable. Given your focus on material culture and candid admission that you are seldom amused, we were certainly an unlikely pair. Thank you for taking a chance on me. My dissertation committee members at the University of Maryland, College Park (UMCP), all informed and shaped this project and process in important ways. Thank you to Nancy Struna, Ronit Eisenbach, Martha Nell Smith, Jeffrey McCune, and Faedra Carpenter. There were many dedicated readers who commented on my work throughout the process and without whom this process may have been untenable: Amelia Wong, Mark Sgambattera, Jill Dolan, Laurie Frederick Meer, Marcus Krefting, Erin Meyers, Nitin Sawhney, Beau Breslin, Greg Pfitzer, Dan Nathan, Tillman Nechtman, and Marla Melito. Students enrolled in courses I have taught on humor at UMCP and Skidmore College have undoubtedly prodded me to think about these ideas in new and valuable ways. Allison Otto, Rebecca Stern, Veronica Monroe, and Jung-Hee Schwartz all have offered fantastic research assistance over the past several years; it has been a pleasure working with each of you in varying capacities.

Visits to the New York Public Library for the Performing Arts, University of Washington, Seattle's Suzzallo Library, the National Women's History Museum in Dallas, Texas, UMCP's Hornbake Nonprint Media Services, and the June Mazer Lesbian Archives in Los Angeles, California, gave me access to dozens and dozens of important comic performances and artifacts. I would be remiss not to offer a big thank you to the accomplished and efficient staff in all these locations. To the publishers at Parlor Press, thank you for granting permission to publish chapter 4: "When Women Perform Charged Humor: The (Gendered) Politics of Consumption." An earlier and rather condensed version of this chapter is published under the title "Laughter in the Final Instance: The Cultural Economy of Humor (or Why Women Aren't Perceived to Be as Funny as Men)" in the edited collection *The Laughing Stalk*, edited by Judith Batalion (2012). I have received incredible support, both financial and moral, from my colleagues and administrators at Skidmore College. From generous start-up funds to faculty writing groups to a faculty-student research collaboration grant, I have never been at an institution that says "yes" more than it says "no," a rarity in this day and age. Let's hope that the same "can do" spirit exists among staff members who decide things at *The Daily Show*. Though there are no hard and fast plans for this (yet), I would like to thank Jon Stewart (in advance) for inviting me to be on his show. I promise not to cuss too much and will even wear makeup. Okay, fine, I'll also throw in a free autographed copy of the book.

I must pay special acknowledgment to my grandmother, Margaret Krefting— a die-hard Freddie Mercury fan whose legacy as lead singer for Queen prompted her to ask that I refer to her as the Queenmum. She not only cracks me up but she was also a faithful reader and fastidious editor as I went through versions of each chapter. I am wildly grateful to the students involved in Comedy Academy programs in Silver Spring, Maryland, with whom I worked for six years while earning my doctorate—you were my teachers as much as I was yours. Deepest gratitude goes to Harry Bagdasian and Robbie McEwen, who championed me throughout, and who are, as it turns out, two of my champions. To Amelia Wong, my soul sister, if this project meets with any success, you are certainly partly to blame. You eviscerated my work and talked me down from many a ledge afterward, epitomizing a perfect blend of honesty and compassion. To my friends, who gave emotional support throughout (you know who you are): thank you. You all are my lifeline, my anchor, and when I am with you I laugh the loudest. A special thanks to Scott Gilmore (who will hate me for thanking him): you gave me moral support and ink when I needed it most . . . je t'aime. Any blame for my preoccupation with comedy can be attributed to my parents, Bob Krefting and Christine Anne, who instilled in me and my three brothers the value of humor and made laughter as important as eating broccoli. Finally, I am deeply grateful for and quite possibly not deserving of the incredible support of my longtime partner and wife, Teresa. Thank you for walking around the earth with me. Let's keep going until our tickers stop. You are my best friend and my muse—when I am with you the world glows.

All Joking Aside

The Laughscape of American Humor

There's a lot of things that people find funny that are really just bullying. When people get bullied, there are people that laugh. And I think that is a lot of comedy. Whenever people come up to me and say I don't really like comedy, but I love what you do, it tells me two things. One is that's someone who has had really bad experiences either with bullying or with going to a comedy club and being made to feel uncomfortable because something is directed toward them.

Hari Kondabolu, "The Feministing Five"

It's just a joke. Come on, I was only joking! Geez, why can't you take a joke? Likely, you have heard this dozens of times. It is a statement most commonly dispensed when the unlucky butt of the joke offers protestations. Some of the most hateful vitriol passes under the guise of joking—someone's truth, but certainly not *the* truth, masquerading as humor. When Kevin Rogers detailed, in a post on Facebook, Tracy Morgan's homophobic tirade at the Ryman Auditorium in Nashville, Tennessee, on June 3, 2011, he publicly called into question what is and is not a joke. In Rogers's estimation, Morgan's worldview felt like an attack against his lifestyle and person. While Rogers understands that comedy can level criticism, he was unprepared for the angry onslaught against queer folks, a segment at the end of the show, which according to his post, ceased to express itself in comedic terms and instead devolved into a string of slurs aimed at the gay community, making him feel intensely uncomfortable.

Comics often use the stage to broadcast worldviews. Tracy Morgan's beliefs about gay people are part of his worldview. The difference between comics Tracy Morgan and Hari Kondabolu, whose statement opens this chapter, is that Kondabolu refuses to use the stage to promote intolerance or bigotry. Ultimately, every comic wants to elicit laughter from an audience, but there are some who give careful consideration to the means by which they achieve that laughter. Humor has always taken aim at its surrounding culture, exposing societal discontent, be it Morgan's antipathy for gays or Kondabolu's open hostility toward bigots of any ilk. All humor locates itself in social and political contexts, but not all humor does so self-consciously or with specific intentions to promote unity and equality or to create a safe and accepting space for people from all walks of life. I take as my jumping off point the Kondabolus performing in the United States—not the Morgans—the comic performers who intentionally produce humor-challenging social inequality and cultural exclusion, what I call "charged humor."

Some jokes are tears in the fabric of our beliefs. They challenge the myths we sustain about how fair and democratic our society is and the behaviors and practices we enact every day to maintain that fiction. In other words, we are all supposed to be equal, but social, economic, and political forces collude to maintain inequality. Jokesters unmask inequality by identifying the legal arrangements and cultural attitudes and beliefs contributing to their subordinated status—joking about it, challenging that which has become normalized and compulsory, and offering new solutions and strategies. For example, Gloria Bigelow, a lesbian African American comic, writes and performs comic material intending to unmask such inconsistencies and remind us that things are not fair or equal for the lesbian, gay, bisexual, transgender, and queer (LGBTQ) community.

> I recently came out at my job, you know. Thank you. Thank you [*applause and whistles*]. Yes, I'm what you call a preemptive gay. I drop big gay bombs whenever I get the chance. "I'm GAY!" [*makes sound of bomb dropping*]. You gotta do it because otherwise if you don't tell heteros that you're gay and they find out [*drops voice to a conspiratorial whisper*] . . . they feel violated [*loud laughter*]. Imagine that. I have no rights, but they feel violated [*laughter and applause*].[1]

Here, she uses her comedy to unveil the heterosexism inherent in the expectation that queers must reveal their sexual orientation to others. While heterosexuals are not expected to make official announcements to friends and family regarding their sexual desires and proclivities, LGBTQ persons are subject to the "coming out" narrative, reifying compulsory heterosexuality, fueling American culture's preoccupation with defining sexual taboos and locating deviance, and assuming the necessity of disclosure so loved ones can cope with this knowledge. The painful reality is that there is threat of ostracism and alienation caused by such a disclosure. Dealing with sexual orientation on a personal level bears its own difficulties, but, as Bigelow demonstrates when she refers to her heterosexual friends who "feel violated" if she does not come "out," one must also contend with familial, social, and cultural backlash about this designation. Importantly, charged humor offers strategies and solutions for combating cultural and legal exclusion. In Gloria Bigelow's joke, dropping "big gay bombs" is one way of increasing gay visibility in the workforce and larger community; it also humanizes political efforts made on behalf of the LGBTQ community and undermines stereotypes. In chapter 1, I further define and explore the characteristics of charged humor, particularly the value and imperative of charged humor as a practice that enacts cultural citizenship.

Stand-up comedy is a mode of performance for which there are many variations and styles. Just one of those many variations, charged humor can work in tandem with other comedic styles and frequently does. The right cocktail of charged comedy and shock humor or charged humor and modern-day minstrelsy can buoy a charged comic seeking mainstream audiences. Since profitable comedy appeals to the largest swath of the American public, and charged humor can have a polarizing effect on audiences, diminishing its widespread appeal, comics may want to consider limiting or omitting profligate use of charged humor when starting out. With some exceptions historically and today, women and men who employ charged humor as a mainstay in their routines struggle to successfully commercialize their comic personae. Comics who throw in a charged zinger here and there have better chances of success than others whose material is charged throughout an entire show. Louis C.K., who happens to be a White heterosexual able-bodied male, has achieved enormous success by most industry standards; however, his use of charged humor, while laudable, is not consistent throughout his shows. The same can be said of Bill Maher, who performs a great deal of political humor but not as much charged humor. In the comedy industry, comics pandering to middle America create "safe" comedy or material, which is typically characterized by apolitical jokes that focus on shared social concerns and experiences without calling into question the terms of their construction or exclusivity. Safe comedy capitalizes on innocuous shared comic frames like Jake Johannsen's feel-good comedy on topics like marriage, fatherhood, aging, taxes, and health.

> In a marriage you gotta learn how to fight . . . guys are not so good at fighting in a marriage at first because we have to learn it, because we learn how to fight from fighting with guys, right? [*pause*] Where you could win [*laughter*]. But in a marriage you don't win, you just get a rematch [*laughter*].[2]

He avoids politicizing content and importantly, his comic persona is a combination of nonthreatening dufus and affable boy-next-door, ensuring widespread appeal of his comedy and clearly the reason why he holds claim to the most number of visits on the *Late Show with David Letterman*. Johannsen is one of many made famous by this style of comedy, including Sinbad, Ellen

DeGeneres, Bill Engvall, Brian Regan, Jim Gaffigan, Paula Poundstone, Frank Caliendo, John Heffron, and Jerry Seinfeld.

While family-friendly comics offend no one, shock comics offend everyone (or at least try to) by projecting personae steeped in the profane, a marketing move much like safe humor that can prove quite lucrative. While having lunch in a restaurant and seated next to a mother whose child runs amuck at a neighboring table, White comic Michael McDonald recounts to his audience that he turned to his lunch-mates and said rather loudly: "Apparently that woman doesn't remember that her abortion is still alive."[3] Formerly playing the recurring role of Stewart on *MadTV*, McDonald laces the comedy special *Michael McDonald: Model Citizen* with controversial and offensive observations and opinions, firmly situating himself as a shock comic alongside contemporaries such as Jim Jeffries, Sarah Silverman, Ralphie May, Whitney Cummings, Daniel Tosh, and Lisa Lampanelli. Shock comedy seldom includes thoughtful cultural critique and instead gains favor and audience loyalty by appealing to a sense of antipolitical correctness. Are you frustrated that you have to be careful with terminology when referring to other races, sexualities, or the differently abled? Tired of having to choke back your antipathy for diversity, multiculturalism, or anything resembling a non-White, non-heteronormative issue, person, or topic? Well, then you are sure to enjoy the increasingly popular genre of shock comedy from comics who take no prisoners and are what Russell Peterson calls "equal-opportunity offenders." When everyone is the target there is little substantive critique and thus shock comedy maintains profitability by being "nihilistically 'neutral,'" refusing to cater to social justice issues or any single community, ideology, or set of politics.[4] This does not mean shock comics lack a conscience or even believe or practice everything they say nor does it mean that charged comics cannot and do not also employ shock humor as rhetorical strategy from time to time. Ralphie May and Daniel Tosh whose mainstay performance mode relies on shock humor also pepper their comedy with charged humor. Each joke stands alone and seldom does a comic employ a single style to the exclusion of every other style. Furthermore, comic personae are mutable. A comic performing safe comedy or shock humor with zeal one year may not be doing so the next.

Comics deploy varying degrees of self-disclosure. Those that clearly portray comic personae differing from off-stage personalities gain audience favor not vis-à-vis identification, rather through an appreciation for a zany, surreal, or Dadaist approach to comedy—also known as character comedy. Some character comedy greats (living and deceased) include Bobcat Goldthwait, Emo Philips, Andy Kaufman, Sandra Bernhard (to an extent), Steven Wright, Mitch Hedburg, Murray Langston ("The Unknown Comic"), Judy Tenuta, and Kristin Schaal. By and large, these are not the comics producing charged humor. They are playing with conventions. It is a style equivalent to safe humor or shock comedy and largely a vehicle to laughter with no agenda to politicize, edify, or unite—the more elaborate and contrived the construction, the less likely the comic performs charged humor. The reasoning: charged humor relies on identification with struggles and issues associated with being a second-class citizen and rallies listeners around some focal point be that cultural, corporeal, or racial/ethnic similarities; this requires drawing from personal experience, if not firsthand than at least access to, understanding of, or empathy with those having these experiences. It is not that character comics do not have comic personae—what Bambi Haggins defines as "the performance of the intersection of multiple ideologies and lived experiences," a construction influenced by "acculturation, individual choice, and industrial imperatives"—rather that charged comic personae more accurately reflect real lived identities.[5] Revenue yielded from character comics electing to portray oddball or eccentric comic personae indicate that viewers do not have to identify with the comic in order to appreciate their work. Kristen Schaal, the new darling of character comedy, serves up a buffet of wacky stories and impersonations ranging from a faux mother to Anne Boleyn to a sandwich (possibly ham), in her premiere half-hour special on Comedy Central:

> I wanted to make sure that my act was family friendly for tonight, but I don't have babies. So I thought that maybe I could pretend that I had babies and that way I could appeal to the people in the audience who have babies and to the people who like to pretend they have babies [*laughter*] . . . My baby was born a twin set so I had to eat the other one [*laughter*]. Naturally. That joke is special because that is specifically for any panda bears that are in the audience tonight [*laughter*].[6]

Making choices to remain politically neutral and culturally ambivalent, as Schaal does so well, may enhance commercial viability—not because identification is not important in comedy (it is), but because the ridiculousness of character comedy obviates the possibility of identification. We laugh because the humor is silly, incongruous, and quirky, not because we relate to the comic personae. Plus, being politically neutral means you are not as likely to offend or make enemies.

Part of what works in favor of charged comics, part of their own unique appeal, is the ability or capacity of the audience to identify with someone like them or having experiences like them. They open possibilities for identification *through shared experience*. Identification is not prerequisite for appreciation or commercial success by any account, but for comics whose personae bear greater verisimilitude with actual lived experience, identification is a key factor in engaging viewers and one way to establish a loyal fan base among minority communities. Though identification is not the only prerequisite for enjoying a joke, it can certainly make for successful comedy. Writ large, this translates to I hear what you are saying and my laughter signals agreement or affirmation. When charged humor repels there is a breakdown in identification between audience and performer. The ensuing arguments are predicated on the notion of identification: how people consume the material of comics with whom they identify and the resulting economic consequences; and how the cultural economy facilitates and rewards identification with certain comics, further promoting certain identities as ideal and desirable, that is, male, wealthy, White, heterosexual, able-bodied, and so on. Charged performances are costly; the types of humor produced and the ways comics perform their social identities often determine their marketability. Charged humor has a limited market in part because it reminds viewers that all is not right in the world. It reminds viewers of the illusion of equality and of the fragility of freedom in the United States.

The Economy of Charged Humor

This is not simply a book about a kind of humor, this is a book about the politics of humor—an analysis of American stand-up comedy and a treatise on the fault lines in the economy of humor in the United States. For example, understanding why women's humor is not as commercially viable shows us why men's humor is. Likewise, understanding why modern-day minstrels whose humor capitalizes on stereotypes can find a market for their humor shows us why defying or undoing these stereotypes will not yield similar opportunities for profit. One main objective here is to examine the economy of charged humor. Economy being defined as the production, exchange, and consumption of charged humor, the primary focus is thus its production (i.e., comics performing charged humor) and its consumption (i.e., the marketability and commercial viability of charged humor). The real puzzle is why some kinds of humor are more commercially viable than others. Is it simply content that informs profitability or the identity of the practitioner as well? Or both? Or something else? How does a performer's position in the national body politic and the willingness to comment on that position inform the economy of charged humor?

The twentieth century birthed a national celebrity culture as technological innovations in communication exported identities to the masses, converting individuals into celebrity chattel for purchase in entertainment's marketplace. Since that time, comic actors fashioned humorous personae like Charlie Chaplin's "lovable tramp," Jackie "Moms" Mabley's role as sassy grandmother, Roseanne Barr's "domestic goddess," or Rodney Dangerfield's self-deprecating "I get no respect" shtick. More formally these could be considered commercial auto-ethnographies—a presentation of self engaging in cultural critique and interpretation. Personae are continuously plopped into the American market-place offering a smorgasbord of identities for consumption. The fact that this puts us (read: consumers) in the position of placing a monetary and cultural value on someone else's identity is fascinating as much as it is potentially disturbing. In the case of comic personae as commodity, what sells and what does not lends commentary about a country that likes to imagine itself as a harbinger of democracy, even as its constituents eagerly declare postracial bliss and pooh-pooh the need for feminism.

Examining the economy of charged humor gives us information about which identities (and values) are commercially viable and also offers a new explanation for the somewhat pervasive belief that women are not as funny as men. Since there is currently a limited market for charged humor, women comics who use charged humor will struggle to rival the success of their male counterparts. If women comics frequently use charged humor and men (especially straight White able-bodied men) are not as likely to use this humor, an examination of the economy of charged humor helps explain this popular perception that men are (inherently) funnier than women. This popular debate surfaced in *Vanity Fair* (January 2007). The late Christopher Hitchens gave voice to this general cultural perception in the controversial piece, "Why Women Aren't Funny." This article sparked public discussion both online and in print, introducing physiological, sociological, and psychological answers for women's presumed inadequacy as producers of humor. Largely overlooked in this ongoing debate is an analysis grounded in material terms that examines the economy of charged humor—how we are taught from a young age what to value; the advantages of learning to identify with those in power; and how laughter in the final instance is shaped by economic forces because identifying with certain points of view bear the promise of material and cultural capital and this influences whose humor is successful and widely consumed in the United States today. Irish American comic Kathleen Madigan describes this positioning for women as "walking up on stage in a total hole."[7] I suggest that the gender gap may be explained by the lack of economic incentives to identify with or consume charged humor—much of which is produced by women. There is no payoff for buying into women's points of view, especially if it reminds audience members of continuing inequalities. This creates a market favoring male humor and those performing apolitical (safe), shock, or character comedy and modern-day minstrels who secure laughter by selling caricatures, recapitulating stereotypes, and reinforcing the worst of audience beliefs and expectations.

That women's humor and charged humor (at times) is less popular or profitable is neither coincidental nor unrelated. Certainly, there are examples of female breakthrough comics like Sarah Silverman, Joan Rivers, Whoopi Goldberg, Margaret Cho, Lisa Lampanelli, Whitney Cummings, and Kathy Griffin, and lesbian comics such as Paula Poundstone, Rosie O'Donnell, Ellen De-Generes, and Wanda Sykes. But when it comes to long-term success as a head-liner in comedy clubs, booking concert venues, and opportunities in television and film, men—Black, Latino, White, Asian, Arab, Jewish, etc.—have histori-cally been its greatest recipients. Not to belabor this point unnecessarily, but consider the following male actors whose careers in television and film began performing stand-up comedy: Bill Cosby, David Letterman, Robin Williams, Billy Crystal, Jay Leno, Dane Cook, Jon Stewart, Adam Sandler, Woody Allen, Eddie Murphy, Jeff Foxworthy, Bernie Mac, Ray Romano, Jerry Seinfeld, Carlos Mencia, Jim Carrey, Tim Allen, Jamie Foxx, Bob Saget, Steve Harvey, Steve Carell, Dennis Miller, D. L. Hughley, David Alan Grier, Jim Gaffigan, Dana Carvey, Dave Chappelle, Dave Attell, Chris Tucker, Colin Quinn, Kevin James, Rob Corddry, Keenen Ivory Wayans, Jeff Ross, Craig Ferguson, Denis Leary, John Oliver, Lewis Black, Martin Lawrence, Daniel Tosh, Judah Friedlander, Zach Galifianakis, Michael McDonald, Bert Kreischer, Aziz Ansari, Wyatt Cenac, and Steve Byrne. I could go on and on.

This male-driven economy of comedy reveals itself in a number of ways, not the least of which is a host of people who perceive men to be funnier than women, a phenomenon that is hardly surprising when popular discourse aug-ments and perpetuates this belief and when each subsequent generation is ex-posed to humor and comic devices generated by men, but marketed to men and women alike. I am all too happy to concede that a few women such as Tina Fey, Kristen Wiig, Annie Mumolo, Kay Cannon, Diablo Cody, and Lena Dunham make important contributions as comedy writers, but I continue to be cautious of asserting women's parity in comedy—it is improving, but it will take more than a spattering of vulvas in the sea of dicks writing our world every day.

Contemporary laugh-makers hail from diverse backgrounds, cultures, na-tionalities, and race/ethnicities. They are able-bodied and differently-abled; they are men and women; they are heterosexual and queer. Yet, national noto-riety and success as a comic favors able-bodied, heterosexual men. In this in-stance, correlation indicates causation: people consume more male humor and charged humor is not as widely marketable as safe shock or character comedy; therefore, in general, men (especially White heterosexual able-bodied men) are less likely to perform this kind of oppositional humor. This does not mean they will not perform charged humor (see George Carlin, Lewis Black, Patton Oswalt, Louis C.K., Bill Maher, Steve Hofstetter, Nato Green, Eugene Mir-man, Dylan Brody, and Jimmy Dore), it just means that such humor from White heterosexual, able-bodied men is rare, in main because people not expe-riencing oppression or exclusion directly have little cause to produce this kind of humor. Being female and/or marginalized by virtue of race/ethnicity, sexuality, creed, ability, age, or class all contribute to the likelihood of creating charged humor.

Analyzing Charged Humor: Methods and Means

Humor is not a science. It is subjective and shifting; that is why we have a "sense" of humor. Comedian Judy Gold puts it aptly: "it's called a *sense* of humor. It's a sense, like smell. Like some people like pizza, some people don't. Some people think some things are funny, some people don't."[8] How you deploy humor and how you respond to others' comic interventions—be they staged, deadpan, parodic, raunchy, physical, shocking, ironic, or satirical—becomes what you can own as your sense of humor. Everyone, of course, experiences senses differently. It is unique to your experience even as it intersects with shared experiences—locally, nationally, and transnationally. It is ephemeral, contingent, and often mood-based, making any analysis of humor a tricky one. This is not an attempt to define what is funny to Americans nor chart an "American" sense of humor—such conundrums are mired in the contested terrain of who counts as American and far too many gross generalizations. Instead, the focus rests on the motives for producing charged humor and the patterns of charged humor consumption, particularly via the cultural practice of stand-up comedy and its stage cousin, the humorous one-woman/man show.

The comedic landscape of charged humor necessitates closer examination of many social identities and the ways categories of difference shape our everyday lived experiences. Since producers of charged humor cut across every category of difference, I do not focus exclusively on one category of difference (i.e., Black comedy, gay comedy, women's comedy, etc.). Therefore, this analysis is intersectional, just as it is interdisciplinary. Power stratifications and the underpinnings of social subordination as it shifts over time have been studied and documented in feminist, disability, queer, materialist, and critical race theories, all of which support, inform, and shape this investigation. In particular, feminist scholarship considers intersecting multiple categories of identities, offering a useful lens and central framing device for studying charged humor and the comics who perform it.

Employed throughout is a mixed-methods qualitative approach using ethnography (interviews and participant-observation), archival research, and audience and critical discourse analyses. Ethnographic methods allow for protracted examination of the production of charged humor. I interview comic performers and examine off-stage interviews in print and visual media in which comics reflect on their material. This examination should stand out as one that foregrounds what the jokester desires to accomplish with a bit—her comic intent.

Most scholarship about comic performance and performers focuses on the content of jokes. Without attending to comic intent, scholars argue that humor is satirical or resistant. This is especially true of analyses of women's stand-up comedy, but just because a woman performs stand-up does not mean that her jokes will be subversive.[9] By not consulting the laugh-maker in question, such analyses rest on the same premise given toddlers who want to know why they cannot have a pet elephant: "Because I said so." In contrast, this work offers authorial context, drawing from performers' lives, background, and personal accounts, inviting them to discuss artistic and political intentions behind their work. As such, this project focuses on what the jokesters want and intend their viewers to get, and why they speak on behalf of themselves and sometimes their communities. In a field as subjective as comedy, one of the few places we can look for assurance as to how comics intend humor to function and operate is from the authors' own perspectives.

Audience and critical discourse analyses assist in understanding why and how the public does or does not consume charged humor. Widely disseminated and broadly consumed cultural effluvia work to situate us in the national imagination and shape identity formation. Stuart Hall argues that "the 'subject' is differently placed or *positioned* by different discourses and practices."[10] Likewise, the cultural discourses circulating about humor treat subjects differently, including the belief that women are not as funny as men. Practitioners of humor, such as stand-up comics, solo performance artists, and those belonging to improv and sketch comedy troupes, and theater collectives are influenced by their subject position and its relationship to the environment around them—culturally, politically, and economically. Examining popular discourses, such as the manifold voices reacting to the idea that men are inherently funnier than women, reveals that such a belief is culturally derived and contingent.

Popular discourses circulating about humor offer perhaps some of the most useful though ephemeral and diffused primary sources because they directly inform production (how comics develop comic material) and consumption (the kind of humor most popular and therefore profitable) in the United States. For instance, when comics like Michael Richards, Daniel Tosh, and Tracy Morgan drew national attention for open bigotry on stage, the ensuing discourses about what is acceptable language and allowable sentiment during a show becomes a matter of popular discourse. Public outcry and backlash can affect the content of performed comedy in the future as well as the consumptive proclivities of audiences. I agree with Roland Martin, a journalist, author, and news analyst for CNN, who wrote in defense of Tracy Morgan's right to free speech on his blog "A Fresh Perspective for the 21st Century," arguing that comics should not have to censor themselves on stage; however, we make the choice to patronize or purchase a comic's point of view. Tracy Morgan's hateful attack on the LGBTQ community will cost him customers and by the same token will potentially yield some new ones. Comics have a right to free speech, but the consumer ultimately decides whose speech to support. The push-pull exchange or terms of agreement between comic and audience is most evident while watching these popular discourses unfurl.

Having performed as a stand-up comic, improv actress, and director for over a decade, I draw from first-hand knowledge and direct personal experience in the comedy industry, which in turn informs my approaches to studying comedy. Throughout I will often write in first person; as with any ethnography, this should signal that analyses cull from my experiences, observations, and interpretations. I began performing stand-up comedy and improv in 2001, just weeks before 9/11, earning my chops at local open mike shows in Nashville, Tennessee. I became a regular at Zanies Comedy Club and The Sutler, getting paid to perform in weekly stand-up and improv shows. After performing in Nashville for a year, I moved to Columbus, Ohio, and continued performing from 2002 to 2004. During that time, I performed at a range of venues. including weekly shows at Norah's Coffee Corner in Grove City, Ohio, a number of all-women comedy shows, which I produced and emceed for LadyFest Ohio, and an occasional appearance at the Columbus Funny Bone. I performed sporadically and infrequently in the District of Columbia while earning my doctorate at University of Maryland, College Park, and instead of stand-up comedy, I devoted any spare time to teaching and directing comic theater.

My comedy style has changed over the years, but early on it was unapologetically feminist, with acerbic critiques of patriarchy, the media, institutions, and social mores. Now, I insert myself more in my comedy and strive to strike a balance—I want to edify not preach. These days, when I do perform (which I still do on occasion), it is for universities, fundraisers, or nonprofit organizations with which I am associated. However, I do not actively promote myself or seek comedy gigs nor do I have a website or an updated headshot and no, you cannot find me on YouTube. Most of my current material, which draws from my own life and US history and culture, is tested in the classroom, where I use it to generate interest in a subject matter, to educate, and to disarm listeners into considering other points of view. At times, throughout this book, I include my own experiences performing. My brand of charged humor elicits strong reactions, both favorable and, well . . . not. I want to define and chart charged humor, in part, because of my own experiences performing the same material to wildly different effects—roaring approval or total disdain (or worse, silence)—depending on the venue and the crowd.

I have been a faithful devotee of comedy since childhood and can recite Bill Cosby's "The Chicken Heart That Ate New York" and Bob Newhart's "Introducing Tobacco to Civilization." Aspiring to stand-up comedy as a teen, I began following comics doing interesting, new, or radical things on stage like Bobcat Goldthwait's screeching frustrated persona, Pablo Francisco and Michael Winslow's cavalcade of sound effects, Margaret Cho's withering analysis of the entertainment industry, and Denis Leary's early drug-addled politically incorrect rants. In the last ten years, I have watched or listened to thousands of hours of stand-up comedy on television, LPs, and filmed comedy specials, and attended live performances in bars, comedy clubs, coffee shops, and performance halls all over North America. Some of the most valuable primary sources for this project include interviews with comedians, documentaries, comic performances, print and electronic media about comedy, and audience surveys. I have made every effort to watch a variety of comics ranging in popularity, style, talent, and identity, though it is impossible to view and catalogue every comic performer.

Early on, I began taking an inventory of jokes, searching for and documenting charged humor in the filmed and live performances I frequented. What follows is not a scientific or quantitative analysis of charged humor; rather, I record who performs charged humor historically and currently, communicate with charged comics about their work, parse out the jokes to get a pattern of usage, and track the consumption of this humor. Herein, charged comics reveal their objectives for writing and performing comedy and the performances offer useful information about audience response to charged humor. Monitoring the success and popularity of comics over the last sixty years indicates what kind of funny fares well in the market, historically and today.

While I emphasize the importance of authorial intent for charged humor, audience interpretations may not coincide with those intentions. I use various methods to assess the exchange between comic and audience members. At times, I "read" audience reception through audible and physical cues, such as laughter, applause, booing, hissing, heckling, head-shaking, and, in some instances, body convulsions.[11] At times, postperformance evaluations contribute to my analyses, providing useful demographic data and feedback about shows. When examining televised comedy, segments posted online, and comedy concert films this tool is neither practical nor possible. This poses limitations on the claims I or anyone can make as to the efficacy of performances. But, my central claim is not that charged humor is efficacious; rather, that its progenitor intends it to be and therefore it *could* function in this way. Performers and scholars alike share my belief that popular culture has the capacity to transform people; indeed, humorist Emily Levine says, "really what a trickster is, is an agent of change."[12]

Part of the value of this investigation lies in its social justice agenda. To that effect, some goals for this project include bringing greater visibility to obscure comics, filming interviews and performances in order to build an archive of work that might make these comics accessible to larger audiences and scholars, creating performance opportunities for charged comics, and focusing on tactics and strategies that minority communities can employ in order to gain full incorporation in the United States, culturally and legally. A strength of cultural studies that holds true for identity-based disciplines, including American Studies, where I situate my own work, is the way it attends to the "development of conscious struggle and organization as a necessary element in the analysis of history, ideology and consciousness."[13] These struggles play out in dimly lit bars and pizzerias, in auditoriums, in world-class performance venues, and in comedy clubs across the nation and stoke the fires of discontent by revealing social, economic, and political inequalities.

Coming Attractions

This book begins by defining charged humor and exploring terms of national belonging, arguing that performing charged humor illustrates one method of enacting cultural citizenship.[14] The study of cultural citizenship explores "what motivates people to action, what gets them moving and inspires mobilization and under what circumstances."[15] Charged humor expands what constitutes cultural citizenship and places importance on the way performance and fine arts can shape our sense of self—reflecting who we are in ways that confer value and worth or reflecting who we are in ways that signal inferiority. Like other methods of engendering cultural citizenship, charged humor redresses the balance, compels action, and highlights the historical and contemporary struggles, double standards, and disenfranchisement experienced by minorities.

After exploring the theoretical underpinnings of charged humor, the focus in chapter 2 turns to historical origins and investigates charged humor emanating from comic practitioners during the mid-to-late twentieth century, while also attending to shifts in the commercial viability of charged humor during this time period. Chapter 3 examines the production of twenty-first century charged humor and provides a "who's who" of contemporary charged comics hailing from multiple minority communities, including Middle Eastern, Muslim, and Arab Americans, Latino/a Americans, Asian Americans, African Americans, differently-abled persons, LGBTQ folks, and those who are economically disenfranchised. Examination of multiple minority communities reveals that the means of exclusion and methods of subordination differ for each; yet, they are united in their desire to illumine diversity within minority communities and to advocate inclusion without having to mute cultural differences. Chapter 4 focuses on the gender gap in comedy to explore how Americans consume charged humor and the larger implications of these patterns and trends in US entertainment, shedding light on the continuously debated question of why men are perceived to be funnier than women.

This book features three case studies, each constituting a chapter and allowing for in-depth examination of contemporary performers using charged humor, all of whom take very different approaches to make similar appeals. The case studies are presented in roughly chronological order or sequenced by age of the subjects, beginning with Robin Tyler, a Jewish lesbian comic and activist who surprised everyone by performing off-script on *The 1st Annual Funny Women's Show* on Showtime in 1979, reciting several jokes about being a lesbian. Foiling any plans to censor or edit her material, Tyler was the first person "out" on television. She was the initial plaintiff in the case that legalized same-sex marriage in California for nearly six months in 2008, and she is currently a key player in the marriage equality movement. By examining Tyler's comedy and activism over forty years, this chapter offers a uniquely personal, insider's vantage point on the gay liberation movement as it changed in response to various presidential administrations, economic upswings and downturns, and technological innovations.

The second case study features Micia Mosely, PhD, a lesbian Black comic whose self-authored one-woman show, *Where My Girls At? A Comedic Look at Black Lesbians* (2008–present) offers diverse and dynamic representations of Black lesbians. For Mosely, charged humor defies simple unitary categories of analysis, insisting that we deal with and confront the complex ways that race, class, gender, and sexuality overlap, contradict, and intersect. Because she does not identify as exclusively Black or exclusively lesbian, she picks at the simple understanding of these categories to transmit more complicated manifestations of how identity is often a braided set of identifiers. Her show evinces the need to consider the complexity of difference, particularly among those occupying more than one subordinated category of difference. The final case study explores the comic corpus of Hari Kondabolu, an up-and-coming South Asian American stand-up comic, by focusing on the evolution of his stand-up comedy from performing modern-day minstrelsy to scathing charged humor. This chapter takes the rather indelicate topic of minstrelsy—be that raceface or queerface—and examines its current usage and marketability in today's entertainment industry.

The study concludes with suggestions for future scholarship in related fields, actions we can take to advance social equality, and contemplates ways comics can harness emergent technologies to increase profit and visibility. All the performers assembled here use charged humor to educate, challenge, unite, and transform, though they do so using different forms of self-authored comedic performance: stand-up comedy, one-woman shows, and humorous vodcasts (video podcasts). While I have made every effort to be comprehensive and inclusive, stand-up comedy holds court to thousands of itinerant jokesters who float in and out of the various scenes, so it is likely that I overlooked the work of some really important voices. I apologize in advance and look forward to discovering where those omissions lie. The diversity of comics in this analysis not only allows for examination of multiple comedic forms but also present together comics addressing issues of gender, race/ethnicity, religion, age, class, ability, and sexuality. The case studies broaden the scope and potential of charged humor by locating it in many different ways. The span of ages among research participants included herein offers a unique cross-sectional and intersectional look at humor produced by folks ranging from twenty-something to performers eligible for senior discounts. The variety of comic forms, the range of communities addressed and the wide span in age among participants demonstrate the multifaceted ways charged humor proliferates and rejects the notion that charged humor is unique to a specific community, generation, or form of comic performance. This inquiry tracks the production and consumption of charged humor whose market value fluctuates in accordance with popular demand. The arguments throughout have implications for how each and every American consumes humor—why we make the choices we do and the collective power of our consumptive practices.

CHAPTER ONE

Making Connections
Building Cultural Citizenship through Charged Humor

> One of my main contentions is that any analytical consideration
> of how ideologies of belonging are forged and sustained through
> cultural forms needs to give comedy a prominent place, since
> laughing together is one of the most swift, charged and effective
> routes to a feeling of belonging together. Comedy is a short cut to
> community.
>
> *Andy Medhurst,* A National Joke: Popular Comedy
> and English Cultural Identities

It feels good to belong in our families, workplaces, social scenes, and even our nation, but not everyone does. Legal citizenship reflects a struggle to determine membership in a national community and what that membership means; put another way, citizenship is the answer to the question: "who belongs and what does *belonging* mean in practice?"[1] Citizenship is understood, articulated, and experienced in a variety of ways at different periods in time by different people. A property-owning White man in the early nineteenth century had a different experience of citizenship than did an enslaved African American woman. Today, a US naturalized Trinidadian transgender man will have different difficulties to negotiate in our society than a Black Muslim teenage girl. They are both United States citizens, though the way they understand and exercise rights as a citizen will be quite different. When we do not belong, we find other means of creating community. As Andy Medhurst suggests in the quote above, comedy is one way of facilitating community, of reminding us that we matter somehow, somewhere.

Fostering community based on shared ethnicity, religious beliefs, and sexual orientation is one means of mitigating experiences of social and political exclusion. Cultural practices used in an effort to build cultural unity and assert rights are part of a larger effort to create cultural citizenship. Draft concept papers about cultural citizenship, written by early members of the Latino Cultural Studies Working Group (LCSWG) in the late 1980s, offer primary sources that lay the groundwork for thorough consideration of how cultural forms can enact cultural citizenship. Cultural citizenship recognizes that while some inhabitants of the US and US territories are not legal citizens, they are, in fact, cultural citizens existing in the daily workings and maintenance of the United States as an economy, society, and culture. Additionally, there are legal citizens who, historically and currently, have not been granted full rights as citizens based on age, sexuality, race, religion, and ability. The theory of cultural citizenship—more widely disseminated in the book *Latino Cultural Citizenship: Claiming Identity, Space and Rights* (1998), edited by William Flores and Rena Benmayor—has been borrowed and applied by scholars researching small- to large-scale mobilizations, such as grassroots initiatives and social movements focused on changing public policy and securing resources and social services. Seldom, if at all, have these studies of cultural citizenship addressed popular cultural forms, though some scholars do cite community cultural development as vital to the project of cultural citizenship. Applying this theoretical construct to an analysis of comedy helps to broaden what constitutes cultural citizenship, incorporating cultural forms like stand-up comedy that have been formerly dismissed as innocuous, irrelevant, or merely entertaining.

People practiced cultural citizenship long before scholars began theorizing and naming it as such. Labor unions organized strikes in canneries, mills, slaughterhouses, and mines to secure a living wage, safe working conditions, and respect for their professions; during the Reconstruction Era and after, African Americans lobbied for access to housing, jobs, and education; and first and second wave feminists defied social expectations by demanding suffrage, education, child custody, and property rights for women. With a specific focus on the social and cultural exclusion of Latino/as in the United States, scholars in the 1980s began giving a name to these strategies for seeking economic, social, and political equality. Members of the Latino Cultural Studies Working Group found themselves frustrated with the limitations posed by existing theoretical concepts in citizenship studies—none of them quite articulated the importance of linking cultural struggle to empowerment and enfranchisement.[2] Seeking remedy for these lacunae, they define cultural citizenship as:

a process manifested in particular types of cultural practices that embody symbols, discourses, practices, values and identities by which a subordinate community establishes a social and cultural space within which to affirm its collective sense of identity, solidarity, common historical experience and struggle to reclaim their rights. The term cultural citizenship recognizes and affirms both the legitimacy of a dominated people's culture, their resistance and their innate rights which have often been ignored in the legal canon of a society. . . . Rather, cultural citizenship identifies the claims of social, human and cultural rights made by communities which do not hold state power and which are denied basic rights by those who do.[3]

Building cultural citizenship involves taking control of a public image created by others to maintain hierarchies; it is about empowering otherwise marginalized social identities, a means of locating and asserting oneself within a specific social, cultural, and political matrix in order to counteract inequitable treatment, develop community, acquire rights, build identity, and experience a sense of shared cultural belonging. When stand-up comics or anyone else do this, they are enacting cultural citizenship.

The definition of charged humor hinges on the practice of enacting cultural citizenship. Charged humor illumines flaws and disparities between the promises of citizenship and the fulfillment of those promises. The term "cultural citizenship" emerged from oppositional cultural practices seeking to empower communities, raise cultural awareness, celebrate a common history, and promote belonging. Lauren Berlant writes that "the populations who were and are managed by the discipline of the promise [of democratic citizenship]—women, African Americans, Native Americans, immigrants, homosexuals—have long experienced simultaneously the wish to be full citizens and the violence of their partial citizenship."[4] And Stuart Hall and David Held write that "this issue around membership—who does and who does not belong—is where the politics of citizenship begins."[5] This chapter explores membership—legal and cultural—as it is conceived by scholars in the field of citizenship studies and unpacks the meaning and deployment of cultural citizenship. I argue that cultural citizenship is a defining feature of charged humor that distinguishes charged humor from other types of humor such as satire, which for important reasons should not be conflated with charged humor, though charged humor can employ satire as comic device. Furthermore, I discuss the characteristics of charged humor such as varying audience reception to it, comic intentionality, subversive content, orientation toward solutions, and its availability in mainstream popular culture. This humor, present since the advent of stand-up comedy as its own distinct cultural form in the 1950s, reveals national contradictions and presents possibilities for restructuring citizenship that accomplishes what it already claims to do—address everyone as equal.

Why Cultural Citizenship?

Why cultural citizenship and not some other term? After all, scholars studying citizenship previous to and concurrent with the Latino Cultural Studies Working Group had already differentiated between legal citizenship and the sense of inclusion one may or may not have in one's country of residence, so there were/ are other alternatives to the concept of cultural citizenship. For example, while LCSWG members penned the tenets of cultural citizenship, sociologist Rogers Brubaker was studying citizenship models practiced in Europe and North America. Where working group members distinguish between legal and cultural citizenship, Brubaker distinguishes between *formal* and *substantive* citizenship. Formal citizenship signals legal ties to a nation-state and, according to Brubaker, "should be egalitarian, sacred, national, democratic, unique, and socially consequential."[6] Brubaker notes that, in practice, national membership does not conform to this model, generating the need to discern between formal and substantive citizenship.[7] He writes:

> There are, besides aliens, other categories of noncitizens. These are persons who belong to the *ville* but not to the *cité,* who belong to the state as a territorial administrative unit, but not to the state as a ruling organization. The definition of citizenship is substantive, not formal. Citizenship is constituted by the possession and exercise of political rights, by participation in the business of rule, not by common rights and obligations.[8]

In other words, you can be a formal citizen but experience de facto or de jure exclusion from civil, political, and social rights. For example, while I am delighted at the repeal of the Don't Ask Don't Tell policy by President Barack Obama in December 2010, I suspect that the practice of keeping silent about one's sexual orientation for fear of informal persecution will remain de facto (although I hope I am wrong). Brubaker's nuanced distinction between formal and substantive citizenship clearly reflects that citizens experience membership differently (it is not always egalitarian); however, the term substantive citizenship does not have the same generative, proactive, and mobilizing qualities as cultural citizenship. Agency, affirmation, and empowerment are critical components of cultural citizenship and the reason other terms such as substantive citizenship are not as optimal. Cultural citizenship is not just about assessing one's rights but *asserting* one's rights.[9]

Modern citizenship—considered so when during the Middle Ages Western civilization became organized into territorial states and later nation states— proffered citizenship as legal means of inclusion into a national body. Echoing Brubaker, working group member William Flores writes that "being a citizen guarantees neither full membership in society nor equal rights. To be a full citizen one must be welcome and accepted as a full member of the society with all its rights."[10] All legal citizens do not feel welcomed and accepted. We experience citizenship as both a legal arrangement and a cultural arrangement unique to our social coordinates (this varies based on the intersection of categories of difference like race/ethnicity, class, sexuality, gender identity, sex, age, religion, and ability).[11] For instance, being poor or queer impacts the way we practice and experience citizenship. While it is illegal to prevent citizens from voting, for folks who cannot afford to miss an hour or more of work, voting is financially impossible or a sacrifice they are unable to make. In this case, the federal government makes legal arrangements that do not account for economic differences impeding civic participation. While the Defense of Marriage Act was repealed, and polls indicate the public's increased acceptance of gay marriage, same-sex couples face legal obstacles to marriage in most states. Polls released by *Politico* and George Washington University cite social approval for gay marriage or civil unions at 70 percent, yet as of 2013 only 20 percent of states confer some kind of legal recognition of these unions.[12] In this case, legal rights lag behind cultural acceptance. Legal and cultural arrangements shift over time, changing our relationship to the practice and experience of citizenship based on where we stand in relation to legal rights and social treatment.

Importantly, cultural citizenship allows that members of marginalized communities may enact cultural citizenship regardless of legal standing as US citizens; in other words, one's legal status does not preclude one's ability to agitate for and participate in developing cultural citizenship. This intellectual strategy of expanding the definition of citizenship beyond one's legal status acknowledges that many people are legal citizens but feel like cultural outsiders, while conversely many residents of the United States are extralegal but remain active in their communities and are participating in the nation-state solely as cultural citizens. In his 2009 comedy special titled *Maz Jobrani: Brown and Friendly*, performed live at The El Portal Theatre in North Hollywood, California, Persian American stand-up comic Maz Jobrani recalculates the borders of belonging:

> This is a great country we live in guys. It really is [*whistles, clapping, and cheers*]. It is. And you know we're all citizens, we are all citizens. I mean some of us have green cards, some of us have green cards but that's alright [*laughter*]. Some of us are illegal. That's fine [*laughter*]. It's all inclusive alright. We're not building any walls here. Lou Dobbs is not in the house. Don't worry about it! [*laughter*].[13]

Legal status notwithstanding, Jobrani makes all US occupants citizens, if only cultural, a rhetorical strategy that confers value and importance to everyone, not just the privileged, card-bearing members of the United States.

To establish parameters for recognizing which cultural practices enact cultural citizenship, working group members specified that "while there may be forms of cultural practice in certain communities that challenge the dominant cultural forms, we reserve the term cultural citizenship for those that emerge within communities with a historical experience structured by their domination by a hegemonic power."[14] When I refer to charged humor or humor enacting cultural citizenship, I mean humor that seeks to represent the underrepresented, to empower and affirm marginalized communities and identities, and to edify and mobilize their audiences. This may manifest as jokes addressing social inequalities, national contradictions, and negative representations or in calling attention to hateful language, power relations, and cultural grievances. Not all comic performance can be characterized in this way—as subversive, oppositional, or mobilizing (think: *Jackass*). Some humor strives to do this, other humor does not. Comedy can function as comedy for comedy's sake: a fart wellplanted, a visual gaffe, a jab at personality quirks or character flaws, or public derision of those deemed different or inferior. An example would be male sexist humor (for examples of this you can look to the performances of Jim Jeffries, Noel Elgrably, Andrew Dice Clay, Pauly Shore, Brian Posehn, Robert Schimmel, Jay Mohr, Adam Carolla, Patrice O'Neal, Daniel Tosh, etc.), which assumes women's inferiority and availability as a passive sexual object and reinforces sexist beliefs and social practices founded on those beliefs, like the humorous cultural sanctioning of rape, which has been and continues to be the subject of debate among comics and comedy fans. Comics performing modern-day minstrelsy (see chapter 7 for a discussion of this topic) are most likely to take on a stereotypical and highly recognized racialized or queered affect for comedic effects. Relying heavily on stereotypes associated with popular stock characters like the Sambo or Queen, this kind of humor confirms rather than questions negative assumptions about marginalized identities. As illustration, Mike Faverman performs queerface minstrelsy during an appearance on *Live Nude Comedy* (2009), a show with comedians and burlesque dancers.

> I had a gay boss too. He told me he was haunted by a gay ghost in his house. How gay is that? [*laughter*]. What, does a gay ghost haunt you from the closet at first? [*laughter*]. Came out late at night and was like: [*assumes a "gay" voice and places a hand on his hip*] "Booo . . . Booo!" [*laughter*]. [*Resumes normal voice*] Woke up and your room is all re-decorated. Had Gucci sheets and gummy bracelets on [*laughter*].[15]

A common style employed by comic performers and popular among audiences, most modern-day minstrelsy is not charged humor, though in some circumstances it can help offset the critique imposed by calculative charged humor.

Cultural citizenship and the humor that enacts it allows room for the many members of minority communities who wish to maintain both full citizenship and a strong and proud cultural heritage distinguishing them as different. George Lopez, perhaps the most visible and well-known Latino comic today, fosters cultural citizenship among his Mexican amigos/as residing in the United

States, regardless of legal status; first, he qualifies Latinos as industrious—projecting positive attributes to replace negative ones—and second, connects an outbreak of E. coli to a form of resistance from agricultural workers tired of working hard only to be disparaged as inferior and excluded from a political process that affects their lives and livelihoods.

> Let me say this. The country is not what you thought it was. Everything you touched first, Latinos touch. We're there, every day, early [*people start cheering and whistling*]. Let me give you some examples—Taco Bell had some tainted green onions, [*assumes a mock "White" accent*] "Oh god, I got *E. coli* from them." [*Resumes normal voice*] Some tainted green onions showed up at Taco Bell, okay, White people get *E. coli*—the whole world fucking stops. Who picks the onions? [*Cheers*] Latinos! You talk shit about us it gets down to the fields [*laughter and cheering*]. I didn't hear you, what did they say about us? They don't want us here, we're lazy, and we're depleting the system? Oh yeah? [*Pick imaginary onions and rubs them on his crotch; laughter*] Here, take that shit to Taco Bell. Take it! [*Laughter*] There's your chalupa right there. Here let me put some hairs [*Pretends to pluck pubic hair and tosses it on the onions; audience roars with laughter*].[16]

Since cultural citizenship encompasses actively producing new representations, celebrating cultural practices, and building community, stand-up comics are in a powerful position to advance cultural citizenship.[17] Like Lopez, they can challenge one-dimensional or negative representations and stoke the fires of resistance to exclusionary and second-class treatment, all under the guise of good ol' fashioned fun.

Laying claim to cultural and ethnic differences may seem contrary to national unity. However, many inhabitants would love their country more if they could just be American *and* everything else they are, without have to mute, self-edit, or censor parts of themselves.[18] It is not necessary for cultural and legal citizenship to exist as a binary in which one defers to the other, where being loyal to our nation comes at the expense of our culture or being loyal to our culture is at the expense of our nation. Working group members argued that cultural differences should be treated as "a resource, not as a threat," and that the nation is made richer and stronger due to diversity.[19] Difference is seen as productive, yielding new cultural forms that in turn shapes America in important ways. The United States is what it is because of its diverse populace and the ingenuity and cross-pollination of peoples and cultural traditions. The beautiful thing—and a commonly overlooked fact in debates about multicultural curriculum today—is that we can allow for cultural differences as citizens while still asserting unity—communal and national. Cultural citizenship reminds of the value, indeed the imperative, of community for instilling belonging.

Humor enacting cultural citizenship not only builds community, but for outsiders looking in, it can combat misrepresentations about that community and, in the process, humanize its members. Charged humor reimagines a community, disrupting the stereotypes associated with various communities and how these communities are positioned in the national imagination—in other words, the way we conceive of others' social, cultural, and political positioning in relation to ourselves and the larger nation. For example, as a queer woman, I situate myself in the larger imagined LGBTQ community. I do not know everyone in that community, therefore it exists in my imagination, but it is based on the real presence of LGBTQ folks throughout the country and in this way I belong to something bigger than myself. You may imagine yourself as belonging to a community of sports fans or an ethnic community or within a community of those living with HIV/AIDS. We all place ourselves within these imagined communities as well as maintain an ongoing imagined construction of other communities to which we do not belong. How we imagine these communities can be damaging and wholly inaccurate, as when a White couple I know, upon arriving in New Orleans and seeing Black folks going about their business on a weekday afternoon in the streets of the French Quarter, immediately turned the car around and drove home. Their imagining of Black people as dangerous and violent was so powerful it deterred them from a vacation planned for months, so strong that they were willing to lose their deposit on the hotel. They did not elect to find another neighborhood where the residents looked more like them; they left the city. In the face of such staunchly held stereotypes, charged comedy functions as a viable and effective tool for disarming listeners into refiguring how they imagine other communities. Therein lies the potential (though not guaranteed) for charged humor to foment social change.

While comics may intend to educate or challenge the worldviews of audience members, we have limited methods of ascertaining success on this count. One of the dilemmas of examining comic performance, specifically comedy aimed at generating social change, is the difficulty of assessing its efficacy, that is, does it change one's opinion, motivate people to become more active in one's community, or help people understand and apply the information being offered by performers. Real social change is difficult to quantify in any case, but more so with performance. Take this joke, for example, in which Hari Kondabolu challenges sexist rhetoric about women's leadership skills.

I find it amazing that we have never elected a female president. And a big reason for that is that we have men in this country that are so sexist that they say things like, "Oh we can't elect a woman. Because you know what's gonna happen if we elect a woman, right? Like once a month she's gonna have her period and have

PMS and go crazy. She'll ruin the country!" There are men who believe this. There are men who believe that a woman because of her biology has her judgment impaired once a month. Well I am a man who happens to have a penis and testicles. My judgment is impaired every five to seven minutes [*laughter*]. And I'll be honest with you. . . . I wake up some mornings with my judgment impaired [*laughter*]. And that is a feminist fucking joke.[20]

Kondabolu challenges biological arguments about females' capacity to lead the country, but it would be difficult to assess whether audience members may change their minds about whether or not a woman would be as good a president as a man. The seed is planted but whether it grows . . . well, this is a big unknown. Sometimes anecdotal evidence surfaces revealing the impact charged comedy can have, like when Richard Pryor's jokes were used to diffuse tension during an arrest, a time when Black men have historically been vulnerable to physical attack. Two Black police officers attending a performance by Pryor shared a story with him backstage about the arrest of another Black man. Faced by police, the suspect, who knew full well the danger posed to African Americans by jumpy cops who assume every Black man is packing heat, he began reciting one of Pryor's jokes that apprises listeners of the care a Black person must take under such circumstances: "Nigger got to be talking about, 'I—am—reaching—into—my—pocket—for—my—license!' You know? 'Cuz I don't want to be no motherfucking accident."[21] The officers recognized the bit: they completed the routine and gales of laughter wafted into the night. Importantly, the man getting arrested took Pryor's advice verbatim. Quoting directly from Pryor's set, this man put into action advice dispensed by Pryor about how to avoid violence between law enforcement and Black folks. Given the difficulties of collecting and assessing such evidence, I do not attempt to offer quantitative analyses of the efficacy of charged comedy; rather, to illumine how and why comic performers opt to create charged humor, to assemble examples of this kind of humor, and where possible supplement this with audience feedback on a particular joke or comic.

In the United States today, the terms of legal citizenship hinge upon civic reciprocity. You are granted rights as a citizen and in exchange you need to conduct yourself in a certain way. Stuart Hall calls membership "two-sided, reciprocal: rights in, but also responsibilities towards, the community" and this becomes a credo for some stand-up comics who insist on generating comedy that strives to make the world a better place, though they would never put it in such trite terms.[22] I could have called this social justice or activist humor or based on their many similarities I might have been content to label it satire. However, as I will explain below, charged humor is characterized by qualities that render other terms insufficient. Charged humor enacts cultural citizenship, making the theorizing of the LCSWG working group central to this analysis. It is not just about illumining social justice issues and prompting action or attacking individuals and institutions that stand in the way of social justice; it functions to create community and validate identities among the culturally and legally disenfranchised.

Defining Charged Humor

I propose to accomplish two things: establish a genre of comedic production—charged humor—and chart its pathways from production to exchange to consumption. To be clear from the outset, examining charged humor provides one lens through which to examine humor, though certainly not the only lens through which we can understand the economy of humor. The term charged humor is a suitable descriptor for a number of reasons. One, it is a metaphor calling upon basic energetic principles of attraction and repulsion that mimic audience response to charged humor. Two, charged humor is self-locating, presenting viewers with (usually personal) examples of feeling like a second-class citizen that on one hand charges audience members with complicity toward social inequities, and on the other offers solutions for redressing the balance by conveying strategies for challenging inequality. Third, charged humor springs from a social and political consciousness desiring to address social justice issues. The humorist in question seeks to bring new worldviews that eschew inequality into public consciousness and discourse. It is humor deployed in the service of creating cultural citizenship, which is especially important for communities whose legal citizenship still feels like an economy class seat while everyone else flies first class. This kind of humor is intentional, meaning the humorist has designs on an outcome, specific or general—a change in attitudes or beliefs or action taken on behalf of social inequality. Finally, charged humor can limit the commercial potential of a comic persona, meaning that there may be a charge, a cost imposed upon those comics incorporating such humor into their performances.

Terms such as satire, political humor, or biting humor do not quite capture the proactive qualities of charged humor, a metaphor I use to describe humor intending to incite social change, develop community, and lobby for civil rights and acknowledgment. Why a metaphor? "Charged" signals the active quality and loaded potential of this humor. Chemistry class taught us that in order for an atom to be charged there must be some sort of disturbance or environmental shift causing the removal or addition of electrons or protons. Similarly, a performer produces charged humor when she foregrounds her marginality in order to call into question and *disrupt* the terms of her subordination; *charged humor both repels and attracts*. This disturbance can be welcome and resonate with audience members, particularly with those sharing similar experiences of marginalization, but it can also elicit feelings of distanciation, alienation, apathy, or anger.

Consider a joke by Louis C.K. in his special *Hilarious*, filmed live at the Pabst Theater in Milwaukee, Wisconsin:

> We have White people problems. That's what we have, White people problems. You know what that is? It's where your life is amazing so you just make shit up to be upset about [*laughter*]. People in other countries have real problems, like, "Oh shit, they're cutting off all our heads today" [*laughter*] . . . We make up shit to be upset about like [*in a sullen voice*]: "How come I have to choose a language on the ATM machine—this is bullshit" [*loud laughter and applause*]![23]

C.K. trivializes the plights of White folks (i.e., bilingual ATM machines, wonky cell phones, and flight delays) for being contrived, globally myopic, and self-centered, urging viewers to consider their woes in a larger social context. Doing so may generate a happier White populous grateful for the privileges and access to resources we have. He targets not just those privileges bestowed by living in the United States, but those accorded to White people in particular. In this instance, charged humor repels viewers who either disagree with the joke's premise or lack awareness of privileged social locations and attracts viewers who know all too well the validity of his critique.

Charged humor asks viewers to think critically. According to communications studies scholar and humor expert Judith Yaross Lee, "American humor reveals the state of the nation."[24] In the case of charged humor, it locates the humorist in the national imagination and shows us where there is trouble. It is intended to be self-situating and a call for viewers to refigure dominant beliefs and stereotypes about minorities and their respective communities. Moreover, it is not simply resistant; it can unite, edify, and rally on behalf of minority communities. Charged humor reveals one's immediate experience of second-class citizenship and gives us proactive means of addressing inequality. Moreover, charged humor can reveal how a person belongs and conversely how and where they do not belong, showing us how they fit into the national body politic. In the concert film, *Chris Rock: Kill the Messenger*, Rock happily reports:

> This is the first time in the history of the world where White men have to actually watch what they say. White men are getting in trouble for saying the wrong words, man it's unbelievable man. And a lot of White guys [*in a mock "white" voice*]: "Hey man that's not fair. You can say whatever you want. You can say nigger" [*resumes normal voice*]. Yeah, when I last checked that was the only advantage I had to being Black [*laughter*]. You wanna switch places [*laughter*]? You scream nigger and I'll raise interest rates [*huge laughter, clapping, cheers, and whistles*]. . . . Sometimes the people with the most shit have to shut up and let other people talk shit about them [*laughter*]. That's how life works.[25]

Rock's argument in a nutshell: so, you cannot say "nigger" . . . big deal, you still own and plunder the universe. Control of public speech (a censoring not observed privately by many people) pales in comparison to control of a financial system whose history is wrought with myriad means of disenfranchising African Americans and other people of color. Chris Rock's charged humor locates and situates himself as Black and a subordinated subject in the United States, invokes cultural heritage by hearkening a shared history of oppression, reveals the real locus of power as the almighty dollar, and calls for economic restructuring. It is activist humor, even if the speaker may not be a formal activist and is simply using the stage as a platform to advocate on behalf of a political cause or social issue. This humor can be satirical, self-deprecating, shocking, or tendentious; it is *always* political and strives to offer solutions.

Charged humor edifies and instructs so it does not simply point to the trouble, but often conjures creative and humorous means for reconciliation or social change. This means that charged humor is a solution-oriented style of comic performance tapping into personal experience and drawing from cultural analysis and interpretation. Nato Green, a heterosexual White man, spent much of 2011 on the road with Janine Brito and W. Kamau Bell on the comedy tour: Laughter against the Machine. From White privilege to xenophobia to the gap between the rich and the poor, Green's wry charged humor deftly points to social inequities *and* supplies possible solutions.

> But when they talk about immigrants . . . the right wing always says illegal aliens and they don't mean alien in a good way, like Alf [*laughter*]. The word alien conveys an image of invasion and conquest. But I've actually known a lot of illegal immigrants in my life and my friends are not here to invade and conquer America, in my experience they are here to clean up America's shit, make America's food while America sleeps [*laughter*]. So if we ever talk about groups of people using metaphors we should at least use an accurate metaphor. Not aliens [*pause*] . . . elves [*laughter*]. How would it change the public policy debate if we all said illegal elves [*laughter*]? [*In a mocking voice*] Close the borders for those magically industrial beings [*laughter*].[26]

Language like "alien," "foreigner," and "illegal" immediately establishes an individual as not belonging in a legal and cultural sense. In this joke, he attacks terminology and beliefs circulating about undocumented immigrants in the United States, exposing these as ways to dehumanize them and make it easier to dismiss or justify exploitation, abuse, and belittling. The language he proposes instead—"magically industrial beings"—recharacterizes a denigrated community performing thankless difficult work. If language creates our reality as sociologists and semioticians suggest, a linguistic substitution would be an important step to change the living conditions of undocumented workers in the United States.

Cultural citizenship helps distinguish charged humor from satire as its own style of humor production; there are similarities but also important distinctions. Like satire, charged humor passes judgment, targeting individuals and institutions with overt critiques. And while charged humor and satire "mean it" and want it to do something beyond eliciting a chuckle, charged humor invokes cultural citizenship. When George Lopez uses the stage to celebrate Latino/a cultural practices and identity—sprinkling jokes with Spanish, castigating anti-immigration sentiments and policies, and openly mocking the superciliousness of dominant (White) culture—he kindles cultural citizenship through charged humor. While charged humor struggles in the economy of comedy, satirical performances abound in twenty-first-century popular culture demonstrating that satire may or may not be charged humor. The popularity of infotainment or news shows using humor to impart information like *The Daily Show* and *The Colbert Report* attests to the public's desire to consume political and social satire, some of which *is* charged humor. More often than not though, the comedy performed by late-night television talk show hosts (excluding the hosts of the shows just mentioned) is more aptly defined as pseudo-satirical, a brand of humor that caricatures celebrities and well-known political figures without actually being critical or taking a stand on salient issues.[27] Perhaps dismissed as an innocuous form of entertainment, comic performances, whether charged, satirical or pseudo-satirical, communicate messages. For charged humor but not necessarily for satire, these messages privilege agency, community, and redress. Like shock comedy, self-deprecating humor, minstrelsy, or performing marginality, charged humor can be satirical. In fact, by evoking aggression, judgment, play, laughter (all key elements of satire) as well as relying on a knowledge base and offering strategies and solutions for change, you could argue that charged humor and satire are one and the same. While these blur in definition and performance at times, both foisting judgment and making an attack, charged humor seeks to remedy experiences of second-class citizenship by celebrating and developing cultural citizenship among minorities—be they sexual, racial, ethnic, corporeal, material, or otherwise—and their allies. In 1962, when Mort Sahl quipped: "Here we are at the new frontier—Cuba," he attacked the US government's global imperialist practices that would threaten the autonomy and independence of Cuba, criticized America's foreign policy, and simultaneously drew attention to the Space Race beginning in 1957 between the Soviet Union and United States (also called the "new frontier" and the title of Sahl's album).[28] The joke functions as satire but not as charged humor. If he had gone on to make a connection between domination of "inferior" people domestically and abroad, uniting folks based on shared disenfranchisement and considering possible solutions for such disparities—that would have made it both satirical *and* charged. Comics wield charged humor on behalf of social justice, seeking to remedy inequality and, importantly, doing so by creating community, fostering cultural citizenship, and generating solutions.

Of equal importance, here, is comic intentionality. Part of what makes this humor charged is that it is done so consciously—the performer is in one regard *charging* her audience with social crimes, indictments of a stratified and prejudicial America. This is not necessarily conducted in a hostile manner. In fact, humor offers gentle rebuke, like a mama bear cuffing her cub. I reserve the designation of charged humor for the material of jokesters whose counterhegemonic material aligns with their artistic objectives. In other words, it is important to examine what a comic says onstage as well as offstage. In this way, I attempt to avoid specious recuperations or readings for resistance of comic material that may be many things, including satirical, but does not intend to be resistant or effect social change. In an interview published in the *New York Post*, Adam Carolla, stand-up comic and creator of *The Man Show*, says, "The reason why you know more funny dudes than funny chicks is that dudes are funnier than chicks." He goes on: "If Joy Behar or Sherri Shepherd was a dude, they'd be off TV. They're not funny enough for dudes. What if Roseanne Barr was a dude? Think we'd know who she was? Honestly."[29] His opinions offstage clearly express male superiority and he corroborates these sexist views in comic material on stage and in the television shows in which he has a hand. Any analysis of his comedy as subversive, antisexist, or feminist would be shortsighted and ignore the evidence available. It is important to examine the comic material circulating and the intentions and values of the jokester in question. Doing so can reveal that while sometimes comics make jokes that at face-value are racist or sexist or homophobic, these are not necessarily world-views they believe or to which they adhere. Such a disconnect might instead point toward what audiences *want* to hear. An aggressively sexual shock comic, Lisa Lampanelli may bash people of color and gays fondly in her sets, but in her interviews, public life (she donated $50,000 to gay rights organizations in 2011), and moments in her performance reveal sympathies toward communities experiencing second-class citizenship by virtue of race, gender, sexuality, etc. These moments belie what might otherwise appear to be virulent bigotry. Investigating Lampanelli onstage and offstage reveals the divide between her personal politics and the comic persona she portrays. It is worth noting that Lampanelli's style of shock comedy proves lucrative for her and others performing similar material; there is a reason she employs this style instead of performing charged humor, which she certainly could do given what we know about her worldviews.

Charged humor occurs in a country divided, whether by political affiliation or ideological differences. Some folks are going to love prochoice material and others will take umbrage, just as some viewers may agree with gay marriage and others will not. One night in 2003 as I was leaving a live performance by Margaret Cho at Ohio State University, I ran into some acquaintances also leaving the show. They raved about the performance, except one White man who remained quiet. When he did speak up, he wondered aloud if comedy was a place for politics. He had enjoyed the show up until Cho rebuked the Don't Ask Don't Tell policy (which was reversed in 2010). Cho was indignant that someone who was willing to die for their country was not even allowed to be honest about their sexuality, as if that had any bearing on their aptitude in the military, as if being gay somehow conflicts with patriotism or the ability to do one's job. "She was funny until she got political," he said. In other words, she was doing her job as a comic until she made political or social commentary contradicting his own worldview. During those same bits, many members of the audience were laughing, cheering, and applauding, demonstrating an ideological divide at play: proponents of gay civil rights signaled agreement while opponents stiffened in their seats.

In general, comics performing charged humor have a harder time becoming mainstream because their material calls into question social hierarchies, builds community, and lobbies for social change. Communications scholar Linda Jean Kenix compares mainstream media to alternative media, arguing that "mainstream media have been traditionally viewed as maximizing audiences through pack journalism that is conventional and formulaic, relying on content that would appeal to the most number of readers and therefore ignoring the issues that are perhaps more important to smaller, minority groups;" whereas alternative media "advocate programs of social change through the framework of politicized and in-depth social commentary."[30] The simplest barometer for classifying a comic as mainstream is to assess whether or not they have name cachet or recognition with a significant portion of the public. Can they pull off their own half-hour Comedy Central special or a full-length concert comedy film; are they invited to perform on late-night television talk shows on the major networks; are they headlining in comedy clubs in major urban centers or better yet a larger performance venue like the Apollo in Harlem or DAR Constitution Hall in Washington, DC; are they offered comedic film roles or can they carry a sitcom or reality show? If you can answer yes to more than a couple of these about any comic, then most likely they are mainstream.

Perhaps it is most accurate to say that charged humor does not help your chances of achieving mainstream recognition, status, and fame. But, it does not preclude those chances—some charged comics like Richard Pryor, Dave Chappelle, Wanda Sykes, Chris Rock, Margaret Cho, and Kathy Griffin are household names in spite of the odds. But many other practitioners of charged humor struggle at the regional level, traveling the national circuit of comedy clubs as forever a feature comic or "road dog," or are making a living cobbling together corporate, cruise line, and college gigs along with special performances for human rights organizations, freelance writing work, and online web projects. How one circumvents an unwelcoming market and an audience potentially at odds with one's agenda varies based on the comic's response to and navigation of said obstacles, political and social conditions, and the technologies used to enable and enhance self-promotion, for example, independent recording labels and social media.

While advertisers and network executives can be fairly indifferent to political worldviews—they support whatever programming is most likely to generate profit within the confines of Federal Communications Commission (FCC) regulations—they are incredibly attuned to the consumptive proclivities of target demographics. An entertainment industry executive put it this way: "You know, getting Latino shows in English on TV is a mathematical formula. When there is enough money to justify it, it will happen."[31] He was referring specifically to Hispanic programming but his point is generalizable. Similarly, in an interview, Lily Tomlin said:

> The bottom line is the dollar. It's just a reflection of the culture. . . . why do they make big blockbuster, you know, action adventure movies? Because they make the biggest box office. There are more people in the culture who want to see that kind of a film. . . . And you're right, every now and then they'll be a blip on the screen and something comes along that just happens to make money, happens to catch on and do well. But by and large, they can count on it [action adventure movies]. They can count on bringing in the dollars with that kind of film, generally. So there are more of those produced. . . . It's not like they're anti-anything, they're just pro-dollar.[32]

Charged humor can be divisive, eliciting strong reactions, both positive and negative, which makes it a risky commercial venture when its material can alienate a good portion of a target demographic. Late-night television talk show hosts like Jay Leno and David Letterman take potshots at Democrats and Republicans, but only usually to target a personality quirk or flaw, rather than to spur reform. Such apolitical material ensures talk show hosts are well-loved and able to transcend and appeal to a nation divided on political issues and candidates.

Television and film are subject to censorship not just by the Federal Communications Commission; a film's or show's content is also subject to network standards that are in turn supported by advertisers. If the content is polarizing, advertisers may lose out on a portion of a desirable market. Networks choose content carefully to avoid objectionable material that could cost them advertisers.

Writing of satire's place in 1950s and '60s television, Gerald Nachman reports that the "networks declared that hip satirical humor was beyond the grasp of The People" and describes television in the mid-twentieth century as a "medium not known for playing to the box seats . . . in those days of white-bread TV."[33] Not a whole lot has changed. Sometimes satirical, but always politicized, charged humor, especially coming from an unknown comic, is not conducive to prime time television, historically or today. Musing on mainstream media in the twenty-first century, career funny lady Maria Bamford makes similar, though more humorous, observations about the restrictions put in place by the gatekeepers of the entertainment industry:

> But you know how it goes—you need health benefits so you start working for the man. You know, I was just typing out what he had to say. I felt like I was taking back the night from *inside* the machine, because it makes a difference to *this* starfish. And then you get a promotion. And my ego says uh, I wanna be on TV and it turns out the man owns that. He just wants to make you do a couple changes to your jokes so as not to upset his buddies/corporate entities. And I made those changes. And then the man says, "I'll give you a big bag of money if you just say what I want you to say." And I took that big bag of money and I said exactly what he wanted me to say. And now I'm re-decorating my house in shades of gray! [*Feigns maniacal laughter*] HA, HA, HA, HA [*laughter*] (emphasis hers).[34]

According to Bamford, to be successfully mainstreamed, comics must either compromise or eliminate polarizing material or find alternative means of building a fan base—both are strategies with which she is familiar. The latter strategy can pay off over time when a comic has enough name recognition to compel advertisers, network executives, and producers to hire her. The former strategy often proves a more clear and expeditious route, which is to perform apolitical material until a solid fan base has been established. Anticipating marketing difficulties, George Lopez elected to perform safe comedy until becoming well-established, after which he had more freedom (read: commercial power) to insert more charged humor.

> I think I kind of compromised myself a little bit in some of the material coming up because you gotta get in. I don't think I was as hard-edged in the beginning, as I would have liked to be now. I've been in meetings with Warner Brothers where I wasn't particularly happy with what I was hearing. And the Chicano would say, "You know what, fuck this! Fuck you guys, I'm leaving." When you leave, you're out. So, I'd make myself stay. Probably a lot of people would say that's selling out but it isn't selling out, it's the way the business is set up.[35]

The arc of Lopez's comedy is testament to this with early work consisting of mainly noncharged family-friendly humor, whereas his later comedy specials,

America's Mexican (2007) and *Tall, Dark and Chicano* (2009) are chock full of charged humor celebrating Mexican culture and heritage and lobbing acerbic critiques at dominant White culture. The same observation can be made of the careers of Wanda Sykes and Margaret Cho, both well-known charged comics but whose early, attention-grabbing comedy incorporated fewer instances of charged humor or trafficked in other comedy styles consumers found appealing, like Cho's use of yellowface minstrelsy. This appears to be a solid strategy for getting a foot in the door.

In sum, charged humor is not as economically viable as noncharged humor. Karen Ripley, a White lesbian comic who started performing in 1977, performs a bit that captures the monetary toll placed on stand-up comics whose comedy draws attention to social identities as marginalized: "I wanted to tell some gay and lesbian jokes because I don't ever want to be rich and famous [*laughter; pause*]; and it's working [*laughter*]."[36] However, the potential charged humor has to be economically viable is contingent on historical context (e.g., different moments in history allow for some charged comics to emerge as national icons) and the individual comic in terms of her identity, stage persona, or point of view, and the frequency, style, and critique of her charged humor. If a comic headlines at Carolines on Broadway, a club in Times Square known for pulling in tourists from across the nation and around the world, she must have either a modicum of notoriety (in that case she could include charged humor) or the jokes must appeal to the majority assembled there. A sure-fire way of garnering said appeal, is to steer clear of polarizing content—a tall order for a kind of humor whose task it is to politicize, edify, and confront audiences about social inequalities. While market gatekeepers may hold the purse strings and seem to dictate what is made available to us, they continually look to us to decide what or who will be featured next on America's "It" list. The public supports comics whose personae reflect their worldviews and ideologies. Noting who is popular in any period of time will in turn indicate popular consensus about what is funny and whose points of view are worthy of support. In the next chapter, I argue that some mid-twentieth century charged humor found favor with audiences, allowing a few charged comics to emerge as cultural spokespersons even, at times, in mainstream media. The popularity of charged humor during this era, relative to the latter twentieth century, reflects a significant enough portion of the population willing to "buy" into the worldviews of charged comics. This coincided with the social rebellion fueling a number of civil rights movements and the (then) emergent technologies granting access to charged comedy beyond television—like the long-playing record.

The critical work of Americanists continues to be the intellectual engagement with "how American national identity has been produced precisely in opposition to, and therefore in relationship with, that which it excludes or subordinates."[37] Citizenship has long promised inclusiveness while remaining hierarchical in practice. An examination of the production and consumption of charged comedy through the lens of cultural citizenship offers a proactive means of identifying those on the fringes of the national imaginary and the methods they employ to feel like they belong. Because I focus on comics who produce charged humor, they range wildly in success in the entertainment industry and hail from every social group imaginable—from household names like Richard Pryor and Louis C.K. to those like Janine Brito, Gloria Bigelow, and Hari Kondabolu, who are recognizable only among a base of loyal fans. Part of the attraction of cultural citizenship as framing mechanism for analysis of charged humor rests on its inclusiveness and ability to encompass such a diverse range of comic practitioners. I focus on the content of their humor, namely on how they reveal their social positioning in the United States and what we can learn and know from them. The strategies they devise to achieve visibility (and even fame) while deploying charged humor has implications for entertainers in many other cultural forms who seek to produce substantive popular entertainment. Humor production is just one cultural form of many having the capacity to reveal who we are, as individuals and as a nation.

> But [Black writers and film-makers] insist that others recognize that what they have to say comes out of particular histories and cultures and that everyone speaks from positions within the global distribution of power. . . . And the question of ethnicity reminds us that everybody comes from some place—even if it is only an "imagined community"—and needs some sense of identification and belonging. A politics which neglects that moment of identity and identification—without, of course, thinking of it as something permanent, fixed or essential—is not likely to be able to command the new times.[38]

This book echoes the clarion call made decades ago by Stuart Hall, a call for a politics recognizing every person's need to connect, identify, and belong. Charged humor is predicated on those needs. Indeed, the impetus for theorizing cultural citizenship grew out of a desire to build community and secure rights among those experiencing exclusion from the larger national body.

It is not a foregone conclusion that second-class citizens will take up arms or rhetorically combat the system or groups maintaining their subordination. While many minority comics perform charged humor, they do not have to and we should not assume that they do or will; they are under no obligation to use humor to engender community or speak out against bigotry. In fact, minority comics seeking a professional career in comedy face extraordinary commercial and social pressures to perform in ways that corroborate stereotypes and satisfy audience expectations about "otherness," for example, a gay man who ratchets up the gay to gain audience approval (think: Jack from *Will and*

Grace) or a Black comic who acts gangsta' although she has never set foot in a ghetto. Whether an exaggerated performance of identity or a form of minstrelsy, the pressure to gay it up, Black it up, or don a raced or queered affect to make fun of your own or another minority group comes primarily from watching other comics do it successfully, which means they are meeting the demands of the public, the people . . . us. Public desire to support social parity can be a game changer in the field of stand-up comedy, shifting how and who we constitute as mainstream, thereby making charged comedy more readily available and accessible. Americanist T. J. Jackson Lears writes that it "is part of our task as well, to listen to those voices (however dissonant and confused) and try to reconstruct the human experience of history."[39] Comedy is telling and there is much we can learn from these cultural critics in jester's clothing. Charged comics are thinking hard and talking harder. They perform charged humor for a variety of reasons, though they do have one thing in common . . . to them, it is not just a joke.

CHAPTER TWO

Twentieth-Century Stand-Up

A History of Charged Humor

I volunteered to go to outer space. When Ike was president I flew over to Washington and I said Mr. Ike can I get on your outer space program? And he said what for? And I said well I can't go to school down here.

Dick Gregory

Football is my favorite sport, the only sport in the world where the Negro can chase a white man and 40,000 people stand up and cheer.

Dick Gregory

In the early 1960s, a veteran and former postal worker by the name of Dick Gregory took the profession of stand-up comedy by storm. A comedic tour de force, in five years time he released seven comedy albums and published three books—one an autobiography and the others, print collections of his jokes set alongside pictorials—while also performing frequently and becoming increasingly involved in the African American civil rights movement. The jokes opening the chapter are not an aberration from his traditional material; they are reflective of the style and charged content of the comedy he performed around the country after getting his first big break in 1961.[1] In his own words: "If I've said anything to upset you, maybe it's what I'm here for. Lenny Bruce shakes up the puritans, Mort Sahl the Conservatives, and me—almost everybody!"[2] His charged comedy was fearlessly critical of what he called "your stinking White racist institutions," and with a gentility that added to his appeal, he was instrumental in bringing pleas for social justice and civil liberties for Black Americans into the homes of White Americans.[3] He eventually left stand-up comedy for a full-time position as an activist in the movement, a position—though the causes have changed over time—he maintains today. From the release of his first comedy album in 1961 to nearly half-a-century later, his messages and convictions remain consistently focused on healthy lifestyle practices, institutionalized racism, better treatment for Native Americans, economic disenfranchisement, world hunger, and the medical and military industrial complexes. I saw Dick Gregory at a speaking engagement held at the American Film Institute in Silver Spring, Maryland, in 2005. These days he is not operating under the auspices of being a stand-up, and it is clear that is not his priority, though he still manages to hijack laughter from his audience, something he does rather easily. During his stint as a stand-up comic, he was among a handful of stand-up comics committed to performing charged humor and many others whose edgy material was a mix of charged humor and satire.

This chapter focuses on the landscape of charged comics performing from the 1950s to the mid-1980s—beginning with Mort Sahl, famous for his political humor, who also, at times, incorporated charged humor in his routines— and explores popular reception to charged comedy. I elected to focus on the charged comics whose comedy and careers are foundational to understanding charged humor as a comedic style and strategy, and whose delivery of charged humor greatly influenced generations of stand-up comics to come. Since I attend primarily to comics deploying charged humor regularly, if not as a mainstay in their routines, this means that some popular comics using charged humor sparingly like Redd Foxx, Moms Mabley, and Rusty Warren are not featured prominently. Revered and reviled alike, charged comics performing during this time like Dick Gregory, Lenny Bruce, Robin Tyler, George Carlin, Lily Tomlin, and Richard Pryor used the stage to promote social justice (some still do). Tyler championed gay liberation, Gregory played the wise oracle of race relations, and after Gregory left stand-up for full-time activist work, Pryor took up a similar mantle. They performed during a time when audiences were increasingly hospitable to critiques of institutionalized inequality, particularly around indices of race and ethnicity. Public support for these critiques allowed charged comics more opportunities for achieving mainstream status. Indeed, the rock-stars of stand-up comedy during this era included charged comics who used their visibility for more than just securing the yucks. It was a fecund period for experimentation, a Garden of Eden for stand-up comedy and particularly for charged comics.

This history of charged humor, its practitioners and its public's reception, begins with the advent of modern stand-up comedy in the 1950s. I track charged humor at this juncture where stand-up comedy became a distinctive cultural form, separate from other modes of performance and enticing the public to support shows exclusively comprised of stand-up comics. As such, I am most interested in how charged humor was produced and consumed in the mid-twentieth century. The period from the 1950s to 1980s saw a surge in the number of comic performers and public interest in what they had to say. This is not to say that earlier popular forms of entertainment did not find ways of sticking it to the man vis-à-vis humor—a trusty device of the oldest order to challenge authority in a nonthreatening way. Lineups for vaudeville and variety shows, whose heyday spanned the latter nineteenth and early twentieth centuries, usually included at least one comic or comedic duo; however, comedy acts were sandwiched between a motley crew of entertainers: jugglers, contortionists, regurgitators, tumblers, ventriloquists, animal acts, minstrels, sketch artists, and musicians. Comedy acts were often but not always apolitical, as when the popular female comic sensation Trixie Friganza used the stage to champion women's suffrage. Vaudevillian comic performers and humorous orators like Mark Twain were the precursors to the stand-up comics so familiar to us today. Indeed, Judith Yaross Lee argues in *Twain's Brand: Humor in Contemporary American Culture* (2012) that stand-up comics today resemble Mark Twain in style and content in addition to borrowing from Twain's strategies for self-promotion and branding that secured his status as an American comedic icon. Charged humor also appeared in the cultural forms emerging from new technological innovations. Fred Allen used radio comedy to attack the wealthy, and Stan Freberg, capitalizing on the newest innovation for entertainment in 1948, the long-playing record, created parodic jingles satirizing the increasingly heavy-handed commercialization of everything. These early humorists and comedic performers unquestionably influenced the new wave of comics emerging in the 1950s, putting stand-up comedy on the map as a popular cultural form strong enough to hold Americans' attention, a form of entertainment that would become a booming business by the 1980s and an irreplaceable and significant influence on national consciousness by the twenty-first century.

Having examined a host of comics performing a variety of comedic styles, some patterns emerge in the usage and deployment of charged humor by comics. There are those that do not perform charged humor at all or sparingly and instead rely heavily on one or a combination of the following styles: shock humor, family friendly (safe) comedy, absurdist or character comedy, and modern-day minstrelsy. Other comics use charged humor with greater frequency, but it does not account for the entirety of their material. Other comedic styles just noted can certainly be enlisted but they are also more likely to employ satire or political humor, which they couple with charged humor (think: Lewis Black or Bill Maher). Finally, there are those comics that use charged humor almost exclusively, like Robin Tyler, Micia Mosely, and Hari Kondabolu (all case studies here). I am most interested in what happens to comics—that is, reception from the public and commercial viability—operating out of the latter two categories. Focusing only on die-hard charged comics eliminates many vital contributions to the historical corpus of charged humor. The ensuing chapters focus on the comics employing charged humor (historically and in the twenty-first century) and the cultural climate and economic environs in which they perform. I examine the substance of their humor, the content of their critiques as well as considering the variability in their respective successes or failures to become mainstream comics.

Shifts in the entertainment industry like the centralization of stand-up comedy after the Comedy Strike of 1979, the rise of neoliberalism and the decline of Keynesian economics, a boom in the commercial airline industry that made it easier for comics to travel from one urban center to another, and the explosion of new programming on cable television all precipitated changes in the marketability and demand for charged humor, making the work of charged comics increasingly difficult to find in the emerging glut of comics striving for professional careers in the field. Furthermore, public interest and support for myriad social movements flagged in the 1980s; up-and-coming comedians seeking to use the stage on behalf of social justice were considered more of an annoyance and out of touch with yuppies' preoccupation with material goods and social status. Some, like Margaret Cho and George Lopez, performed sans charged humor until they secured a following or slipped in charged humor periodically, while relying primarily on jokes and content audiences were eager to hear—like material about airline peanuts, the Scarsdale Diet, and Molly Ringwald. Since the mid-1980s, devout charged comics desiring a wider audience have had to be resourceful and creative in finding venues and creating a fan base outside of mainstream avenues for exposure like the national comedy club circuit, television specials, and comedy concert films.

Mid-Twentieth-Century Charged Humor: 1950s–1960s

Bebop music was the musical style emerging in the 1950s, making quite an impression for its improvisational aspects. Spontaneity seeped into many cultural forms: experimental theater was on the rise, artists flirted with abstract expressionism, and the Beat Poets got their jollies from drugs and the heady high of artistic collaboration, playing around with the written word and breaking all kinds of literary rules. Though the '50s have been characterized as a conservative decade segueing into the more radical 1960s, historian Alan Petigny offers evidence to the contrary, calling the years following World War II until 1965 the "Permissive Turn," a period birthing the civil rights movements and prefacing the more overtly rebellious youth countercultures that would characterize the 1960s. An interest in the individual or self, the ascendancy of social sciences, especially modern psychology, a rise in enrollment in higher education, and theological shifts emphasizing love and forgiveness over discipline and self-abnegation all contributed to the desire for spontaneity and improvisation and fostered investment in "the principles of democracy, diversity and individual autonomy."[4]

In comic performances, stand-up comics began moving away from traditional jokes both in formula and content. Instead of the standard—set-up and punch line, then repeat—comics began telling stories using anecdotal humor to amuse their audiences. According to Gerald Nachman, early storytellers, the progenitors of this shift in style, like Jean Carroll, Danny Thomas, and Sam Levenson "helped create a new, civilized environment for the wild band of revolutionaries who were slowly gathering on the horizon just over the mountains."[5] This more confessional style of comedy prompted audiences to identify with the comics as people; audiences felt like they knew the comic personally. In a style wholly familiar to today's consumers of live comedy but one not as commonly employed before the 1950s, some comics interacted with audience members, asking them questions and using the exchange as comedic fodder. Others, like Lenny Bruce and Jonathan Winters, improvised entire sets, employing a fly-by-the-seat-of-your-pants method that mirrored the improvisational qualities becoming infused in so many other popular culture forms. Accustomed to sharing billing with other kinds of entertainers like contortionists, jugglers, magicians, and musicians, comics sought refuge and carved out spaces in small venues in major metropolitan areas like the hungry i and the Purple Onion in San Francisco, the Bitter End, the Village Gate, Bon Soir, the Blue Angel, the Duplex, and the Café Wha? in New York City, and Chicago's Playboy Club and Mister Kelly's, many of which catered primarily to folk singers and stand-up comedy and showcased young comic hopefuls like Mort Sahl, Bill Cosby, Dick Gregory, and Lenny Bruce.

> So, I think the reason the hungry i became what it became and why it was so widely copied was because in the Eisenhower/McCarthy/Nixon era and the early '50s that it was a springboard of dissent. You didn't find it in the legitimate theater. You didn't find it in a novel. You didn't find it on a television. You didn't hear it on the radio. But I think the hungry i and the spin-offs of the hungry i were the first signs of an opposition to the Cold War forming.[6]

Borscht Belt comics and aging vaudevillians, who had long ago learned to adapt to new forms of communication like film and radio, earned a living by recording comedy albums and in the emerging television programming that included late-night talk shows and variety shows like *The Ed Sullivan Show*, *The Tonight Show*, and *Laugh-In*. But a new kind of comedy was taking hold, mirroring the public disquiet that began to seethe in the youth countercultures and civil rights movements during the mid-twentieth century. Social unrest and upheaval was not around the corner; it had already arrived and could be seen in the satire and the charged humor of this decade's comedians.[7]

Mort Sahl, Lenny Bruce, and Dick Gregory captured the nation's attention in the late 1950s and cemented their respective places in the annals of comedy with their cutting-edge, now-classic routines recorded and sold widely in the early 1960s. Longtime owner of San Francisco's legendary hungry i, Enrico Banducci started off hiring only musicians and singers but was convinced to give Mort Sahl a regular spot. Initially unimpressed with Sahl but recognizing his potential, Banducci felt sympathy for the waifish rookie in need of a job and, as he did for so many other hard-up artists, including Maya Angelou, Banducci hired him. It was the winter of 1953 and thus began a working relationship that would span many decades. Years later Banducci still admired Sahl's faith in what Banducci saw as social satire: his steadfast belief that comedy can help change the system.[8]

A loquacious satirist, Sahl spared no one, least of all acting presidents and other government and religious officials. A charged joke told during one of many hungry i reunion shows (this one in 1981), he waxes indignant at the censoring of the word "lesbian" on *The Tonight Show* hosted by Johnny Carson's stand-in John Davidson in 1980:

> So, uh, I sit there and say to Fred McCourt, the producer: "What's the matter?" And he says: "You were out there didn't you see? We tried to bleep it all in time. He said 'lesbian' on the air." And I said, "Yea I know." So he says, "Well, you can't say that on the air." So, uh, I say, "Why?" So he says, "Because we've got a middle class audience and we could offend their sensibilities" [*laughter*]. I said, "Really?" and he says, "Yea, this is not a night club where you can get up and curse" [*laughter*]. So I want you to know where television is coming from. Isn't that the example? What they think of that—the audience. The audience of course they are referring to is us. They think that's gonna bother us. Whether she says female homosexual on the program or the chiding of John Davidson, she said she is a practicing lesbian. That's gonna upset us? Remember what we've been through here. We went to Vietnam for fourteen years: cost $171 billion, 50,000 dead, 30,000 casualties and we lost. Came in second. Is that better? [*laughter and clapping*].[9]

Drawing from his vast knowledge of American politics, Sahl uses political satire to execute this piece of charged humor demonstrating the symbiotic nature of the two styles of comedy. This comic bit goes on to indict the government and military, detailing a litany of abuses foisted on the American people like rising inflation, expansion of the military industrial complex, and gas shortages. He concludes the bit with a rhetorical question: "And now I ask, in light of the forgoing atrocities, what's one more lesbian on *The Tonight Show*?" In this joke, making mention of a marginalized sexual orientation pales in comparison to aggrandizing "family values" domestically while destroying families in developing nations. In the words of Dick Gregory, "America's the only country that lies about what she is . . . we say we're about one thing but we do something else."[10] The entertainment industry's protectionist stance against topics and words deemed inappropriate veils the sinister agenda to maintain power differentials that favor the rich and the White (often these go hand-in-hand) and dismiss marginalized social identities. Individuals can and will assume their abject status when they are convinced that they are impure, insignificant, and inferior and will find it difficult to mobilize if they are unaware of how to unite to redress inequality. Identity-based organizations, like the NAACP, lobbying for adequate and positive representations in television and film believe there is a direct relationship between equal and fair representation and social acceptance. A commanding presence and influence on many people, the representations we see in film and television can impact how we see ourselves and others. Sahl's joke strips away the façade of television, reminding viewers that content is heavily edited and moreover, the implications of that editing—who and what is rendered invisible.

Because Mort Sahl's humor was far more political than charged, examining his humor helps differentiate between political humor and charged humor. Sahl was nothing if not a keen observer of American politics. Listening to his successive comedy albums offers its own lesson in American history. He lampoons presidents as they take office—from Eisenhower to Nixon—and a cavalcade of political officials and intellectuals such as former press secretary James Hagerty, General Curtis LeMay, and Bertrand Russell. While he waxed eloquent on political figures, international affairs, and the government, his focus was seldom inequality and he took few measures to develop cultural citizenship among any swath of disaffected constituents. With fleeting references to women (who he only refers to as "chicks" or girls) "being attacked as a minority," in general his performances convey latent skepticism for the women's movement.[11] In the nearly dozen albums released in the late 1950s and throughout the 1960s, he says little on the topic of race relations, gay liberation, or access issues for the differently abled, but to be fair, when he does, his is a clear point of view that spurns bigotry. In 1960, he derided Tennessee governor Buford Ellington, for stalling desegregation in Tennessee schools.[12] Supported by his White constituents, Ellington's response mirrored many other state officials stubbornly opposed to integration. Sahl superficially addressed the status of atheists—a group historically reviled by the public—but not by attacking their persecution or offering possibilities for change; nor did he include himself as an ally. Responding to the evangelist Reverend Billy Graham's accusation that Sahl was an atheist, Sahl assures the audience he is not because, "It's too hard to be [an atheist] in society [*pause*] because you don't get any days off."[13] On a later album he quips: "I'm not really an atheist—I believe in a higher power . . . electricity."[14] While humorous, to be sure, both jokes dodge the question and neither is charged because there is no substantive critique nor does he foster cultural citizenship among atheists or any marginalized religion. In the late 1950s and early 1960s, he shared a status as American cultural icon with the famed Lenny Bruce, whose material was less about politics and more oriented toward social and cultural commentary.

Introducing Lenny Bruce at his Carnegie Hall performance in 1961, the announcer defends Bruce's bad-boy reputation and the salience of his comedy:

> The one thing I'd like to say about the label of "sick comedian," which I think is a misnomer, what Lenny does perhaps as a short explanation to the people who don't understand what he does; it is not that Lenny Bruce, per se, is a sick comedian, but that Lenny Bruce comments, reflects, holds up the mirror so to speak, to the sick elements in our society that should be reflected upon and that should be spoken about.[15]

Bruce's records with the most charged humor are ones performed for audiences in 1960 and 1961 like *I Am Not a Nut, Elect Me! Lenny Bruce—American*, and the nearly two-hour performance recorded at Carnegie Hall on February 2, 1961. In these albums he addressed class inequality, comparing his income to that of schoolteachers and calling it a "disgrace" and assuring audience members that if teachers were paid a fair wage, "then the education system would change immediately."[16] On the same album he introduced a comedic sketch featuring a Black man (Randy) and a Jewish man, both escaped prisoners who, shackled together, are on the run. We drop in on them having a conversation outside of the clink. Randy wonders aloud "if they'll ever be any equality?" The Jewish escapee argues that equality already exists, citing that they stand an equal chance of being drafted for the Vietnam War. Randy replies: "Yeah . . . but what about the schools and segregated housing?" His Jewish mate dismissively responds: "Well those things take a little time [*laughter*]. You can't shove everything down people's throats."[17] Using comedic characters to illustrate the stagnancy and absurdity of advancement for people of color, Bruce avoided didactic remonstrations of prejudice and substituted them for an equally effective, though passive, means of citing systematic inequality. Similarly, in another set, he enacted a conversation between a White man and Black man at a party. Struggling to make the Black man feel comfortable at an event where he is in the minority, the White man only introduces every cliché and stereotype circulating about Black people.

IMITATING WHITE GUY AT PARTY: You know what I'm gonna get you something to
    eat. I didn't notice any fried chicken here, watermelon [*laughter*], but uh, I'll get

something you'll like. I'll get a watermelon for you. I'll get you all the watermelons in the world 'cause I love ya [*laughter*] . . . Now, I'd like to have you over at the house.

IMITATING BLACK GUY AT PARTY: Thank you, I'd like to come over.

WG: Yeah, it'll be dark soon [*laughter*]. [*Pause*] Look you can come over to my house if you promise you won't do it to my sister. You don't want no heeb plowing your sister, and I don't want no coon doing it to my sister [*laughter*]. You can understand that can't ya?

BG: It doesn't make any difference to me just as long as she's nice.

WG: [*Pause*] What do you want weed or something?[18]

This sketch illustrates what not to do when socializing in racially mixed crowds. It is humorous because it's ironic: White man attempts to make Black man comfortable; his every overture clearly reveals his discomfort. Illuminating the ridiculousness of these stereotypes, the joke makes us laugh, first because we recognize the stereotypes as such, and again, at the foolishness of the White man's ignorance.

For his 1961 album, Lenny Bruce borrowed a campaign slogan from Governor Earl Long of Louisiana, who was thought to have gone crazy when he checked into a mental institution in 1959. Long's slogan while running for a fourth term as governor was, "I am not a nut, elect me!" Bruce mocked his platform by arguing that the slogan is as ineffectual as running with a slogan of, "I don't wet the bed, elect me!"[19] Not unlike Sahl, Lenny Bruce was progressive and political. But, Bruce, who laced his comedy with Yiddish idioms and shared first-hand knowledge of Jewish persecution, frankly discussed queer folks (Lenny himself courted both sexes), conveyed a clear point of view regarding racial inequality, and directed attention to abuses wrought by organized religion, performed more charged humor than Sahl. In 1959, on *The Sick Humor of Lenny Bruce*, he chided the country for making such a fuss over a young White boy stuck in a well for six days: "You still see in the classifieds: Orientals may buy here, Negroes may buy here. And one schmuck gets caught in a well and everyone stays up for a week!?"[20] As he implies, the fate of a lone boy when compared to that of entire racial groups marginalized in the United States, seems rather shortsighted.

Throughout the 1960s Lenny Bruce's political insights and charged humor began to wane. In San Francisco in 1961, the police arrested Bruce for saying "cocksucker" at the Jazz Workshop, an obscenity charge for which he was later found not guilty. Several more arrests followed, some for drugs and two more for obscenity (Chicago in 1962 and New York in 1964). He was found guilty for these later charges. By 1965 he had been arrested nineteen times and had one conviction; his legal battles had left him bankrupt and embittered. Almost as if prepping for closing arguments, his performances became lengthy remonstrations against the charges made against him. Painful to watch and hard to follow, in his next-to-last night club appearance, filmed at Basin Street West in Hollywood, Bruce brought a detailed memo of charges leveled against him, explained each joke condemned by the court, contextualizing it further and showing how it was misunderstood. He bristled at the accusation that his comedy was "insulting" and "lacking in redeeming social importance."[21] The audience seldom laughed; the whole thing feels awkward, then and now. On stage, Bruce shifted from using charged humor that commented on social stratification and the human condition to a fever-pitched rebuttal of the criminal charges that, like his life (he died in 1966) in the last four years, occupied most of his attention.

While Mort Sahl was politically savvy and Lenny Bruce broke taboos, Dick Gregory holds the title of champion charged comic during this time period. It was Hugh Hefner who spotted Dick Gregory, placed him in the Playboy Club, and helped him achieve the visibility and fame that got him on the cover of *Time* magazine just months after he left an unsatisfying career as postal worker to become a full-time stand-up comic. Starting out in African American clubs, Gregory became one of the first Black cross-over comics (along with Moms Mabley), a move he was ridiculed for by contemporaries like Nipsey Russell, Timmie Rogers, and Slappy White.[22] But Gregory seized the spotlight with a clear objective: "I didn't come here tonight to impress you, only to inform you."[23] Given this agenda, Gregory captured the ears of precisely the audience most in need of these messages. The Black civil rights movement needed allies, and Gregory's comedy proved one way to make White audiences hip to the need for social justice. His style and comic persona regaled audiences on both sides of the color divide, a good thing as otherwise he might have been just preaching to the choir.

On his first album *In Living Black and White*, recorded at Hefner's club in Chicago and on best-seller lists for over six months, Dick Gregory rips one zinger after another, discussing integration, the Ku Klux Klan, sit-ins, voting rights, and access to education. When a heckler interrupted him repeatedly near the end of his performance, Gregory replied: "Trying to get you to shut up is like trying to explain integration to a lynch mob [*loud laughter*]!"[24] His charged jokes packed a serious wallop throughout:

> A lot people don't understand how we can own so many Cadillacs with them inferior jobs. Well, racial segregation buys us Cadillacs. You have a country club you can join—I can't. So I save $500 a year [*light laughter*]. You know damn well I'm not taking my family to Florida this winter so that's another $1500 I save [*laughter*]. Walk out here tonight I get hit by a bus, I'm not going to the best

hospital where they're gonna charge me $2500 so I go to City hospital for free. Pick it up—I save $2,500 plus $2,000. $4,500 dollars and General Motors sell me anything I want [*laughter*].[25]

In under thirty-five seconds, he indicts institutionalized racism, which comes at a cost, a cost that he humorously quantifies at $4,500; however, he alludes to the psychological tax imposed on oppressed groups that is impossible to quantify. Line item by line item, he makes lemonade out of lemons, calculating the so-called profit gained when you are barred entry into elite organizations and clubs; when traveling poses the threat of verbal or physical assault and lack of access to restaurants, hotels, and stores; and when your station limits your access to the best health care. Knowing that White folks who believed Black people should not own nice things were angered by seeing a Black person own a Cadillac, Gregory exposes that a luxury car is hardly compensation for being treated as a second-class citizen. The responding laughter is bittersweet, sweet because it is funny, bitter because it is true.

Commerce is color-blind, or so Gregory intimated, reminding audiences of their powerful role as consumers. As long as efforts are focused, united, and determined, leveraging collective buying power can be one of the swiftest ways of creating desired social change, as when Black folks in Alabama forced integration on buses by boycotting public transit and organized elaborate carpooling schedules as an alternative. This is one among many strategies for empowerment that his charged humor advocated; others included boycotts, sit-ins, supporting the lowering of the voting age, and creating reform by organizing, educating yourself and others, and corresponding with local representatives. Summoning the promises made by the Declaration of Independence, he suggested that anytime someone sees a riot on television, they should stand and read the Declaration, which he goes on to movingly recite. The real injustice, he says, comes when Black people take a stand and do what the Declaration says, and they are called hoodlums, and that, he goes on to say, is "when we know the Declaration is for Whites only."[26] Some of his best advice promoted coalition building, as when he implores listeners to "get concerned about *all* people [emphasis his]," including his "White hillbilly brothers" in Appalachia and other rural areas. Calling for freedom and rights for Native Americans, Puerto Ricans, Mexicans, Jews, African Americans, and the impoverished, he promises that "Together we will solve my problems."[27] Recognizing that a racial order comes at a cost to everyone, Gregory's charged humor confronted multiple forms of racism and classism and its myriad targets.

While Gregory transitioned into the role of full-time activist, the next crop of charged comics earned their chops in the local scenes in New York City, the Midwest, and the West Coast during the sixties and early-to-mid seventies.

Robin Tyler, Lily Tomlin, Richard Pryor, Paul Mooney, and George Carlin each sought exposure as comics, sketch comics, actors, or droll drag queens. On the political front, the Civil Rights Act of 1964 had outlawed de jure segregation; in fact more constitutional amendments were ratified in the 1960s than any other decade, excepting the 1910s when Congress passed multiple amendments, for example, allowing the federal government to collect taxes, direct elections of US Senators by the people, and prohibition of alcohol. Civil rights movements came into full swing, promoting a culture of protest aimed squarely at the government and its domestic policies of tiered citizenship and foreign involvement in Cuba, the Soviet Union, and Vietnam.

During this era of protest cultures and cynicism toward the government, audiences clamored for substantive comedy. In the time period that birthed the folk protest movement, which made protest anthems in the style of Woody Guthrie a distinct genre of music, charged humor was highly sought after by coming-of-age baby boomers, though not always welcomed in mainstream mediums like television and film. Fortunately, the comedy album, which did not face as many restrictions from the entertainment industry to maintain family-friendly entertainment, was a hit with people of all ages, especially younger generations; politicized or rebellious content did not necessarily inhibit sales. In fact, several best-selling and successive recordings could turn a commercially risky enterprise (someone like Richard Pryor) into a known quantity, convincing network executives to take a risk and cast a long shot in a TV guest spot or a film role.

Twentieth-Century Charged Humor: 1970s–1980s

Comediennes during the 1960s and '70s took advantage of the freedom and lawlessness allowed by the comedy record, though women hardly constituted a statistically significant number of working comics during these times. Seen as an aggressive form of performance and antithetical to women's delicate sensibilities, women were less likely to pursue a career in stand-up comedy. Other factors contributed to the paucity of women comics like the shared cultural belief that men are naturally funnier than women, a society that promoted a gendered division of labor that made women responsible for childcare and domestic duties that effectively kept them at home, and tough conditions on the road for comics. Phyllis Diller, Moms Mabley, Joan Rivers, Rusty Warren, Totie Fields and Lily Tomlin, were a few of the women who succeeded as professional comics at this time. With rare exceptions (Tomlin perhaps), successful female comics mainly performed in gender-appropriate ways that were palatable to mainstream audiences. Self-deprecating humor was one tactic for overcoming audience opposition to a funny lady commanding the stage, and diminished the threat of a female comic asking a coed crowd to give her audience, to listen to her, to value what she says, her point of view. This was not easily done in a society where men were accustomed to commanding attention, barking orders, and amusing starry-eyed ingénues. According to Albert Rapp, a classical literature scholar exploring styles of humor in the 1951 study *The Origins of Wit and Humor*, self-deprecating humor communicates the performer's inferiority; it is one of three ways a comic puts the superiority theory of laughter into action. You can laugh at people that are "better" than you, turning the tables and making you feel superior; you can laugh at people that are "lower" than you (i.e., stupider, inferior in some way) and maintain your social standing; or you can draw laughter at your own expense, that is, you invite the audience to feel superior to you.[28] There is a subversive element at play in using self-deprecating humor. At first glance, you are making fun of yourself, but therein lies a criticism of a society that constructs ideals impossible to achieve.[29] When Phyllis Diller mocks her fright wig and stick legs, she simultaneously draws attention to the impossibility of fulfilling socially constructed standards of beauty, and disarms her audience by making them feel superior to her. Phyllis Diller and Joan Rivers made careers out of self-deprecating humor, while Rusty Warren and Moms Mabley both performed blue, meaning the content of their material contained sexual innuendo or was considered "dirty." In a live performance at the Greek Theater in Los Angeles, California, Mabley humorously recalled: "Had a brother older than he was—ninety-nine. He married a girl fourteen—fourteen! He didn't live but five days. Took three undertakers a week to get the smile off of his face."[30] Central to her commercial appeal and success, Mabley pushed an irreverent granny persona that made her seem harmless. In the process, she managed to say all manner of things on stage deemed inappropriate in other social settings. She started performing on the chitlin' circuit at a young age, was the first woman to perform at the Apollo Theater, and like Dick Gregory, was one of the few African American comics (and the first female) during the 1960s to secure patronage from both Black and White audiences.

It is understandable that these women pioneers poked fun at themselves or flirted with the profane; women had a hard enough time getting stage time, let alone the gumption to become mouthpiece for issues like women's liberation, gay rights, and civil liberties. But that was not the case with Robin Tyler, who began writing charged material in the late 1960s for comic sketches she performed with Pat Harrison. As a comic duo (billed as sisters rather than the lesbian lovers they were), they recorded two albums, *Try It, You'll Like It* (1971) and *Wonder Women* (1973), performed antiwar material for troops in Vietnam, and played a select number of university and college shows. Robin Tyler went on to develop her career as a stand-up comic and later became a full-time activist for gay civil rights. She was the first openly lesbian comic and one of the only early female comics to be as committed to charged humor as Dick Gregory. Indeed, their career paths are eerily similar with the principle difference being Tyler's obscurity relative to Dick Gregory. An omission in the history of popular culture I seek to remedy, I chronicle her life and career in chapter 4 in great detail, attending to the multipronged strategies she has employed in order to create social change on both political and cultural fronts.

Mild-mannered and sensitive, Lily Tomlin was everything the unapologetically brash Robin Tyler was not, though both sought to educate and entertain using stand-up comedy, sketch comedy, and one-woman shows in order to do so. Jane Wagner, Tomlin's longtime partner, comedy writer, and author of much of Tomlin's work, preferred to operate more subtly when trying to communicate a message. She believed that a story line or narrative nudged audience members to identify with people cut from all kinds of cloth. Identification serves as a humanizing force engendering empathy and accordingly, "the people on the stage, in the movies, represent humanity, so the people in the audience themselves, somehow they are changed by watching," says Jane Wagner.[31] With Tomlin as the face and Wagner as the voice, together they brought a peace-loving feminist-lite charged humor to an appreciative and now aging body of hippies in the mid'70s and early '80s.

Influenced by the likes of Ruth Draper, Beatrice Lilly, Lillian Gish, and especially Lucille Ball, in 1969 Lily Tomlin was an instant sensation on *Laugh-In*, beginning at a salary of $750 a week and three seasons later boasting a salary of $2,500 a week. This variety show would be her creative playground, a place for her to develop the characters that would go on to make her famous, like Edith-Ann, a precocious and observant five-year old, and Earnestine, a nasally operator whose snorts signaled derision toward the poor soul on the other end of the line. Before making it on the show, Tomlin had early training in theater at Wayne State University, skills she honed while performing stand-up comedy for years in Detroit, Michigan. Her first one-woman show *Appearing Nitely*, cowritten with Jane Wagner, uses humor to negotiate universal topics like coming of age, parenting difficulties, and the ubiquitous passage of time. In offering us multiple subject positions with which to identify, Tomlin accounts for the diversity both within and between individuals and their respective communities without passing judgment and without making claims to objectivity. Tomlin describes her work as "comedy that is relevant and comments on our lives," but avoids being too topical, meaning the content can stand on its own decades later and for generations to come.[32] An important piece of cultural work for feminism, scholar Jennifer Reed argues that Tomlin's *Appearing Nitely* serves up a "critique of patriarchy, capitalism, conventionality, naïve politics, and selling out."[33] Inspired by women's liberation and civil rights movements, Tomlin's performance appealed not just to a niche audience of feminists, hippies, and performance art hounds but to the masses as well, which helped bring the goals of these movements into the homes of millions.

The Search for Signs of Intelligent Life in the Universe (1985), also written by Jane Wagner, was considered "the first feminist comedy ever to appear on Broadway."[34] (The same feat has not been accomplished since, although Whoopi Goldberg's *The Spook Show* [1984–1985] may not have gotten the credit it deserved for tackling issues about race and gender too.) Other shows since then like Kathy Najimy and Mo Gaffney's *Kathy and Mo: Parallel Lives* (1989) and Eve Ensler's *Vagina Monologues* (1996) were certainly popular but played off-Broadway. Responding to this description, Tomlin explains that in this show "there is no hierarchy . . . it's connected . . . The conflict is not someone triumphing over someone else, or whatever the classic definition of drama is, etc. Yet, the play is cathartic, which is staggering you see."[35] Staggering because in the theatrical genre of drama, catharsis has been assumed to be achieved only by introducing conflict—for example, man loses battle, man loses woman, man loses dog. Tomlin and Wagner illustrate otherwise and show that a celebration of humanity in all of its complexity and quirkiness may yield catharsis not achieved at the cost of someone else's life or dignity.

In *The Search for Signs*, Tomlin portrayed a cast of twelve characters addressing the need for developing and strengthening community, and commenting on pollution, male chauvinism, advertising/trends/fads, suicide, drug abuse, gay bashing, women's liberation, reproductive rights, and a world rapidly globalizing. Many of the same themes pervade Tomlin's early recordings. Beginning on *Laugh-In*, and especially on her comedy albums, Tomlin used her characters to communicate her own values and/or cast aspersion on societal elements supporting unjust systems. One such character in the show: Lyn, a hippie women's libber turned yuppie coping with a midlife crisis, says to her general physician:

> But doctor, [*pause*] pre-menstrual syndrome? [*Pause*] I'm getting divorced, [*pause*], I'm raising twin boys [*pause*], I have a lot of job pressure. I've got to find one. The ERA didn't pass. Not long ago I lost a very dear friend [*pause*]. And the woman, [*pause*] my husband is in love with is quite a bit younger than I am. And you think it's my period and not my life?[36]

In this bit, Wagner and Tomlin attacked the medical establishment's tendency to, when confronted with women emoting anything other than congenial affability, connect their emotions to menstruation or menopause, never recognizing them as a valid response to the situation at hand. As if losing a dear friend to suicide, leaving your husband of ten years, having few job prospects other than low-paying and unreliable pink-collar work, and learning that your government refuses to make equality for women a constitutional priority, or any one of these things alone is not enough to drive even the most stoic to distraction. Desiring to communicate the possibilities of "feminism, and new age . . . and gay rights," Lyn becomes mouthpiece for the feminist wordsmith Jane Wagner.[37]

One-woman shows remain somewhat popular today among select audiences. In 2007, I attended a solo female performance called *Family Secrets* by Sherry Glaser, a Jewish lesbian performance artist, in which she portrays five characters in a Jewish family: Mort (father), Bev (mother), Fern/Kahari (eldest daughter), Sandra (younger daughter), and Rose (grandmother).[38] Much like Tomlin, Glaser's characters are bound by a certain time period and span multiple generations. For Glaser it is the early 1980s in Los Angeles and for Tomlin it is the mid '70s in New York. Period jokes and references keep the audience chuckling— who wouldn't laugh when reminded that track suits became hugely popular in the '80s and folks did *not* turn the radio station when they heard Duran Duran? Glaser, like Tomlin who was among the first female comics to perform in male drag, takes on the male persona of Mort, who stubbornly refuses to accept his daughter's bisexual lifestyle and teeters on the brink of being the family boob, especially when it comes to nontraditional beliefs. Tomlin and Glaser explore a range of subjectivities that convey the powerful lesson that acceptance and tolerance are key to maintaining a family, community, and nation. It is cultural citizenship writ large. It is also worth noting that Glaser's charged humor in the twenty-first century, despite deploying a similar style and mode, has not come close to rivaling the successes of Lily Tomlin.

In 1970, during Lily Tomlin's second season on *Laugh-In*, Richard Pryor spent some time in Berkeley, playing around with performance, writing, illegal drugs, and even playing the trumpet. (He would later meet Lily Tomlin and always thought highly of her and her work.) At that point, still early in his career, he had only recorded one comedy album, *Richard Pryor* (1968), live at the Troubadour in Los Angeles.[39] In it, you can hear early iterations of famous bits like "Super Nigger"—featuring a Black man of heroic proportions who can "see through everything except Whitey" and lives in a model city, which, according to Super Nigger, "means we have niggers under control here [*laughter*]"—and the "Prison Play," wherein the prison warden, upon hearing that a play to be performed is about a White woman who falls in love with a Black man, is placated only when assured, "It's quite alright, the nigger gets killed." (When the play does not, in fact, end with a lynching, the bamboozled warden warns: "If I don't get a damn nigger out here we're gonna hang a homosexual."[40]) After his brief stay in Northern California, Pryor returned to Los Angeles at the end of the year. In his memoir, he recalled: "For the first time in my life, I had a sense of Richard Pryor the person. I understood myself. I knew what I thought. I knew what I had to do. I had to go back and tell the truth. The truth. People can't always handle it. But I knew that if you tell the truth, it's going to be funny."[41] He recorded one of the earliest video recordings of his stand-up comedy at The Improvisation Night Club in New York, *Richard Pryor: Live and Smokin'* (1971), where you can hear little outbursts of opposition to his charged humor, which is gritty and seasoned with coke-addled anger. Confessing that he "always wanted to be something different than a nigger. 'Cause niggers had it so rough," he also began using a junkie character (not Mudbone, who surfaced later in his 1975 album, *Is It Something I Said?*) whose observations serve as cultural critique: "I'll be alright. I can handle this White world then—I get a little shit in my veins, I can take all this shit."[42] Exploring a conflict that must have resonated with many African Americans—the desire to belong regardless of racial identity—he opens the set stating:

> Always wanted to be something. Never wanted to be White. Hope not all along.
> No, I always wanted to be something different than a nigger, 'cause niggers had
> it so rough. I tried to be a Black cat with neat hair [*soft laughter*]. I thought that
> was a problem—the hair. I said if my hair was straight, then they dig me. So I
> got it processed [*pause*] . . . wrong.[43]

He went on to point out the spurious treatment of Black folks—inequitable housing, lack of access to education, negative assumptions based on race and so on—and closed with: "Black people have a lot to overcome. And it ain't just a mountain. Martin Luther King said, 'I have been to the mountain top' [*laughter*]. I've been to the mountain top too and I looked over the top and what did I see? More White folks [*laughter and pause*] with guns."[44] In his memoir, he writes that his second album, *Craps after Hours* (1971), "also explored race, sex, and drugs, but with even more shape and sting."[45]

On *Bicentennial Nigger* (1976), the album Pryor referred to as his "most political album," he criticizes the recently released blockbuster *Logan's Run*, a cinematic romp through a futuristic world where no one is allowed to live past thirty and instead of seeking monogamous relationships, people celebrate free love and women cannot seem to find enough fabric for skirts longer than mid-thigh.[46] Pryor lamented: "White folks ain't planning for us to be here," and based on the all-White cast of *Logan's Run*, he would be right. In response, he urged people to make movies that include African Americans and that do not depict them as criminals or pimps. Recalling a history of being sold as chattel and another century of economic exploitation and second-class treatment, Pryor cited White folks as being the biggest pimps yet, saying: "We the biggest hos they got." Pryor played a blackface minstrel in the final bit that doubles as the album's namesake, "Bicentennial Nigger," detailing centuries of abuse and malignment received at the hands of "Whitey." To end, he broke minstrel character. "I ain't never going to forget," he said, emphasizing each word to the hushed crowd.[47] There is a moment of silence before you hear any flutter of air and then, deafening applause.

Surprising then that fifteen years before that Pryor, in 1962, was honing his craft in New York City and invited to perform on *The Ed Sullivan Show* and *The Tonight Show Starring Johnny Carson* with material very different than what you hear on albums like *Bicentennial Nigger*. Pryor enjoyed a modicum of success performing family-friendly material, but for him that material did not feel honest. Honesty about the racism he observed would not grant him access to television shows, but over time he did build a fan base with his charged humor. Fast forward and by the end of the 1970s, Pryor was well on his way to adding movie star to his resume. He had small roles throughout the mid '70s, but after his concert film *Wanted: Live in Concert* (1978), Pryor became Hollywood's new sweetheart. This comedy special, along with subsequent shows like the 1979 concert recorded live at the Terrace Theatre in Long Beach, California, and back-to-back tours in the early 1980s, *Live on the Sunset Strip* (1982) and *Here and Now* (1983), show us a Pryor who has settled into himself, found a distinct point of view. Actively working to stay off drugs (although he went through a period where he began freebasing in the early '80s), seeking to continue securing choice film roles, enjoying several life-changing trips to Africa, and recovering from the loss of his grandmother who raised him, all these factors shaped Pryor into a man who maintained his convictions but whose comedy was less punctuated by or focused on social justice—though by no means was it unclear where Pryor stood. Most fans were so because they were acquainted with his early charged comedy, but even new converts would recognize his point of view that emphasized equality, community, and antiracism. His charged humor, included more sparingly in later concert films, focused on a racist criminal justice system that looks the other way when police officers "choke niggas to death," and schools White listeners on the dangers faced by Black people at the hands of law enforcement officers.[48] Just as Dick Gregory revealed the hidden costs of racism, Richard Pryor takes inventory of the psychological toll of racism.

> Racism is a bitch. White people you gotta know. It fucks you up—but what it does to Black people is a bitch. Because no matter what it—it is hard enough being a human being [*laughter*]. It's really fucking hard enough just to be that [*clapping*]. Right? Just to go through everyday life without murdering a motherfucker is hard enough. It's hard just to walk through life decent as a person. But here is another element added here when you're Black. Got that little edge on us. It's enough to make you crazy [*laughter*]. If you're in another argument with another man—he could be White—and it's man on man for a minute, get rough, ending up calling you nigger. You gotta go, "oh shit. Fuck. Now I ain't

no man no more. I'm a nigga'. Now I gotta argue with that shit [*laughter*]. Fuck. Throwing my balance all off" [*laughter*]. No, but it's an ugly thing . . . I hope one day they give it up [*clapping*].[49]

Recognizing the skills necessary to make difficult topics like racism palatable for mixed race audiences, fellow comic and talented writer Robert Townsend explains that "when Richard exposed how ridiculous racism is you had to laugh . . . that's being a master comedian."[50] Aside from these charged moments, and they really do feel like moments, which bookend the shows, the rest of the material on later specials focuses on Pryor's life, stories about his pets and children, his childhood, an occasional appearance from the long-standing character Mudbone and, of course, his many, often volatile, relationships with women. Notably, his material during this time focused on the lasting impact of his trips to Africa, where he confesses he understood "how White people feel in America now [*pause*] . . . relaxed."[51] It was a trip to Africa that provoked Pryor's change of heart about use of the term "nigger." He announced in 1982 that he would no longer use the word, "Because there aren't any. . . . We never was no niggers. That's the word that's used to describe our own wretchedness." and as a result Pryor suffered backlash from his community, fellow comics, and family.[52] "[Paul] Mooney and David Banks," he writes, "told me that people thought I'd gone soft, sold out, turned my back on the cause, and all that political, militant shit."[53] This was no grand gesture of complacency; for him it was a redemptive move meant to reinvest Black subjectivity with worth and value, conferring cultural citizenship where otherwise denied. It was a plea for acceptance, honesty, and unity, themes he continued to include in live performances as long as he performed (he died December 10, 2005). Testimonies from family members, former wives and lovers, and fellow entertainers indicate that though he struggled with addictions which made him difficult at times, he was a good person striving to live and perform with integrity.[54]

Coming onto the scene around the same time as Richard Pryor, George Carlin's career trajectory was fairly synchronized with Pryor. After only ten months of radio comedy, George Carlin scored an appearance on *The Jack Paar Tonight Show* as part of the comedy duo Burns and Carlin, just months before Dick Gregory appeared on the same show. The public eagerly embraced Gregory, whose protestations anticipated the social rebellion already in full swing. In contrast, Carlin was a bit of a buzzkill—as hacky as he was apolitical—and he was still working to develop his comic voice, his stage persona, his point of view. Carlin and Jack Burns parted ways and Carlin began pursuing stand-up comedy as a solo career in New York City. In two years time, coveted comedy venues like Bitter End and Café Wha in Greenwich Village welcomed Carlin. He began releasing comedy albums around the same time as Pryor. Both nursed a cocaine habit and both initially performed mainstream-friendly material. Pryor fashioned himself after Bill Cosby and Carlin donned a more conventional appearance, style, and content. Pryor was moved to make his comedy more honest, more of a reflection of himself and his worldviews, and Carlin, having realized that audiences were demanding antiestablishment humor, felt he could also be more honest on stage, which prompted an overhaul in image and comic persona that made him less appealing for mainstream gigs but a huge success with the public. Early on in Carlin's career, he was arrested and hauled off to jail after mouthing off to the cops in defense of Lenny Bruce when he was arrested for obscenity while performing at the Gate of Horn in Chicago. Afterwards Carlin took up a similar mantle in the '70s with his "Seven Dirty Words" bit, which attempted to secure the right to free speech for comics.[55] Sporting a longer coif, dressing down in jeans and t-shirts, and peppering his comedy with drug culture references (his 1974 album *Toledo Window Box* was named after a kind of marijuana) and hippy idioms like "hey man," "yeah," and "cool, dude," turned out to be a genius marketing move. Audiences wanted someone edgy and rebellious, a voice that would challenge the norms and traditions that baby boomers were eager to slough.

Incredibly clever with language, Carlin admitted that he was always trying to make up for dropping out of high school by being articulate, smart, and well spoken. And so he did, for not long after Peter L. Berger and Thomas Luckmann published the now renowned sociological text, *The Social Construction of Reality* (1966), Carlin was applying its arguments in his comedy routines, making Americans think about morals and values as cultural constructs, deconstructing society as deftly as any professor. If you combined Stan Freberg's commercial jingles with Lenny Bruce's yen for the taboo, and Mort Sahl's political satire, you would get groovy Carlin in the 1970s. Commenting on reproductive rights for women, arguing that being gay is not abnormal (or, rather, that abnormal is relative), and pondering the extermination and relocation of American Indians, Carlin delivered some charged humor in his repertoire (usually one track on each album that detoured from his stock mock commercials and commentary on human foibles, bodily functions, and vernacular idiosyncrasies). But, his real beef was with Christianity, specifically the Catholic Church, most likely since he was raised Catholic and sent to parochial schools. His early religious satire seems more light-hearted and good-natured as when he assumed a Brooklyn accent to play Jesus being interviewed for a radio show. Those barbs hastened to sting as Carlin aged and later comedy specials convey less patience and more frustration when confronting the topic. Mark Twain became so angry at the inconceivable inequities and unfair things he knew about the government, society, and world that he ceased to be able to insert humor in his speeches and writings. Carlin never lost the funny but his comedy got heavier and sometimes preachy—usually on the topic of the government and religion.

Carlin was politically incisive at times, wielding satire like a weapon, but in main his jokes on religion zero in on problems without offering solutions; they critique without building anything in the process, making religion appear more silly and superstitious than an impediment to social equality. In contrast, Bill Maher, a man who is today's comedic critic of organized religion, does not just criticize religion; rather, he uses charged humor to demonstrate how religious practices perpetuate inequality. Like Carlin did, Maher makes a living commenting on political officials, cultural issues, and the economy with a similar I-make-no-apologies-for-myself attitude. Both are openly critical of organized religion (Maher released the documentary *Religulous* [2008] on this topic), but Maher also lambasts religion for its role in perpetuating inequality. His solutions center on critical examination of religious doctrine and practices that sanction oppression. He gets flack from the public about the criticisms he levels against religion and uses the stage to explain his opinions. Regarding a trip to Africa taken by Pope Benedict XVI, Maher complains: "I'm mad at him for going to the continent most ravaged by AIDS and telling them they couldn't use condoms. So don't tell me that religion doesn't do any actual harm [*cheers and clapping*]."[56] He details a litany of abuses stemming from religious practices or actions taken in the name of religion, which, according to him, include:

> most wars, the Crusades, the Inquisition, 9/11, arranged marriages to minors, blowing up girls' schools, the suppression of women and homosexuals, fatwahs, ethnic cleansing, honor rape [*people start wooting and clapping that intensifies throughout the rest of the list*], human sacrifice, burning witches, suicide bombings, condoning slavery, and the systematic fucking of children. There's a few little things that I have a problem with [*crowd claps and cheers*].[57]

Among those infractions includes collusion in the systematic oppression of women, LGBTQ persons, African Americans, and children. Carlin may have agreed with Maher, but his own comedy targeting religious institutions seldom makes the connections Maher does between faith practices and oppression. On the other hand, Maher and Carlin find common ground connecting US global relations to ideologies of exceptionalism, or the belief that the United States is innately superior by pedigree, skills, and power to other nations and their inhabitants. On this topic, they both generate charged humor.

Three years before Carlin hosted *Saturday Night Live* during the show's inaugural season in 1975, he performed in Santa Monica, California, taping the show for a LP record entitled *Class Clown*. This second album, like his first, went gold. It is this album that contains the infamous "Seven Words You Can't

Say on Television" routine that secured Carlin a place in American collective memory. Addressing US occupation of Vietnam during this performance, he likens Vietnam to a woman with whom the United States has its way. In less delicate terms: the United States is fucking Vietnam.

> Then you have to remember the sexual side of Vietnam, which a lot of people don't notice . . . they're always afraid of pulling out, that's their big problem you know [*laughter*]. [*Talking in different voice*] "Pulling out doesn't sound manly to me Bill [*laughter*]. I'd say leave it in there and let's get the job done" [*makes explosion sound effects and then resumes normal voice*]. Cause that is, after all, what we're doing to that country, right [*clapping*]? Yeah [*heavy applause, whistles*]! And we have always been good at that, you must admit, we uh, took care of uh, took care of the Blacks, uh took care of the Indians. I consider the South just another minority that was screwed by the US government. I have no prejudice against them. They got it too [*makes same explosion noises; sparse laughter*].[58]

Drawing a parallel between the conflict in Vietnam and slavery, the treatment of the Vietnamese, and treatment of racial minorities here at home, Carlin connected global and cultural imperialist practices. Carlin revealed the patriarchal underpinnings of global conquest and social stratification by gendering this relationship—by feminizing Vietnam, emasculating social identities construed as inferior (i.e., we "took care of the Blacks"), and rendering military occupation and social dominance as the terrain upon which masculinity is secured. Nearly forty years later, Maher's charged humor reflects changing discourses on racism, highly politicized discourses emanating from right-wing conservatives allowing White men to lay claim to victim status. Maher explains this phenomenon while also pointing toward the flaws in this argument:

> A lot of this birther stuff [Tea Party politics] is obviously just racism [*crowd cheers*]. It's funny the way racism has really grown up, if you will, you know from the Jim Crow days. It's just more subtle. . . . The only racism they [conservatives] can see now is reverse racism [*laughter*]. Right, this was the big problem with Supreme Court Justice Sonia Sotomayor is that she was a reverse racist. [*Sounding exasperated*] Yes, that's the problem. For too long Puerto Rican women have had their boot on the neck of the White man [*laughter, cheers and clapping*]. . . . You have to understand the Teabagger mindset. They have this nostalgia for this America they think was stolen from them that used to be, that was better. It's really the 1950s, okay. That's what they think was Shangri La. You know what they never get is that it's kind of insulting to a lot of Americans to pine for this era because it wasn't that good for a lot of people. It was good if you were a White man. It wasn't that good if you were Mexican, [*audience claps and the clapping is sustained throughout the list*] or Black, or Jewish, or disabled, or gay, or a woman [*audience hoots, hollers, and claps*].[59]

If supporters of the Tea Party movement pine for a time when women, people of color, gays, and religious minorities knew their place, they have to go farther back than the 1950s, because revisionist history reveals a 1950s bubbling precipitously with social rebellion, a precursor to the radical countercultures that would soon manifest. Inequality has always been met with resistance, but in varying ways—there is no Shangri La of yore. These jokes by Bill Maher and George Carlin both confront issues of racism, illustrating the various ways it manifests over time. In a supposedly "postracial" country in the twenty-first century, Maher's observations may meet with greater skepticism than Carlin's did in the 1970s. By the late 1970s, Carlin, Pryor, and Tomlin were rising stars whose charged humor had found favor with the American public. They managed to get a foot in the door of mainstream entertainment before charged humor began its decline in popularity in the 1980s. The Comedy Strike of 1979 precipitated this economic and cultural shift about take hold in the United States.

The Comedy Strike of 1979

Civil rights movements in the mid-twentieth century demanded political and social equality for minority groups and modeled successful strategies for subsequent social movements, including one fought by stand-up comics seeking economic redress and standardized club practices in the late 1970s. In March of 1979, the Comedians for Compensation led by Tom Dreesen, comprised primarily of comics in Los Angeles, picketed the Comedy Store, owned and managed by Mitzi Shore, for fair wages. At the time, many of them, except major headliners, received no compensation other than the exposure and opportunity to develop and hone new material. Mitzi Shore called it a "workshop" for comics and even established the Belly Room, a smaller room where women, whom Shore believed audiences had trouble liking, could work on their material in order to eventually strut their stuff in the main room.[60] The strike lasted nearly six weeks and was supported by many comic notables including Richard Pryor, Jay Leno, and David Letterman. Shore finally conceded to compensate the comedians and a settlement was reached on May 4, 1979, to pay $25 per set, but these promises were not enforced with any regularity. However, other comedy venues, in order to lure in the talent and maintain competition with other local and national comedy clubs, began standardizing their pay for the three positions of opener/emcee, feature, and headliner. Comedy clubs, including chains like Budd Friedman's Improvs, the Comedy Zone, Punch Line, and Funny Bone began popping up in the Midwest and all over the country. In order to get the big names to travel, club managers had to provide travel stipends and a living wage. Only a few years after the strike, there were over three hundred new comedy clubs in the country and many more on their way. Within five years time, by 1985, a job as a stand-up comic feature or headliner went from being synonymous with "broke" to a potentially financially stable profession, whereby someone could earn a decent income.[61]

This certainly does not mean that life on the road was without problems. Comedy club managers stiffed the comics or flaked when it came to providing promised lodging. There was no standard reimbursement for travel, which was out of the question for openers and possibly negotiable for feature comics. Personal accounts of life on the road in *I Killed: True Stories of the Road from America's Top Comics*, testify to the myriad difficulties comics continued to encounter in the 1980s. A better, more stable life might be found on television, whose market had recently ballooned dramatically as entrepreneurs successfully launched new cable networks. The availability of acting roles especially comedic ones surged and lured in not only road comics, but new talent taking advantage of this low-hanging fruit. A glut of television roles and the rising popularity of live comedy meant that comedy veterans were getting television roles and appearances, but so were novices, otherwise "green" comics with little to no stage time under their belts. Televised comedy, unless you were fortunate enough to land a special on HBO, curtailed the kind of free speech found in live performances and on the long-playing records that put charged comedy on the map thirty years earlier. Considered unsuitable for television, the rebel comics of the 1950s, '60s, and '70s cultivated a cultural form that could not be adapted for television while retaining its contempt for a corrupt government, cynical view of politics, and critique of social inequalities. And comedy clubs, while growing in number, booked comics most likely to appeal to their audience, that is, middle-class White folks. Ergo, the rise of pseudo-satire (which poses as rebellious, but is not) and family-friendly comedy illustrated that the project of securing equality as citizens is antithetical to the success of capitalism. T. H. Marshall waged such an argument in the 1950s and concluded that capitalism and citizenship are inherently contradictory: political action taken to redistribute wealth or compensate workers adequately is a right guaranteed by citizenship but is one antithetical to the maintenance of class stratification, a hallmark of capitalist systems.[62] In short, comedy on television avoided aggravating advertisers, even if this meant silencing or editing humorous material. In other words, new spaces for entertainment accelerated by capitalist efforts to secure consumers exercising brand loyalty placed restrictions on the messages of comedic material. Jokes were vetted for controversial, lewd, or questionable content. Charged comics in the mid-twentieth century revealed gaping fissures between our moral code touted abroad and the moral code enacted domestically—not exactly a topic welcomed with enthusiasm by network executives. Careful review of content was not new protocol for network television, but there were more people tuning into the television and for longer periods of time. With most of

Americans owning a television by the 1980s, and the rise of the global market for television, the entertainment industry supported programming that played a central role in producing consumers.

But, the aims of the TV networks were only one of many factors influencing a decline in the performance of charged humor relative to the number of professional comics, whose ranks inflated alongside a rise in comedy clubs and network channels. Others include Reaganomics, new probusiness policies, greater investment in the military industrial complex, aging Baby Boomers having kids of their own, and shifts toward conservatism. These trends ushered in the age of neoliberalism, a political philosophy and practice cogently described by Lisa Duggan in these terms:

> The raising of profit rates required that money be diverted from other social uses, thus increasing overall economic inequality. And such diversions required a supporting political culture, compliant constituencies, and amenable social relations. Thus, pro-business activism in the 1970s was built on, and further developed, a wide-ranging political and cultural project—the reconstruction of the everyday life of capitalism, in ways supportive of upward redistribution of a range of resources, and tolerant of widening inequalities of many kinds.[63]

Legislation had been put in place that dictated de jure equality, despite de facto experiences of cultural and political exclusion, and was used as evidence that everyone had equal opportunities to succeed. When the pay gap between men and women did not diminish or when people of color continued to be overlooked for promotions, this new conservatism placed responsibility squarely on the shoulders of "those people who didn't work hard enough" rather than any institutional or societal flaws. The comedy record, so popular in decades prior and a format conducive to delivering material ill-suited for television, fell out of favor with consumers. Records were replaced by cassette tapes, but it was hard to compete with the plethora of alternatives available for watching your favorite comics perform, for example, television, concert films, and live performances in comedy clubs. Given the restrictions imposed by television censors, charged comics eager to disclose these truths were more likely to be able to do so via live comedy, but even performing live in comedy clubs they could incur the wrath of audiences and risk losing an invitation to perform there in the future. It was far easier and commercially successful to tread carefully or to avoid controversial topics or critiques altogether. The combination of these forces changed the landscape of comedy—the content and the modus operandi of comedians. Not challenging the status quo allowed plenty of comics to flit back and forth from comedy clubs to television and film acting. Migration between these entertainment forms became the new gold standard for success as a comic.

Comics with the cultural cachet of national notoriety had arguably more freedom to employ charged humor—after all, this is the humor that helped comics secure a national following in the first place; you would think a savvy agent would capitalize on that market potential. For example, Pryor, Tomlin, and Carlin were championed by audiences because of their charged comic personae. They achieved national fame before or just at a time when audiences clamored for comedy with substance, reflecting an era of civil discord, social unrest, and a declining faith in the political system. Already having market cachet, they managed to maintain careers firmly ensconced in the mainstream in the ensuing decades. Charged comics emerging on the heels of their success in the mid '80s, like Kate Clinton, Marga Gomez, and Karen Williams, found themselves locked out of the game and were forced to find alternative means of establishing themselves without compromising their charged points of view. Presciently, Jane Wagner said in the early 1980s: "I still have this urge to be moralistic [*she laughs*] and want things to mean something. And I know that it's, pretty soon it's not gonna be fashionable at all."[64]

Comedy Centralizing: A Shifting Market

A decline in the popularity and frequency with which comics use charged humor has everything to do with the predilections of consumers, who are in turn influenced by the unique confluence of social, political, and cultural forces around them. In the 1980s, many factors contributed to changes in the availability and consumer demand of charged humor, including the neoliberal conservatism that proved to be a backlash to the prevailing social movements of the 1960s and '70s, the decline of the Keynesian welfare state and the rise of Reaganomics. At this time, the explosion of channels on cable television, which, while supplying greater opportunities for national exposure, simultaneously demanded comedy (and lots of it) appealing to the widest demographic possible. While I am leery of and aim to avoid any claims uniformly declaring pre-1980s stand-up comedy as libratory and post-1980s as restrictive, there are connections between the institutionalization of stand-up comedy as big business (largely spurred by the Comic Strike of 1979) and the styles of comedy deemed more profitable, that is, absurdist humor, apolitical safe comedy, shock humor, and modern-day minstrelsy in the mainstream. Charged humor found fewer opportunities to flourish in comedy clubs and on television, but entertainers knew how to adapt and they did in this rapidly shifting market.

While subject to the moral leanings of its rulers, popular entertainment has also challenged those rules, introducing public debates about definitions and standards of decency and propriety. Performed comedy has a long history of pushing the boundaries of social acceptability, of toying with the taboo. Lenny

Bruce and then George Carlin became household names and comedic icons because of their public battles with law enforcement over language used in sets. Not unlike vaudeville's decency standards, which were imposed as a means to expand its target audience to women and children, today's censorship focuses on preventing obscenity, for example, use of foul language, pejoratives and sexual innuendo, and questionable content, whether explicitly sexual, political, or violent, from being broadcast. By contrast, ratings systems are far more forgiving of violent content and the Hays Production Code of 1934 and today's film rating system is more likely to request an "R" rating for a show with "adult content," that is, sex, language, drugs, gender nonconformity, than they would for a movie in which viewers might see a dozen or more people die throughout the film.[65] For instance, after his first appearance on *The Ed Sullivan Show*, wherein Elvis Presley was captured gyrating his hips suggestively and which elicited a number of complaints from viewers, he was filmed from the shoulders up during subsequent performances. For his appearance on the iconic show, Bob Dylan refused to change the lyrics to his music at the request of network executives and was barred from performing, and when The Doors reneged on their promise to substitute another word for "higher" in a live performance of "Light My Fire," they incurred the ire of network executives; according to keyboardist Ray Manzarek, they lost out on a contract for six more appearances on the show.[66] During the mid-twentieth century, charged comics like Lenny Bruce, George Carlin, and Richard Pryor were wooed cautiously or not at all for television and film roles largely because their acts included profanity and incorporated taboo topics like drug use, sexcapades, and illegal activities. Although Pryor assisted in writing the screenplay for *Blazing Saddles* and Mel Brooks advocated on his behalf, producers passed him over for one of the lead roles because they feared he was too controversial.

Even when embraced by the masses, comics performing charged humor may encounter career complications. When Dick Gregory began his ascent to fame he was invited to perform on *Tonight Starring Jack Paar* in the winter of 1961. Gregory declined because Paar never allowed Black guests to talk with him postperformance as he did White guests. Gregory reports that Paar called him personally to let Gregory know he was welcome to come sit on his guest couch following his performance. It was the first time Americans saw a White man and Black man on television engaged in real, civil, humanizing casual conversation, according to Gregory. The public response was overwhelming (studio lines could not handle the volume); more importantly, it was overwhelmingly *positive*.[67] Undoubtedly the public played a role in sustaining Gregory's prominence as a comedic voice—Paar would never have made concessions on his show were it not for Gregory's rising popularity. The substance of his comedy resonated with many during a time of social unrest. The confluence of

Gregory's early soft-spoken yet incisive musings on racial inequality, a spirited and increasingly progressive public eager to consume this comedy, and the novelty of his approach and content, all ushered him into the mainstream at precisely the same time when other comics using charged humor were struggling. Lenny Bruce was being blacklisted from nightclubs all over the nation as was Mort Sahl, whose envelope-pushing political and charged humor television executives had determined too controversial. After extending a short-term contract to Sahl in anticipation of more opportunities for exposure on network TV, executives later rescinded and opted to forego any further commitments to him for fear of losing sponsors, ratings, profits, and viewers. Sahl also refused to pander to any political party, making some fans, and especially the Kennedy family, furious since they had assumed him an ally.[68] Sahl and Bruce suffered professionally but for different reasons unique to their careers, comedy styles, and personal choices; performing charged humor contributed to but does not account entirely for their stalled careers when it came to televised performance opportunities nor can charged humor be solely credited for Gregory's career taking off. Gregory opted to retreat from the comedy scene, favoring a career promoting civil rights and healthy living, so it is unknown the extent to which he could have maintained his status as popular charged comic. It is questionable whether his material on racism coming from an unknown comic would be welcomed by the public. Richard Pryor's early comedy was safe by his own estimations and sought mainstream recognition but did not reflect Pryor's point of view. Chris Rock, in an interview filmed for *Richard Pryor: I Ain't Dead Yet, #*%$#@!!* (2003), suggests that "Pryor didn't make his early albums to cross-over like *That Nigger's Crazy*, but he did cross-over and get mainstream."[69] When he did cross-over, making a national splash with his third album, *That Nigger's Crazy*, which sold over a million copies that year, he did not stop politicizing his jokes. That the charged content of Pryor and Gregory garnered such enthusiastic support reflects more than just their skills, but also the ideological propensities of their fans.

Charged humor that arises from or addresses issues germane to one's identity appeals to minority communities because in most cases, they "get" it in a very real way. In 1969, while civil rights activists pressured the government to make good on civil rights laws passed in 1957, 1960, and 1964, statements from Dick Gregory like, "We [African Americans] tired of these insults. All we doin' is reacting to them," and "We trying to work to change this racist structure," appealed to Black audience members who shared Gregory's frustration and ire for system changing too slowly.[70] Whether the same content can and does find favor with audience members not sharing similar experiences rests on the individuals digesting the humor and on the tenor of the jokes—the more aggressive a joke, the more likely it is to be off-putting. Similarly, a penchant for the didactic to the exclusion of the funny (all talk and no jokes) can sour reception. African Americans lend a sympathetic ear to Richard Pryor, Dave Chappelle, Chris Rock, and Katt Williams, a demographic pull that helped to ensure their eventual cross-over to the mainstream and subsequent rise to stardom. To that effect, Pryor writes: "I was hot in the Black community long before I cracked the mainstream."[71] Of course, you have to be talented too. It is not as if minority communities usher in every performer simply because they share a phenotype, gender identity, or sexual orientation.

What Lily Tomlin and Whoopi Goldberg did in the 1980s continues with Sherry Glaser, Judy Gold, Monica Palacios, Micia Mosely, Marga Gomez, Anna Deavere Smith, Sarah Jones, and Lisa Kron, but these ladies are barely blips on anyone's radar. Tomlin and Goldberg fared well in part because the timing was right; in the early-to-mid '80s cultural forms continued to reverberate with the revolutionary oeuvres evoked in earlier decades. This became increasingly muted as the '80s marched on and folks declared feminism dead, which was wishful thinking encouraged by the glut of images of women on television and film as either deadly seductress (read: men have no power) or in positions of power that totally belied the reality of women's professional careers. Susan Douglas identifies these images as emblematic of two prominent narratives in US culture right now: embedded feminism—we have achieved gender parity—and enlightened sexism, which ironically condones sexist images because they are considered outmoded.[72] Either image sends the message loud and clear: women are in control, so effectively, in fact, that some men (mainly White) in the 1990s and after became angry at what appeared to be a threat to their long established dominance and a takeover of their livelihoods by women, immigrants, and people of color.[73]

Mid-twentieth century comedians explored charged comedy and owing to a favorable zeitgeist for it, charged comics gained the popularity necessary to strut this material before receptive American audiences. Manifold shifts in American political, technological, ideological, and cultural climates facilitated a decrease in the commercial viability of charged humor in the late twentieth and early twenty-first centuries. Stand-up comics committed to using the stage to foment social justice either resigned themselves to other careers or learned to promote themselves within a market increasingly catering to niche demographics. Longstanding popularity in a consumer niche can, as it did with Pryor, launch a comic performing charged comedy onto the national stage. This is how the charged humor of Chris Rock and Dave Chappelle made its way into White Americans' homes. Unfortunately, women have less success with this tactic because, while there have been attempts to create women-only reviews (always billed as a "girls night out") meant to appeal to a female audience base, generally women do not rally behind other female comics in numbers necessary to impel crossover to the mainstream. Acculturated to regard men as the standard bearers of humor, women learn to laugh at men's jokes and like many other men, share their skepticism for women's capacity to successfully generate humor. Some solutions for charged female comics in this predicament are to lean heavy on another niche base, that is, Jewish, Latino/a, LGBTQ, differently abled; develop one-woman shows they can perform in a variety of venues outside the comedy club scene; or revise material (limiting charged humor) in ways more palatable to mainstream audiences. The latter strategies apply to male charged comics as well. This is the climate in which charged comics learned to operate in the 1980s and '90s and arguably where we are now in the twenty-first century, which explains why many of the comics discussed in the next chapter on contemporary charged humor may be unfamiliar. Those that are household names most likely made concessions with their charged material in order to achieve that status.

I grew up listening to Bill Cosby, Louie Anderson, Eddie Murphy (without parental consent . . . sorry Mom and Dad), Bob Newhart, Paula Poundstone, and Sinbad. They are still some of my favorite comics, as are Keith Alberstadt, Bill Burr, Kristen Key, Bob Marley, Ellen DeGeneres, and Jim Gaffigan. I love how their comedy makes me laugh at human foibles, awkward interactions, and family drama—the mundane stuff of life. Their humor unifies listeners and makes for great entertainment, but in most cases does not politicize or enact cultural citizenship. It is not charged humor. You have to be true to yourself when you go on stage as a comic performer, and I hold no judgment against comics opting to perform safe comedy or using styles that make sense to them. There is nothing wrong with this kind of humor, and comics are sure to make successful careers from this family-friendly apolitical comedy. But many writers and scholars have tackled these topics, focusing on mainstream comedy, and so now I want to look at what does not lend itself easily to mainstream incorporation in the twenty-first century.

In 1998 while I was in college, I traveled two hours from north Alabama to Nashville, Tennessee, to attend my first live comedy show featuring Beth Donahue, a talented comic and radio personality at the time. She blew me away and not just because her tagline was "Whooooore" (a bumper sticker I sported on my car for years). Before then, I had only been exposed to what I saw on television, select concert films and my father's collection of comedy albums; the comics I had access to were almost exclusively men, save Rosie O'Donnell's stint as host of VHI's *Stand-Up Spotlight* and Elayne Boosler's comedy specials (I was most familiar with *Party of One* and *Live Nude Girls*). I had never seen a female comic so irreverent, but moreover, who spoke directly to my identity as a woman and commented on society's maltreatment of women. Having realized the power of comedy to promote social change, I began a quest to find more of this kind of comedy. Some of my favorite charged comics include Kate Clinton,

Patton Oswalt, Kate Rigg, Chris Rock, Maria Bamford, Margaret Cho, George Lopez, DeAnne Smith, Kathleen Madigan, and Maz Jobrani. These charged comics and others like them sought and continue to seek myriad methods of securing a fan base outside of mainstream comedy, and over time, some of them have garnered enough of a following to warrant television and film roles, placing them alongside mainstream comic contemporaries. Emergent technologies in the twenty-first century like social media sites facilitate wider exposure, bearing the promise of greater access to charged comics and perhaps, even portending the reshaping of what constitutes the mainstream. Charting how and where charged humor succeeds or fails reflects changing attitudes, popular discourses, and social issues. The relative marketability of charged comedy—the fact that this shifts over time or based on who delivers the charged humor—indicates fluctuating consumer demand.

CHAPTER THREE

Laughing into the New Millennium

We use our humor to speak the unspeakable, to mask the attack, to get a tricky subject on the table, to warn of lines not to be crossed, to strike out at enemies and the hateful acts of friends and family, to camouflage sensitivity, to tease, to compliment, to berate, to flirt, to speculate, to gossip, to educate, to correct the lies people tell on us, to bring about change.

Daryl Cumber Dance, Honey, Hush! An Anthology of African American Women's Humor

Meet Patton Oswalt, a White forty-something male comic, who situates himself as an atheist, a belief system held by few in the United States, where 95 percent of the population cite some form of religious or spiritual affiliation.

I'm an atheist. And I love religion. I really do. And I don't love religion in a snarky mean-spirited way. I unabashedly, sincerely love that we have religion. Because if we didn't we wouldn't be here right now being all postmodern and ironic [*light laughter*]. There'd be no civilization.[1]

He locates himself as atheist and now (unless you are among that 5 percent of nonbelievers) what little information you have about atheists stirs and like carbonation begins popping into your thoughts, perhaps things like unscrupulous, confused, or hedonistic. Documentarian Morgan Spurlock, in an episode of *30 Days* (season 2), took public polls on opinions toward atheists and found that they are among the least trusted of people and thought to have little moral grounding. Yet another common misperception is that atheists are antireligious, because to be disassociated with religion somehow implies an aversion to or condemnation of religion. Countering this false perception about the way atheists are imagined, Oswalt professes his appreciation for religion and launches into a laughable history of religion making the kingdom of heaven analogous to eternal dessert. He continues:

> If no one invented religion we would've been fucked right now. Because at the dawn of man, civilization was [*beat*] the biggest and the strongest. And that's as far as we were going to go. It was whoever was the biggest fucked, killed, ate anything they wanted [*light laughter*]. That was it. Civilization was a huge psychopath with a club going: [*in a "primitive" voice*] "I'm going to have rape for dinner" [*laughter*]. That was it. That's as far as we were gonna go. And then, one of my ancestors, some weakling [*laughter*] said: [*in a conspiratorial voice*] "Look, there's no way I can beat that guy but what if I trick him into thinking that if he doesn't kill and rape people while he's down here, when he dies there's a magic city in the clouds, and he can go up and have all the cake he wants" [*laughter; resumes normal voice*]. Now that's not a very well formed plan but he went and told the big psycho and the psycho heard that and said: "Yeah I like cake." BOOM! [*laughter and clapping*]. There you go. That was the beginning of civilization. Now we can work on fire and writing and agriculture. That's religion. It's the old "sky cake" dodge. It worked [*laughter and clapping*]. . . . So the next time you see some douche bags in front of an abortion clinic or trying to ban a Harry Potter novel. Just say, [*in a patronizing voice*] "Oh sky cake [*laughter*] why are you SO delicious?" [*laughter and cheers*].²

Using humor, Oswalt reduces all religion to a ruse—the ol' "sky cake" dodge—hollow promises meant to seduce the strong into submission so we could all work together to create a safe, productive, and sustainable society. Importantly, he ends his bit with a directive for how to contend with extremists that use religious doctrine not shared by everyone or even the population as a whole to curtail civil liberties. His mode of resistance is a nonviolent passive aggressive way of pooh-poohing not simply the issue (i.e., abortion rights and banning books) but the entire religious engine that drives this nation. The subtext reads: religions are contrived and even silly but there are also values and societal benefits gained from such systems, so why not be tolerant of each other and respectful of others' beliefs and right to participate in whatever kind of religious practice they choose. Charged humor such as this works to enact cultural citizenship, affirming individuals and communities and unpacking some of the stereotypes and misconceptions associated with them, as when Oswalt does this for a minority community like atheists.

Now, meet Kate Clinton and Karen Williams. They are both lesbian charged comics and political satirists who started performing in the early 1980s and whose social identities could not be more different from Patton Oswalt's. Ideological congruence, however, means that despite cultivating vastly different fan bases, their charged humor tackles similar social justice issues. Though benefiting from multiple privileged social categories (i.e., male, White, heterosex-ual, able-bodied, wealthy), Oswalt makes keen observations about sociological marginality. On the other hand, it is Clinton's and Williams' positions as lesbi-ans (for Williams this is further compounded by her being African American) that reminds them daily of the importance of their comic locutions in a social location that is not protected in the workplace or in the streets, or legally recog-nized in the United States. Eager to address issues of power—who has it, who does not, and how we can get it—both offer the audience tools for addressing bigotry and challenging worldviews that limit the rights of others. Kate Clinton jokes:

> I believe in the power of laughter in a democracy. 'Cause what it does, is it takes the tyranny of the things we are given and it just blows them apart. So, and you can do it too. The next time you're talking to somebody who's telling you the biggest line of crap you've ever heard . . . be a faith-based comedian and just go like this [*mimes a prolonged ingratiating guffaw*]: "Good one [*said as if the person were joking only to realize that they were not*]! Oh my God, you mean it" [*laugh-ter*]! *And they will never say those things again with any degree of confidence.* It's time to bring 'em down. God told me. She did [*whistles, cheers, and applause*] (emphasis hers).[3]

Here, Clinton subversively renders God female and designates laughter as her weapon of choice against hate speech. Her contemporary, Karen Williams, advocates using one set of rights (the right to bear arms) to challenge the ero-sion of another set of rights (a woman's right to choose).

> I'm all about power to the people, really, totally power to the people. We need to use our rights while we still have them. Like we have the right to bear arms so the next time somebody says something stupid to you, just shoot 'em. Just fuck-ing shoot 'em while you can. *Because you can't get an abortion but you can still shoot an idiot.* Just shoot 'em [*laughter and cheers*]. . . . I'm a Buddhist, I just wanted to declare that off the bat (emphasis hers).[4]

Clinton and Williams demonstrate agency as performers and offer instruction to viewers—though Clinton's advice is more productive and plausible—for responding to ignorant comments, using humor to instruct the audience in ways of contending with bigotry, hearsay, and moral platitudes. The lynchpin here is action. Not a specific action but that you consider taking some action in defense or on behalf of making society equal for everyone, a place where no one must experience second-class citizenship.

Kate Kendall, executive director of the National Center for Lesbian Rights, who introduces comic Kate Clinton at the launch party for her twenty-fifth anniversary tour, says: "If you can laugh about difficult and scary times, there's hope in that laughter. And that is what [Kate Clinton] is able to do. And make us think. And make us laugh. And make us commit. And make us feel this sense of community."[5] Charged comedy affirms and mobilizes one's community to redress inequities, to compel viewers to work for social justice. Intentionality is key here. For example, Karen Williams reports that she sees her comedy "as an expression of political activism because our voices just aren't heard."[6] René Hicks, also a Black lesbian, veteran comic, states: "There were two things that I said to myself about comedy. One, I had to get to the point where I was as funny onstage as I was off-stage. And two, I had to become the activist onstage that I was offstage. Those were my two goals."[7] For them, comedy offers a forum to express their activist sensibility, a way to coax members of the audience to engage with social and political issues germane to their own lives as Black, lesbian, and female. Consider this example in Hicks' performance where she works to de-stigmatize the word "nigger":

> A negative word can be turned into a positive if you attach it to something everybody loves. And that's one word, [nigger] I had to find something and I did, I'm a genius. Know what I came up with? Snack foods. Think about it. We love Cheetos, Doritos, Pringles . . . why not niggers? Does that not sound like a snack food? That way we could get the racists to eat their words [*hearty applause and cheers*]. Because let's get real, they're not going to be able to resist cheese niggers, sour cream and onion niggers, nacho niggers. But um, there's not going to be any barbecue niggers. I don't like the way that sounds [*ohhhhs and laughter*].[8]

Her playful attempt to refigure this racial pejorative now reduced to the euphemism: "N-word," seeks to expand the use of the term in a positive manner instead of imposing a syntactical change that does not alter the original meaning of the word. By making this comic proposition, she is able to communicate other important information: that racism is an issue we should proactively address; and that language shifts over time and collectively we can transform words formerly imbued with negative meanings. Hicks' open admission to being an activist on stage, to use her humor to instruct, supports interpretation of her humor as charged. This chapter explores contemporary charged humor while also attending to the intentions and values of charged comics supplied by off-stage interviews.

Comics can and do use their humor to inform and instruct audiences about citizenship, politics, the law, and social interaction from the perspectives of minority communities. They explore the everyday lives and practices of the polis, playing the roles of observer and cultural critic. My objectives for this chapter include an analysis of the production of charged humor (chapter 4 turns to a focus on reception) and an exploration of the current landscape of charged comics performing in the twenty-first century. The first section considers the shifting economy for charged humor during the comedy boom in the 1980s and '90s, the various forces influencing a decline in the demand for charged humor, and the comic strategies for which audiences clamored. The rest of the chapter explores the range of goals, tactics, and strategies implemented by comics performing charged humor in the twenty-first century from various communities including: Middle Eastern, Muslim and Arab Americans, differently abled comics, LGBTQ comics, African Americans, Latino/a Americans, Asian Americans, and comics addressing issues of class and wealth disparities. Though the impetus for performing charged humor may vary between communities, this kind of humor is united in its effort to affirm identity and develop community. It may be used as a coping mechanism for cultural exclusion and oppression, and to mock social conventions, particularly conventions excluding them or reifying bigoted beliefs and practices. Examination of specific social identities should not be read as an attempt to silo these identities. Many comics belong to more than one marginalized category of identity, for example, a queer Asian American comic or a differently abled Muslim comic. Rather, exploration of various indices of marginalized identity illumines the basis upon which many claim an experience of second-class citizenship. The production of charged humor means to accomplish two things. First, it garners chuckles and second, it simultaneously reflects the imposition of second-class citizenship while invoking cultural citizenship, a social and rhetorical strategy meant to bolster a sense of belonging for marginalized communities.

A New Era of Comedy

The Comedy Strike of 1979 set a precedent for compensating comedians, offering stipends not just to headliners, but emcees and feature comics. In the wake of the strike, business entrepreneurs established hundreds of comedy clubs across the nation. By 1990, you could go watch live comedy in every major city and many towns. The line-up became standardized usually consisting of an opener, the emcee, who warmed up the audience with some jokes and promoted future shows. Next was a feature comic (usually a road comic) who performed stand-up anywhere from 15 to 30 minutes. The headliner performed last, typically for 45 to 60 minutes, and tended to be a comic with more experience or notoriety than the feature act. Mirroring the rise of comedy clubs, the 1980s also saw an explosion in cable programming offering more opportunities for comics to perform on television, including premium channels like Showtime, HBO (Home Box Office), and Cinemax whose status as pay cable networks (customers had to pay additional fees to access these channels) allowed them greater freedom in programming. Eager to take advantage of the cash cow that stand-up comedy was becoming, HBO and Showtime began producing comedy specials and filming live comedy shows like Russell Simmons' *Def*

Comedy Jam and airing them repeatedly on the channel. These premium channels had the luxury of fewer restrictions on its content, allowing comics to perform as they would in a club, complete with expletives, sexually explicit content, and other material deemed offensive and inappropriate for major networks. Comedy Central was launched in 1990, giving viewers comedic programming around the clock. Cable networks and the advertisers supporting now-abundant programming sought new markets, niche demographics that broke down by age, sex, race, personal interests, political affiliations, sexual orientation, and gender expression, although programming catering expressly to LGBTQ communities was not available until producers launched Logo TV in 2005. Exposure on cable and premium channels helped catapult comics into the national limelight and could move a comic from feature status to headliner practically overnight. Between these various modes of transmission, there was no shortage of opportunities for comics to perform in the 1980s and 1990s. By the mid-to-late 1990s, given the variety of ways comedy fans could now consume stand-up comedy without having to leave the comfort of their homes, some comedy clubs closed their doors, but we were still left with plenty of options for watching stand-up comedy either live or on television.

During this time, public desire for and support of charged humor waned, a surprising turn of events given the numerous outlets for performing comedy that could offer a platform for the proliferation of charged humor. But, as the social rebellion so characteristic of the last several decades began to ebb, people no longer craved comedy advocating for human rights, at least not in numbers great enough to impel comedy club managers or network executives to book comics performing mainly charged humor. As such, many of those outlets were (and in many regards still are) inhospitable to this kind of content due to its polarizing effects. Charged comics with name recognition and cultural cachet like Richard Pryor and George Carlin were unaffected by this turn; having proven themselves indispensable as comic commodities, they still had ample opportunities to perform across the country and moonlight in television and film. Comics using primarily political satire like Bill Hicks, George Carlin, Lewis Black, and Bill Maher could get away with throwing in some charged humor, but charged humor was scant and took a backseat to their roles as satirists. While charged humor may have become increasingly harder to find, this was not for lack of comedic performers desiring to impart sociopolitical critique that drew attention to existing inequalities. All the essential ingredients were present: charged comics, new venues for exposure, and market gatekeepers eager to satisfy consumer demands, but those demands (at least en masse) no longer included comedy that belied the growing certainty that social equality had been achieved.

Instead, in the late twentieth century, people clamored for apolitical comedy: prop comics using sight gags, family friendly jokesters, shock comics, and character comics employing absurdist humor. Vestiges from an older era, prop comics and magicians surged in popularity. Gallagher's wacky observations and signature "sledge-o-matic"—a large wooden hammer used to smash all manner of food items—made him one of the most famous comedians during the 1980s. During the same time, the now infamous comedic duo, Penn Jillette and Raymond Joseph Teller (more recognizable as Penn and Teller) wowed audiences with their illusions. Bill Cosby secured a sitcom on NBC developed from his comic persona, a guy anyone could get along with telling a mix of stories about his upbringing and newfound role as a father. *The Cosby Show* aired for nine years (1984–1992) and was (and still is) immensely popular. Little known at the time, a young woman by the name of Ellen DeGeneres began worming her way into the hearts of Americans in the early 1980s with her gender neutral comical observations about life and human interactions. Other comics making a name by performing family-friendly material included Billy Crystal, Louie Anderson, Paula Poundstone, Tim Allen, and Rita Rudner. It proved a fertile period for shock comics—this generation's version of "blue" comics speaking candidly about sex and drugs—like Sam Kinison, Denis Leary, Robert Schimmel, Eddie Murphy, Bob Saget, Bernie Mac, Jim Carrey, and Andrew Dice Clay, who all successfully gave voice to taboo topics allowing audiences to gratify impulses they were taught to repress. Roseanne Barr's penchant for raunch made her a popular addition to the growing list of shock comics during this era, but she also peppered performances with charged humor that illumined gender inequities—though not enough to dampen the appetites of Americans. Following in the tradition of Andy Kaufman, character comics peddling absurdist humor emanating from the likes of Emo Philips, Mitch Hedberg, Judy Tenuta, Bobcat Goldthwait, and Steven Wright, found a welcome audience in America during this time. Being zany was a given and they did, at times, shock their audiences, but their humor was seldom tendentious.

Stand-up comedy in the twenty-first century featured more of the same investment in observational and family friendly humor, shock humor, and character comedy, but in the wake of 9/11 humor also began to spring from our collective pain and uncertainty owing to this and other global atrocities. This period of time has been dubbed the age of the ironic and the age of the awkward, wherein the public finds humor in the exploration of tragedy and in moments of heightened self-consciousness. Tig Notaro's comedic, but dark revelation in 2012—she had breast cancer forcing a double mastectomy, ended a relationship, and lost her mother in an accident; all during a span of four months—made her an overnight sensation with the American public. Ironically using tragedy as comedic fodder, Notaro also capitalized on our growing penchant for the awkward—that is, deadpan humor, uncomfortable silences and pregnant pauses, and being self-reflexive about laughing at something so tragic. The age of the awkward is perhaps best represented in the spate of mockumentary sitcoms like *The Office, Parks and Recreation,* and *Modern Family* that have become wildly successful in the twenty-first century. These shows are distinctive in style and production. There are no laugh tracks or studio audience, and shows are filmed with a single camera. Just as in a real documentary, actors make direct eye contact with the camera and sit down for camera confessionals. This helps to achieve a sense of realism aiding the comedic effect derived from awkward exchanges. *The Office,* set in Scranton, Pennsylvania, at Dunder Mifflin, a paper company, follows the goings-on of a small eccentric staff. A single glance at the camera from work associates Jim or Pam, while their boss Michael Scott speaks to them, communicates discomfort or disapproval.

Saturated with so many styles of comedy emerging from a growing body of jokesters, comedy fans in the twenty-first century sought fresh approaches to the cultural form and unique perspectives. A motley band of adventurous comics cultivated an alternative comedy scene in the 1990s in West Coast venues like the Un-Cabaret in downtown Los Angeles and Largo and Luna Park in West Hollywood. Kathy Griffin created a weekly comedy revue called "Hot Cup of Talk," and Laura Milligan did the same at a venue in Los Angeles called Tantrum. Alternative comedy was more intellectual, satirical, and even charged at times, requiring a knowledge base from audiences. The anecdotal and stream-of-consciousness style of delivery may have felt new compared to the modus operandi of so many comics featured on television and hired in comedy clubs, but storytelling was and has been a central feature of stand-up comedy since it emerged as its own distinct cultural form in the 1950s. Alternative comedy caught on, and by the twenty-first century many comedy fledglings experimenting in these venues were achieving mainstream success, like Kathy Griffin, Patton Oswalt, Dana Gould, Sarah Silverman, Andy Dick, Margaret Cho, Janeane Garofalo, Andy Kindler, David Cross, Jack Black, and Jeff Garlin. It is no surprise, then, that if charged humor was going to find an audience it would do so vis-à-vis this alternative comedy scene nurturing cerebral, anecdotal, and edgy forms of comedy, which rose in popularity in the twenty-first century. Some comics catering to niche identity markets performed charged humor to a consumer base that could identify with the critiques waged. Chris Rock spoke to the conditions of the Black and African American communities, while Kate Clinton spoke to the conditions of queer communities. To call it a revival or resurgence of charged humor would mischaracterize the amount and relative exposure of this kind of humor production. More accurately, if you knew where to look you could find charged humor. With the advent of social media technologies, something I discuss more in the book's conclusion, we have myriad ways to discover and follow the kinds of comedy we most enjoy. This is how I have managed to locate many of the contemporary comedians discussed in the following sections, what could be considered today's "It List" of charged comics.

Muslim, Arab American, and Middle Eastern American Charged Comics[9]

Islamic, Middle Eastern Americans, and Arab Americans were made all too aware of their tenuous status as citizens following the attack on the World Trade Center on September 11, 2001. It is not as if Arab Americans had not already been subject to exclusion from citizenship or had their rights as US citizens infringed upon prior to this event. As recently as 1994, President Bill Clinton's counterterrorism bill targeted Middle Easterners in the United States by calling for the "deportation of non-citizens based on evidence known only to the government."[10] Middle Eastern and Arab Americans have had a conflicted relationship with the United States for centuries, the outcome of which are wild oscillations between being White and becoming racialized and depicted as evil, exotic, primitive, and threatening. Arabs and Arab Americans have a unique relationship with the United States, reflecting the constant state of flux between the US and Arab countries in the Middle East, Southwest Asia, and Northern Africa. Not only does this ethnic ascription or designation as an Arab homogenize what is a widely diverse group of nationalities and cultures, since 9/11 it has seriously compromised the freedoms and liberties guaranteed Arab American citizens (and anyone "looking" Arab or Muslim), regardless of national origin. Since then, Arabs, Muslims of all ethnicities, and Persians have taken on Italian and even Latino nicknames like "Tony" or "Hector," hoping to be identified as something other than Arab or Middle Eastern (read: terrorist). Mohammed "Mo" Amer, a Kuwaiti-born Palestinian comic whose family emigrated to the United States during the Persian Gulf War when he was nine, shares that his mother begged him not to perform political comedy: "We come over here so afraid. . . . And what she is afraid of is that they are going to send us back [*laughter*]. . . . I was like, 'Mom, we're Palestinian [*loud cheering and whooping*], we're stateless' [*laughter and clapping*]."[11] Maysoon Zayid, a Palestinian Muslim with cerebral palsy, reports that since 9/11, "we as Arab-Americans and Muslim-Americans edit . . . there's a big fear when you run a charity or when you are on the phone and just talking to your friends that the things you will say will be misconstrued."[12] It is not just fear of persecution that drives Middle Easterners and Arab Americans to perform Italian or Latino and impose self-censorship. In other words, these are not precautionary measures that are unfounded. These fears are based on the reality that incidences of physical assault against anyone looking Arab or Muslim skyrocketed post-9/11, as did ethnic profiling like when a Persian American woman speaking Farsi in an Apple store in Georgia was refused service in 2012.

Uniquely situated by one's local and national history and one's social locations, while many comics use charged humor or humor enacting cultural citizenship, they may do so for very different reasons and to achieve different ends. Middle Eastern American comics enact cultural citizenship through their performances, discussing ethnic profiling, unfavorable public scrutiny, government surveillance and detainment, and cultural stereotyping. There are currently a handful of Muslim, Arab American, and Middle Eastern American comics performing charged humor in the United States (among other countries), including Dean Obeidallah, Tissa Hami, Ahmed Ahmed, Maysoon Zayid, Maz Jobrani, Maria Shehata, Max Amini (sparingly), Aron Kader, Mohamed "Mo" Amer, Azhar Usman, Sarah Arafat, Sherif Hedayat, Elham Jazab, Preacher Moss, Eman Morgan, and Nick Youssef, all of whom, with varying frequency, produce charged humor, using their stand-up comedy to address concerns germane to being Arab American or from the Middle East and at times (if applicable) being Muslim in the United States. For example, Egyptian American comic Ahmed Ahmed teaches his audience not to assume Muslims are always Arabs: "People don't realize that there's a big difference between Arabs and Muslims. I'm sure most of you know the difference. You would be surprised how many people do not know the difference. Most Arabs are Muslims, most Muslims are not Arab."[13] He disrupts the misguided notion that Muslim=Arab and repopulates Muslims in the national imagination, expanding membership beyond inhabitants of Arab countries in the Middle East, Southwest Asia, and North Africa.

Comics develop material to criticize stereotypes and the lack of positive representations in United States visual culture, as when Dean Obeidallah, comic and cofounder and coexecutive producer of the New York Arab American Comedy Festival, humorously observes:

> Look at the news stories about Arabs. You've got the bad ones; we're described as gunmen, militant, or terrorists. Then there's the good ones; we're described as "alleged" gunmen, militant, or terrorists [*laughter*]. I wish there were fun things in the media that would show a fun side. Maybe a fun story about an Arab Muslim family, like a sitcom called *Everybody Loves Ramadan* on CBS [*laughter*]. It'd be a big hit.[14]

Azhar Usman, an Indian American Muslim comic also known as the "Ayatollah of Comedy" takes up a similar mantle and criticizes media representations of Muslims during an international tour called, Allah Made Me Funny— Official Muslim Comedy Tour. The tour began in 2003, and cofounder Usman, along with several other stand-up comics traveled to over twenty countries on all five continents performing charged humor.

> I feel like the media always stereotypes us, profiles us, and the one group that gets it the worst—Iranians [*clapping and laughter*]. I'm surprised they responded [*loud laughter*]. Iranians don't like to be called Iranian, they like to be called Persian. Cause Persian is associated with nice things like cats [*loud laughter*] and rugs, not nuclear bombs. But truthfully when was the last time you saw them in the media show a normal Iranian family just hanging out. No, it's always a big mob, pissed off [*laughter*]. They don't like America and there is a big sign, "death to America" [*laughter*]. Is that even grammatically correct? I have never been so angry at somebody that I am like, death to you [*laughter*]. Death to me, death to you [*loud laughter*]. And why do they always spell America with a "k." What does it mean; what are they trying to tell us? These people have no jobs, not familiar with the rules of grammar; they don't even have spell check. These people are so backwards they don't even have Microsoft Word [*laughter*].[15]

Usman challenges primitivism, a narrative commonly associated with Arabs, Muslims, and Middle Easterners and an association used to dismiss these identities as uncivilized and thus inferior to the civilized practices and people of Western nations. His latest performance venture is a one-man show titled: *Citizen of the World*, an apt title for a performance seeking to harmoniously unite audience members regardless of nationality, ethnicity, and religious affiliation.

Arab and Middle Eastern American comics offer a unique view of how one's experience of inclusion and belonging is subject to change . . . over night. Stand-up comedy provides a nonthreatening forum for them to educate and entertain audience members and depict their own experience as an Arab or Persian (and in some cases as a Muslim) living in the United States. Cynthia Willet, in her monograph *Irony in the Age of Empire: Comic Perspectives on Democracy and Freedom*, writes that "when non-Middle Easterners in audiences laugh with (and not at) the Islamic American humorists, the laughter humanizes the 'enemy' . . . the laughter disables power, stymies arrogance, and strikes a blow against the pretend manliness that dominates the political field."[16] Preacher Moss, a Black Muslim charged comic who toured with Azhar Usman compels his audience to identify the links between maltreatment of Muslims and other minority groups, uniting the persecuted from many communities against their persecutors.

> Folks don't feel special. Muslims don't feel special. Here is the scoop. Haters have been around for years. Eh? Listen to me. Haters have been around for years. And believe me the same people that hate Muslims, hated Asians, hated Latinos, hated Blacks, hated Jews [*clapping*]. I read this book and in this book it

said that haters cling to poor values, they cling to the hate. And the Arabic word for cling is "imsak." And the word imsak ironically comes from the Arabic root word, which means constipation [*loud laughter*]. So let us say that we are dealing with some people that are full of, themselves [*laughter*].[17]

Other comics use irony to depict the fragility of national belonging for Middle Eastern Americans, like Maysoon Zayid who responds to the re-election of George Bush Jr. in 2004 by joking, "great, I'll be the funniest chick in the internment camp."[18]

Maz Jobrani, who reports being influenced by comics such as Richard Pryor, George Carlin, and Lewis Black, weaves into his humor a celebration of Iranian culture and community, encouraging people to visit Iran and Arab countries and lauding the accomplishments of folks like Anousheh Ansari, the first Iranian in space and the first self-funded woman to travel to the International Space Station. A self-professed watchdog for the Middle Eastern community, he is highly invested in keeping informed and using the stage to broadcast instances of cultural aspersion like when he recounts the story of a White woman at a McCain rally in 2008 who took the microphone and told the crowd that then-Democratic presidential nominee Barack Obama was not to be trusted because he was Arab. Taking back the microphone, McCain (in Jobrani's words) corrected her saying:

> "No, no ma'am, he's not an Arab, he's a good family man" [*laughter*]. It takes a second to sink in right [*laughter*]? Because the logic of that is that Arabs are bad family men [*laughter*]. Because I watched and I was like: "Yay [*pause*] . . . what the fuck!?" [*sustained clapping, cheers, and laughter*]. His response should have been: "Ma'am, he's not Arab but there's good Arabs and bad Arabs. You need to go home and take your pills because you're fucking crazy" [*laughter*].[19]

He points to a publicly ethnocentric faux pas and importantly, refigures what should have happened or what McCain should have said, refusing to leave his audience with what is status quo and instead substituting accurate information for McCain's harmful generalization (there *are* good and bad Arabs just as there are good and bad Europeans and South Americans and Africans, etc.). While corresponding with Maz Jobrani about personal objectives and intentions for performing charged comedy, he wrote:

> I continue to read the news all the time and see social and political injustice. I feel that a comedian's job is to point out hypocrisy. We all know it's there, but if you can point it out in a funny way I think the audience laughs, but also learns something. . . . If they're able to laugh though and also leave thinking, "Hey, that guy was Middle Eastern American and he didn't try to kidnap me or hijack anything or throw any rocks," then I think I've achieved a higher goal. I think

that these are stereotypes etched in peoples' minds in the West and we need to break them bit by bit.[20]

With few exceptions, Middle Eastern American, Arab American, and Muslim comics are informed and visible members of their communities opting to produce humor illumining their history, politics, and cultural beliefs and traditions. Like Persian and Arab Americans, other minority groups in the United States have seen such fluctuations in status and similarly produce humor documenting their precarious relationship with their nation.

Charged Comics Who Are Differently Abled

Josh Blue, winner of *Last Comic Standing*, season 4 (2006), is a terrifically funny comic who also happens to have cerebral palsy. Before taking the stage for one of the many competitions with a live studio audience that narrow down the pool of potential winners for the show, Blue opines: "I don't know of any other comics with disabilities who have really got on national TV and said what they have to say." This means the stakes are high for him. Having no differently abled comic role model, he could be one of the few or even the only comic with a disability visible to a wide audience. On stage, he promptly addresses his cerebral palsy, as one might expect because it is noticeable, but in a way that challenges the audience to consider their own responses to persons who are visibly differently abled: "People ask me if I get nervous before coming up on stage. I say, 'heck no, I got this many people staring at me all day' [*laughter*]."[21] The material and psychic issues for persons with disabilities include but are not limited to social stigma, always being subject to the gaze/staring of others, discrimination in employment and hiring, the difficulty acquiring monies, services, and access for a disability, and a medical system that seeks to "normalize" differently abled bodies, which conveys a message of deficiency or being substandard. Because of these issues, persons with disabilities are more likely to be impoverished, an economic condition forcing dependency when, in main, persons with disabilities are and can be independent as long as the built environment accommodates and employers hire them. Many differently abled performers used comedic modes of communication to dispel the myths surrounding disabilities like being asexual or nonsexual, weak and dependent, and an object eliciting pity or inspiration—a common dramaturgical device used in films and TV wherein a differently abled character is sacrificed in the end or fulfills some narrative of hope. Differently abled performance artists ask their audience to grapple with the issues relevant to disabled bodies—what assumptions are made about these bodies; what are the medical discourses that circulate to regulate and normalize disabled bodies; what does the goal of normalizing disabled bodies assume (i.e., that persons with disabilities want to be corrected or made "normal") and also why might some persons with disabilities not opt for corrective medical measures (e.g., cochlear implants for the hearing impaired, prosthetic limbs, or plastic surgery for a cleft palate or highly visible scars). Comics who are differently abled cite various reasons for producing charged humor and though they may not say they are enacting cultural citizenship, many express motives to use comedy to edify audiences, to define themselves, and by pointing to their similarities encourage audience members to incorporate them culturally, politically, and legally in a way that accepts difference, rather than mute it.

Acknowledging diversity within communities (a recurring trope in the production of charged humor) proves particularly important for persons who are differently abled who find themselves stigmatized by virtue of disability, but who do not necessarily share the same disability or the same experience of disenfranchisement; for example, life for a tetraplegic poses different challenges than for someone who is blind, deaf, or disfigured. According to performance studies scholars Carrie Sandahl and Philip Auslander, having a disability constitutes its own identity category in the same way that we are marked by race, ethnicity, sexuality, and gender. They posit that disabilities are "something one *does* rather than something one *is*," (emphasis theirs) arguing that disabilities like other identity categories are performed.[22] We perform our gender by wearing gender markers appropriate to our sex; we do so by choice, but society expects and condones our obedience and deference to these performances of identity. Performing disability comes with social expectations that persons with disabilities will act strong in the face of adversity, accept any assistance offered but not requested, and exhibit gratitude for any accommodations made, whether legal, medical, structural, or educational, even when these fall short of their actual needs. For persons who are differently abled, acknowledging that disability is performed offers them the freedom to perform their disability in ways inconsistent with dominant notions about persons who are differently abled, challenging stereotypes and cultural assumptions. As Sandahl and Auslander aver, the "self-conscious performer" works to be an active agent of meaning, "manipulating and transforming stereotypes . . . since the available 'scripts' of disability— both in daily life and in representation—are frustratingly limited and deeply entrenched in the cultural imagination."[23] These tactics are used by differently abled performance artists like Mary Duffy, Carrie Sandahl, David Roche, and Marie Wade as well as charged comics who are differently abled like Kathy Buckley, Josh Blue, Benjamin Stuart, J. D. England, Alexis McGuire, Chris Fonseca, Greg Walloch, Alex Valdez, Geri Jewell, Kenneth Littleton Crow, Nikki Payne, and Brett Leake.

Differently abled comics (charged or not) seldom achieve national acclaim because booking agents do not believe the public wants to purchase tickets to see someone on stage with a disability, especially if it might make audience members uneasy or depressed. In *Look Who's Laughing*, a documentary focusing on differently abled comics, Bob Fisher, a comedy club owner also in charge of the club's bookings, admits that when hiring someone with a disability he has concerns as to whether the audience will be able to overcome their own discomfort.[24] John Cooney, the comedy club owner who booked Chris Fonseca confesses to judging Fonseca at first and being legitimately surprised at how funny he was. Tetraplegic White comic J. D. England counters that the owners are not the one taking the risk, it is the performer who has to win everyone over, and White deaf comic Kathy Buckley says: "I think Club owners take a risk when they don't put people with disabilities on the stage."[25] As with women comics, differently abled comics do not have the same economic viability that an able-bodied or male comic has in this particular cultural form and entertainment industry.

For many reason, comics with disabilities are motivated to write and perform charged humor. Geri Jewell—a White lesbian woman with cerebral palsy and the first person with a disability to have a regular role in a television sitcom (*The Facts of Life*)—articulates her objectives for comedy in an interview, chief among them "the responsibility to educate."[26] Jewell wants to instruct and uses comedy to teach her audience about disabilities and ableist attitudes and behavior. Alexis McGuire, a White dyslexic performer and teacher said of her experience performing comedy: "When people laugh, they are not laughing at us, they are laughing with us, in recognition of what's happening in their own lives. None of us make fun of ourselves; we make fun of our situation."[27] Brett Leake, a White headlining comic who has muscular dystrophy and perhaps the most accomplished and successful differently abled comic on the national comedy circuit, says that "being on stage, being able to tell jokes about my disability allows me an opportunity to define my own terms;" and Chris Fonseca, a Latino with cerebral palsy, reports in an interview that his intentions for comedy are to relate to the audience so they can see that he is "one of them."[28] Maysoon Zayid, a Palestinian woman with cerebral palsy, shirks the label "political comedian," for the same reasons I do not conflate political comedy and charged comedy. Her charged comedy is certainly political but it also has an agenda to illumine social inequalities. Attempting to draw attention to the way her comedy purposely seeks to challenge social stratification, she self-identifies as "a human rights comic" and comments on the capacity for humor to promote social change saying, "Humor is the voice of the oppressed from generation to generation."[29] Alex Valdez, a blind White man and the first disabled comic to work the professional comic circuit, speaks at length in an interview about the opportunity comedy affords him to show people a little bit of his world, who he is and what he is about.[30]

The opportunity for social critique and commentary to reach large audiences and to do so under the auspices of humor make stand-up comedy especially appealing to charged comics who are differently abled. It should not be assumed that being differently abled presupposes deployment of charged humor, and there are comics with disabilities that prefer not to talk about disabilities—theirs or anyone else's—because they would rather focus on shared human experience. This is the same stance Ellen DeGeneres took as a stand-up comic; however, while this would not be considered charged humor, I would argue that comedy uniting folks based on shared experience does its own work to nurture investment in shared humanity, which can help bridge social and political divides. Recognition of our similarities, our shared humanity, makes it more difficult to justify social and political inequality, which is one possible social outcome of comedy that unites its audience members despite social, economic, and political differences. It will be easier to support legislative efforts aimed at ending discrimination, if people can imagine themselves in similar circumstances.

LGBTQ Charged Comics

Bridget McManus, a White lesbian twenty-something comic relatively new to the scene, says of her intentions for comic performance: "If I could make anyone think 'Wow, we're all the same' . . . cause we *are* all the same. I want to bring people together with my comedy if I can" (emphasis hers).[31] McManus clearly wants her audience to identify with her and her life and thus calls attention to similarities across the sexual spectrum, versus differences. Sabrina Matthews, also a White lesbian, expresses sentiments similar to McManus, saying she is "very proud of [her]self for how many straight people [she's] stood up in front of and made them realize that they have something in common with [her]."[32] Audience identification—indicated by laughter, cheers, smiles, whistles, and applause—relies on shared activities and experiences (i.e., raising children, being a son or daughter, going to work, being in a relationship, cultural treatment of racial and sexual minorities, etc.) and mutual feelings and ideas (i.e., social irritants, acquiescence to or the shirking of behavioral protocol and ideas of civility, political beliefs, etc.) and in general signals success to the comic. Just moments before he performs at the Renenburg Theater in Los Angeles, Edison Apple, a gay American Indian, turns to the camera filming him backstage and says of performing comedy: ". . . it's the hardest form. You know if you can sing it's one thing. If you have a script it's another thing. But to go out there and you know give these people your ideas and your thoughts and your heart and your life—you hope that they connect."[33] Here, laughter is a product of human connection; it does, of course, rely on the set-up, language, and delivery of the joke, but in this cultural practice of performing charged humor, laughter is a nonverbal but very audible response signaling identification and agreement, confirming appreciation for the comic script being performed.

Because how any group is perceived in the national imagination dictates and determines the level of incorporation—whether cultural, political, or legal—for that group in society, LGBTQ performers utilize performance as a means to solicit acceptance and civil liberties not yet afforded our community. Janet Bing and Dana Heller argue that—much like other minority communities—lesbian communities have a different set of cultural beliefs and practices than mainstream America, which are expressed in their humor. These jokes "constitute an imagined cultural community based in resistance, transformation, and survival" in order to create a sense of belonging traditionally missed by minority viewers consuming limiting representations of the LGBTQ community in mainstream media.[34]

Like any minority humor, queer humor draws from cultural scripts and experience specific to a social identity, that is, quotidian behaviors, activities, and beliefs, and at times becomes charged when it challenges legal and cultural exclusion and inequity. Not all LGBTQ comics perform charged humor and if they do, it is not necessarily the only kind of humor they write and perform. For DeAnne Smith, a White lesbian comic born in the United States but now living in Montreal, it is a matter of striking a balance.

> I think it's important to be conscious of social justice issues, but I also don't want to fall into the trap of haranguing the audience or "preaching to the converted." I work to include social justice issues subtly, as part of a larger and more general joke. It's this approach which means my otherwise observational comedy is peppered with phrases like "third world genocide," "rich, white privilege" and "participatory economics."[35]

One does not need to be queer to advocate on behalf of LGBTQ communities; in fact, many heterosexual comics vocalize support for gay civil liberties, just as there are White comics who speak out against racism. Take for example a bit performed by Margaret Cho, a vocal Korean American ally of the LGBTQ community who is frustrated and confused why homophobia is still so prevalent despite the visibility and seeming acceptance of LGBTQ culture in the mainstream—a troubling paradox revealing that gay culture can be commercially co-opted even while under attack and that there can be cultural visibility even as LGBTQ persons continue to fight for legal equality. And who is to blame, according to Cho? Well, for one, the prior Pope Benedict XVI for his public castigations of LGBTQ persons and lifestyles:

> And he [the Pope] is always saying, "Oh it's abnormal. Gays are abnormal." It's like, oh yeah you a real good judge of normal [*laughter*] with your gold dress

and matching gold hat [*laughter*] . . . livin' up in the Vatican with your 500 men [*laughter*] . . . surrounded by the finest antiques in the world [*laughter*] . . . Queen, please! You live like Versace did [*laughter, whistles, and cheers*].[36]

Her stand-up normalizes LGBTQ persons as compared to the outlandish garb and bizarre lifestyle Popes have led. This kind of humorous contextualization illustrates the absurdity of their vitriolic comments and makes them the object of ridicule instead of "fags," "dykes," and "trannies" commonly made the butt of homophobic humor. This reversal of fortune is fairly standard in queer comedy. Suzanne Westenhoefer (White lesbian comic) often concludes her shows saying: "We don't choose to be gay. We're chosen," flipping the heteronormative script positioning her and other LGBTQ persons as deviant and instead lauding them as special, important, or the religiously imbued "chosen" ones.[37] Westenhoefer is one of many LGBTQ comics using charged humor to enact cultural citizenship, including Lily Tomlin, Kate Clinton, Judy Gold, Rosie O'Donnell, Tig Notaro, Lea DeLaria (at times), Sabrina Matthews, Vicki Shaw (at times), Elvira Kurt, Julie Goldman, Amy Tee, Bridget McManus, Karen Ripley, Jen Slusser, Stephanie Howard, Robin Tyler, Page Hurwitz, DeAnne Smith, and Jerry Calumn. As with some differently abled comics, many LGBTQ comics belong to more than one minority community like Kate Rigg, Karen Williams, Micia Mosely, Edison Apple, René Hicks, Gloria Bigelow, Wanda Sykes, and Marga Gomez.

Like other cultural practices connected to the study of cultural citizenship (e.g., protests, strikes, rallies, voting initiatives, cultural traditions, etc.), comedy can affirm our social activities, political leanings, consumer choices, and identity. Elvira Kurt, the Canadian daughter of Jewish Hungarian parents, has a joke about the lesbian "uniform" of blue jeans and a t-shirt that she sports on stage illustrating a simple but good example of how jokes confirm for insiders (read: fellow lesbians) that they are or are not doing what they should be doing for their subject positioning.[38] Cultural citizenship is about "identifying those types of cultural practices that have been or can be the basis of a community's claiming and affirming the political and cultural space that challenges the dominant culture's interpretation of them, their history and the norms and practices that reproduce their subordinate status."[39] Therefore, comics exercising their positions as cultural citizens will opt to use their comic material to negotiate a respected space for themselves and their community in the national imagination. They do this by identifying the cultural attitudes and beliefs contributing to their subordinated status like when Wanda Sykes notes the additional burden LGBTQ folks bear in having to reveal their sexual identities should they deviate from heterosexuality.

It's harder being gay than it is being Black [*clapping*]. It is cuz there's some things that I had to do as gay that I didn't have to do as Black. I didn't have to come out Black [*laughing, clapping, and cheers*]. I didn't have to sit my parents down and tell them about my blackness [*laughter*]. I didn't have to sit them down . . . [*in a dispirited voice*] "Mom, dad, I got to tell ya'll something [*laughter*]. I hope you still love me [*laughter*]. [*Pauses and shakes her head*] I'm just gonna say it. Mom . . . dad . . . I'm Black" [*laughter*].[40]

Sykes then plays the role of shocked and disturbed mother who cries out to the Lord to give her daughter cancer, to be "anything but Black Lord," and laments her blackness blaming it on watching too much *Soul Train* and hanging out with Black people. Her humor cites the multifarious ways society enacts compulsory heterosexuality—that is, that being gay is contagious, parents have done something wrong, the imperative of "coming out," that disease or terminal illness is better than being gay, that gays are defective heterosexuals—setting a litany of heterosexist beliefs and attitudes in front of an audience with humor and aplomb. Sykes was not always known for such acerbic critique. In earlier performances, she presented as heterosexual and incorporated fewer charged jokes. Knowledge of what sells and what does not surely influenced Sykes to perform commercially viable humor until achieving some modicum of notoriety, after which time she had the economic security and cultural cachet to say more about her personal politics, identity, and values. Having visibility like that of Sykes makes the impact of charged humor all the more profound (and subversive).

When Sykes openly declared herself a lesbian, a member and ally of the queer community, she also reminded the public not to assume that persons of color are automatically straight. In an interview, Gloria Bigelow explains that she feels compelled to share that she is a lesbian because people assume she is straight *because* she is Black, which they also do of Bridget McManus because she performs "femme" on stage. Unlike racial minorities in the United States, sexual minorities can opt to "pass" as heterosexual, as Sykes did for some time, by presenting themselves as appropriately feminine or masculine or as Bigelow, asserts, just by virtue of being a racial minority in a culture representing LGBTQ persons as predominantly White. René Hicks, born and raised in San Francisco, discusses the number of people who are still not comfortable coming out, even as tolerance and acceptance of LGBTQ communities has increased. She believes this is especially true for queer Black folks whose experience of coming out is very different than the celebrations her White counterparts appear to have upon coming out to friends and family. This is the subject of one of her jokes, which cleverly reveals the way one's experience is compounded by multiple oppressed subject positions: "Black people have sort of like a revolving door on their closet. Sometime we in; sometime we out. See because we already have one burden to deal with, sometimes it's hard to deal with two. I mean we're already openly Black [*laughter*]."[41] Again, we see an allusion to the choices available to White sexual minorities, which are unavailable to racial/ethnic minorities.

Queers of color must navigate a different set of waters, as they contend with being both a racial and sexual minority as well as those experiences affected by one's biological sex. Gloria Bigelow frames this dilemma in comedic terms:

> It's tricky being Black and being gay because Black folks, we, we're homophobic [*laughter*] you know, cause we've been oppressed so we know how to oppress. You know what I mean? It's like we were in the slave quarters taking notes. [*Feigns pensive deliberation over a writing tablet and then to herself*] "Use religion! Don't forget the Bible!" [*laughter*].[42]

Facing potential exclusion in racial/ethnic communities due to their sexuality and in queer communities due to their race, queers of color often find themselves in social and political quandaries forcing them to choose between queer or race loyalty. As evidenced by Bigelow's humor (and many others) comic performance provides an opportunity—albeit limited in scope depending on the success and notoriety of the comic in question—to give voice to these dilemmas, making clear the effect this exclusion has on the individual and pointing toward various technologies of oppression, for example, Bigelow cites the role of religion in oppressing racial *and sexual minorities*.

LGBTQ comics opting not to pass as heterosexual—such as veteran comic Sabrina Matthews, a White butch lesbian born in Baltimore, MD, and raised in Rye, NY—use their appearance to call attention to the stereotypes that people harbor about other groups. On one hand, this functions as a tactic to identify stereotypes as reductionary and generalizing fictions, while also identifying which beliefs and assumptions constitute stereotypes. On the other hand, stereotypes can be used to confirm one's cultural belonging while also useful as a comic device since it capitalizes on shared comic frames or existing beliefs and knowledge people have about various communities. For example, during her performance, Matthews confesses: "Yes I have a truck and a cat. I know the surprises just keep on coming [*laughter*]. This is like the only shirt I own that's not flannel."[43] The enjoyment of that joke derives, indeed relies, on the shared set of cultural beliefs about lesbians. Lesbians and heterosexuals alike can chuckle at their mutual knowledge (regardless of its veracity) of the cultural construction of lesbians in the United States. Since stereotypes about various groups and communities will vary across cultures, the joke is successful because knowledge of the stereotypes affirms a "we," a cultural belonging less associated with categories of difference and more a signal of national belonging. In an interview, Matthews acknowledges that she capitalizes on these stereotypes:

In front of a straight crowd it's a lot of fun to do stereotypical jokes like that because, one thing, it hits on the things that they're expecting to laugh at. I bet it sometimes surprises a lot of straight people that we might have a sense of humor about our own stereotypes. I certainly have a sense of humor about my own stereotypes.[44]

Combating the cultural axiom that feminists and lesbians do not have a sense of humor or that they cannot laugh *at* themselves, Matthews purposefully destabilizes this stereotype even while joking about other stereotypes that are, in her case, accurate.

African American / Black Charged Comics

In an episode of *Comics without Borders*, hosted by Canadian Russell Peters, Black comedienne B-Phlat rails against breast implants, championing natural beauty instead, and in a joke about adopting kids reminds audience members of the need for good homes for children in the United States. Her charged humor is at times undercut by the use of stereotypes like reducing native Africans to ignorant cannibals, but then again it is in those moments she gets the heartiest laughter. It gives one pause. At times a comic chooses to sneak messages into a joke guaranteed to get a laugh, that is, the joke capitalizes on a stereotype about another group. Charged humor can be presented alongside pseudo-satire or outright mockery, and this is not uncommon particularly for comics desiring (and achieving) national success. They know what works and what sells. The following bit begins innocently enough with B-Phlat pointing out that money makes it easier to exercise—an incisive critique of the resources (i.e., disposable income, time, childcare, transportation, exercise accessories, etc.) needed to belong to a gym, to get fit via privileged means. She goes on:

> And see I live in the hood. When you live in the hood, you can't just get up and go running and go exercise. I live in the hood—all Black people. If they see me running, they gonna think something happened [*laughter*]. They be like: "What the hell, why she runnin? Ya'll get in the house! Go in the back yard [*laughter*]! Something happened out here . . . someone runnin', they runnin'" [*laughter*]![45]

People running in the "hood" signals danger, a warning of police activity or a public altercation down the street or worse. In any event, B-Phlat suggests it would be misinterpreted because of a particularly violent history shared by African Americans and associated with living in lower income housing. Using a more overt style of performing charged humor, Dave Chappelle's stand-up comedy special *Dave Chappelle: For What It's Worth* (2004) is peppered with charged humor such as:

I spoke at my old high school and I told them kids straight up, If you guys are serious about making it out of this ghetto, you got to focus, you gotta' stop blaming White people for your problems and you've got to learn how to [*falters and waits a beat*] rap or play basketball or something nigger, you're trapped [*laughter and clapping sustained through end of joke*]! You are trapped. Either do that or sell crack, that's your only option, that's the only way I've seen it work. You better get to entertaining these White people. Get to dancing [*laughter while he dances*]! Go out there and be somebody![46]

Chappelle's admonition to Black youth is startling in a society relentlessly touting the myth of meritocracy—that you can do anything, be anything you want to be. The humor derives from his play on the audience's expectations that he will dispense with uplifting platitudes. In most contexts, his claims are not in and of themselves humorous, but by introducing an incongruous moment he counters audience expectations *and* the myth of meritocracy, rendering the myth laughable even when this reality is not.

The experience of being wrested unwillingly from their homeland directly impacted African American humor, "rooting the group's humor in an inversion of experience of a dislocated and stolen people," according to historian Elsie Williams.[47] African American humor reflects the time period in which it was exercised, pointing toward the epochal social, cultural, and political limitations placed on African Americans. Historian Robert Pratt argues that humor "says something about the African American experience, defines us in new and creative ways."[48] In her monograph on Moms Mabley, Williams identifies four major features/typologies of African American humor emerging over the course of the last 150 years: the plantation survivalist, accommodationist, in-group social satirist, and integrationist of the '60s and '70s.[49] All of these typologies served to depict, explain, and qualify blackness to audiences.

Being visibly marked by alterity presents struggles unique to one's social, political, and historical positions. Regardless of verisimilitude, comedy has long been means to communicate ideas about identities. In an interview with W. Kamau Bell, Black comic and formerly the host of *Totally Biased with W. Kamau Bell* on FX, he and radio hosts of *Jordan, Jesse, GO!* discuss audience expectations when it comes to addressing race:

> HOSTS: It speaks in part to the burden of expectation, you know, when a comedian and part of your job is explaining the world and add to that that you're Black, and thus, if you're not performing for a specific Black audience then you sort of have to shoulder this other burden of "oh god I have to explain blackness to White people and be funny."
>
> W. KAMAU BELL: Yeah, and some of those people are probably your agents and managers . . . when the biggest comedian in the country is Jerry Seinfeld,

White people aren't necessarily like: "He speaks for our whiteness. He's an icon for us. He's important." You know, they just go: "He's funny!"[50]

W. Kamau Bell cannot extricate himself from his blackness; he is raced regardless of how he self-locates and whether or not he shares a sense of belonging with Black and African American communities (though, in his case, he does). When I perform, being a woman and a sexual minority makes me a token member speaking on behalf of women and queers. Whether I perform marginality or not, for example, call attention to my queerness or womanness, if physiognomy indicates "otherness," whatever I say will somehow be linked with that otherness. Arab American comic Dean Obeidallah observes this in his standup when describing the period following 9/11 during one of his performances:

> For the people who aren't Arab I can just tell you this. I hope you never come to a time where you feel self-conscious or uncomfortable in your own country. And that's been the weird thing about a post 9/11 world for me. . . . People ask me. They go, well has your life changed since 9/11? It has changed in a couple ways. . . . If you're of Arab heritage, the difference is, for those of you who were here before, you're not White anymore because White people aren't subject to racial profiling, ever. And if you are White you should feel lucky about that. You never suffer as a group for the sins of a few. Like Oklahoma City, remember Timothy McVeigh and his redneck buddies. There was no "Operation Hillbilly" after that [*laughter*]. And think about the bad things that White people have done: presidential assassinations, corporate scandals, country music [*laughter*] . . . someone should be in jail [*laughter*].[51]

Obeidallah points out that when a White person makes a mistake, their poor behavior or performance does not become a reflection of all White people. This is perhaps most noticeable to groups subject to this discrimination. In a study of African American stand-up comedy performed in the wake of 9/11, Lanita Jacobs-Huey found Black comedy less jingoistic than that of other comics. Instead, Black comics cautiously considered America's own culpabilities (past and present), commented on the redirection of racial profiling from Black to Arab, and questioned the terms of their own national belonging.[52] Knowing that audiences read individuals as token or representative of any group often means that members of minority groups subject themselves to self-censorship and editing; we are afraid our idiosyncrasies will be generalized to an entire community.

Audience reception has other ways of shaping, if not dictating representations of identities. When it comes to racial/ethnic minorities performing stand-up comedy there seems to be two comic personae that routinely sell well to middle America: race neutral, wherein race is never called directly to the

attention of the audience (think: Bill Cosby or Wayne Brady), or a performance of race that satisfies existing beliefs and stereotypes about racial categories (think: Eddie Murphy or Martin Lawrence). This topic arises later in
their podcast as Jesse Thorn and Jordan Morris continue their interview with
W. Kamau Bell.

> HOSTS: There's this big world of African-American comedy that is very grounded
> in this sort of def-comedy jam idea that Black comedy is. And then there is sort
> of another world of Black comedy that is maybe inspired by Bill Cosby when
> part of the premise is that this transcends race; that it's not about race, it's
> about human experience and we've all been, we've all seen children say the
> darndest things. . . . I imagine that it must be tough to find a third path that
> is very much conscious of race and identity but isn't about, you know, quarter
> waters and growing up in the hood or whatever.
>
> W. KAMAU BELL:. . . I never wanted to be the def-jam school, which is unnatural
> to me. I never wanted to appear to be the other thing [race neutral] at all. And
> think that's something I struggle with. . . . So, that was I think a hard part,
> trying to find that place. Which is ironic cause it's not that long ago that the
> two biggest comics in the country were [Chris] Rock and Dave Chappelle, who
> I feel were that third thing, and I felt like, oh wow with these two guys like
> they'll be some sort of trickle-down theory. And then it never trickled down.
> It's like Reagan's trickle-down economics and it never trickled down. I think I
> assumed it would open up doors for a lot more comics like me. And there are a
> lot more comics, not exactly like me, but Black comics that sort of speak to a
> different history than others. Like, how do we get through? It's like Dave
> Chappelle and Chris Rock were the special ones.[53]

Micia Mosely, a Black comic whose comedy easily falls into that third category
Bell and hosts Thorn and Morris describe makes a similar observation saying:
"I also recognized that like I do a lot of what [Chris Rock] does except he's a lot
more famous than I am." There does not seem to be public demand enough to
sustain more than a handful of charged comics, and those that do manage to
achieve mainstream status and consistently employ charged humor also tend
to be men. Thus there are fewer visible examples of the third category of comics, those addressing race and identity in ways that neither neutralize nor caricature race. Mosely continues to work on her material refusing to omit or limit
charged humor from her sets, passionately declaring, "It's more important that
I actually get the message across, than it fits a traditional joke pattern."[54] Her
status as female, feminist, Black, and lesbian charged comic in many ways determines where and to whom she can perform.

While African Americans share a common history of persecution, collective
experiences of enslavement, political and cultural disenfranchisement, and

institutionalized racism, Black men do not suffer from the same difficulties posed to Black women seeking careers in comedy, and in general have traditionally achieved rights before women in the United States. This does not mean that Black men do not produce charged humor; on the contrary, some who are most adept at using comedy to point toward cultural and national contradictions have been African American male comics such as Dick Gregory, Richard Pryor, Chris Rock, Paul Mooney, Katt Williams, B.T., Preacher Moss, Wil Sylvince, D. L. Hughley, Lavell Crawford (sparingly), JB Smoove (sparingly), Baratunde Thurston, and Dave Chappelle. But there are plenty (more) Black male comics who do not perform charged humor. Some that spring to mind are: Alonzo Bodden, David Arnold, Kevin Hart, Patrice O'Neal, and others. Just because a comic performs charged humor does not mean s/he is the paragon of parity or s/he understands other forms of subordination. Anyway, understanding and identifying which social identities are marginalized still does not preclude attacking members of those groups. I attended a comedy performance at Carolines on Broadway in New York City in May 2011 wherein Paul Mooney's stinging charged humor illumined racial inequality while alternately feeding the audience misogynistic and sexist jokes.

Black comediennes continually have to negotiate a distinctive voice and performance aesthetic, in part because they are repeatedly occluded as subjects of analysis by virtue of sex when studying comics (read: male) and by virtue of race when studying female comics (read: White). As both Black and female, comedian Paula Jai Parker reports: "every time I've experienced sexism I wondered if there was a little racism attached to it. I don't know. It all goes hand in hand to me. I experience them daily."[55] Due to these intersecting oppressions, scholar Carol Allen found that "African American female comedy tends to be critical and deconstructive, recoding both white supremacist and masculinist ideologies" and "plays with and against the atrocity of slavery and the ensuing packaging and sale of all things Negro."[56] African American women comics must combat an untiring legacy of misrepresentation construing Black women as lascivious or hypersexual and unapologetically aggressive, characteristics that fly in the face of Victorian ideologies of true womanhood that continue to bear currency like piety, submissiveness, domesticity, and purity. Consequently, Black comediennes use their position as cultural soothsayers to undermine the validity of these dominant images and to inflect these perceptions with positive associations and attributes. Thus, where dominant culture paints the picture of Black female dominance, a Black comedienne may respond by qualifying this as a necessary strength deployed to battle infidelity or protect loved ones from domestic abuse. Black women comics focus on corporeal issues, sexual and personal relationships, "and racial and gender authenticity" as a way to attend to the misrepresentations pervasive in dominant culture.[57] According to L. H.

Stallings, in *Mutha' Is Half a Word: Intersections of Folklore, Vernacular, Myth, and Queerness in Black Female Culture*, women's humor is pivotal to "contemporary Black women's self-definition and struggle" and Black female culture offers possibilities for the discovery, celebration, and dissemination of radical Black female subjectivities.[58] Charged comedy produced by Black women reflects the social and historical restraints placed upon them as they contend with presenting themselves authentically while trying to circumvent the trappings of essentializing Black womanhood.

Black women comics achieve a wider audience willing to listen, relate, and even adopt their views when they present themselves as nonthreatening and socially engaging on stage (Wanda Sykes is the perfect example of this), which in a subversive turn allows them the freedom to be more direct, honest, and even political, displaying behaviors traditionally considered unladylike. Contemporary Black women comics performing charged humor include Whoopi Goldberg, Loni Love, Luenell, Melanie Comarcho, Aisha Tyler, Sommore, Mo'Nique Hicks, René Hicks, Adele Givens, Laura Hayes, Sheryl Underwood, Gloria Bigelow, Paula Jai Parker, Micia Mosely, Wanda Sykes, B-Phlat, Erin Jackson, Demetria Dixon, and Karen Williams. Using comedy that is proactively antiracist and antisexist and seldom employs self-deprecating humor often results in a celebration of Black womanhood and contests the terms by which Black women are defined by the dominant culture.

Latino/a Charged Comics

The number of successful Latino/a comics is small relative to the Latino/a population in the United States, which is around 15 percent and growing. George Lopez, Cheech Marin, Carlos Mencia, Gabriel Iglesias, and Pablo Francisco are the most successful and nationally recognized Latino comics. While there are a handful of Latinas performing in amateur and professional circuits, none has the name recognition achieved by these men (particularly the first three) for performing comedy, though Anjelah Johnson is gaining traction with American audiences. One reason may be that Latinas employing charged humor frequently opt to work out of a genre of performance particular to Chicano/a culture, which brands their style of performance as alternative, operating outside the frames of traditional stand-up comedy and foreign to mainstream American audiences.

To find the Latinas employing charged humor, one must look beyond the traditional stand-up comedy format. Departing from the first Chicano theater movement (most popularly El Teatro Campesino) arising in the 1960s, which was largely spurred by the Chicano civil rights and united farm workers movements, Chicana performance art, which is often humorous, seeks to foreground the politics of a specifically female Chicana identity versus a working male Chicano identity. Chicana theater has its own genre of performance fusing poetry and theater, called teatropoesia, which "reflects their ethnic and historical position" and stems from the Chicano/a community's interest in poetry whether print, spoken word, song, or performance.[59] Teatropoesia uses poetic form to make the personal public and developed in response to social barriers such as the wide-spread exploitation of Latino/a labor. Contemporary Latino/a comic performers like George Lopez, Sandra Valls, Marga Gomez, Lisa Alvarado, Gabriel Iglesias (at times), Marilyn Martinez, Sara Contreras, Chris Fonseca, Monique Marvez, Felipe Esparza, Eva Morales, Jesusa Rodriguez, Monica Palacios, Diana Raznovich, Astrid Hadad, Larry Torres (minimally), Ela Troyana, and Carmelita Tropicana all use charged humor in teatropoesia, performance art, and/or stand-up comedy.

The sold-out AT&T Center (1,400 seats) in San Antonio, Texas, erupts in cheers as George Lopez struts confidently onto the stage and begins yelling "Viva la Latinos!" in *George Lopez: Tall, Dark and Chicano* (2009). Infusing his comedy with a smattering of Spanish, he delights in the addition of Sonia Sotomayor to the Supreme Court and rails against the Republicans voting against her nomination by President Barack Obama (including John McCain), saying, "Fuck you putos [*screams, clapping, and cheers*]! You will NEVER get the Latino vote now! You're fucked! [*Cheers continue*]. . . . Tell them you will not vote for them [*he points the microphone toward the crowd as they explode in cheers and whistles*]!"[60] Throughout the performance, he calls upon viewers to take notice of the ways people and the government "bastardize our culture," enjoining them to vote for Democrats, boycott restaurants that include "border" in the name, and to celebrate Latino/a culture. The content of his humor is far more charged than the stand-up he performed in his first full-length comedy concert film: *George Lopez: Why You Crying?* (2005), which details the tribulations of growing up poor in Los Angeles. His early humor errs on the side of crowd-pleasing, apolitical, safe humor. Looking squarely at the camera filming for the documentary *Brown Is the New Green: George Lopez and the American Dream* (2007), George Lopez opines: "There's the 'pass' and then there's the 'can't pass.' And you know what? [*Points to face*] This can't pass. And this performing and achieving at this level is harder because of this [*points to face again*]."[61] As his popularity swelled, he became increasingly vocal in his support and devotion to Latino/a communities and now makes every effort to specifically champion the Mexican American community. The crowd appreciates this and he is rewarded with cheers, whistles, standing ovations, and applause after nearly every sentence he speaks. Choosing to curtail, limit, or even eliminate charged humor in earlier specials, now makes him one of the most prominent as well as savvy practitioners of charged humor. Similar to Margaret Cho and Wanda Sykes, he exercised caution in establishing himself as politicized until he garnered a strong nation-wide following. Having done so he can now take more liberties on stage, performing charged humor with greater frequency and openly using his fame to instill cultural pride, solidarity, and political action; in other words to enact cultural citizenship through charged humor.

Latina jokesters continue the tradition of politicized Chicana performance, using humor as a satirical device and a way to entertain while instructing audiences. Performance studies scholars Diana Taylor and Roselyn Constantino argue that Latina performances, many of them comical, demonstrate the diversity of Latinas as well as the complex history of colonization and its effects. One of the Latina divas of comedy, Marilyn Martinez, now deceased, reported: "I think it's hard when you're a woman and especially . . . that I'm a Latin woman."[62] All Latino/a comic performers must choose whether they will perform charged humor. This humor would educate about a history of colonization, genocide, and forced assimilation and combat stereotypes and misrepresentations like that anyone looking "brown" is here illegally or that Latinas are tempestuous and hypersexual. For example, Lisa Alvarado jokes, "I'm not the typical Latina because I got pregnant in my *late* teens" (emphasis hers).[63] Hers is a moral lapse vindicated by her superiority to younger Latina mothers. The joke is funny because it sets up a false expectation with audience members (read: what she is about to say will stray from how we imagine Latinas in the national imagination) only to have that expectation fulfilled. The joke is both a stereotype constitutive of communal identity and an aberration from the stereotype, albeit minimal.

Felipe Esparza, winner of NBC's *Last Comic Standing* (2010), comes across as a bumbling ultra-chill dude preoccupied with stereotypical cis-gendered male subjects like women, cars, and sex, but his comedy is also sprinkled with charged humor dealing with class issues and being Mexican American in the United States. During an appearance on *Comics without Borders*, he says: "I live at home for one reason; someone needs to answer the phone in English. That makes me the manager [*laughter*]."[64] English fluency is lingual and cultural currency. We live in a society that perpetually grumbles about nonnative English speakers (think of the complaints people have anytime they deal with someone with an accent: doctors, auto mechanics, teachers, professors, tech support) and the increasing antipathy toward US residents who will not learn to speak English. My stepmother, who emigrated from Russia nearly twenty years ago and teaches math at a community college in Florida, lives in constant fear of being fired because each semester students gripe about her accent on evaluations. Just to reiterate: she teaches math. Speaking English allows for better navigation of American culture and business (read: success), and everyone knows that speaking English poorly can seriously limit the occupations (read: success) available to you. Esparza recognizes the power conferred by one's fluency in English, and regardless of his parent's skills, abilities, and experience that surely exceed his own, this singular skill of fluency makes him the manager. It is a disturbingly accurate depiction of how power flows in this nation, where pedigree and cultural capital far outweighs skill, natural talent, or time on the job.

Asian American Charged Comics

Like other race/ethnic based minority communities, the Asian American cultural tradition of performance varies based on country of origin, region of relocation, and proximity to urban centers. Asian American comics like Vijai Nathan, Margaret Cho, Ali Wong, Edwin San Juan, Bobby Lee, Samson Koletkar (who is also Jewish), Dr. Ken Jeong, Hari Kondabolu, Sheng Wang, Tapan Trivedi, Aparna Nancherla, and Kate Rigg have used comedy onstage to develop community among Asian Americans, voice dissatisfaction with stereotypes, and where the women are concerned, challenge the objectification and hypersexualization of Asian women. Americanist Lisa Lowe in *Immigrant Acts: On Asian American Cultural Politics* documents Asian Americans and their particular history of exploitation and exclusion, arguing that culture presents a possible if not advantageous site for constructing new subjectivities, undermining the nation's desire for docile immigrant bodies, and "question[ing] those modes of government."[65] To demonstrate, Aparna Nancherla—a South Asian Indian American stand-up comic who wrote for and sometimes appeared on FX's *Totally Biased with W. Kamau Bell*—uses her comedy to recall India's history of colonization and its lasting imprint on the collective psyche of South Asian Indians.

> I have this thing that whenever one of my Caucasian friends apologizes to me I automatically assume it's for imperialism on some level [*laughter*]. It's totally my issue but it does lead to some awkward situations. Like if one of them is like, "Oh, Aparna here's your CD that I lost sorry it took me so long to replace it. Do people still use CDs?" and I'm just like, "oh . . . and . . . [*pauses and nods encouragingly*]" [*laughter*]. And they're like, "Oh I'm sorry I thought it was just the CD. Is it something else? Oh man I feel like a bonehead." And I'm just like, "Remember your people [*takes her fist and crushes it into the palm of her other hand while making sounds like an explosion*]? And then my people [*emits whimpering and crying sounds*]" [*laughter*]. And they're just like, "This again?" And I'm like, "History's wounds never heal!" [*laughter*]. And they're like, "Why are we still friends?" And I'm like, "I ask myself this every day" [*laughter*].[66]

She, like other comics using charged humor, recognize the potential that entertainment has, specifically a cultural form allowing comics to author their own performances and speak from personal histories, to wage war on cultural fronts. Placing importance on such cultural battles, Karen Shimakawa, author of *National Abjection: The Asian American Body Onstage*, considers representations of Asian-ness on stage as well as the ways Asian American performers confront the paradox of living as both an outsider and "at some fundamental level, an undifferentiable part of the whole."[67] The dominant culture or "the whole" relies on the practice of "othering" Asian Americans and this othering constitutes the whole. They are known by what they are not: "read as abject, Asian-Americanness thus occupies a role both necessary to and mutually constitutive of national subject formation—*but it does not result in the formation of an Asian-American subject or even an Asian-American object*" (emphasis hers).[68] Sheng Wang, a Taiwanese American stand-up comic, illustrates this in a charged joke that illumines what W. E. B. Du Bois defined as double consciousness, meaning he views himself through the eyes of others, imagining how his actions may be corroborating or even introducing new negative stereotypes about Asian Americans.

> One night, I was at the Milwaukee airport waiting for a connection flight, and I had uh this crazy idea because I found this random can of tuna in my backpack [*laughter*]. And I was like let's make this a heartier meal, I'm gonna put that in my salad, right because it's protein and it's gonna fill me up but it's also smelly unorthodox behavior [*laughter*]. Like, no one does that. And I was worried because if you're White and you're weird, you're a weirdo. But, if you're an Asian dude at the Milwaukee airport and if you start to step out of line, then you just started a whole bunch of new stereotypes for your people [*laughter and applause*]. Folks, will look at that guy [*shakes his head disapprovingly*]: "They all do that" [*laughter*]. So I was paranoid. I was really concerned that people were watching me, judging me, thinking I was being cheap or weird, whatever. Then I got to a whole new level of fear. I got worried that people thought I was eating cat food [*laughter*]; for no reason. I was just sure people were thinking, "Hey that Chinese dude is putting Friskies in his Caesar salad [*laughter*]. Everybody take a picture. Put it on the Internet and tag 'Asia'" [*laughter*].[69]

In this exchange, as Wang proposes it, Asian Americans do not emerge with any sort of subjectivity intact. He is scrutinized and his behaviors reduced to uncivilized and backward.

To counter limiting cultural stereotypes and subsequent social alienation, Asian American comics are raising funny voices, stepping up to confront cultural invisibility, misrepresentations, stereotypes, and perceived political impotence. Bobby Lee, an energetic Korean American gains audience affection with his buoyant personality and playful self-deprecating humor such as one of his popular openers: "I look like a Native American with Down Syndrome [*laughter*]." While his comedy is primarily fun-loving and innocuous, he foregrounds his allegiance to the Asian American community and occasionally inserts charged humor.

I hate Asian porn. I don't like the titles of the magazines; they're so fucking racist [*light laughter*]. I want to masturbate to a magazine called: *Girls Who Happen to Be Asian* [*laughter*]. But no, these magazines are called: *Kung Pao Titty* [*laughter*] or *Beef and Broccoli and Pussy* [*laughter*]. I don't get horny, I get hungry [*louder laughter and applause*].[70]

This joke echoes the common resentment of any minority citizen reduced to their race/ethnicity, sexuality, or disability. While these identity categories are certainly important, they are not the sum of our parts; they are just one part. Similarly, the beliefs that all Asians look alike and can communicate with one another despite the heterogeneity of the Asian American community functions as another reductionist practice. Dr. Ken Jeong, who performs stand-up comedy and practices internal medicine (usually not at the same time), offers an example of this:

The thing I hate about my job is translating for other Asian patients. Apparently someone has made me the go-to-guy to translate for every Asian motherfucker they wheel in the hospital [*laughter*]. I tell my boss: "Sir, I don't know if you understand. See, I'm Korean and the family there, they're Vietnamese, you know? [*Chuckles uncomfortably and draws his eyes back up and then down in a slant*] You know what I'm saying [*laughter*]? Chink? Nip? Hello?" [*laughter*]. He doesn't care. He goes [*speaking slowly and patronizingly*]: "Hi this is Dr. Jeong. He going to speak Asian to you" [*laughter and clapping*].[71]

The non–Asian doctor proceeds to offer an extensive medical report steeped in jargon and motions to Dr. Jeong to translate. Springing into fighting stance, perhaps recognizable as a "ninja" pose, Dr. Jeong summarizes the medical report, translating for the Vietnamese family with exaggerated gestures speaking slowly in English with an "Asian" accent: "Eberyting . . . Okey-dokey [*laughter, clapping, and cheers*]."

Kate Rigg, a Canadian, queer, bicultural, biracial comic performer living in the United States identifies herself as a "cultural terrorist" who works on the "deconstruction and reconstruction of language."[72] She uses her stand-up comedy to challenge phallocentrism and reconstitute her subjectivity, in part by negating common fallacies about Asian women.[73]

I am so happy actually to be part of this show [*cheers*] for real because I mean, well I'm a very naughty delicate oriental lotus petal first of all. And I get to talk about my pussy for the whole fucking set which I'm really, really excited about. . . . Because you know it's not just to like gratuitously flap my pink bits on the stage at you, you know what I mean [*some chuckles*]? I'm not trying to take us all on a trip to tuna town you know and to be vulva, I mean vulgar. There's a point to it, okay. There's a point because in our culture we are penetrated by penis references you know all the time you know, in comedy clubs man. If you go to comedy clubs all night long, I swear to God it's like: dick, dick, dick, smack my Internet, whacking off, porn, perineum, scrot, jizz load, cumshot, long duck dong, right? [*one person claps*] . . . As a woman in comedy, you know, I feel like it's my duty to, you know, redress the balance, you know, kind of take back the night, like vaginally feng shui every room [*laughter*] that I go into, you know like [*her voice switches to what is considered an Asian accent*]: "Take a candle shaped like clitoris; place in northeast corner of room" . . . I know about feng shui of course because I'm Asian [*she emits a fake laugh*] and some of you now are probably waiting for me to shoot some ping pong balls out of my cooch, [*some men cheer*] but that's not going to happen![74]

On and offstage, Rigg desires to be "winningly subversive" but as the audience response indicates, being subversive is not always well received. Performing in *The Naughty Show: Bad Girls of Comedy*, viewers may have expected beautiful women cursing and talking explicitly about sex (and what is wrong with that?) but did not expect her to wax on about a phallocentric world and women's limited say in that world. Admittedly Rigg speaks quickly but when an opening bit and nearly the first two minutes of a set is met with such long periods of silence, you typically have one of two situations. Either the comic is simply not funny. Period (this is not the case here). Or, the audience is caught off guard or uncomfortable because they feel attacked or uncertain of where things are going—expectations are going unfulfilled. At times, depending on who you are, charged humor repels viewers from a worldview that challenges their own, one that they do not care to give much thought. These are worldviews that reveal privilege, power, and authority; they are views that hold little cultural or political currency. In main, we are not used to being held captive by any worldview against our will, not when you can change the channel, put down the book, or close that tab online. Walking out of a performance is another thing. Because it is unlikely for audience members to exit a performance prematurely (unless severely agitated), silence becomes a useful indication of the degree to which the audience identifies and agrees with the performer. Laughter signals both identification and agreement. As Rigg demonstrates in her stand-up comedy (even if some folks do not want to hear it) and as Karen Shimakawa and Lisa Lowe argue, performance opens opportunities for Asian Americans to negotiate their abject status, to assert the Asian American subject and transform national subject formation in the cultural imagination.

Class Matters for Charged Comics

There seems to be a general reluctance to acknowledge and openly discuss class differences and growing class inequality in the United States. Seeking to avoid social stigma, those located on either end of the economic spectrum self-identify as middle-class. A sociologist studying poverty, labor, and inequality, Gregory Mantsios identifies four common myths circulating about class: that we are a classless society; we are a middle-class nation; everyone is getting richer; and anyone from any class background can be wildly successful.[75] Indeed, the rich downplay their wealth and the poor, ever aware that things could be even worse, see themselves as middle-class folks facing temporary financial setbacks. Wealth begets wealth, which is why rich people stay rich and poor people stay poor. With a growing chasm between the "haves" and the "have-nots," and since there is a finite supply of money, it is a fallacy and numerically infeasible that everyone could be getting richer. The myth of meritocracy also known as the myth of the American dream works hard to console the economically downtrodden, assuring the working poor that if they work hard enough fortune lies just around the corner. For those who never reap the rewards of the so-called American dream, the onus of their failure lies squarely on them instead of economic institutions and systems structured to maintain class inequality. Nearing the end of a half-hour special on Comedy Central, South Asian American comic Hari Kondabolu shared his personal dislike for 1960s protest music, which his friend describes as the sound of the revolution. Kondabolu disagrees saying: "I always assumed the revolution would be a bit louder. I assumed gun fire, and bombs blowing up, and the blood-curdling screams of rich people having their throats slit and their land taken away and maybe even their organs eaten."[76] This became his segue into the final bit for the show, wherein he details who would die in the revolution based on our current class order:

So I was telling that joke at a small liberal arts college recently and this young woman came up to me and she was very upset and she was like, "You know there's a lot of really good rich people in the world and I don't think it's fair that you just grouped everybody together." And I get what she was saying. She was saying me, my family, my siblings, the people in my country club, the kids that went to my private boarding school. And I thought I would compromise with her so I made a list of exactly who would die in the revolution that I wanted to share with you tonight. [*Takes out a piece of paper and reads*] List of people that will die in the revolution, by Hari Kondabolu. I really shouldn't put my name on it. [*Laughter*] Alright, alright. List of people who will die in the revolution: Number one. Anyone who has called their car "ghetto" because their built-in GPS didn't work will die in the revolution. Two, anyone whose first real job was being the star of a reality television show and the name of the show wasn't *Inner-City Youth Unable to Find Work and Forced to Star in a Reality Television Show* will die in the revolution. Three, Jimmy Buffet. Four, [*pause*] (that one's kind of obvious), four: anyone who has used the phrase "my grandparents' cottage" in a sentence without it being preceded by the phrase "we had to sell" will die in the revolution. Five, the young woman who inspired the creation of this list, her parents, her siblings, the people at her country club, and the kids who went to her private boarding school, with the exception of the affirmative action and financial aid students, will die in the revolution. [*Cheers and laughter*] And finally, the woman who boarded the Jet Blue flight in front of me and turned to her husband and said, "I hate flying Jet Blue, because Jet Blue does not have first class." It's Jet Blue! Jet Blue is like the best airline in the world! I mean everybody gets a comfortable seat, everybody gets ample legroom, everybody gets a television, everybody gets unlimited snacks! This woman's issue wasn't that there wasn't first class; her issue was that there was finally equality in the world! This woman will die in the revolution [*cheering*]![77]

Turnabout is fair play. Society blames people for their impoverished status; instead, Kondabolu reproaches rich people for their role in perpetuating class inequality and condemning the poor. Aware that network executives may balk at the joke's content, Kondabolu intentionally performed the joke at the end of his set. While portions of the performance may be edited out of these half-hour specials, opening and closing bits are always left intact for visual and aural continuity. Placing the joke last ensured that viewers at home would have access to this inflammatory charged humor. Kondabolu debunks the myths about class that Mantsios cites as problematic, strategically reaching a different audience than his scholarly counterpart to educate on the same issues.

Examining wage and earnings data from the US Census Bureau shows that being a racial or ethnic minority correlates negatively to income, meaning racial/ethnic minorities will earn less for the same work and hence are more likely to be impoverished than White folks.[78] Rather than treating poverty as a misfortune requiring economic change, media narratives glamorize a difficult upbringing, showcasing the few who escape poverty as inspirational and proof that the American dream works. African American stand-up comic Gloria Bigelow exposes this hypocrisy while performing on *AfterEllen*, focusing on the co-optation of the term "ghetto" commonly bandied about to signify low-class.

> I don't know how you're gonna feel about this, but, uh, I've been thinking lately that we should take the word "ghetto" out of the popular vernacular. I know it's pretty sad for some people; it's very sad. But the thing about the word ghetto is it's kind of like making light of a misfortune. Ghetto is not a good thing. And out in the suburbs the kids have ghetto parties. Did you know this? They have ghetto parties and they drink out of brown paper bags and they're like, "We so ghetto" [*laughter*]. No! Could you imagine other misfortune parties [*laughter*]?

Like if we had a Bernie Madoff party. People bringing ripped up 401Ks and shattered dreams and they're like, "It's a party—Madoff!" [*laughter*]. No, it seems to me that people don't know how to use the word ghetto in context.[79]

Comparing the working poor to middle-class people now facing financial ruin, Bigelow conflates the two, showing that neither deserves social disparagement nor should we celebrate their economic travails. Daniel Tosh, White comedian and host of Comedy Central's *Tosh.0*, observes the way money grants access to specific kinds of recreational and sporting activities and the ways this intersects with race/ethnicity. White people do not intrinsically gravitate to skiing and ice skating nor are African Americans naturally better suited to run track or play basketball; racial status and ethnic heritage does not explain desire to play and/or success in specific sports, but, as Tosh points out, money does.

> The Winter Olympics are pointless. I'll say it. Are you kidding me? I assume the only reason we have them is so White people feel relevant in sports [*laughter*]. Because other than that the only thing the Winter Olympics show me is which country has more rich White kids [*laughter*]. What's it cost to go skiing, nine hundred dollars a day? [*Sarcastically*] I can't believe that's not more popular in inner cities [*laughter*]! Hey Latrell you wanna play basketball today? "Nah man I'm going to Breckenridge." Ooooh . . . laddy-Uncle-Tom-dah [*laughter*]. Latrell is going to Breckenridge.[80]

Wage disparity, which affects people of color, persons who are differently abled, women and gender nonconforming folks, is one of many structural forces maintaining economic inequality. Nikki Payne proffers environmental classism as another example of structural inequality. A White Canadian female comic born with a cleft palate and raised in a trailer park in Nova Scotia, Payne uses comedy to teach the audience that vulnerability to bodily harm and material devastation correlates directly to income and affordable housing.

> The thing that bothers me the most about growing up in a trailer park is the misconceptions. All the things that the common people say about people who live in trailer parks, right. I remember watching the comics on TV, they're always like: "Why do the people who live in trailer parks always live in tornado alley? [*emits an exaggerated laugh*] Hahhahahahaha." Why? Why? Because we're poor! That's why [*laughter*]. Land comes cheap when there is a sixty percent chance you're going to DIE on it! [*laughter and clapping*].[81]

Lower-income housing anywhere coincides with higher crime rates, poorly funded elementary and secondary education, and closer proximity to toxic waste dumps and other environmental health hazards. Prolonged exposure to airborne and waterborne toxins increases the likelihood that poor people of all ages will suffer from temporary and permanent illness, infection, and disease.[82] This means that the population least likely to have comprehensive health insurance is the most likely to need medical care. A single visit to the emergency room sans insurance can be the financial ruin of a family for years to come.

Comics were making jokes about the millions unable to afford health care long before President Barack Obama's Affordable Care Act passed in 2010, but in the two years leading up to that time as the public debated the merits of this legislation, stand-up comics weighed in on the matter with even greater frequency. All too aware that she does not have access to preventative medical care, Maria Bamford, a White stand-up comic, shares homegrown methods for sick care or dealing with major medical issues.

> I got a couple things: an air conditioner unit and a scuba diving mask and I figure, I could set that up in any situation. You know, let it cool the cancer [*laughter*]. 'Cause cancer is hot, right? And then, um, if I get pregnant, I got a level. Uh, [*laughter as she stares down at her belly*] looks good from here. And uh, then, there is a lot of mental illness in my family so if you catch schizophrenia you get four boxes of Mike and Ike, a Bible and a cage [*pause*] . . . wait it out [*laughter*].[83]

Jeff Caldwell, a White comic performing mainly family-friendly material, supplies another creative method of handling medical care without health insurance which he and his family went without for years because it was an expense he could not afford. He says that while he had no health insurance, "I did have auto insurance that covered health in the case of an accident. So every time I got sick I dragged myself into the car [*laughter*]. Run her into a tree again [*laughter*]. Not a shrub left in my neighborhood [*laughter*]."[84] Some stand-up comics had personal stakes in the outcome of this legislation for a couple reasons. One, because stand-up comedy is a form of entertainment requiring little start-up capital making it an appealing profession to those without a financial safety net. Not all comics come from working class backgrounds, but many do. Two, because professional stand-up comics are classified as independent contractors (meaning they do not have an employer to help subsidize insurance), health insurance remains unaffordable for many stand-up comedians, even career comics with steady income, like Hari Kondabolu who has prestigious comedy credits on his resume and formerly wrote for FX's *Totally Biased with W. Kamau Bell*. Here, Kondabolu openly criticizes what he perceives as a piece of legislation that barely accomplishes what President Obama sought to do—diluted public policy that will do little to effectively remediate economic stratification in this country.

I don't like my current level of health care, which of course is NO health care [*laughter*]. I was really hoping for the public option, but of course we weren't going to get it because we started the debate in this country with the public option. And when you start with a reasonable idea it goes through the legislative system. It gets negotiated back and forth, it gets watered down; you don't get what you necessarily wanted. You started with the public option. It went through the system. What do we have now? Echinacea, prayer and hug [*laughter*] all on the free market, right? And it's frustrating because the critics were deriding the public option for being a redistribution of wealth and I don't agree with that. And I wish we had started with my health care proposal. Because my health care proposal wasn't so much about a redistribution of wealth, my health care proposal was more about a redistribution of organs—from rich to poor [*laughter*]. Oh and you think, oh after rich people die we would take their organs from them? Yes, of course, friends, after the rich people die [*laughter*]. And after we kill them [*laughter and clapping*]. Like a bunch of scalpel wielding Robin Hoods in the night. We would kill these rich people and take their organs from them [*laughter*]. 'Cause there are a lot of poor people who need those organs for transplants and of course for food [*laughter*], and as we all know, rich people's organs are a delicacy [*laughter*]. We would force feed them organic grains and get them all plump and fat, their organs juicy and succulent and then we'd have them walk around their large estates—so they would be free range, free range rich people [*laughter*]. Then very humanely, very humanely, we'd kill them, a single slash to their throats, very humanely. And then we'd rip out their entrails and pull out their organs. And we'd FEAST. We'd eat a little meal I call JUSTICE [*laughter*]. And you're thinking, Hari, this proposal sounds unreasonable. Yes, and if we had started with it, we'd have the public option by now.[85]

Violence may not be the best solution to our economic woes, but Kondabolu is not advocating the actual slaughter of rich people; this analogy invokes the need for radical public policy that does not just scratch the surface of the financial train wreck in which many Americans find themselves.

Comics using charged humor to shed light on existing and increasing class stratification hail from many social identities. They are men and women, people of all races/ethnicities and nationalities, queer, gender nonconforming, and straight, differently abled and able-bodied, and pledge faith to diverse religions. Some of those include Daniel Tosh, Nikki Payne, Maria Bamford, Emily Levine, Jeff Caldwell, Tapan Trivedi, Hari Kondabolu, Kathleen Madigan, Gloria Bigelow, Micia Mosely, Chris Rock, George Lopez, Kate Clinton, Roseanne Barr, W. Kamau Bell, Nato Green, and B-Phlat. They all speak to the limitations and difficulties faced by the economically disenfranchised working poor, whose numbers are on the rise and whose ranks they sometimes occupy, if not now, then before or potentially in the future. If the economic recession in 2008 showed us anything it was how close so many of us are to financial instability. While it may not be popular to discuss socioeconomic status openly, charged comics fight this stigma, using humor to expose class inequality and urging viewers to consider their own roles in maintaining economic disparities.

The conditions supporting noncharged stand-up comedy as commercially viable remained fairly stable through the 2000s. Despite that comedy clubs continue experiencing a decline in revenue and the live comedy boom is well-over, public demand for stand-up comedy has not abated. It is simply being consumed in other ways like via online mediums. The comedy for which the public clamored in the 2000s seems to, with some exceptions, still be a combination of safe, absurdist, shock, or modern-day minstrelsy humor. However, a sea change in such inclinations to consume charged humor in the 2010s seems as good a possibility as any. In the twenty-first century, major events like the attacks on 9/11, subsequent wars in Afghanistan and Iraq, natural disasters that devastated New Orleans, Indonesia, Japan, and Haiti, an economic recession that strained our pocketbooks in an already gravely stratified economy, and impending threat of virus and disease, all these factors have taken a toll on the collective psyche of Americans. Examining filmic representations of the apocalypse in the 1990s and comparing them to the same kinds of visual texts produced after 9/11, film studies scholar James Aston and John Wallis, an expert in millennial cultures, argue that these representations indicate a turn toward pessimism. During the twenty-first century there has been a decline in the faith we place in science, technology, military, and government to stave off or save us during an apocalyptic event.[86] The public flocks to stand-up comedy to escape and also to seek catharsis, a way to process conflicting emotions that result from the (constant) fear of global annihilation and conflagration. As cultural spokespersons, comics have long been obligated to comment on poltical, historical, and social events. Our best comics are the ones that can do this so well and the aughts were no exception. Some spoke out on behalf of Muslims and Arab Americans, while some declared open season on Middle Easterners, reflecting domestic discord regarding the ensuing international conflict. American's appetite for comedy grew under these circumstances and a growing sense of vulnerability and skepticism is paving the way for contrarian voices that belie the American Dream. Rapidly changing cultural, technological, and political climates may yield another period of social unrest and rebellion that, like the mid-twentieth century (1950s–1970s), could create more hospitable reception to charged humor in the near future. Should we enter another fruitful era of charged comedy there exist even more methods for communicating to massive audiences. Comics can avail themselves of various social media tools that provide creative means of self-promotion and allow for exposure difficult to obtain through traditional methods vis-à-vis managers, agents, and booking staff at comedy clubs.

Charged comics summon the courage to speak truth to power and are out there working hard, in most instances taking a serious pay cut and flack from audiences across the country for performing this humor. Each comic represents a unique perspective about how they belong and offers diverse tactics for illuminating this humorously on stage. The production of charged humor enacting cultural citizenship reflects the individual and communal effects of the burden imposed by second-class status in the United States. These comics translate political and social issues for their listening public and offer possible psychological, political, and social means for combating ostracism and being maligned by the media. While hailing from disparate communities whose struggles are unique to their culture or nation's history with the United States, these humorous voices on the fringes are united in their quest to enact cultural citizenship vis-à-vis comedy. These are the producers of charged humor.

The end goals are the same for comics producing charged humor. Sommore says, "I just want people to know that I gave it my best and I intend to make a difference" and Chris Rock says it is his job as a comic to "examin[e] the human condition and brin[g] light to it."[87] Charged humorist Emily Levine states: "And what I hope to do when I make these connections is short circuit people's thinking. Make you not follow your usual train of association."[88] Their motives for being comic performers and writing the jokes they do coincide in an effort to enact cultural citizenship. In doing so, they draw attention to the ways they do not feel included or acknowledged in the national imagination. This humor will not change material conditions or reverse discrimination per se, but it can indicate where and how to start. These producers of charged humor want their jokes to be meaningful: build communal solidarity, reflect corruption and hypocrisy, promote parity and tolerance, and replace cultural fictions with fact or at least the complexity and dynamism of identity. All joking aside—they (we) just want to belong.

CHAPTER FOUR

When Women Perform Charged Humor

The (Gendered) Politics of Consumption

Do women and men laugh at the same jokes? Will a hermaphrodite meet you half way? I can't answer that but I can tell you that female comics have a harder job than male comics. It's that simple.

Lewis Black, History of the Joke

I kept thinking to myself, why was she [Elaine May] not as big a comedic actor as, say, Will Ferrell or Adam Sandler? And the question remains to this day. I think the unfortunate answer is that women just don't get as far being hilarious as men do. Period.

Merrill Markoe, We Killed: The Rise of Women in American Comedy

In *Vanity Fair* (January 2007), Christopher Hitchens published the derisively titled editorial, "Why Women Aren't Funny," echoing a long-held general cultural perception that men are funnier than women. Humor, on his terms, is best pursued by men, is understood most clearly by men, and should include only those issues pertaining to men. His insight into the gender divide in humor consumption is as follows: "Male humor prefers the laugh to be at someone's expense, and understands that life is quite possibly a joke to begin with— and often a joke in extremely poor taste. . . . Whereas women, bless their tender hearts, would prefer that life be fair, and even sweet, rather than the sordid mess it actually is."[1] Hitchens's essay articulates an argument that upon closer inspection quickly unravels. He is correct in saying that women are *perceived* as less funny, but he offers (sexist) biologistic and otherwise deterministic arguments to explain a cultural and economic phenomenon. In doing so, he reduces audiences' reception to and consumption of humor to something natural, innate, predetermined, and therefore moot, which for him is ideal because it leaves him and every other swinging dick with the upper hand, the "equipment" necessary to incite laughter and the arbiter of precisely what should elicit laughter.

Christopher Hitchens's article sparked public discussions both online and in print, introducing arguments from the biological and sociological to cultural and psychological explanations for public perceptions of women's inadequacy in the realm of humor production. What Hitchens overlooks and what the current public/print investigation of mixed audiences favoring male humor over female humor indicates, however, are cultural explanations of the economy of humor or the way consumption of humor is shaped by the cultural economy, the material incentives shaping popular cultural forms in the United States. How we belong shapes our identity and its material accessories, for example, shoes, jewelry, and cars. The artists we consume also shape our identity, whether a style of music, an aesthetic created by attraction to certain fine arts, and yes, even comics. To that effect, Lauren Berlant, writes that "identity is marketed in national capitalism as a property. It is something you can purchase, or purchase a relation to. Or it is something you already own that you can express."[2] Stuart Hall agrees that a "greater and greater number of people (men and women)—with however little money—play the game of using things to signify who they are."[3] Just as we can buy or obtain an image by wearing certain clothes and consuming certain music, we can also shape that image by buying into and supporting certain comics. This consumption is irrevocably wedded to and props up our ideas of who we are, including our national affiliations and where we see ourselves fitting into the national imagination.

Mainstream markets, comprised of the White middle-class (often referred to as middle-America though this is not entirely homogenous) and multiple niche markets like those targeting blue-collar workers, religious groups such as Muslims, Christians, and Jews, racial/ethnic communities, the differently abled, sexual minorities, and young adults, together constitute which comics achieve visibility. While these markets generally operate based on the profit potential of comic performers, there are exceptions to this, and some cultural gatekeepers do take financial risks on comics in whose work they believe or want to invest for personal or political reasons. Yet, a single vote of confidence from a booking agent, producer, or entertainment executive will not maintain itself for long if the comic yields little revenue or lacks a loyal fan base.

Mainstream audiences—here defined as those having purchasing power regardless of sexual orientation, race/ethnicity, nation of origin, or religion—tend to affirm the perspectives and identify (read: invest in and economically support; laugh or otherwise respond favorably) with male comics. It is important to situate "mainstream" in economic terms because booking agents, producers, network executives and industry entrepreneurs make hiring and casting decisions based on the perceived marketability of a comic, which is determined by their proven ability to appeal to a wide consumer base—middle-America or niche. While there are minority communities that do not necessarily consume comics appealing to middle America, they do, however, still support male comics more so than female comics also performing in the same niche market. For example, members of the African American middle-class exercise buying power in the market and though they may not be tuning in to watch or buy tickets to see Jim Gaffigan or Greg Proops, they *are* showing up to support D. L. Hughley and J. B. Smoove. Though I say this with caution, the only minority community where investment in male experience and points of view does not appear to be a foregone conclusion is within the LGBTQ community. While the focus here lies in public predilections for male comics over female comics, I include other categories of identity like heterosexual, able-bodied, and White to reference and recognize the multiple dimensions of power and privilege operating in society and to paint a complete portrait of other privileged social identities in the United States.

Ideal citizens—able-bodied, heterosexual men of some means—in general, are afforded privileged experiences and worldviews that would not necessarily prompt them to write charged humor. A man who has never experienced heterosexism or been threatened because of his sexuality has little cause to invest in understanding the manifold dangers and problems created by intolerance, bigotry, and legal discrimination. What reason does one have to be critical of a system from which one benefits? As such, female comics will be more likely than men to produce charged humor, just as differently abled comics (male or female) will be more likely than able-bodied men to produce charged humor. There is a causal relationship between the public belief that women are not as funny as men and the tendency for women to perform charged humor. Comics, especially female comics, using stand-up comedy as a forum for revealing their second-class status, will struggle to achieve success equivalent to men, even as men who corroborate this sex hierarchy will succeed like when Daniel Tosh speaks candidly on the topic during a stand-up performance:

> At least we're not women. Right fellas [*laughter*]? Geez. What is that like? Is it horrible? Is it awful? To know you're number two [*laughter*]. By the way, these aren't my beliefs. These are my observations of the world I live in. If it changes, I'll adjust the material accordingly [*laughter*]. I like when you [women] try to rationalize it: "No it's great being a woman, free drinks is worth not having equality" [*laughter*].[4]

Despite collective desire to imagine we have achieved gender parity, charged humor and our consumption of it (or not) give us away. We prefer not to be reminded that women are not equal to men and that feminism is in fact not dead—subjects that women's charged humor routinely broaches.

Part of the project of cultural citizenship, a defining element of charged humor, is to negotiate increased access to the cultural economy. Engin Isin and Patricia Wood, in *Citizenship and Identity*, "establish cultural citizenship as a field in which the rights to access to production, distribution and consumption of culture become a field of struggle and conflict."[5] Gaining access and visibility is a difficult enterprise for comics whose worldviews are not widely shared or who refuse to pander to an audience ready to laugh at dick and fart jokes served with a side of misogyny (e.g., the jokes that begin, "I love my wife but . . ." or the ever popular strategy of describing women as powerful, beautiful, and smart only to launch into how rotten, devious, and controlling they *really* are). To see which identities and values are most desirable (to be or to emulate) in the United States, one has simply to look at which comics achieve success. Most that do are able-bodied persons packing privilege like male privilege, class privilege, heterosexual privilege, and many have White privilege.

Maria Bamford, a White heterosexual female comic, is self-reflexive about her social identities and the ways they confer privilege. In a live performance at the El Ray Theater in Los Angeles she says: "I love my country. Maybe that's because I'm White and rich [*laughter*]. Things are really working out for me. . . . I'm not technically rich but I do have a lot of shit that I don't need that I refuse to share with anyone and that feels solid somehow [*laughter*]."[6] She attributes her own attachment to her country as favorable *because* of her income and status as Caucasian, and not ironically either. The laughter elicited yields to the following explanation: "It's funny because it's true." But then she goes on to say she is not actually rich, merely suffering from material excess as a result of her selfishness, which she has in a true new age fashion, reconciled within her spirit. This kind of movement back-and-forth and qualifying of terms, that is, rich and not rich, is the bedrock of Bamford's narrative style, which is adroitly accompanied by an infinite cast of characters, both real and imagined. She is continually demonstrating a higher social consciousness in her comedy, telling jokes about sweatshops, gender inequalities, institutionalized racism, homophobia, access to healthcare, and the like, and yet as she herself reports, terrifically fails to live up to many of the social ideals she waxes on about. This becomes a source of amusement for audience members who can see themselves in similar arrangements, if not before then certainly now, because Bamford's comedy works simultaneously to inform you of the social and political issues she deems important. Even if she herself cannot live up to them, your exposure to new information and issues challenges you to try to do the same. Maria Bamford, one of the funniest people performing comedy today, has indeed made a career of comedy employing charged humor but her charged content and quirky nonconformist style inform her status in the comedy world: pressed tight against the laugh ceiling.

A connection between nation (who constitutes the ideal) and cultural economy to audience preferences for male comics is conspicuously absent from public and academic discourses on the matter. Contemporary humor scholarship in the humanities addressing gender differences largely focuses on differences between male and female comics such as content and stylistic differences, and still does nothing to address the fundamental question of why female comics fail to meet with success equal to their male counterparts. What are the cultural explanations for the belief that men are funnier than women and how does this affect humor consumption, particularly charged humor? What are the rewards—material, social, or otherwise—for engagement with or identification with comics, and how does this influence the consumption of this kind of humor? Interviews with and articles about stand-up comics, print media, public commentary, and documentaries on stand-up comedy all assist in mapping out the debate proposing men are funnier than women, paying particular attention to the various cultural explanations advanced to explain this perception. Starting from popular discourses circulating about men's higher aptitude for comedy, I counter that audiences' lack of enthusiasm for women comic performers is symptomatic of power differentials, that there is no economic or cultural incentive for buying into women's perspectives, particularly when they draw attention to their status as marginalized by producing charged humor. Moreover, the same factors influence and inform the public's hesitancy to consume charged humor at rates equivalent to other styles of humor like shock humor, character comedy, family-friendly humor and modern-day minstrelsy. Because many of the comics producing charged humor are women, examining why women are not perceived to be as funny as men is another way of understanding why charged humor struggles for the same economic viability as other kinds of humor.

Why *Are* Men Perceived to Be Funnier Than Women?

Are men threatened by funny women? So reads the title of an article written by Emily Wilson, journalist and freelance writer for the liberal online news source *Alternet,* published on September 4, 2007. Those offering counsel on this matter included me, Jewish lesbian comic Judy Gold, *Bitch* cofounder and editor Andi Zeisler, and women's humor scholar Regina Barreca. Interviewees affirmed that women struggle to achieve similar popularity and success performing comedy in the United States. There are many reasons contributing to this, but Andi Zeisler provided what I believe to be the primary reason for this disparity: "we need to look at *who* is defining what is funny" (italics mine).[7] This means we need to pay attention to the prognostications of folks like Christopher Hitchens or other widely read writers as they define what is funny and identify the *ideal* candidates for humor production (hint: for him that would be men).

It also means we should look to the public for their thoughts on this debate. Is Christopher Hitchens reinforcing existing beliefs or does he ring hollow with his public? Emily Wilson's article, which discussed the power dynamics and fear behind the acceptance of female comics, elicited a great deal of comments from readers that offer insight into the range of opinions the public has about women's capacity for humor and whether said humor constitutes a threat. Some readers leaving comments seemed to agree with Hitchens's position that women are not as funny as men for a variety of reasons, though not necessarily for the same reasons posited by Hitchens.[8] An overview of the 198 comments reveals that those who believe women are not funny or not *as* funny as men cite the following reasons: lack of interesting subject matters—"there seems to be a glut of bad female comics who are obsessed with relationships, and think rambling on about them is funny" or "I'll be very happy when female comedians drop the subjects of shoes, purses, shopping, dieting, urinary incontinence, and PMS"—and gender expectations, for example, women are not supposed to be aggressive. One individual commented:

> As a culture we (men AND women) are uncomfortable being put in that position by a woman. . . . OR, to quote Brett Butler, when she described rednecks squinting at her from the audience and what was clearly written across their sour faces: "You wouldn't be talkin' that trash if someone had taught you how to make biscuits."[9]

Few of those commenting chalked it up to biology and those that did offered little in the way of scientific evidence: "There are funny women of course but just fewer. Men are better than women at 3 things, stronger, funnier, and math" or "It *is* an anomaly to be funny and female, just like it's an anomaly to be an NFL linebacker and female."[10] One of the lengthier responses argued that women are biologically unsuited or less suited than men for humor production and attributed this to the aggressive nature of comedy, which he argued men are better equipped to handle and went on to write that the women who are funny are lesbians, "further adding weight to the argument that perhaps testosterone levels contribute to humour."[11] Other comments express indignation that such a debate even exists.

> We know we're funny. . . . The question is why so many men have such a hard time acknowledging that what women (including feminists) find funny really is

funny, even if the guys aren't laughing. The reason this is important is that the same question can be asked about any other damn thing: "Why do so many men have such a hard time acknowledging that what women (including feminists) find important really is important, even if the guys don't take it seriously."[12]

This comment clearly echoes Andi Zeisler's suggestion that we look to *who* is defining what constitutes humor or what counts as funny.

For the most part the lengthy discussion threads indicate a thoughtful and conscientious debate over the merit of the article's contents and whether the public agrees that female comics are threatening and why. A handful of those commenting discuss the power dynamics and impact of culture on audience reception of humor. In response to the individual positing that favorable reception of male humor versus female humor was a biological given, one person wrote:

> To ignore or refuse to acknowledge the impact and contribution of sociali[z] ation and interaction and culture on human attitudes and behavior is to miss half the picture. And it is the social/cultural aspects of human life that we can actively change. . . . No comedian is objectively more or less funny than the other, regardless of race, cultural, gender, sexual orientation or disability differences. It is the subjective experience of the audience that determines whether they think the comedian is funny or not. You personally think men are funnier overall than women. Fair enough, that's your opinion, but be aware it is YOUR subjective opinion, not fact.[13]

These comments reflect the ongoing debate and the variety of reasons women are perceived not to be as funny as men. This debate turns up in print media, film, and television, and among those making a career of stand-up comedy.

This debate is addressed in *The History of the Joke with Lewis Black*, a documentary on stand-up comedy produced by the History Channel, and a host of comics comment on the issue, echoing similarly wide-ranging responses. First, viewers hear from Dr. Richard Wiseman of the University of Hertfordshire, who discusses gender differences in humor citing research showing that 71 percent of women laugh when men tell a joke (based on recorded conversations at parties) and 39 percent of men laugh when a woman tells a joke. Lewis Black counters this by saying that if men were smart they would laugh at women's jokes so they could get laid. For Black, though he jests, women should be perceived as funny as a means to a nuptial end. Another veteran comic, George Carlin says, "specific and individual women are as funny as any specific and individual man. The difference is in the acculturation and conditioning that people go through and for a long time there weren't many female stand-ups because it was somehow too masculine a job, too aggressive a job."[14] A seventeen-year White veteran of stand-up comedy at the time, D. C. Benny haltingly testifies that a higher percentage of male comics make him laugh than female comics, wondering aloud whether he is biased. Marina Franklin, a Black woman and fellow comic, sitting next to him mouths the word: "chauvinistic." Popular ventriloquist Jeff Dunham uses his puppet (Walter) to say that he does not think women are funny. During a joint interview with comics Robert Kelly and Lynne Koplitz, Kelly professes an exasperation at the complaints women have about not being accepted or as validated as male comics. Kelly thinks Koplitz is funny when she talks about human experiences but when she starts speaking from a female perspective (performing charged humor), he does not think she is as funny: "When you talk about your own experiences, you're not being a woman, you're actually just being Lynne."[15] The problem with this logic is that she *is* a woman and her life is shaped by this sex and gender assignment and construction. The underlying request seems to ask her to strip woman-ness from her comic material, arguably one of the fundamental social positions contributing to how she experiences the world. You can be a woman telling jokes, just do not call attention to your woman-ness or any other category of difference that might force listeners out of their comfort zone, because that forces them to learn from another perspective or identify with someone unlike them. Male humor is humor genera, and humor arising from any other position becomes "Other" humor, topical, or special interest. When men fail at comedy, failure is not seen as a product of their maleness or endemic to men as a whole; however, when women bomb, the default explanation is her being a woman. For example, while traveling from one comedy club to another, Janeane Garofalo reported that it was not uncommon to hear the following: " 'We had a woman here last month and she did terrible so we weren't going to have women again.' You would never hear, 'We had a man here last month and he really bombed so we're not having men anymore.' "[16]

Female comics take umbrage that they are always already up against popular cultural beliefs that women are not funny or if they are, that it is an anomaly. Kathleen Madigan, an Irish American comic headlining clubs all over the country, chats with Lewis Black stating:

> I did not know that half of the population thinks women aren't funny. I was not given this information. I had no idea. The more successful I become, the more people come up to me after the show and go: "Usually I hate women comics, but you were hilarious!" And I'm like, really? So, all these years I've been walking up on stage in a total hole?!"[17]

Sara Benincasa, a young White comedy writer and performer, is equally troubled by such statements.

> To tell me that most people with the same genitalia as me aren't funny, but I'm the exception is just bullshit. In our culture, men are still socialized to only find one another amusing. I'm not sure why that is, but part of me thinks it's because the person who makes you laugh has some degree of power over you. . . . So if you're laughing at someone, you're in some way subservient to them. For so many reasons, some men—and some women—don't necessarily want to give control to women.[18]

To some it has become a tired and outmoded debate, particularly when evidence to the contrary abounds, as Kathy Griffin cheekily states, "The notion that chicks aren't as funny is ridiculous and comes from men who aren't as funny. But I enjoy dispelling the myth and I hope that I do and I try to and it's one of my favorite things to hear: 'Hey, you're funny and you have that vagina.'"[19] This debate informed the production of *The History of the Joke with Lewis Black*. Coexecutive producer, cowriter, and director of the documentary Dave Greene fought to keep some of the women's comedic material in the documentary because his colleagues (men) did not find it amusing. In an e-mail exchange with me, he writes:

> The most interesting fights were my insistence on keeping female comedians in the show. Some male staffers just didn't think they were funny, and I had to make an argument to keep them in. I used a demographic, rather than a comic rationale to explain my decision; some of the bits I didn't find funny, either—but someone might.[20]

Greene wisely capitalized on the argument that humor is subjective, gently reminding his colleagues that their opinions about what constitutes funny cannot be generalized to the populous.

There is evidence that society finds men more facile in the realm of humor production (pace: Hitchens) in part because it is considered inappropriate or out of line for women to not only demand attention and visibility, but to even speak about or reference certain sensitive topics like sex (they could laugh at men) or gender roles (they could expose the artifice of gender) or politics (they could be smarter than men in the audience or hold controversial opinions). Julie Goldman, a lesbian Jewish comic and cast member of LOGO's *The Big Gay Sketch Show* interviewed by Andi Zeisler in *Bitch* says, "in comedy, [that] translates into this weird [situation where] women can only talk about certain things. The men can talk about anything they want, but when women start talking about [the same] stuff, somehow it becomes offensive. There's a double standard and I'm tired of it."[21] Robin Tyler, a longtime comic, producer, director, and activist, comments on the current social climate for women comic performers saying: "You have women comics, but at the same time because it's such a reactionary period and non-feminist period, you have the sexism that has reared its ugly head. And if you go to the comedy clubs again, you'll see the SM [sadomasochism] jokes, and you'll see the denigration of women."[22] Thirty-something White comic Jen Kirkman reports that she has been booed for telling jokes about female masturbation, experiences she now incorporates into her jokes. In an endearing way, she mocks the antiquated or conservative viewer who finds women's sexuality threatening, frightening, or lacking in gentility saying, "I feel like I am going to turn around and someone is going to be inventing the wheel behind me. I'm like how long do women have to live on earth before they can talk about the same things dudes talk about."[23] Women who broach sensitive or offensive subject matter or attempt to counter sexism in the industry may find themselves in a struggle to garner positive reception from their audience and as these examples show, audience members may have difficulty identifying with her point of view. Women will have difficulty competing with men in a genre of performance that makes certain (masculine) topics off limits while at the same time discouraging and devaluing the humor produced from a woman's standpoint, like when Robert Kelly told Lynn Koplitz that she is funny when she does not talk about being a woman.

Women comics must work to counteract the belief that women are not funny onstage with audience members and backstage with skeptical booking agents. Sommore, African American host of *Comic View* and stand-up comic for over twenty years recalls: "Well, when we did *The Queens of Comedy* we came together and we knew that we were trying to prove a point. First of all it was stated that all-women shows do not sell. So we wanted to prove them wrong with that and then we wanted to prove that women can be funny."[24] As a result, Darryl Littleton, producer of the documentary *Why We Laugh: Black Comedians on Black Comedy*, notes that "*The Queens of Comedy* put a spotlight on female comediennes and showed their viability. So despite comments from comedy icons such as Jerry Lewis that females weren't funny . . . lady comics were making headway, but just how far was another question."[25] Similarly, one person commenting online relayed the following story: Janeane Garofalo challenged Bill Maher on his show *Politically Incorrect* when he "posited that the dearth of female comedy writers on TV had less to do with sexism and the 'old boy' club than the 'fact' that women 'just aren't as good at that kind of comedy.' Janeane Garofalo shot back, 'Yeah, I watch TV written by men, and I'm not laughing my ass off.' To his eternal credit, Maher fell over laughing, and told her she was right."[26] Garofalo chides Maher for forgetting that not everyone appreciates or shares the same experiences with male humorists and comics. He may have forgotten; after all this is humor de rigueur. According to Dave Greene:

The only real debate that my fellow comedy writers and producers tend to have is the "are women funny" one, but it's always circular. Of course women can be funny. But men find male comedians funny in the same way they find male rock stars awesome: Complaining that not enough men laugh at Wanda Sykes is like complaining that not enough of them listen to Melissa Etheridge.[27]

Beneath this comparison is the genuinely troubling question that even if men are capable of admiring and looking up to women entertainers, why would they? What incentive do they have other than perhaps Lewis Black's earlier point that you might have more opportunities to "get lucky" if you laugh at women's jokes.

The sum of this ongoing popular discourse constitutes the debate as to whether women are as funny as men and the various reasons people think they are not. This debate holds sway in the public, informing consumption trends, and, as the testimony from Dave Greene indicates, it can determine whether viewers even have access to consume certain kinds of humor in the first place. Online comments and discussion in response to online articles dealing with this debate expressed a range of opinions varying in intensity, were comprised mainly of American and British readers, and included a number of posts by those self-identifying as comics. Interestingly, every comment posted by someone identifying himself or herself as a comic agreed that the industry is sexist, that women have a difficult time achieving equal success in stand-up comedy and that this is mainly due to cultural values assigned to gender in most Western nations. Print and film media sources corroborate the pervasiveness and strength of this popular discourse about women's aptitude for humor production, and interviews with comics in the industry do the same.

Nearly a year after the publication of Emily Wilson's piece, I received a lengthy e-mail from a cordial engineer living in Maryland who read the *Alternet* article, located me through the university, and e-mailed me with questions about why women are not as funny as men. In his e-mail, Kenneth Winiecki shared that he finds women comics to be irritating or at least more so than most male comics and was earnestly "trying to figure out why [he] find[s] a significantly higher proportion of female than male comedians unfunny."[28] The tone was apologetic but firm; many women comics are annoying and he thought my research would lend some insight to the matter. From the *Alternet* article he became acquainted with one of the leading arguments for why women are more likely to be perceived as not funny, namely, that women who are funny are seen as potentially threatening. He found the argument to be less than thorough in addressing his ambivalence toward women comics and countered the hypothesis saying: "Usually when I am threatened I think I feel fear and/or defensiveness, but my negative responses to comedians usually seem to include boredom and/or irritation, which don't seem to me much like a threat response."[29] I considered his queries seriously and placed them in the context of my own work, which among other objectives seeks to look beyond the very useful and oft employed discussion of women's comedy as resistant. It *is* resistant and we can gain much from these thorough and insightful analyses of what women are resisting. The tenor and quality of that resistance gives visibility to how these resistant practices can lead to social change. Performances intending to resist often enact cultural citizenship but simply reading for resistance shows us how and why individuals produce humor, not how the nation consumes humor and why consumption patterns favor men or comics opting not to produce charged humor. Simply elaborating this argument would never address the real question which was publicly framed by Christopher Hitchens, echoed in Kenneth Winiecki's e-mail, and now the subject of this investigation: Why are men (perceived to be) funnier than women?

The Answer . . .

To address this query that resounds in various ways in public and private discourses, I would defer first to Andi Zeisler and her question of who is defining what is funny and second to cultural explanations for the current economy of humor or the way culture influences the economy of humor. I define the economy of humor as the production, exchange, and consumption of humor. Communications scholar Joanne Gilbert elaborates on this definition.

> When a stand-up comic performs for a paying audience, money is exchanged for laughter, social criticism is embedded in the material eliciting the laughter, the comic/social critic gets paid, the comedy club makes money, an economic symbiosis has been achieved. Perhaps it is not surprising that a comic's jokes are called "material," for, within the commodification of cultural performance, jokes are exactly that—the material of capitalist currency. The economic dimension of humor illuminates the various exchanges—aesthetic, monetary, sociopolitical—that occur in the context of stand-up comic performance.[30]

In this case, the product is a brand of humor, an identity, or lifestyle you can relate to by attending live shows or simply by setting TiVo to record the latest material by your favorite comic. The product here is a human, and as Stuart Hall points out, the consumption is both material and symbolic: "Even consumption, in some ways the privileged terrain of reproduction, is no less symbolic for being material. . . . In a world tyrannized by scarcity, men and women nevertheless express in their practical lives not only what they need for material existence but some sense of their symbolic place in the world, of who they are, their identities."[31] Our wardrobe conveys messages about who we are, as does the consumption of comic material. Male comics fare better in the market but why?

When humans are the product (entertainers), the exchange of those products in the economic realm will be as equally fraught by power relations as they are in the sociopolitical sphere. Based on existing social inequalities there is simply no reward for engaging with or learning to identify with women whose power is already determined as secondary to men in this society. The same is true for comics (male or female, but more often female) producing charged humor. The willful adoption of views, opinions, and behaviors requires incentive, a payoff of sorts. French sociologist Pierre Bourdieu recognized that material gains and advantages are not easily calculable or reflected in one's bank statement. He dissected the many forms capital takes, generating the terms "cultural capital" and "social capital," as forms of capital gain that yield benefits (e.g., prestige, networks, education, opportunities, experiences, and proximity to power) not quantifiable in dollars or relative currency.[32] This thinking places the discussion right where it should be . . . in the shifting realm of culture as it plays out in the economy, rather than Hitchens's biologically deterministic explanations. Women and/or comics producing charged humor are clearly lacking in power, in opportunities, and in prestige—all the criteria necessary to ensure that viewers will be motivated to (learn to) "buy-in" or identify.

English scholar Norman Holland argues that "*interpretation is a function of identity*," or that personality traits and "differences in age, sex, nationality, class, or reading experience will contribute to differences in interpretation."[33] Who we are—the sum of our parts—shapes our reception, thereby determining what (or who) we are likely to consume. On the one hand, we consume things "like" us, things with which we identify. The Blue Collar Comedy Tour with Bill Engvall, Jeff Foxworthy, Ron White, and Larry the Cable Guy (Daniel Lawrence Whitney) features four White men whose comedy capitalizes on appealing to a specific working-class blue-collar ethos. This is not to say that they do not reach viewers outside of this class-based demographic (since class status is not fixed and there is a certain nostalgia attached to this ethos that can appeal to viewers who have transitioned into white-collar labor or who can identify based on regional, affectational, or gender similarities), rather that they are more likely to appeal to viewers sharing similar categories of identity. It is interesting to note that these four comics have all achieved enormous success in the comedy industry, making them incredibly wealthy. Since their comedy relies on cultural references to a certain class-inflected lifestyle (though they also capitalize on regional identity: rural and not urban; southern and Midwestern states rather than East Coast or West Coast), they have had to make choices about self-presentation in their stand-up. I attended a live performance by Ron White in 2007, noticing that jokes inadvertently calling attention to his wealth were not as successful as his "old" jokes or the misogynist humor he uses throughout. Fans cannot identify with such an opulent lifestyle (i.e., bits that reveal he has his own plane) so instead White has to keep reminding audience members that he is still just a "good ol' boy" who likes sex, whiskey, and sports just like the rest of them.

On the other hand, identification and reception is primed early on so that we consume things we wish we could be, things that signify power. Consumption favors what is "like" us and what is most ideal, that is bearing the greatest cultural and political cachet. We cannot deny the overwhelming power of our economy—a hypercapitalist republic—to dictate popular culture forms, including who and what we enjoy (read: consume). Shane Phelan, in *Sexual Strangers: Gays, Lesbians and Dilemmas of Citizenship*, argues that

> struggles for inclusion are shaped not only by the needs of the excluded and the fears or needs of the excluders, not only by whether demands can be framed within the rhetoric of the polity, but by *whether state actors have an incentive to include the excluded* [italics mine]. The incentives of those actors will not only affect whether a group is included, but will importantly shape the terms under which inclusion will occur.[34]

Based on women's proximity to power or their tacit social standing as inferior to and subordinated by men, there is simply no economic incentive for anyone, men and women alike, to learn to identify and "buy in" to a woman's point of view. Understanding male perspectives and experiences—which are more recognizable as the standard or norm by which we measure all other experiences—whether or not you are yourself male, bears the promise of incentive or Pierre Bourdieu social and cultural capital. Women's experiences and identities as marketable commodities will fail every time when placed alongside their male counterparts, whose lives and identities bear far greater promise for cultural and economic viability. *Last Comic Standing*, the longstanding and popular reality show canceled in its eighth season, has in all its seasons had one female winner, Iliza Schlesinger (winner of season 6, 2008)—a situation I attribute to an audience's propensity to identify more strongly and in most cases, with male comics, rather than any lack of ability on the part of the women to be humorous.

Popular representations of male lives and experiences abound whether in literature, television, or film, and consumers learn to identify with these normative representations, finding means of accessing the cultural capital concomitant with having the privileges of being male, White, heterosexual, and able-bodied.[35] We recognize privileges bestowed by virtue of money, access to resources, powerful networks, and the protection provided by belonging to the dominant culture; more than that, we strive for it, seeking the secrets of success, wanting to assimilate by mimicking the techniques, attitudes, and even the speech of the successful. The message is that if you do what "they" do, you might achieve some modicum of success, too. Audre Lorde made this observation thirty years ago: "For in order to survive, those of us for whom oppression is as American as apple pie have always had to be watchers, to become familiar with the language and manners of the oppressor, even sometimes adopting them for some illusion of protection."[36] If women's experiences are subordinate to men's, then when it comes to a form of performance like stand-up comedy, whose success is dependent on audience identification with the comic, audiences will respond (read: identify) less enthusiastically. Their logic: why would I need to or want to understand and identify with women's and/or minorities' lives and experiences when society continually reinforces that they are of little value. As consumers, even though we may not be thinking of ourselves as such while watching television or attending a live performance, we must have incentive for our investments, whether monetary, emotional, psychic, or time-based.

Last Comic Standing has never included an equal number of male and female contestants and in their weekly battles (between three comics, where one is sent home) often two or more females are voted into the battle ensuring that one or more leaves nearly every week in the first several episodes of each season. Frequently, the final three ratio is 3:1, male to female. Some may argue that there are fewer successful female comics because they comprise a smaller percentage of those attempting to pursue comedy as a career, creating a smaller pool from which to extract talent. Fewer numbers of female comics may be the result of public skepticism toward lady jokesters but does not adequately explain the general public's lower rates of consumption of women's stand-up comedy. British comedian Jimmy Carr offers one explanation, and Kathleen Madigan agrees, that the life of an itinerant road comic is difficult for anyone and not necessarily a lifestyle women would be drawn to particularly if they have partners and/or children.[37] Practical concerns aside (but not made irrelevant), the bottom line is that if the public believes—and shored up those beliefs with cold hard cash—that women are as funny as men, then we would be exhausting our female comedy reserves to accommodate for the demand. Generally the market is neutral, a capitalist engine insouciant to creed, race, gender, or sexuality. The market or the economy, in this case, is not inherently sexist or any other -*ist* or -*ism*; the market supplicates to the dollar. However, the market *is* influenced by consumers whose consumption choices reify social inequalities. Cultural perceptions influence audience reception and in turn determine the economy of humor, meaning that gender anxieties inform who audiences are most likely to favor and this determines the economy of humor. The cultural capital yielded as a product of identification with male comics and the incentive to identify with and consume the stories, activities, and ideas of the powerful will continue to ensure that audience reception will favor men.

While the numbers fluctuate, women generally constitute anywhere from fifteen to thirty percent of those in the field of comic performance. Drawing from thirty years of experience in the comedy business, Caroline Hirsch, the owner of Carolines on Broadway, says, "there are less women comediennes around than men" and estimates that "it's 20% women comediennes compared to men."[38] Shaun Breidbart conducted a statistical analysis of gender differences in comedy and was among the many individuals responding to Christopher Hitchens's inflammatory article(s). Breidbart's analysis indicates that "one third of amateur comedians are female," though the percentage decreases for professional female comics. And this despite his concomitant findings that women are more likely than their male counterparts to take a comedy writing or improv course and to approach the craft more seriously than their male peers. He concludes, writing: "As a male-dominated industry, it's a long, hard fight for women until the numbers start to even out. What will help to even them out? If people would stop publishing articles claiming that women aren't funny. It's clearly not true."[39]

Higher numbers of male career comics alone cannot explain an audience's predilection for male comedy, a phenomenon reinforced by the simple evidence of who is hired to emcee, feature, and headline in comedy clubs across America—men. While more men in the industry could certainly be a product of the persistent notion that men are categorically funnier than women, this gender inequity does not by itself explain and/or create this cultural perception. It is true that audiences have more opportunities provided them to identify with male comics, making this process more commonplace or making it appear a more natural connection, but more exposure to male humor does not explain the general reluctance to invest (economically and personally) in women's humor.

One could also argue that the cultural perception that men are funnier than women functions to dissuade women from pursuing comedy professionally. If the odds are stacked against you, why even bother to combat the odds. Another argument could be that women are acculturated differently. With an enormous list of television and film credits, African American stand-up comic and author Aisha Tyler thinks fewer women take a stab at stand-up comedy because "women are not socialized generally to be assertive. . . . We're very much kinda told by culture like: 'be precious, be pretty, be cute' and so comedy's not precious or pretty or cute."[40] However, women are not homogenous and while Tyler accurately describes the way society perpetuates codes of femininity, these gendered norms vary among communities distinguished by race/ethnicity, national origin, region, creed, and education. A young Black girl raised in Chicago by nouveau hippies may be given more latitude in her expression of femininity than a young White girl raised in Selma, Alabama, by Pentecostal parents. Changing the ways we construct gender and socialize young people can do its part to encourage more women to enter the field of stand-up comedy but audience members will still require some kind of incentive in order to identify, that is, the humor produced must draw from and reference the most profitable comic frames, namely, what stands in for the ideal—the ideal citizen, the male ideal, the heterosexual ideal.

Gender determines incentive because each audience member has to "work" to identify with and share in the humor and laughter. If there is no payoff, no capital gains—culturally or otherwise—to be had, audiences will opt out or experience distanciating or negative emotions much like those described by Kenneth Winiecki as apathy, boredom, annoyance, and/or disapproval. Cultural attitudes affect economic choices and this includes buying tickets to see comics or purchasing the opportunity to identify in humorous terms with individuals. As a result, topics addressed by women comics specific to the female condition are ghettoized and seen as "special interest" comedy. During a phone interview with a reporter from *The Columbus Dispatch,* prior to an all-women comedy show I produced and emceed in Columbus, Ohio, in spring 2004, the reporter asked if men were welcome to attend the show, assuming that since it featured an all-female line-up that men may be unwelcome (or perhaps disinterested). I assured her that men were welcome and added that precious few think to ask the same of the typical all-male line-ups at local open-mike shows and comedy clubs across the nation.

Successful comedy relies heavily on affirmation of and identification with the comic. According to Americanist Lawrence Mintz, a comic leads her audience "in a celebration of a community of shared culture, of homogenous understanding and expectation."[41] The key here is that these comic cultural frames are *shared* or else viewers cannot affirm or identify with the performer. Laughter signals identification or belonging and affirms that one "gets" where you are coming from—that is, the jokester relies on comic conventions and works within comic frames recognizable to viewers. L. H. Stallings writes, "In order to recognize the humor of any comic, the public audience must be privy to the personal and private identity and subjectivity of the performer as well as the hermeneutics the comic may be using."[42] We laugh because we simultaneously appreciate the lawlessness of comedy *and* because we "get it," and through our "getting it," we also belong. Humor issuing from the mouths of women and members of minority communities that falls flat with audience members can reflect a culture's lack of desire to acknowledge the experiences of the Other, signaling their tacit exclusion from the national imagination. Success in comedy serves as a litmus test or cultural index for belonging. Group laughter in response to a joke affirms one's position in the national imagination by signaling group belonging and agreement; this is Mintz's "community of shared culture."

The experience of being part of a live audience offers audience members a more participatory and authentic community of shared culture than televised performances, which undergo serious editing to add laugh tracks and remove any unfavorable or lackluster responses from the audience, leaving only a stream of cackling patrons not necessarily laughing at the joke just performed. Laughter is dubbed into the background much like the canned laughter associated with sitcoms and favorable audience responses are carefully selected to present a pleasing and positive response to the comic performing. And yet, we are compelled to make many assumptions at the point of engagement with the humor we see on the silver screen. First, that since I belong to a national community and this is being aired nationally, my laughter is shared by and with my imagined national community. If this is not compelling enough, also implicit here is the niggling suggestion that if I do not find this funny I may not belong; in other words, I risk being an outsider. Second, that comics are selected based on their talent and any comic on television, particularly with their own show, must be highly skilled; implicit here is that if I do not find this very funny, this may speak to my ability to assess the quality of comic performance. Based on this evidence, the responses of audiences during live shows are the most useful indices of gauging the success of the jokes and the extent to which audience members identify with the comic performer. Audience identification illumines cultural/social outsiders and determines who sells and who does not.

A patriarchal society producing White male norms that are taken to be the natural order of things ensure that masculinity, whiteness, and heterosexuality prevail as superior and desirable and determines who belongs and who does not. Loosely translated, this means that when it comes to comic performance, socially constructed notions of how we belong in the national imagination dictate success with the live audience. Comics occupying privileged social locations in the national imagination, that is, male, able-bodied, White, heterosexual, advance a position and bear identity markers that audiences recognize as dominant in the shared national imagination and thus bear the promise of incentive. For example, if I can understand dominant modes of being I will increase my chances of gaining access to the power and prestige of the dominant class or ideal citizens. Heterosexist, sexist, racist, classist, and ableist ideas of nationhood work to create an economy that supports these beliefs. In time, the market reflects social inequalities. It comes as no surprise, then, that most comics touring the national circuit are heterosexual men. White is not part of the standard here, not because Black, Hispanic, and Asian men do not experience racism and marginalization, but because men of color, especially Black men, have achieved an inordinate amount of success in stand-up comedy compared with their female and queer counterparts. The DC Improv in Washington DC, where I lived for six years, booked five female comics (Sheryl Underwood, Erin Jackson, Sommore, Aisha Tyler, and Loni Love) in a three-year span (August 2008–August 2011) constituting approximately five percent of their bookings (several women returned each year). With some exceptions, I attribute this to the overwhelming majority of folks identifying with a heterosexual male standard because *affirming a male identity bears the greatest incentive and cultural cachet in society.*

Comedy is just one of the many popular cultural forms that offer us a particular view of our cultural history and our own unique position in this nation's social matrix. Artistic interpretation of women's lives—whether via performance art, stand-up comedy, theater, or dance—functions to put substance where there is absence, to replace fiction with nonfiction. Women's visibility in humor production marks a contribution and a disruption, indeed reminds audiences of exclusionary constructions of citizenship, challenging and "transforming the gendered rhetoric of belonging in new ways."[43] They are framing life as they know it and in the process exposing their position in the national imagination; it is cultural work that according to social scientist May Joseph illumines "yet another dimension of the possibilities, anxieties, and contradictions of cultural citizenship within the modern state."[44] Stand-up comedy is an intentionally humorous performative iteration of (national) identity and audiences vocalize affirmation or dissent consonant with dominant constructions of national belonging. It is an exchange between performer and audience, a dialogue signaling acceptance and rejection, and usually predicated on the performer's perceived proximity to the straight male standard.

In *Vince Vaughn's Wild West Comedy Show*, Vince Vaughn hits the road for thirty days of consecutive live shows with four male comics—Sebastian Maniscalco, Bret Ernst, Ahmed Ahmed, and John Caparulo—most of whom have achieved feature status (at that time) in comedy clubs nationwide. In Austin, Texas, one of the many cities on the tour schedule, Sebastian Maniscalco mocks men who wear flip-flops and who order "feminine" drinks, as characterized by fruit juices and garnishes.[45] Though they laugh at his mockery of men buying wussy beverages, the crowd boos him following the flip-flop joke and he commences to cut that particular segment short so as not to lose the audience entirely. Here he is reinforcing what he sees as cis-gender appropriate foot apparel for men, an opinion not shared by the majority of those in the audience. Maniscalco employs the strategy of using humor to reference concepts of staid masculinity and to ridicule questionable behaviors that undermine "real" men as macho, caring little for their outward appearance and participating only in consumptive practices acceptable for men (i.e., electronics, cars, tools, etc.). In an interview following that show, he shares that he routinely performs this joke because it has proven successful in the past and with audiences in other cities on the same tour. This joke typically meets with success because it draws from stereotypical notions of masculinity circulating in contemporary culture. Humor expert Trevor Griffiths noted in 1972 that "when a joke bases itself upon a distortion—a 'stereotype' perhaps—and gives the lie to the truth so as to win a laugh and stay in favour, we've moved away from a comic art and into the world of 'entertainment' and 'success.' "[46] Maniscalco did not consider the ways masculine gender markers shift from region to region. It is, after all, quite hot in Austin, Texas, making flip-flops the shoes of choice for women and men.

Jokes emerging from and capitalizing on gender stereotypes and differences are used frequently and continue to be successful, particularly if they make women the butt of the joke.[47] In my own experience of performing stand-up comedy there are two sure-fire ways to get a laugh: use obscenities and make fun of women. Despite drawing from a well-spring of easily identifiable gender conventions, audience members in Austin did not identify with Maniscalco's parameters of masculinity as set forth in this joke because it made questionable the masculinity of a number of those in attendance (most likely those men, Maniscalco's gender truants, wearing flip-flops at the time). In this way, there is a palpable exchange between audience and performer where laughter signals affirmation and negative responses such as booing, hissing, or shaking one's head signals disagreement, disapproval, or lack of identification with the comic frame or the fundamental premise of the humorous material. Both the blessing and the curse of live comedy is that not all audiences will respond similarly, and the comic must be prepared for this.

While audience responses can be telling about who is included in our shared national imagination, comic performances themselves reveal the ideologies and discourses constituting national belonging or citizenship and the ways these are expressed—reified, interrupted, and unsettled. The stuff of comedy draws from the everyday lives of its practitioners and from this we can bear witness to the way citizens are marked by race, sexual orientation, gender, class, and ability, all of which inform one's experiences and constructions of nationhood. For example, Bonnie McFarlane who appeared on season 2 of *Last Comic Standing* and since then has been touring nationally with her now husband Rich Vos (also a comic), tells the following joke: "Stop judging people by the color of their skin and judge them by the way they act [*whistles and cheers*]. And if they act White, let 'em stay [*laughter*]."[48] We laugh because she flipped the script—her opening line bears the promise of tolerance, which is belied by her next sentence. It is humorous because it is unexpected and also because it illumines racist axioms of who does and does not belong. It also points toward the

American legacy of extending legal and social rights to racial/ethnic groups most willing to assimilate and comply with White male Western behaviors, norms, and values. Our notions of national belonging are built upon racist, sexist, classist, heterosexist, and ableist assumptions of who constitutes the ideal citizen, and this is aptly reflected in the circulation of contemporary humorous discourses (i.e., jokes such as McFarlane's) and discourses about humor production (i.e., the widely read essay by Christopher Hitchens).

Audiences populating the comedy clubs across the nation will identify with and affirm the perspectives of the comics whose beliefs and lifestyles reflect mainstream, socially acceptable norms—values shared, condoned, and exhibited by many. Since these dominant ideas and values arise from a mainly White patriarchal epicenter of power (and based on the hiring trends in comedy clubs across the United States), we can conclude that the humor emitting from the mouths of men has been and will continue to be highly sought, an economically viable investment, and a safe bet for mixed race and gender audiences who are well trained in what *should* make them laugh. British popular culture scholar Andy Medhurst writes:

> Nation construction is also involved in the business of identifying internal others, who are seen by those subscribing to an imagination of national community wedded to closed, fixed and impermeable versions of belonging, as threatening groups that are *on* the inside but must on no account become *of* the inside.[49]

Critical here is the understanding that comic performers situated as outsiders on the inside are going to struggle and have to work harder to establish mutual points of identification with their audiences and in the process be perceived as less competent or funny—in this case, that would be the ladies and/or minority subjects performing charged humor.

To be clear, I am not arguing that all male comics will be successful and all female comics unsuccessful; in fact, there is evidence contrary to this. Many US female comic performers such Wanda Sykes, Kathy Griffin, Margaret Cho, Chelsea Handler, Sarah Silverman, Tina Fey, Ellen DeGeneres, Amy Poehler, Molly Shannon, and many more have found national recognition and acclaim. However, when placed in their respective entertainment venues, such as national comedy circuits, talk shows, sitcoms, and variety shows, they are the sexual minority. However, I *am* suggesting that success is largely predicated on audiences' ability to identify with the jester in question, and there is a greater likelihood of this when the subjects and topics broached are gender neutral or fulfill existing stereotypes about women, for example, women are high maintenance, nagging, submissive, innocent, bitchy, and so on. The women comics garnering success have done so by and large in one of three ways. First, they appeal to broadly dispersed niche markets comprised of like-community members that when combined make a strong consumer base (e.g., Kathy Griffin enjoys a fan base of primarily LGBTQ persons, women, and popular culture enthusiasts, of which she belongs to the latter two, and while she is not herself a lesbian, she is very supportive of the LGBTQ community). Second, if their comedy is gender neutral (read: male) and therefore nonthreatening, it becomes culturally acceptable and while coming from a female body, seldom focuses on specifically female issues unless to collude in their silliness and irrelevance, for example, Sarah Silverman's shock comedy that targets everyone with equal vehemence so as to render any real satire or critique moot. This is not a new phenomenon. Twenty years ago, Ellen Hopkins, then a journalist writing for the *New York Times* and now bestselling author of young adult fiction, assessed that of all women comics performing, "the best tend to have material that isn't gender specific at all."[50] In an interview with Andi Zeisler, an editor of *Bitch* magazine, fellow comic Kate Rigg comments on Silverman's comedy: "A lot of women comics out here in L.A. are angry at Sarah Silverman because she androgynizes herself to the point that she can . . . pass. It's like doing blackface—she's doing dickface. . . . As a comedian, I don't give a shit. But as a feminist, I care, because I'm aware that she's set up to erase her perspective as a woman in order to pass."[51] Third, women achieve industry accolades when they caricature women, using themselves and other women as the butt of the joke; in other words, when their comic persona capitalizes on stereotypes about women, fulfilling a highly circulated demoralizing narrative about women's ineptitude, frivolity, and obsession with, say, communication and snuggling.

By winning season 6 of *Last Comic Standing*, Iliza Schlesinger demonstrated that women can secure audience identification and success; however, her comedy routinely depicts women as vapid and hyper-feminized, fulfilling preexisting perceptions audience members may have of women and further enhancing the likelihood that audience members will identify, if not with her, then at least with her worldview. Her own performance of gender, a woman spurning high heels, laughing at her social foibles, and speaking with confidence, often defies the very stereotypes she deploys each time she mimics a female friend or persona on stage. She asserts herself as one of the gang, someone who herself participates in the gendered social customs even as she pokes fun at the social demands she cannot live up to. While her comedy may offer subtle critiques of codes of femininity impossible to achieve and maintain, her performances for the nationally televised show revolved mainly around targeting women as the butt of the joke, the overarching subtext reading: aren't women silly (and if you think I'm funny then you agree)? Her comedy makes it clear that she belongs, and in some fashion endorses, dominant beliefs about gender held by the majority of Americans.

The promise and potential of comedy is that its progenitors can and do make social critiques; therefore, it is important to note that many women strive to incorporate appraisals of patriarchy, gender norms and stereotypes, capitalism, and bigotry into their comic performances, albeit in varying ways and to varying effects. Feminist humor and lesbian humor "affirms the values, beliefs, and politics of the in-group and forms part of a shared stock of stories and myths that help form, disseminate, and preserve an imagined community."[52] For many of us not "belonging" to the mainstream, humor functions as a way to create community and culture among the marginalized. Kate Clinton, a White lesbian comic whose biting political humor has made her a favorite among liberal and lesbian audiences in alternative performance venues, repeatedly stated at a live performance at Ellington's in Austin, Texas: "You create the world; you invite the people in."[53] In her case, that world is fashioned by her experiences as a female, as a lesbian, as a White American, and as a teacher. The problem she and other women comics face is that mainstream audiences, when confronted with the comedy of the marginalized (by virtue of race, sexuality, gender, ability, class, and age), tend to struggle to find common referents and experiences compatible with their own. If the world created is one based on marginalized subjectivities and experience, you can invite people in, but it does not mean they will understand or value (literally, in economic terms) that world. Audiences tend to enjoy themselves more when they can identify with the comic. Unfortunately, when identification is primed as White, heterosexual, and male oriented, women must struggle all the more to be heard and to legitimate their experiences, let alone have them qualify as being humorous.

The same struggle exists for comics producing charged humor or humor that reminds its audience that not everyone is equal. Humor that foregrounds one's marginality in a way that challenges stereotypes and illumines the history and consequences of one's exclusion disrupts the illusions of American claims to democracy and meritocracy. This is, perhaps, unsettling for privileged viewers occupying dominant categories of identity, but audience members sharing a similar history of exclusion, scapegoating, and exploitation may be compelled to identify; however, this is not a given and even within minority communities, there is greater cultural cachet associated with a male perspective and worldview than a female one. At the risk of parsing this out ad nauseam, what this means is that given a male and female comic, both of whom perform charged humor, identification with the male comic still yields the greater incentive.

One of my favorite "bits" I perform addresses the lack of synonyms or slang words circulating for discharge or women's vaginal fluids. This is in direct contrast with the plethora of synonyms in play for a man's seminal fluids, for example, jizz, spooge, Petey's protein, spunk, gick, and so on. I consider this disparity in my stand-up and the way the term itself (associated with the firing of weapons and being released from the hospital) alienates women from their bodies. To improve the situation, I offer the audience my own alternative term for discharge and invite them to use the term as a substitute in the future:

> Instead of using the term discharge, I would like to suggest the term "panty soda." Say it with me now: PANTY SODA! It's fun, it's fizzy, it's *you*. I can't create this kind of change on my own, people. I need your help telling others about panty soda. So, tell your family, neighbors, [*pause*] and friends at Bible study or Torah class and together we will spread panty soda all over the nation.[54]

Reactions to this joke vary based on my audience. Performing for LadyFest Ohio (2004), a feminist arts festival, for an audience comprised mainly of feminists (male and female alike), this joke brought down the house eliciting cheers, clapping, hooting, and roaring laughter. Performing at the Funny Bone Comedy Club in Columbus, Ohio the same year, the joke elicited nervous titters from a smattering of women and some applause from a group of women (without any men) seated at a table in the back of the club. Like Maniscalco's failed flip-flop joke, I sensed that I was "losing" the audience with this joke and adjusted my set to jokes less particular to the female condition. This joke, by virtue of its subject matter, has nothing to do with men and unless male audience members are willing to imagine otherwise, namely what it might be like to be a woman, to occupy a body pathologized and considered substandard by Western medicine, there is little pleasurable yield from this joke other than the humorous term itself: panty soda. When there is no point of reference, listeners can detach, which often leads to judgment and alienation, a phenomenon I argue is more likely to occur during the performance of a female comic. Women and men are conditioned to perceive male experience as the norm or template genera and thus when women take the stage and implicitly request or require your attention and/or identification with female experiences, many find themselves experiencing a kind of distanciation, confusion, or simply an ambivalence toward this performance of otherness or what Joanne Gilbert calls a "performance of marginality."[55] This might explain why Christopher Hitchens struggled with such a myopic and sexist view of what constitutes the humorous. His diatribe warrants closer examination in order to understand the fundamental flaws of his claims as well as the public response it elicited from fellow journalist, Alessandra Stanley.

Hitchens Revisited

The debate over whether women are as funny as men (or funny at all) is not a new popular discourse. In the 1890s, newspapers printed editorials and articles speculating that women were born sympathetic, disallowing a fondness for jokes since humor is often mean-spirited. An editorial published in 1901 in *The Washington Post* begins: "The question was an old one: Do women have a sense of humor? They have long been accused of having a hollow where that bump ought to be."[56] The early 1900s delivered more of the same biology-as-destiny argumentation, that is, women are born lacking the DNA necessary to appreciate and produce humor. The debate raged on over the next century: women can exercise wit but not humor; vanity prevents women from pursuing comedy because women can be funny only by sacrificing their beauty; a woman's comic appeal requires she be beautiful otherwise she risks losing male patrons; funny women are unnatural; funny women are manly; women cannot be ladies *and* comediennes—the two are antithetical; women cannot be funny and feminine; women *can* be funny and feminine; women are too emotional to be humorous . . . and on.[57] Justifications made for women's inferiority in the realm of humor production were contradictory from one decade to the next and many were recycled and revived repeatedly over the course of the century. In no way original, Christopher Hitchens, almost verbatim, invokes biological explanations for women's deficiencies in the realm of humor production supplied over a hundred years ago.

Hitchens draws from diverse sources to prop up his argument that women are innately not as funny as men, including the similarly minded early twentieth-century print journalist H. L. Mencken and women contemporaries in the field of literary humor production like Nora Ephron (not actually quoted) and Fran Liebowitz, whose comments contribute less to any premise or argument he makes and more to the sexist conditions under which opinions like his can thrive and generate support. Ephron and Liebowitz believe that we live in and abide by male cultural values that allow for men to be funny (read: aggressive) and women to be pretty (read: submissive), which Hitchens reads as culture reflecting biological destiny. He also draws heavily and quotes at length from a poem by Rudyard Kipling whose arrogant imperialist attitude does a remarkable job of legitimating similar sentiments in the sweeping generalizations, objectifying remarks, and essentialist comments made by Hitchens throughout. Hitchens's argument in brief: men have deep-seated biological urges that compel a need for women to laugh at their jokes; women have no such need. Without the persistent nudging of biology's dictums, women do not have to cultivate the ability to be funny, only to appreciate the humor of men. Adding insult to injury, Hitchens pays mock deference to women's superiority, on account that they can bear children, endorsing biologistic arguments with religious inflected language such as characterizing maternity as a "higher calling." To be fair, Hitchens does allow that some women can be funny, whom he describes as by and large "hefty or dykey or Jewish, or some combo of the three."[58] The implication is, of course, that women falling into one or more of these categories have no need (or desire) to fulfill biological compunctions to achieve a woman's "higher calling."

The bulwark of his more essentialist claims relied on one Stanford study that found that when confronted with humorous material, in this case cartoons, women demonstrated more activity in some brain regions (specifically the left prefrontal cortex) than men, "suggesting a greater emphasis on language and executive processing in women." Further, they found that women could identify the "unfunny" faster than men and since they tended to have lower expectations for the cartoon functioning as humorous, "they were more pleased about it."[59] Hitchens's analysis of the study is summarized as: "Slower to get it, more pleased when they do, and swift to locate the unfunny—for this we need the Stanford University School of Medicine?"[60] That women are quick to recognize when a joke is not funny, which in many cases means that it just made "her" the object of the joke, that they have a higher order of processing and functioning, and are imbricated in a legacy of misuse and abuse that may prime their suspicion of anything shoved in their face and declared "hilarious," speaks less to their inabilities than to their capacity for discerning judgment. Importantly, Dr. Allan L. Reiss, the Stanford University researcher cited by Christopher Hitchens, wrote a letter to the editor protesting that his study was misinterpreted and misused by Hitchens.[61]

In April 2008, Christopher Hitchens's invectives against lady humorists were countered in an essay by Alessandra Stanley paired with a *Vanity Fair* cover of female comedy greats, including Sarah Silverman, Tina Fey, and Amy Poehler. The magazine cover invites you to consider this article in contrast to/with the Hitchens essay published the year before and Stanley references Hitchens's essay repeatedly throughout. Unfortunately, by doing so, she locks herself into an essentialist and tautological debate that make her earnest attempts to unseat his biases appear as feeble as her lengthy and somewhat simplistic contemplation of changing beauty standards for women in the comedy industry.

Alessandra Stanley acknowledges that early- to mid-twentieth-century female jokesters were attractive but notes that their comedy routines required them to be "ugly," that "they couldn't be funny if they were pretty," which prompted them to don outrageous costumes and wigs to achieve comic effects.[62] She then launches into the beauty and sex appeal of contemporary women's comic performers. Her argument in a nutshell—women can be funny and beautiful—fails for a number of reasons. First, this was not the primary argument or issue raised by Hitchens. It was tertiary at best. She seems to have honed in on his comment that funny women are mainly hefty, dykey, or Jewish and seeks to counter this claim by showing us how beauty and humor can come in one package. Introducing this new debate of whether women can be pretty while also funny, does not adequately address or challenge Hitchens's arguments;

rather, she side-steps his initial and far more inflammatory claims that women are *not* funny. Second, since women began performing in comedic roles in the late nineteenth century there has existed debate as to whether funny women had to forego beauty to secure the yucks. Early twentieth-century lady vaudevillians such as Nora Bayes and Irene Franklin demonstrated that beauty and humor could coincide and indeed flourish. Think of the spate of screwball comedies released in the 1930s, wherein the quirky, clumsy, and often hapless heroine was always a knock-out beauty like Claudette Colbert or Katharine Hepburn. Despite repeated evidence to the contrary, journalists and reporters continue to resurrect this popular discourse, which does a remarkable job of illustrating just how invested we are as a culture in women's beauty and any activities with potential to compromise women's beauty. It should be noted that the women selected for this issue are considered the (mainly White) belles of comedy, while other equally notable female comics were not included, presumably because in some way they do not fit the White standards of beauty perpetuated by the media (e.g., where are Ellen DeGeneres, Kathy Griffin, Paula Poundstone, Rosie O'Donnell, Mo'Nique Hicks, Kathleen Madigan, Roseanne Barr, Kathy Najimy, Whoopi Goldberg, and Lily Tomlin). Finally, Stanley ignores the evidence that these women do frequently alter their appearances and not necessarily for the better, for comic effects. *Saturday Night Live*, a live sketch comedy show televised weekly and also the training ground to a third of the women featured in the photo shoot, is chock full of sketches requiring its lady performers (several of whom were selected for the photo spread) to transform into a myriad of other characters more unseemly than sexy such as a longtime resident of a trailer park or a prepubescent teen with questionable social skills and a speech impediment (both played by Amy Poehler). Queen of the grotesque Amy Sedaris, among those featured in Stanley's article, played "fugly" for years as Jerri Blank in *Strangers with Candy* (1999–2000). Stanley does manage to counter Hitchens's claims that funny comediennes are only "hefty or dykey or Jewish." But, then again, we only get to see a limited cross section of women jokesters in the *Vanity Fair* photo shoot. The reality is that funny women run the gamut in conventional beauty standards and what matters most is *that there are many funny women.*

Not to be outdone and certainly unable to allow Alessandra Stanley the final word on the matter, Christopher Hitchens responded to Stanley in a follow-up essay: "Why Women Still Don't Get It" posted exclusively to *Vanity Fair*'s website.[63] The second essay advances a tired reiteration of the first as equally rife with contradictions and misogynistic language that either turns women (including his colleague Alessandra Stanley) into vampish sex kittens or castrating bitches. He reduces Stanley's essay to a flirtatious overture, writing: "Oh

Alessandra, oh angel, if you wanted a giggle or even a cackle, you only had to call me." And in the tradition of great bombasts, he gloats that Stanley's essay coupled with a layout of sexy funny ladies is precisely what he intended: "Did I never tell you this was my Plan A, and was my deepest-laid scheme all along? I forgive you for being so slow to see my little joke because—ah well, just because."[64]

This last line casting Alessandra Stanley as simple-minded or naive is not meant just for her. In fact, he is alluding to the Stanford study and the erroneously contrived "scientific" evidence proffered in his first essay. He has to forgive her because her sex excludes her from being able to see his "joke" (we are slower to get it, remember?). Every woman becomes the butt of this joke, though we may not even know it, and though we may be complicit and laugh along with it. If there truly existed substantial evidence and objective data indicating that women are biologically and genetically inferior in the realm of humor production, I would not waste my time or yours concerning myself with these matters. But I loathe allowing anyone to invoke biological determinism for what is and always has been culturally determined. The premise of Hitchens's jeremiad is hardly original; he follows in the footsteps of other notables using science and genetics to support their racist, sexist, classist, ableist, and heterosexist agendas. Fortunately, women have the advantage in this day and age of being in a position to combat these kinds of views and it is imperative that they do so. For this, we should applaud Alessandra Stanley and the other pundits, scholars, and comic performers who argue, demonstrate, and perform otherwise.

Charged humor incites consumers to invest the same cultural capital in productions of cultural citizenship like charged humor. Audiences will identify with performers representative of the most ideal or desirable citizens, that is, those comfortably situated within the dominant culture and bearing the privileges of not only legal but social inclusion, namely White, male, heterosexual, able bodies, eighteen years or older. While stand-up comedy may appear an innocuous form of entertainment, successful performers often reflect the status quo. Our beliefs about ideal members of the polity influence who we support with our time, energy, and money. It is most advantageous to understand and identify with those with the most access to privilege and power. This phenomenon of the cultural economy, at least for the time being, ensures that male, heterosexual comics will elicit the laughter necessary for continued advancement in the business of humor production. Since many women comics in some way produce charged humor, this may also explain why women comics are not perceived to be as funny as men. As long as women perform humor that reveals their second-class status, builds community, or advocates on behalf of women or any other minority community, they will elicit the same tepid public response because not only is there no incentive to buy into women's points of view but any point of view that calls into question the male ideal or the category of the ideal citizen.

There are (and have been) many highly successful male comics who are Jewish, queer, differently abled, and/or people of color, for example, Jerry Seinfeld, Josh Blue, Cedric the Entertainer, George Lopez, Shawn Wayans, Adam Sandler, Eddie Izzard, and so on. The history of stand-up comedy is full of exceptions, and it is simply inaccurate to say that only White dudes can get a break and achieve success. However, any analysis of the schedules for headliners in the mainstream comedy club circuits reveal that White and Black men outnumber their Arab, American Indian, Latino, and Asian male counterparts. Just as prisoner demographics are not representative of the nation's demographics, comics' demographics are not either. What is most important to recognize is that, despite occupying a marginalized subject position like being a Jewish male or a Black male, being male trumps the subordinated subject position, still making them more ideal candidates for identification and yielding greater social/cultural capital than women. Being White, able-bodied, and/or straight is less predictive of success than is being male.

Evidence indicates that comic success looks different for women comics than for men in professional stand-up and related commercial endeavors. While successful men in this industry command lead roles in blockbuster films and many use their comic material to star in autobiographical sitcoms or host late-night talk shows, for women comics the pinnacle of success today looks more like small cameos as witty best buds in blockbuster films and headlining comedy clubs or larger performance venues in major metropolises where the right advertising aimed at niche markets can draw an audience substantial enough to fill the seats. *Baby Mama* (2008) and *Bridesmaids* (2011) are both movies that defy this tradition and demonstrate that female-driven comedies can fare well in the blockbuster market. In an ironic (and rather ingenious) turn rarely seen in show business, Kathy Griffin built an empire by filming her struggle for notoriety and fame in show business, managing to turn her petering comedy career into an Emmy-winning reality television series called *Kathy Griffin: My Life on the D-List* (2005–2010). It remains to be seen how long she will maintain this level of success; as any performer will say: you are only as good as your last performance, and people have short memories. For men, but even more so for women, the pressure to sustain a career in comedy remains constant, meaning that regardless of whether a comic enjoys national recognition, s/he must devote untold energies to self-promotion and new commercial endeavors in order to remain in the public eye. *Joan Rivers: A Piece of Work* (2010), a documentary offering a behind-the-scenes glimpse of the comic legend, humanizes Rivers by exposing the trials and tribulations of a working comic and illustrates the intense daily rigmarole required in order to maintain a career in comedy. Despite few opportunities for women to strut their comic stuff in women-driven sitcoms and a lack of strong female characters in network television and movies, women continue to take up the microphone and try their hand in a field where the odds of mainstream commercial success are relatively slim.

Women, try as they might, will continue to flounder when placed next to their male counterparts as will queer comics alongside heterosexual comics and comics who are differently abled alongside able-bodied comics. There will be exceptions to this rule but for the most part those exceptions will be minority comics who either play into existing cultural stereotypes or opt not to discuss or bring their marginality to the forefront such as Ellen DeGeneres who has gained national adoration for her quirky, girl-next-door brand of observational humor. These exceptions will be the fodder for the naysayers (like Christopher Hitchens) as they argue either that anyone can succeed in stand-up if they work hard enough or that unequal success between men and women is merely a product of genetic encoding or biology. Both arguments are problematic, the former invoking the myth of meritocracy and placing the blame on the individual for lack of success and the latter making moot any possibility for equity among male and female comic performers. Both are equally strategic and safe arguments to make because neither holds the people or audiences responsible for their lack of desire or willingness to identify and collude with women's perspectives or worldviews, which in turn dictates their success in the business of stand-up performance. Abby Paige echoes this in her article "Laugh Trap," which opens and closes by taking to task the arguments proffered by Hitchens in *Vanity Fair*. She concludes the article writing:

> Great comedians are critical thinkers and deep feelers, and these days that may be precisely why the current crop of female ones are so threatening to so many: They are smart, they have a microphone and they are not afraid of you. In a sense, Hitchens was right: Women are too smart, powerful, and authoritative to be funny. He was just looking in the wrong direction for a fuller explanation. If you want to know why women aren't funny—or why they shouldn't throw their heads back and laugh—don't look toward the stage, but to the audience.[65]

The audience, sometimes contained in a physical space but more often broadcast widely to a national audience or community, determines who is funny, and this audience is shaped by the social relations and material conditions specific to this historical moment.

In sum, Christopher Hitchens presents an argument for which there is no debate, at least on his terms. In the face of such myopia Alessandra Stanley can do little other than point to the history of women's disenfranchisement from the industry of humor production and pay homage to the small but growing army of women jokesters active in the world of comedy writing and comic performances today. Replacing biological determinisms, which have the unfortunate history of reflecting whichever cultural attitudes are in mode, with cultural determinisms, places this debate back into the actual realm responsible for women's *perceived* ineptitude in comic performance compared to men. One reader, commenting on Emily Wilson's article "Are Men Threatened by Funny Women?" profoundly states: "None of us can 'decide' to find something/ someone funny—it's a primal, involuntary response we can't control. We can only hope that subsequent generations provide us funny women and receptive audiences NOT so entrenched in the power bullshit of our culture's outmoded past."[66] Recognizing the influence of culture in the economy of humor and in determining consumption of humor also opens the door for change, the possibility that the cultural economy will shift over time, making charged humor and/or women's ideas and perspectives profitable investments for audiences and in turn profitable investments for agents, network executives, and comedy club owners. In the words of Shaun Breidbart, "comedy is a business; it runs on money. Your money is your vote. Go out and vote."[67] While I cannot say that it pleases me, the extent to which capital—material, social, and cultural—dictates success and opportunity, the way it determines laughter in the final instance, I can say with a certain amount of confidence that it explains the question of why men are (perceived to be) funnier than women.

CHAPTER FIVE

Robin Tyler

Still "Working the Crowd"

> Not since the days of segregation has a whole community faced
> constitutional amendments branding them as non-citizens. . . .
> Even before the latest offensive on our rights, LGBT people
> were not citizens in this country. Citizens, by definition, have
> equal legal rights with others. Not just with respect to marry,
> but in employment, housing and public accommodations, and
> increasingly, adoptions, access to medical care and anything else
> the religious right can dream up, we are not citizens.
>
> *Robin Tyler and Andy Thayer,* The "Gay Marriage" Struggle:
> What's at Stake and How Can We Win?

As of July 24, 2011, New York State, where I now live, began recognizing same-sex marriages. Desiring to be the beneficiaries of rights and tax exemptions made available to heterosexual couples, my partner and I married in August 2011. While I am delighted that the state now finally acknowledges our union, I am all too aware of the tenuousness of this status. What if we move to one of the other thirty-three states that do not recognize our marriage most of which have constitutional provisions or statutes limiting marriage to a union between a man and a woman? What kinds of rights will we have if we are traveling and some calamity befalls us in one of those states or abroad? We still need other legal documents to protect us in those instances such as a durable power of attorney and a medical directive that protects us and our assets should one of us fall ill or pass away. To be safe, all lesbian, gay, bisexual, transgender, and queer (LGBTQ) couples will have to continue doing so until all the states legalize same-sex marriage. The complications are threefold if children are part of the equation and queer couples raising kids must draw up legal protections for their children that the law confers heterosexual married couples immediately.

Protecting ourselves as a lesbian couple is costly—in time, money, and energy—and the extra work and hassle are a tacit reminder that this would all be a lot easier if we were just normal, "straight" like everyone else. After all, if we were not different, then we would not feel like second-class citizens in the first place. While some citizens may be citizens in the legal sense, not all legal citizens feel incorporated into the national imagination and on some level understand that compared to their privileged brothers and sisters, they function as second-class citizens. Appeals for queer equality are predicated on two claims. First, the American claim to and promise of freedom and second, a claim to equality as queer, with queerness intact (e.g., essentialist arguments have been very effective because they line up with the US ideology that people have a right to be who they are, that is, queer is not a choice).[1] Main strategies employed by any cultural outsiders seeking to become a part of the body politic are cultural visibility and assimilation. Boosting cultural visibility is essential and empowering, but there is always the concern of who is visible or who becomes representative of the queer community. Furthermore, history indicates that cultural visibility strategies alone cannot and will not result in equal civil liberties and rights for the queer community. When it comes to the strategy of cultural visibility, questions are raised as to whether this strategy aimed at heightening the visibility of LGBTQ persons does anything to actually change their real material existence or legal rights.

Gay is the new cool in popular culture, but this does not change lack of access to federal rights or mean that queers cannot be fired for being "out" on the job. Indeed, cultural visibility of LGBTQ persons has increased and we enjoy greater visibility in popular visual culture. After all, Ellen DeGeneres hosts a daytime talk show and there are openly gay celebrities like Lance Bass, Patrick Neil Harris, Wanda Sykes, Jodie Foster, Clay Aiken, Ellen Page, and Raven-Symoné. There is now an LGBTQ-focused television network—LOGO, popular television shows with lead LGBTQ characters on broadcast television like *Will and Grace, Glee, Dawson's Creek, The Office,* and *Modern Family,* and a number of films have achieved popularity among the queer and straight alike: *The Rocky Horror Picture Show, Kissing Jessica Stein, To Wong Foo Thanks for Everything, Julie Newmar, But I'm a Cheerleader, Boys Don't Cry, The Kids Are All Right, Brokeback Mountain,* and *Blue is the Warmest Color.* But visibility is not sufficient and means relatively little in terms of rights. Robin Tyler, Jewish lesbian stand-up comic turned activist, opines, "We have no rights. People are talking about gays assimilating in the United States. . . . How can we assimilate? We don't have any rights, it's an illusion . . . this illusion that there's somehow equality out there is, is not true."[2] Thus, acknowledgment that comes from legal inclusion extends beyond visibility and manifests in concrete social and political acceptance and equal rights for the LGBTQ community.

Without consideration of acknowledgment, one can argue (and many have) that LGBTQ persons enjoy all the civil liberties and protections—the right to vote, to marry within a heterosexual union, to call upon law enforcement for protection—guaranteed any other.

On the other hand, assimilationist strategies combat marginalization but have been criticized for asking proponents to adopt the values of the dominant culture. This is the primary strategy of the "new gay visibility" movement that seeks to assimilate LGBTQ persons by emphasizing their normalcy. Two major flaws accompany this strategy; the first is underestimating the vociferous nature—ideological and visceral—of those opposing queer equality.[3] Second, some consideration should be given to the fact that the focus of the marriage equality movement not only prioritizes one issue while ignoring others, but also leaves other sexual strangers and kinship arrangements (i.e., bigamy, polygamy, and polyandry, etc.) without civil rights or protections to be with the partner(s) of their choice. In other words, gay marriage legislation simply reincorporates one group while strengthening another's status as gender and sexual outlaws.[4] Once considered a liberation movement, LGBTQ persons sought to secure social acceptance despite their differences; now, the focus seems aimed at demonstrating similarities and hence suitability for cultural and legal inclusion and assimilation into the dominant culture. Robin Tyler describes this shift in the movement:

> This is a civil rights movement about not being on the back of the bus for anything. And so I think that what's changed in my lifetime is we've gone from being a "gay liberation movement" [*uses air quotes*]—it really didn't get much anywhere—to a lesbian/gay/LGBT civil rights movement that essentially is going after the right to work and the right to marry and the right to have children and the right not to be violated and so forth and so on. And so I think that the marriage movement has wrested it . . . wrested the movement away from the 20 percent of LGBT people that just wanted to be a liberation movement, so that we can be culturally different, into a civil rights movement where we can have choice.[5]

This begs the question of how can strategies be enacted to confer rights without being exclusive to any group or without effacing cultural differences. It is not that either set of strategies—assimilation or visibility—is wholly unsuccessful, but that in most cases they are deployed to the exclusion of the other and both have consequences that do not call into question citizenship as it is currently understood. One possible answer advances a "thorough queering of public culture," rather a move toward the queering of citizenship, altering its infrastructure and effectively broadening citizenship to be more inclusive and to achieve the goals of inclusion.[6] This means that cultural visibility, while less effective if pursued as the only course of intervention, is essential to and should be deployed in concert with the assimilationist strategies such as legal protections and legislation conferring the same rights held by heterosexuals. Arguments and historical evidence supplied here consider the myriad ways Robin Tyler deploys both strategies to advance queer equality.

Since the 1970s, Robin Tyler has waged battle against sexism, heterosexism, and racism on stage and in the streets. This chapter documents the multifaceted career of Tyler, exploring over forty years of her work as both comic performer and activist, from the gay liberation movement in the 1970s to the twenty-first-century marriage equality movement. The terms of citizenship need reform but since those terms operate in the psychic field of our imaginations *and* as legal torts and documents, Tyler believes that efforts must be focused on both arenas.

> Winning legal battles is important, but if they come in a vacuum of next to no public education, relatively little is accomplished from the perspective of the "average" LGBT person in the street, the young person growing up in a homophobic school system, etc. We need to change the social climate in which everyday LGBT people live. When public opinion shifts in concert with legislative advances, then that legislation takes on far greater power and also is much more impervious to reversal. Changing public opinion is the key to civil rights defense, and advance, of our community.[7]

Changing public opinion is no easy feat. Some argue that tolerance coupled with time will breed future generations more willing to accept and incorporate people who are "different" into the national body politic. Others believe dynamic and increased representations, cultural visibility, and public education are important to developing understanding and tolerance for sexual diversity. These are all tactics intended to document and effectively alter the psychic and material conditions contributing to one's position as an outsider—together they are the cultural practices developing cultural citizenship. Robin Tyler combines cultural work and legal advocacy to develop interventionist tactics aimed at queer equality, efforts resulting in legislative changes and greater public acceptance for LGBTQ persons—what women's studies scholar Jane Ward calls a queer intersectional politics and what I playfully term a queer(ful) intersectional politics. Ward defines queer intersectional politics as "an intersectional politics that struggles for racial, gender, class, and sexual diversity while resisting the institutional forces that seek to contain and normalize differences or reduce them to their use value."[8] Similarly, as a pioneer in the entertainment industry and in multiple social movements, Robin Tyler advances a politics of change that does not cater to corporate, institutional, or economic interests, in other words she launches a queer(ful) intersectional politics that seeks radical legislative changes not because queers are "normal" or just like everyone else, but because we are human. For instance, she does not advocate nor believe that LGBTQ inclusion should come as a result of demonstrating our assimilability, an argument that has been used frequently within the marriage equality movement. Nor does she believe any social movement is above reproach and uses her stand-up comedy and prominent role in social movements to critique broader society for disavowing queers and challenge civil rights movements perpetuating homogeneity in membership or focus (i.e., exclusionary) and/or in the pockets of corporate America. The fact that the attack is launched from a stand-up comic makes this approach to social change a queer(ful) intersectional politics.

What makes Robin Tyler so special when there are other activist comics performing and working in the United States right now who also serve up queer(ful) intersectional politics or a politics that seeks cultural recognition without muting diversity—for example, Margaret Cho, Kate Clinton, Karen Williams, and René Hicks? I could have elected to focus on any one of these women, but unlike the others, Tyler's career spans over four decades of engagement with social movements; and through her comedy and activism you can track shifts in these movements and the strategies used to create social change. Additionally, no other comic is as proactive as Tyler on *both* cultural and legal fronts. Robin Tyler's life and career as a performer and activist extend beyond her. Her vantage, her battles, her triumphs are the stuff of history, the history of the gay civil rights movement in the United States. Over the course of forty years on the front lines of the gay liberation movement, now the gay civil rights movement, she has devised and employed a great number of tactics for educating the public about LGBTQ issues, such as providing a safe space for women to gather and celebrate their diversity and for ending the public defamation of LGBTQ persons in the media. She has rallied support for various LGBTQ causes and is a key player in the marriage equality movement in California, challenging California's Prop 8 legislation all the way to the United States Supreme Court.

Presenting: Robin Tyler[9]

"We're not a cute comedy team," Robin Tyler told a reporter from *The Advocate* in 1972. She goes on: "We [she and Pat Harrison] are a revolutionary comedy team. We came here to educate, [and] to entertain."[10] Seven years later, looking dapper and playing coy, Robin Tyler appeared on the *1st Annual Funny Women's Show* on Showtime in 1979, hosted by Phyllis Diller, during which she performed openly lesbian material, becoming the first gay or lesbian to do so on national television. She performed a short set during which she recounts a time when a male audience member, none too pleased to listen to her in-your-face brand of charged humor, stood up and began heckling her. Tyler jokes, "And then he said the one thing that was really supposed to upset me.

He said [*in a deep and gravelly voice*], 'Hey are you a lesbian?' And I said, 'Hey, are you the alternative' [*laughter that moves into sustained hooting, cheers, and clapping*]?"[11] The heckler, who would rather make a public spectacle than suffer the presumed indignity of having to listen to Tyler's feminist charged humor, is made the butt of this joke. Tyler's retort emasculates him by using him—his display of arrogance, buffoonery, and aggression—as clear example of why she is a lesbian in the first place. This joke that brought down the house has no trace of self-deprecation, does not rely on stereotypes to achieve a laugh, and places men (not women) as the butt of the joke. Writing jokes that avoid these sure-fire mechanisms for inducing laughter is a difficult task and part of the struggle to produce charged humor. As a comic you want your audience to laugh, but as a charged comic, you also consider at whose expense the joke is being made. Tyler's production of charged humor is a mainstay of her comic material. She seldom cracks a joke that does not also cut like a dagger, and when a comic refuses to compromise their material, they often find themselves shut out of the mainstream market, a high price for speaking truth to power.

Robin Tyler was born Arlene Maxine Chernick on April 8, 1942. Her parents owned a pet store and raised their family in "farm country" in Winnipeg, Manitoba, Canada.[12] Her grandparents on her mother's side were Russian Jews who migrated to Canada after getting married. In her own words, "My grandmother ended up becoming a religious fanatic and dying in a mental institution. Now my mother, who was always trying to be thin all her life . . . became an amphetamine psychotic trying to lose weight."[13] On her father's side, Tyler shares that while she is unsure of the circumstances or details of the event, she did learn that her grandfather killed her grandmother but does not provide details of when or how this occurred. She professes having a penchant for the dramatic at an early age and by the age of eleven was performing professionally at the Manitoba Theatre Center. At the age of 16 she was cognizant of her lesbian desires and stopped dating boys. In her teen years, she became friends with Terry, a young gay Ukrainian. Without realizing it at the time, she and Terry—two strong—held the first gay civil rights demonstration in Canada in 1959 by standing on street corners and holding up signs saying: "Gay is Good!" Passersby thought "gay" meant happy and some even stopped to give them money.[14] Concerned that she was not taking an active interest in men, her parents sent her to study at the Banff School of Fine Arts.

As a Canadian citizen she had access to the dramatic arts, which, in her own estimation, influenced her desire to be a performer. She says:

> I was raised under socialism in Manitoba, and this affected me to the extent of I got to go to theatre school for free. . . . The reason they call opera and all those other things the high arts—opera and symphonies—it's because of the high

price. But we got to go to symphonies and operas and be very educated culturally because it was free in Manitoba.[15]

She came out as a lesbian in Winnipeg at a time when there existed little understanding or tolerance for LGBTQ persons. In order to pursue show business
and meet other queer folks, she moved to New York City in 1962 at the age of
twenty and began training at the American Musical and Dramatic Academy.
Here, she changed her name to Robin Tyler, a legal change prompted, if not
inspired, by an article written by Del Martin and Phyllis Lyon in *The Ladder:
A Lesbian Review*. This humbly produced publication by the Daughters of Bilitis,
the first lesbian rights organization in the United States, was eagerly read by
lesbians across the country.[16] Their message urging lesbians to become politically active and move to urban centers spurred Tyler's desire to assume a personal
moniker reflecting her burgeoning activist sensibility, which she channeled into
her performances—be they music, comedy, or female impersonation.[17]

> Just working at the 82 Club and having the police chase me, thinking I was a,
> you know, a drag queen, politicized me. And, I never knew about segregation,
> nobody ever talked about it, so I used to go to the park in New York and hear
> people talk about civil rights and about Black civil rights in the '60s and, this
> was like [*gestures wide with hands*] amazing to me. . . . And, so I just became
> politicized by being chased by the cops, by being arrested for impersonation, by
> going to the park and hearing Black civil rights speakers.[18]

While attending the New York Drag Ball put on by the Imperial Court at
Manhattan Center, she was arrested for female impersonation. As she recalls,
the police assumed she was a man and "they took me to jail, and all the queens
were saying, 'She's a girl!' And so they allowed me one phone call. I called the
New York Post."[19] The headlines the next day read: "Cops Grab 44 in Dresses—
And a Real Girl in Slacks." The article, written by Alfred T. Hendricks, details
the raid on the gala and the ensuing confusion leading to the arrest of a "real
girl."[20] The city filed charges against all forty-four men—six for indecent exposure and thirty-eight for masquerading. After being arrested for female impersonation, Tyler began performing professionally in drag under the pseud-
onyms Stacey Morgan and often as Judy Garland.

Her political sensibilities infused her performance work, particularly when
she paired up with the "very famous high-fashion model," Pat Harrison, who
became her partner on-stage and off.[21] Afraid of the consequences of representing two out lesbians, their agents advised them to bill themselves as sisters—
Robin and Rachel Tyler. In their earlier work they performed using mainly
self-deprecating humor, which was a staple comedy style used by women
comics such as Phyllis Diller and Joan Rivers during this time. For women,

making oneself the butt of the joke helped diminish the threat that funny women posed to male audience members, but it also meant women were once again casting themselves as inferior. Tyler and Harrison soon rejected self-deprecating humor instead opting to satirize oppressive institutions.

> Sexist jokes were the mainstay of the profession, and women comics were expected to make themselves, as women, the brunt of their own jokes—witness Phyllis Diller. "But we wouldn't be self-deprecating," says Robin, "and at first we weren't funny. Then all of a sudden feminism came along. In essence what we did then is now called the new women's humour, a humour which finally gave women the opportunity to make not themselves the brunt of the jokes, but rather the society that was oppressing them."[22]

Hearing that they could make $220 a week per person performing overseas for the troops, in 1970 the duo auditioned and were invited on a USO tour to Vietnam (and later to Bangkok) to entertain the troops. Few female entertainers were booked for this tour and Tyler and Harrison may not have been had they auditioned as comics. In fact, Tyler and Harrison, who had since changed their names from Robin and Rachel Tyler to Harrison & Tyler, billed themselves as singers so it came as a surprise to everyone to see them performing comic entertainment and as the tour progressed inserting antiwar material into their sets.

> It's only as we started to play in Vietnam that we started to make comments on what was happening [with the war] and then we really started to do comedy in Vietnam—to the point of, they wanted to throw us out. But the soldiers loved us, you know, because we were doing anti-war material. We didn't even know it, it's not like we came from an anti-war position. It's when you see war close-up, nobody can be pro-war.[23]

Although they "didn't go for any political reasons," the experience politicized them and when they returned they continued to perform antiwar material and became very popular in the antiwar movement, "playing all the free antiwar demonstrations."[24] Before returning home from the USO tour, Tyler accidentally overheard and captured on tape a commanding officer disclosing that the United States had begun bombing Cambodia, an international news item that the government failed to disclose to the media. When she returned home, she called the *Los Angeles Times* to tell them about this breaking story, offering the tape as evidence. Hours later a CIA agent showed up at her doorstep demanding the tape. Fortunately, she had made duplicates and hoping for a better response, she called the *Los Angeles Free Press*, who broke the story the following day.[25]

Their performances before and after the USO tours already incorporated other pressing social issues of the time. Together they put out two LPs of radical feminist sketch comedy: *Try It, You'll Like It* (1971)[26] and *Wonder Women* (1973)[27] and toured universities and colleges around the country in the early 1970s interrogating issues of sexism, homophobia, and heterosexism and inciting audience members to think and act differently about civil rights and equality for women, people of color, and LGBTQ persons. The first two minutes of their act situates them as lesbians and feminists, a move that did not win them additional fans or venues in which to perform:

ROBIN: Who out there thinks we're strange huh? How many out there think we may be "you know what?" Anybody? It's not true. No, it's not true. It so happens that Patty and I met in a very usual way.

PAT: Yeah, I was driving the truck and she was loading it.

ROBIN: Cut that out, cut that out. Most of you who know about us know that Patty and I happen to be feminists . . .

PAT: And that's not a hygiene deodorant.

ROBIN: What it means is that we believe in the women's liberation movement. Now, how many of you brothers and sisters out there believe in the women's liberation movement?

PAT: You know people have the wrong idea about women's liberation. They really do. All it means is that women want to get out of the kitchen and back on the streets where they belong!

ROBIN: Back on the streets, organizing, marching, and protesting. Now, of course, the question that we get asked the most is what made you personally become feminist.

PAT: Well, we were born women . . .

ROBIN: Yeah, that helped.[28]

In their acts, they donned characters and personas to reveal the sexism in advertising and education, wage inequalities, gendered double standards, and homophobia. Looking back on that period of performing with her then-lover Pat Harrison, Robin says: "We took all of the jokes that had ever been done on women and we did them on men. And when a man jokes about a woman it's called funny but when a woman does jokes on men it's called anti-male."[29]

Robin Tyler began performing independently as a comic on the West Coast in the mid-'70s. No stranger to the entertainment industry or successful techniques for comic performance, she quickly made a name for herself, releasing *Always a Bridesmaid, Never a Groom* (1979),[30] "which was the first openly gay or lesbian comedy album."[31] Stepping out on her own and learning to develop her own comedy stylings, Tyler had to learn to shift from the straight woman (as she was when performing with Pat Harrison) to deliver her own punch lines. Using her own life as backdrop and narrative for her jokes, her first album demonstrated her passion for exposing social ills and inequalities, the sexism inherent in the English language, and the limitations of assigning roles and rules to expressions of gender identity. As these examples indicate, her comedy is first and foremost unapologetically feminist and prowoman.

> My mother delivered me. They're always saying doctors deliver our babies. Doctors don't deliver our babies. Doctors receive them, WE deliver them! Besides, women don't have breakdowns, we have breakthroughs. We just get in touch with our anger, right?
>
> Alright now, come on guys. Let's not get insecure about this kind of material. Anytime you're insecure, just do crotch-check, it'll still be there. I mean we've been listening to this tits and ass jokes for sixty years guys . . . you're not going to pull the foreskin over our eyes![32]

This album borrowed from earlier jokes written for her duo comic performances and while funny at times, it is easy to see how her brand of charged humor could alienate audience members not agreeing with her radical feminist beliefs. Tyler, whose life indicates that she was always an activist in her own right, co-opts the cultural practice of stand-up comedy to gain ground and followers for the women's liberation movement and the gay liberation movement. Using comedy as a window dressing for pointed social critique, she, like many others taking this confrontational tack in stand-up comedy, did not get picked up by major networks or launched into the mainstream. She elicits positive responses such as cheers, clapping, whistling, and laughter as much for her punch lines as for stating beliefs with which audience members agree.

> I believe in wages for housework. I believe that women who work in the house, women that raise children, people that raise children should get paid by the government for raising those children. . . . There's no such thing as welfare. We're not giving anybody welfare, we're paying people to do a very hard job to raise those children [*hoots and hollers*]. The only thing wrong with it is that we're underpaid; now that's all that's wrong with it [*clapping and cheers*]![33]

There is no hidden joke in the above passage and no laughter either. It was a statement made about our sexist wage economy, an attack on the stigmatization of welfare recipients, and a challenge to change the way we think about and legislate public assistance. This was hard to sell even to hippie audiences radicalized by the many civil rights movements and enjoying the charged humor of Richard Pryor and George Carlin during the same era. Both Pryor and Carlin found ways of slipping in the critique; Tyler's charged humor was more like a left hook to the kidneys and she made no apologies for it. Plus, Pryor and Carlin's maleness certainly worked to their advantage at a time when the public preferred women's humor to be at their own expense.

Following the release of this album Robin Tyler toured clubs and universities as a lesbian comic. Her second solo comedy album *Just Kidding* (1985)[34] is, as her first was, a humorous indictment of bigotry, homophobia, and Christianity. She used her notoriety as comic performer to buoy her move into a full-time career as an advocate for social justice, mostly related to gay and lesbian rights. She was able to put her burgeoning skills as an activist to the test when Anita Bryant, a well-known singer, led a successful campaign in Dade County, Florida, to repeal an ordinance prohibiting discrimination on the basis of sexuality. Bryant pursued similar campaigns in St. Paul, Minnesota, Wichita, Kansas, and Eugene, Oregon. In an effort to counter Bryant, in April 1978 Tyler called for the first National Gay March on Washington while she was performing in a St. Paul, Minnesota, benefit for the St. Paul Citizens for Human Rights. The show was intended to raise money to "prevent the repeal of the ordinance in St. Paul which protects people from discrimination on the basis of sexual or affectional preference."[35] A planning committee convened the following day to begin organizing the march. Newly elected City Supervisor of San Francisco Harvey Milk called Tyler to let her know that a march was unnecessary. He was elected and for all intents and purposes this battle was won. Tyler disagreed and maintained that the march was essential to rallying support for policy changes giving LGBTQ persons protection and civil rights. She reports that with the help of one of his aides, Cleve Jones, Milk became convinced of the importance of this effort and soon after joined in to lead the march. Harvey Milk was assassinated eleven months before the march took place on October 14, 1979, and in many ways the march became a tribute to him, an event to honor the contributions he made to the gay civil rights movement. In the week preceding the march, founder of the Metropolitan Community Church, a Christian denomination welcoming LGBTQ folks, Reverend Troy Perry and Robin Tyler led the Gay Freedom Train across America, stopping in major cities to demonstrate, rally, and speak on behalf of civil liberties and equal rights for LGBTQ persons.[36]

Thirty years later, Robin Tyler continues to be at the forefront of the LGBTQ civil rights movement, most recently by being the first to file the equal marriage rights lawsuit against the state of California to "include gays and lesbians in being able to marry."[37] She and her partner, Diane Olson, along with their attorney Gloria Allred, announced this decision at 9:00 a.m. on February 4, 2004, only hours before Mayor Gavin Newsome began marrying same-sex couples in San Francisco, California. The case, *Tyler, et al. v. the County of Los Angeles*, went to California's Supreme Court, which ruled on behalf of Tyler and Olson making gay marriage legal for approximately six months, until California residents voted for the passage of Proposition 8—a 2008 ballot initiative amending the constitution and eliminating the right for same-sex couples to marry in California. After five more years of litigation, Tyler and Olson won the case when the US Supreme Court declined to rule and upheld a lower courts ruling on the unconstitutionality of Proposition 8, making same-sex marriage legal in California.

After a twenty-three year hiatus, Tyler returned to the stage, performing *Always a Bridesmaid, Never a Groom* (2007)—a title borrowed from her first solo comedy album—a nearly two-hour long autobiographical solo comic performance. In it she offers a retrospective of her life as an entertainer and activist while addressing LGBTQ social and political history over the course of forty years. She has thrown her hat in the ring as an educator and a writer, developing workshops, lectures, and courses, and authoring and coauthoring a number of articles about the gay civil rights movements. She frequently responds to contemporary issues in magazines, newspapers, and online on *Huffington Post*. As Tyler would tell you, her work as a performer and activist are inextricably linked and the record shows that the marriage of performance and activism succeeded in generating discussion, edifying audiences, enlisting support for LGBTQ causes, and humanizing the movement in order to encourage extending civil liberties to the LGBTQ community.

Radical Politics and Performances

Robin Tyler has never been interested in fitting in and being like heterosexuals, a point to which she will attest and one that her comedy corroborates: "Flaunting . . . isn't that a funny word? When a heterosexual shows us a picture of their family it's called sharing. When we show them a picture of our lovers it's called flaunting."[38] And she does expect to have the same rights conferred heterosexuals: not a fraction, not a few, but *all* rights. In an interview with me she said: "Why did we want to marry? Was it because we could assimilate? No, I just simply wanted civil rights, the same civil rights heterosexuals have, and maybe to choose to raise children. And so I began to work in the marriage movement because I realized that I didn't want to be a movement just talking about sexual politics."[39] Her role in the marriage equality movement was not an overture to assimilate as some might think. Robin Tyler maintains a visible presence in the gay civil rights movement and the marriage equality movement and in both she invokes queer(ful) intersectionality by using radical tactics within assimilationist strategies to bring civil liberties and acceptance to US cultural citizens.

Not everyone agrees that there should be such an intense focus on the battle for gay marriage. Some are uncomfortable with what appears a legal maneuvering to integrate and assimilate queer folks on heterosexual terms and according to heteronormative institutions. Michael Warner, a queer theory scholar, criticizes the gay marriage movement for ushering in what he calls a new era of "homonormativity," a term Lisa Duggan describes as "a politics that does not contest dominant heteronormative assumptions and institutions, but upholds and sustains them, while promising the possibility of a demobilized gay constituency and privatized, depoliticized gay culture anchored in domesticity and consumption."[40] In this argument, gay marriage inducts queers into middle-American complacency and divests the movement of its radical politics and antiestablishment designs. Robin Tyler's active role in the marriage equality movement may seem contrary to Warner's criticisms; yet, she, like Warner, is critical of assimilationist strategies and instead works sometimes within and more often alongside and outside human rights organizations supporting gay civil rights, devising her own radical tactics for intervention and cultural visibility. She wants the whole kit and caboodle and no, she will not apologize for how she secures these rights or what she does or does not do with them once they are secured. For Robin Tyler, "it's not about marriage, it's about showing them that we are full human beings. We are not fighting for the right for sex. . . . This is about our lives."[41] Critiques and concerns about the gay civil rights movement from within have not gone unnoticed by Tyler, but she also values action and the only thing she hates more than not having her rights is to allow criticism and internal politicking to stagnate progress. She will be the first to admit that she does not always get it right and that her tireless advocacy work was (and is) the product of trial and error. Some tactics have succeeded and others have failed—examining both offers fruitful lessons and yields potentially useful strategies for current and future social movements. Robin Tyler's strategies for social change—and what I will explore in this section is not only history but blueprint for future progress—includes marches, performances, unauthorized protests, civil demonstrations, letter-writing campaigns, online mobilization efforts, legal action, and women's music and comedy festivals spanning from the 1970s to the present.

Robin Tyler's production of charged humor and strategies aimed at securing civil rights relies on the premise that acknowledgment—cultural, political, and legal—is a key component of full citizenship. In order to avoid the repeated and rather untrue argument that LGBTQ individuals have full rights as citizens, we need to broaden our understanding of citizenship to include acknowledgment. Doing so illumines an entirely different picture of citizenship, one in which LGBTQ persons are second-class citizens. Legal inclusions and protections (though whether LGBTQ persons have this on their own terms is dubious at best) and acts of civic participation alone—voting, participation in the civic polity, demonstrating social responsibility, and activism—does not a citizen make and there is historical evidence that these acts did not and do not ensure an extension of equal rights nor acknowledgment as citizens. Political scientist Shane Phelan argues that sexual minorities exist as "sexual strangers" in a land resistant to strangers (of any ilk).[42] Strangers occupy an ambivalent space fraught with anxiety that makes strangers "prey to renewed exclusion, scapegoating, and violence."[43] Sociologist Zygmunt Bauman first applied this notion of citizen stranger while studying European Jews, arguing that this designation as stranger exists outside the us/them binary. This means sexual strangers are not national enemies but persons excluded from citizenship legally and culturally, a mostly nonhostile consignment to the fringes of the national body politic. The mere fact that there are citizen strangers—be they undocumented, infirm, queer, or itinerant—illumines the "ways in which official citizens may nonetheless be civic strangers."[44] This further evinces the need for creative tactics that generate visibility and contribute to a "public culture of acknowledgment."[45] Visibility and acknowledgment ensures that when the time comes, there are numbers enough to support changes in public policy.

As early as 1924, when Henry Gerber founded the Society for Human Rights in Chicago, LGBTQ citizens have organized and colluded to carve out a respected space in society, mobilizing to obtain and protect basic civil liberties like the right to be safe from violence, freedom of gender expression, the right to job security, the right to adopt, and the right to marry. The late 1970s was an important moment in the gay civil rights movement. May Joseph considers the 1970s "the moment of rupture . . . for Western states radically renegotiating conceptions of democratic citizenship."[46] Indeed, the civil rights movement, women's liberation, the Chicano movement, and the gay liberation movement cast suspicion upon any claims to real democracy in the United States. The question became: how can any nation boast that it is a democracy while having different rules and allowances for different groups based on gender, race, ethnicity, sexuality, and class? In 1978, the year Robin Tyler called for the first National Gay March on Washington, Harvey Milk was the first openly gay man elected to public office, and the Briggs Initiative—an initiative developed by John Briggs, a California senator, and promoted heavily by musical artist Anita Bryant, which banned LGBTQ teachers and those supporting gay rights from working in public schools—was moving through the court system of several states. The initiative failed in California but passed in Oklahoma and Arkansas. Open attacks on LGBTQ folks on myriad fronts prompted organizing on behalf of LGBTQ civil liberties like the march on Washington. In a brochure detailing the march, the organizing committee published the following five demands for the LGBTQ community:

repeal all anti-lesbian/gay laws; pass a comprehensive lesbian/gay rights bill in Congress; issue a presidential executive order banning discrimination based on sexual orientation in the federal government, the military, and federally contracted private employment; end discrimination in lesbian mother and gay father custody cases; and protect lesbian and gay youth from any laws which are used to discriminate against, oppress, and/or harass them in their homes, schools, jobs, and social environments.[47]

While Tyler was very involved in subsequent marches in 1987 and 1993 as main stage producer and main stage coproducer (respectively), she did not call for another march until 1999, what would be known as the Millennium March on Washington for Equality (MMOW). During her brief stint as executive producer for MMOW (she left the position and had no further involvement with the 2000 March due to irreconcilable differences with the executive committee),[48] Tyler enumerates countless reasons for participating in MMOW "What Are We Marching For?" It was a sobering reminder to hear that the demands made in 1979 at the first national march had yet to be met over twenty years later in 2000.[49]

In 1959, Cornelia Otis Skinner, a comedic actress performing during the mid-twentieth century, presciently suggested that there would be fewer prejudices if we all laughed a little more because "people who laugh together do not tend to hate one another."[50] Likewise, Robin Tyler believes that heightened visibility vis-à-vis comedy leads to tolerance and understanding, which in turn leads to an increased likelihood of legal and legislative changes—a formula she has been documenting and advancing for decades. In an interview for the *Winnipeg Free Press*, Tyler says, "If you can get people to laugh, it's a way to get them to listen to what you have to say, to challenge their thoughts and illuminate lies."[51] Her charged humor broaches social issues in a humorous way— targeting sexist advertising, homophobic attitudes, and hypocrisy in her own community.[52] Robin Tyler began producing charged humor in early performances with comedy partner Pat Harrison.

> ROBIN: Men are very hung up about women saying dirty words.
> PAT: Yeah, the only kinds of words we think are dirty are: kill, war, hate, I mean those are the kinds of words that are dirty.
> ROBIN: But men don't want us to say dirty words and I'll give you an example. For instance, there's one word that begins with "f" that ends with "k" that most men don't like to hear women say.
> PAT: Yeah they want us to do it but they don't want us to say it.
> ROBIN: And I don't think people should be hung up over saying words. I think people should, you know, just let it all hang out and just say words.
> PAT: Say it . . . be liberated.[53]

Gendered double standards, a culture of violence domestically and abroad, and the silencing of oppositional discourses, Tyler and Harrison address all these issues in the span of ninety seconds in their act. When they were not performing, Pat Harrison and Robin Tyler engaged in other forms of civil disobedience; they staged protests, organized sit-ins and sent letters to major print media sources openly indicting public and military officials for their treatment of entertainers and handling of funds for USO and Special Services. On Saturday, August 22, 1970, the same year as the Kent State shootings and two years before Congress passed Title IX, Tyler and Harrison commemorated the 50th anniversary of women's suffrage by staging a sit-in at a Rams-Raider football game. They were removed by force from the playing field, all the while shouting "demands for more sports scholarships for college women; for schools to end discouraging females from participating in athletics; and for women to have the right to form teams or to participate in any professional sport."[54] Not all coverage of the demonstration was as thorough or as objective as the *Los Angeles Times* article just quoted. In another article about the sit-in, published by the *Los Angeles Herald-Examiner* and written by Steve Bisheff, the author describes the pair as "two pretty young things . . . One was a well endowed redhead, the other an equally curvaceous blonde."[55] A sleight of hand erased the substance of their complaints. Clearly Bisheff conferred more worth to their physical appearance than their rationale for interrupting the football game.

The following year, as domestic tensions continued to mount over US involvement in Vietnam, Tyler authored an open letter to the editor of *The Hollywood Reporter*, which was reprinted with her permission on Thursday, March 11, 1971. In the letter she chastises USO officials for not increasing salaries for entertainers, for being out of touch with the kind of entertainment the troops prefer, and for "losing" all thirty-seven (positive) reports submitted following the performances of Harrison and Tyler in Vietnam. The letter ends with a "call for a Senate Investigation into the workings and distribution of funds of both USO and Special Services."[56] From these early interactions with the press Tyler learned to manipulate the press to support various causes, understanding the value of keeping the public informed, especially about the issues she deemed noteworthy. There was no Senate investigation, but her letter became one of many concerns raised about US dealings with and occupation of Vietnam, contributing to growing public pressure to withdraw.

Antiwar activists had a good year in 1972, as did members of the women's liberation movement. The United States withdrew its troops from Vietnam, and hope was ignited for feminists and womanists when Title IX passed and the Equal Rights Amendment moved through the Senate (though it was never ratified by Congress). In the spring of that same year, Pat Harrison and Robin

Tyler filled in for two vacationing deejays at KGBS radio. They went on air with a show they called "The Feminist Forum" an intentional jab at a concurrent KGBS show called "The Feminine Forum" hosted by Bill Ballance, a radio show Tyler and Harrison criticized as "cater[ing] to the worst in feminine fantasies and frustrations."[57] Ballance's radio personas earned him a reputation for being a shock jock, much like Howard Stern and Don Imus, or any radio/ television personality relying heavily on political incorrectness and offensive humor, in other words, shocking their public. On "The Feminine Forum," Ballance was known for excoriating feminists and women liberationists who called into the show, but on "The Feminist Forum" Tyler and Harrison dispensed information about abortion centers, women's clinics, and the women's liberation movement. The show fused practical information for women with radical politics and a healthy dose of humor. The comedic duo created quite a stir when they compared Alabama Governor George Wallace to Adolf Hitler in their comic routine. According to journalist Susan Stocking, this "left management in the somewhat awkward position of having to offer equal time to Wallace supporters. That in itself might not have been so bad, but the next day Harrison and Tyler apologized—to Hitler."[58] Wallace's staunch segregationist stance made enemies out of many people during this time, and an attempt to assassinate Wallace shortly thereafter left him in a wheelchair for the rest of his life. Whether a product of Harrison and Tyler's making a mockery of Balance's show or merely the result of shifting public interests, "The Feminine Forum" was canceled the following year.

Civil disobedience, radical speech, or staged guerilla counterattacks . . . whatever you call it, Robin Tyler has a long history of surprising her audiences while performing, breaking contracts by adding "inappropriate" (read: political) material, introducing unplanned performers to the line-up, and using humor to openly attack major corporations and political figures. Following the success of their stint on USO tours and short-lived careers as radio deejays, Harrison and Tyler took "The Feminist Forum" on the road, performing at colleges and universities across the United States. Maxine Feldman, a folk singer and one of the first openly lesbian musicians, traveled with them opening many of their shows by singing the now-famous lesbian anthem "Angry Atthis," often against the wishes or at least unbeknownst to those coordinating these performances.[59] Tyler makes no apologies for these breaches of contract; in fact, she often concludes live performances as in her first solo-comedy album, in a rebellious Puck-ish fashion by telling her audience: "If I've offended any of you, you needed it!"[60]

Aware of the power of performance, Tyler implemented charged humor to improve cultural visibility and enacted cultural citizenship to improve media representations and make advances in civil rights. Sometimes this is subtle as when Egyptian American Muslim comic Ahmed Ahmed tells the following joke, the subtext of which clearly identifies those experiencing a second-class citizenship (all for different reasons):

> I read a statistic on CBS.com that said right after September 11th, hate crimes against Arabs and Muslims went up over a thousand percent, right after September 11th, which apparently, check this out, which apparently still puts Arabs in 4th place behind Blacks, gays, and Jews. It's true. [*Pauses and chuckles*] So what do we have to do [*laughter*]? We want to be number one in something [*laughter*]![61]

Tyler was less subtle in her comedy routines as when she positions herself as a newly empowered woman who will fight for recognition and inclusion as a woman and as a "dyke."

> The women's liberation movement has given us a new word called assertive, right. Assertion is taking your own power. Aggression is taking power over others. I'm not assertive, I'm aggressive. I intend to take power from the people who took power from me. So, I am aggressive. And it's better to be aggressive than repressive [*cheers*]! But every time a woman is aggressive, self-confident, her own person, they call her a dyke. So, I think it's a compliment, don't you [*clapping and cheers*]?[62]

Turning disparaging language into personal accolades, Tyler's bit reframes the ideal woman in her own radical image. Tyler recorded this bit in 1979, the same year comics went on strike to secure fair wages, the same year Gloria Gaynor released "I Will Survive"—a hit single that would become an anthem for the LGBTQ community—and the same year Margaret Thatcher was elected Prime Minister in Britain. Unfortunately, despite the passage of over thirty years her observations about social treatment of powerful women still resonate.

Tyler's charged comedy is unapologetically feminist, zeroing in on sexist commercials and negative representations of women and using the stage to deconstruct gender and sexuality in Bible stories and fairy tales:

> You know who the biggest purveyor of pornography was in the United States in those days? . . . The biggest purveyor of pornography was Walt Disney. It's true! The first portrayal of women, I'm seven years old I go into a movie theater and there's a princess on stage singing a song [*she sings*]: "someday my prince will come" . . . and then, he leans down. He thinks she's dead and then he kisses her. Now there's a word for that where I come from. And what happens? Snow White leaves the wicked witch who had had a wonderful relationship with her for four years to wash socks for seven little dwarfs. Now come on![63]

For some, her points are well-taken. Corporate Disney has managed to create an empire on fairy tales and fables reinforcing women's dependency and passivity. Whether we can assign this foul play as falling under "child pornography" . . . well that seems far more specious. Her charged humor fared well among the college crowds but not as favorably among mainstream comedy club venues just beginning to crop up on the West and East Coasts. Tyler frequently performed in the Belly Room of The Comedy Store in Los Angeles (a side room established as a workshop performance space for women comics), run by the notoriously business savvy Mitzi Shore, but did not perform in the main room where comics such as Steve Martin, Richard Pryor, and David Letterman were known to headline at the time. In fact, she was one of the few comics who despite not being paid for her performances still supported Mitzi Shore during the 1979 Comedy Strike. The Belly Room offered a space to rehearse but Tyler wanted her messages to be heard and knew there was an audience for her charged humor, just not among mainstream audiences. The public was hip to racism and enjoyed supporting charged humor exposing racial bigotry and government hypocrisy, but homophobia and sexism were different matters. Feminists had long been charged with having no sense of humor, and Tyler made a point of putting men on the receiving end of her jokes, just as men had done and are still doing to women. Locked out of conventional spaces for performing stand-up comedy, Tyler sought out alternate venues where feminist and proqueer charged humor could flourish.

In 1978, Robin Tyler, forged a connection—romantic and professional—with Boo Price, at the time a coproducer of the Michigan Womyn's Music Festival. One thing led to another and soon Tyler was scheduled to perform at the festival. Skeptical that a comic could please the throngs of women gathered at the festival, Lisa Vogel, also one of the festival's coproducers, was at first hesitant to include Tyler in the show's line-up. Despite these misgivings, her performance was successful with many but did anger some for its criticism of the festival's fundamentalist politics like refusal to serve meat, assuming its attendees were all vegetarians. Tyler, herself a butch lesbian attracted to other butches, openly questioned butch-femme binaries perpetuated by lesbians and in general poked fun at the internal standards imposed by the community even as they fought constraining standards placed on them by dominant culture. After two years of experiencing what Tyler describes as "unbendable rules made by a few for the majority—in the name of what is 'politically correct,'" she decided to produce her own festivals for women.[64] In her own words: "intolerance of others' choices was not acceptable. I was a feminist, and to me feminism meant the right to choose."[65] For fifteen years (1980–1995), Robin Tyler produced the West Coast Women's Music and Comedy Festival and for nine years, with some exceptions, produced the Southern Women's Music and Comedy Festival

(1983–1992). In total, she produced twenty-five festivals over the course of two decades, creating women-only spaces where charged humor—hers and many others—could flourish in a way proven impossible in mainstream media outlets.

The 1980s and '90s were tumultuous for Robin Tyler who continually fought to secure the land necessary for the festivals, facing hostility and overt discrimination from surrounding communities especially when the locals caught wind that thousands of lesbians had converged on Camp Coleman in White County, Georgia (property belonging to the Union of American Hebrew Congregations). Some of the general hostility toward these large-scale attempts to gather, educate, and develop community can be attributed to the effects of neoliberalism as it took hold during the Reaganite years. These shifts in the economy and public sentiment also help explain the wane in consumption of charged humor during the 1980s, even as opportunities to perform were on the rise. According to social and cultural analyst Lisa Duggan in *Twilight of Equality? Neoliberalism, Cultural Politics and the Attack on Democracy* late twentieth-century neoliberalism was born out of pro-business activism, which "was built out of earlier 'conservative' activism."[66] This conservative ethos was gaining ground throughout the 1970s and was embraced fully under the Reagan administration. Neoliberal hegemony, what Duggan characterizes as the consent of the people to shift in attitude and policy toward certain communities and sectors of the public, occurred in five phases in the United States: first, with challenges to and legislation undermining New Deal and progressive policies; then building public skepticism and disdain for any movement emphasizing distribution downward, that is, the Black power movement, women's liberation, gay liberation, and so on. This affected Tyler's advocacy work because the women's festivals she organized became the target of public scrutiny, hostility, and overt discrimination. While performing at one of these festivals, Tyler remarked on the stir their presence created saying: "When men think of two lesbians, you know it excites them, and two thousand they're scared to death. So, we are not only their worst fear but we are also their greatest fantasy and they must be in tremendous conflict over us."[67] In the economic sector, the third phase of neoliberalism is increased mergers, acquisitions, and creation of giant monopolies in corporate America. The 1980s was fraught with financial takeovers, fragmentation, and consolidation of business that got us to our current oligopoly market. Remember Richard Gere's character in *Pretty Woman* (1990), the decadent and nonplussed Edward Lewis—that was his job. Fourth, neoliberalism infiltrated the cultural front via the emergence of "culture wars" (1980s–1990s) imposing religious beliefs (and restrictions) on "public institutions and spaces for democratic public life."[68] This was best illustrated during the public controversy in 1990 when John Edward

Frohnmayer, presidential appointed chairmen of the National Endowment for the Arts, vetoed grants slated for four performance artists whose work was considered indecent. And finally, neoliberalism entails a watered-down "form of 'equality' designed for global consumption during the twenty-first century, and compatible with continued upward redistribution of resources."[69] The latter manifestation—otherwise known as neoliberal multiculturalism—can double as the American dream or more cynically as the myth of meritocracy or more recently as the jaw-dropping moniker being bandied about the media: (we're so equal that we live in) "'postrace' America."[70] Following President Obama's first State of the Union Address in 2010, MSNBC host Chris Matthews said: "He is postracial by all appearances. You know, I forgot he was black tonight for an hour. You know, he's gone a long way to become a leader of this country and passed so much history in just a year or two. I mean, it's something we don't even think about." His statement, at best, is a feeble attempt to assert that President Obama can sit at the cool kids table (read: As long as you do not act Black, you will fit in just fine here) and at worst draws from stereotypes about Black affect, speech, and mannerisms, which openly belies the possibility that we are living in anything resembling a "postracial" society.[71] One of the characteristics of neoliberal multiculturalism is that "racism constantly appears as disappearing according to conventional race categories, even as it takes on new forms that can signify as nonracial or even antiracist."[72] The cultural and political zeitgeist during these decades informed Tyler's decision to create workshops and open dialogue during these festivals for important but difficult conversations about intersecting identities and discord between and among identity-based communities. She fought hard to make sure that difference and diversity within and between groups was, if not entirely understood or celebrated, at least respected. This stance was foundational to Robin Tyler's comedy and is the lynchpin of a queer(ful) intersectional politics. She used her comedy and activism to advocate for equal rights and to admonish the movements she associated with when they rejected intragroup differences like lesbians who did not choose to define themselves as butch or femme or feminists who were not vegetarians. Unafraid of being vocal about what were very unpopular views even in her own circles, she also adamantly refused to take on the role of victim as a woman, lesbian, or Jew and criticized social movements, promoting a rhetoric of victimage.[73]

At times throughout these years she was verbally attacked, marched on, and boycotted by women in her own community who accused her of being "a rich Jew trying to get rich off the backs of the women's community."[74] One such event occurred in Yosemite State Park during the second West Coast Women's Music and Comedy Festival in 1981. During a speech, a group of women (about 200) marched on her, threatening to burn down her cabin. Those attending the festival paid $65 for four days and nights of workshops, performances, access to facilities, and fully prepared meals. The complaints centered on what they considered a high price for the event and what was perceived to be racist hiring practices because all the kitchen staff were Black women. Tyler countered that the price for the event was comparable to other events and the festivals were never a business venture as much as a way to develop and educate the women's community. On the matter of the all-Black kitchen staff, Tyler reported that she hired two African American kitchen coordinators who in turn did the hiring for the entire kitchen staff. These positions also happened to be the highest paid positions in the camp.

Just as Robin Tyler led her communities in boycotting orange juice, for which Anita Bryant was a spokeswoman, the women's and LGBTQ communities used the same tactic and no longer booked Tyler at LGBTQ events and boycotted the following year's festival (1982). Tyler stopped performing, "had a nervous breakdown," and "became a periodic alcoholic"; however, she refused to stop creating festivals and using them to educate and politicize attendees.[75] Her second solo album, *Just Kidding*, was a live recording from her performance at the 1985 Southern Women's Music and Comedy Festival and reveals some of the tension Tyler was experiencing within her own community at the time.

> I've been noticing the way you've been responding to the singers, and I'd like to say something as a comic. And Kate Clinton and I were discussing it backstage. They [singers] really get the kind of adoration that comics don't get, yep [*audience moans and disagrees*]. I was a singer, oh yes [*groans continue with boos*]. Sure, yeah. Oh that's good, we're going to do an act by consensus. Shut up [*scattered laughter*]. We're not processing. I'm not glad you're sharing this [*few whistles from crowd*]. Now let me get on [*cheers from crowd*]![76]

Robin Tyler was clearly caught off guard and almost loses her audience, though ends up gaining back their favor and finishing the rest of the performance without any further trouble.[77] Already having a reputation for having a diva personality, it would not be surprising if the audience found her statement to be a silly and pandering proposition—that singers get more adoration than comics—and a means for Tyler to garner celebrity treatment and status from her own community. Surely those in attendance knew of the tenuous relationship Tyler held with major players in the women's liberation movement and the gay liberation movement; tensions were running high. Unlike other live recordings from her performances at festivals, this one reflects the unease between Tyler and her audience. No doubt, her terse response to defection from the crowd was, among other things, also a product of the immense pressure she was under. While she continued to travel, speaking on behalf of the gay civil rights movement, she did not perform again until 2007 when she began trotting out an original one-woman multimedia show called *Always a Bridesmaid, Never a Groom*, to audiences in Los Angeles, California.

These music and comedy festivals showcased talented women eager to find a venue to explore their feminist sensibilities in a welcoming space, but social justice gains went far beyond that. The objectives were to entertain and educate, and each year portions of the proceeds were devoted to various political and social initiatives. The women attending the festivals raised thousands "to fight an initiative that was to put people with HIV into 'camps' in California," helped fund the 1987 National Gay March on Washington, and salvaged woman-owned Redwood Records among other initiatives.[78] Tyler created and led workshops on anti-Semitism, racism, and the civil rights movement. These opportunities to teach were the early seeds of courses she later developed on the history of comedy based on the civil rights movement. The sum of these tactics constitute a queer(ful) intersectional politics that combines legislative campaigns with education and activism (with a dose of humor), asking us to reconsider the terms of citizenship on all frontiers—legal, cultural, and political—in the classroom, on the books, in the courtroom, on the stage, and in the streets.

The movements to which she belonged began changing as the grip of neoliberalism tightened in the late 1980s and 1990s. Political and cultural shifts influenced the definition and experience of citizenship and as such shaped and informed the tactics deployed by Robin Tyler. One of the defter maneuvers on the part of the Reaganites in promulgating the American dream was to connect private/personal success with the nation, which "sets the stage for a national people imagining itself national only insofar as it feels unmarked by the effects of these national contradictions."[79] This means that people subject to marginalization are less likely to achieve the American Dream and more likely to attribute failure to do so to their own actions rather than institutional barriers or systemic flaws. In other words, when bad events occur in our personal lives like loss of a job or an appendage, one's value as a citizen becomes questionable, automatically making it a personal failure and ensuring that people occupying certain (negligible) social locations (queer, people of color, differently abled, etc.) will experience a kind of second-class citizenship that dominant ideologies tell them is their fault in the first place. To that effect, Lisa Duggan points out:

This rhetoric promotes the *privatization* of the costs of social reproduction, along with the care of human dependency needs, through *personal responsibility* exercised in the family and civil society—thus shifting costs from state agencies to individuals and households. This process accompanies the call for the tax cuts that deplete public coffers, but leave more money in the "private" hands of the wealthy.[80]

The end product is a culture of blame placed upon those living in poverty because their destitution either signals their failure to achieve the American Dream because they are lazy, irresponsible, and incompetent or belies the American Dream altogether (it has been far more profitable to foster the former).

The 1980s and 1990s were also characterized by an explosion of new media changing the way movements could mobilize constituents, like the Internet, which was made available for commercial use in the mid-1990s. Robin Tyler capitalized on emerging technologies to reach a large swath of the public for online issue campaigns, keeping her focus on issue campaigns and infrastructural change. It is critical to devote energy to both: infrastructure and issues, otherwise, we run the risk of perpetuating the existing belief that rights alone can and do level the playing field, negating the ways in which state institutions are perpetrators of racism, sexism, and heterosexism. In 2000, Robin Tyler and attorney and political consultant John Aravosis founded the StopDrLaura.com campaign, which coordinated protests all over the nation against Dr. Laura Schlesinger, a radio pundit routinely spewing inaccurate, and disparaging information about LGBTQ persons.[81] This campaign, which ran on a budget of $18,500, focused on coordinating protests against Dr. Schlesinger's radio program, generating petitions with thousands of signatures from people disagreeing with her agenda or program content, and sending letters of complaint to companies buying airspace during her show. At the time of the campaign, Dr. Schlesinger was negotiating syndication of her show on national television. Potential sponsors began dropping their bids for commercial space after supporters of StopDrLaura.com threatened to boycott their products. Proctor and Gamble's decision to retract an offer to sponsor the show quashed any possibility that Dr. Schlesinger would host a television show. Reflecting upon this triumph, Tyler writes with coauthor and founder of the Gay Liberation Network Andy Thayer: "The successful StopDrLaura campaign showed that by leveraging the volunteer enthusiasm of new activists, even a cash-poor campaign can have a dramatic impact on public opinion and ultimately force multibillion dollar institutions like Proctor and Gamble to do the right thing."[82] In total, over 170 advertisers left the show as a result of this online campaign.

Buoyed by the success of this web campaign, on July 15, 2003, Robin Tyler and John Aravosis went on to cofound DontAmend.com, an online campaign aimed at preventing antigay constitutional amendments.[83] This initiative posted articles from newspapers across the country related to antigay legislation and offered a number of ways of becoming active in the campaign for gay civil liberties that included: contact information for California senators, information about upcoming rallies, online petitions, and a pledge against voting for politicians supporting antigay amendments. In 2003, the campaign targeted Pennsylvania Senator Rick Santorum (a Republican presidential hopeful for the 2012 elections) for his vocal opposition to homosexuality. Founders posted contact information for companies donating money to Santorum's reelection campaign such as Gateway, Sprint, and United along with the amount donated. For five years (2003–2008) this web site featured the latest news, information, and ways to intervene on behalf of gaining and fighting attempts to limit civil liberties for the LGBTQ community. The website expired once the Human Rights Campaign took on the task of posting similar data encouraging citizens to become socially aware and politically engaged.

While activists found means of harnessing new media for their own ends, University of Chicago English Professor Lauren Berlant warns that the proliferation of this media "has paradoxically enabled the standards and rhetorics of citizenship to become so privatized and subjective that even privileged people can seem legitimately to claim "outsider," if not "minority" status."[84] With ballooning numbers of people claiming have-not status, there is a risk of not recognizing the ways people enjoy unearned privilege by virtue of race or gender, even if they experience oppression based on another marginalized subject position. According to key players in the gay civil rights movement, too often, an influx of those claiming outsider status leads to fragmentation within the movement, detracting attention from important initiatives and efforts aimed at securing rights that require some modicum of group consensus. Seeking to make important legislative inroads and understand the nature of intracommunity concerns from all its members, Robin Tyler's queer(ful) intersectional politics is often more radical and less cautious than those organizations spearheading the marriage equality movement, who argue that change should come in a package orchestrated and designed by them.

In Terms of Belonging: The Marriage Equality Movement

During our interview, Robin Tyler positioned herself politically as "a very angry democrat," incensed that democrats, "instead of having the courage like Martin Luther King [Jr.] did, to come up against the Democratic Party," have instead "become pawns with the Democratic Party."[85] For this and other public indictments like it, Tyler has *not* emerged as the funny lesbian mascot for the gay civil rights movement, instead waging her own legal battle, *Tyler, et al. v. the County of Los Angeles* (the case that legalized same-sex marriage in California only to be overturned by Proposition 8), in relative obscurity, despite her position at the helm of the marriage equality movement. The case attracted a great deal of national attention; and even made its way to the United States Supreme Court (June 2013) who declined to rule on the constitutionality of Prop 8—this on the same day DOMA was repealed. Tossed out for a procedural issue, this decision upholds a lower court's ruling against Proposition 8, effectively legalizing same-sex marriage in California. Throughout this there was little to no mention of her involvement, let alone her leadership role in the process until *The Advocate* placed Tyler and Diane Olson on the cover in January 2009, five years after the couple filed suit. Even so, for those following the marriage equality movement, she remains relatively obscure.

Historically, Robin Tyler has never curried favor with any political party at the expense of the gay civil rights movement and the marriage equality movement. In fact, her unwillingness to compromise when it comes to issues of equality for LGBTQ persons has made her unpopular with even those within the movement. After filing the equal marriage rights lawsuit against the state of California she was confronted by a number of organizations and individuals working in the movement who accused her of steamrolling an issue they believed the American public was not yet ready to decide.

> And the legal law firms, the gay legal law firms were really angry at us for making the decision, [be]cause they thought it wasn't the time. You know, they kept saying to Martin Luther King [Jr.], "Now's not the time." . . . He used to say, "If not now, when?" And they'd say to Martin Luther King, "There's gonna be a backlash." And he says, "Backlash? We've never gone forward, how can there be a backlash?" So we have the same thing . . . when the Supreme Court of California dissolved the marriages in San Francisco, then the gay legal firms, the City of San Francisco, Lambda [Legal], ACLU [American Civil Liberties Union] filed for people in San Francisco . . . so, they now had a lawsuit going to the Supreme Court. . . . And eventually all the lawsuits were combined, and it's interesting [be]cause all the activists were friends with each other. But the unfortunate thing is that the group that filed in San Francisco tried to make us invisible, like we didn't file first. . . . I mean, we go to San Francisco and they have a press conference and they have the San Francisco couples there but not us . . . they really treated us very badly and tried to make it like it wasn't our case at all, that it was always their cases. These very people that yelled at us for daring to file a lawsuit at this time. . . . But now all the organizations have decided to throw big demonstrations that night—call it a celebration of life— and we haven't been invited to it. It's like we didn't do it and didn't exist. Why not? Because these corporations, these organizations are going to make a lot of money off of looking like they started and put this lawsuit through.[86]

Tyler has been and continues to be assailed for her vocal criticism of issues within the LGBTQ community and for her leadership role in the marriage equality movement by those who oppose assimilationist strategies as well as members within the movement who prefer to take things slowly and to proceed more carefully. The latter folks believe that change will be more amenable over time or that there are more pressing concerns in LGBTQ communities.

The most popular strategies being deployed right now by gay rights organizations fall within the category of assimilationist. Shane Phelan finds this tendency toward assimilation more than a little troubling, writing that "the 'de-gaying' of HRC [Human Rights Campaign] collaborates in the deeper homophobia that motivates resistance to equal rights."[87] The tools employed in the move for gay assimilation include appeals to empathy and of course, the visible normalization of the population seeking inclusion, usually characterized by an ostracizing of bad queers. The marriage equality movement has utilized assimilationist strategies like fighting for same-sex marriage at the state level in the courtrooms and the polls to obtain rights and benefits for LGBTQ communities. Robin Tyler works within the movement, utilizing assimilationist strategies like petitioning for legal recognition of her marriage with Diane Olson (though her activism seldom coincides with the timeline preferred by movement leaders). However, she employs a queer(ful) intersectional politics by criticizing the non-profit industrial complex spearheading (read: funding and representing) the marriage equality movement.

> Until we think of ourselves and act like a civil rights movement instead of the gay industry, and realize that most of these organizations that have taken over for us, that attending a dinner for $150.00 or being an activist on the web . . . does not promote change. Change is promoted in the streets and in the suites. When *Brown v. the Board of Education* happened, when the Supreme Court ruled free integrated schools, they didn't integrate right away. There was this huge civil rights movement in the '60s of people on the streets insisting on their civil rights. And it took years and years of activism. So, so I think what's happened is we've allowed our organizations to take over for us thinking they're acting in our best interests, when I think most of the time they're acting in the best interest of maintaining their jobs. And so, any other corporation where the head of corporation makes a quarter to a third of a million dollars a year, and does not produce a product, they'd get fired. But here we have corporations, gay corporations with great logos, you know—Human Rights Campaign: the equality sign—but they're like Enron: great logo, no product. So, until we demand, until we stop just handing over millions of dollars blindly to our corporations that produce no results, and until we understand that change happens from the bottom up, then we won't change.[88]

Her criticism of the gay industrial complex echoes Lisa Duggan's concern that "many of the dominant national lesbian and gay civil rights organizations have become the lobbying, legal, and public relations firms for an increasingly narrow gay, moneyed elite."[89] This matters because efforts aimed at achieving equality will favor issues benefitting the gay, moneyed elite, for example, a preoccupation with marriage equality that overshadows ending employment discrimination. Not everyone wants to marry, but everyone in the LGBTQ community would benefit from employment protection policies like the Employment Non-Discrimination Act.

Some argue that the gay liberation movement sought to celebrate diversity, while the fight for gay marriage is a legal maneuver humanizing and drawing similarities between LGBTQ persons and the public in order to incorporate LGBTQ folks without any distinctions. Robin Tyler and Andy Thayer combat this stance by suggesting that the "issue is the question of *choice* in joining an institution in US society, not an *obligation* to join it and be 'assimilated.' "[90] For all of those in the movement pooh-poohing the fight for the right to marry, calling it an elitist assimilationist agenda, she argues that "equal access to marriage rights is far more vital to the material lives of working class LGBT people of color than it is to stereotypical, upper middle class white male couples."[91] To those who would rather see the fight for same-sex marriage taken more slowly or attention focused on other issues, Tyler responds that the "point of winning equal rights legislation is not so that we have the ability to repeatedly file lawsuits just in order to secure our rights, but instead, to win a societal acceptance of LGBT people so that such lawsuits are rarely needed;" in other words, if social acceptance is gained alongside marriage rights, a good deal of time, money, and energy can be put toward making other advancements in the LGBTQ community.[92]

> When I was at the Supreme Court three weeks ago, one of the questions . . . one of the lawyers said (on our side) Terry [Teresa] Wright, this brilliant lawyer from the city of San Francisco. She said, "If the word marriage doesn't matter, then when interracial marriage was ruled for on behalf of interracial marriage, instead of calling it marriage, why didn't you call it interracial domestic partnership?" And I need to tell people that in 1948 when they ruled, the California Supreme Court for interracial marriage, 76 percent of the American public was against it. You know, now it's 50/50, but so it wasn't on the whim of the American public that they ruled. And it was only until 1991, in 1991, finally the majority of the American public believed that there should be interracial marriage. So right now it's a 50/50 thing with gay marriage. But we shouldn't be waiting and letting them vote on whether we should have this civil right or not.[93]

The significance of winning marriage equality goes beyond the 1,138 rights conferred in marriage. Tyler and Thayer argue that "the marriage equality issue has become a national litmus test on whether or not LGBT people are going to become citizens in this country."[94]

My interview with Robin Tyler and Pat Harrison took place on Mother's Day, Sunday, May 11, 2008. She allowed me access to her personal archives and library and helped to contextualize the performances and information gathered at the June Mazer Lesbian Archives in Los Angeles, California. On May 15, 2008, two days after I returned to the East Coast, California's Supreme Court announced its decision to legalize gay marriage, declaring it a constitutional right for same-sex couples. While working in Tyler's library and office, the quiet was punctuated with phone calls made to various gay rights organizations and people from the press to organize a press conference on the day the verdict was made public. While the exact date was unknown, Tyler and many others were preparing their public statements and making arrangements to respond to either verdict. Her excitement and anticipation was palpable as was her frustration with a particular gay rights organization that had already arranged for a press conference at an ideal and coveted location for such events. These arrangements were made without including Tyler and Diane Olson, excluding them from the event and effectively securing the best location for a press conference. This kind of ostracism and intracommunity backlash is a recurring trope in Tyler's career, which some might argue as justifiable and others as unfortunate.

Many were shocked when California voters passed Proposition 8 banning same sex marriage in California on November 4, 2008. After nearly six months and thousands of wedding licenses doled out to same-sex couples—among them Ellen DeGeneres and Portia de Rossi—those having married were left uncertain as to their legal status as a couple (later it was determined that any same-sex couples married before Proposition 8 took effect would be treated as a legal union). A week and a half later, on November 15, 2008, Wanda Sykes, a comic and actress, spoke at a rally at the LGBT Center of Southern Nevada in Las Vegas. She responded publicly to the passage of Proposition 8, which coincided with Arkansas passing legislation banning gay couples from adopting and Florida making same-sex marriage unconstitutional.

> I felt like I was being attacked. I was personally attacked. Our community was attacked. . . . If we had equal rights we wouldn't, shouldn't have to be standing out here demanding something that we automatically should have as citizens of this country. . . . Instead of having gay marriage in California, NO, we're going to get it across the country. When my wife and I leave California I want to have my marriage also recognized in Nevada, in Arizona, all the way to New York. . . . Gay is not a choice . . . that's like telling me that I chose to be a woman; that I chose to be Black. Are we saying that if being gay is a choice that people are straight because they chose not to be gay? I am very proud. I am proud to be a woman. I am proud to be a Black woman and I'm proud to be gay! . . . Now let's go get our damn equal rights! Come on![95]

Any social movement demands momentum to sustain any sort of legal policy or legislative changes. It also draws strength and inspiration from celebrities like Wanda Sykes, willing to come out to her fans in order to generate support for the marriage equality movement.[96]

Robin Tyler's outspoken brand of performance and activism has earned her a reputation as tenacious and indefatigable, not necessarily desirable traits to some. She has drawn criticism from within and outside the LGBTQ community, but perhaps this should be the benchmark of successful advocacy work—you know you are making progress when even those within your community think you are moving too fast. Whether or not you agree with Tyler, it is clear that she has launched numerous successful campaigns for changing public opinion and fighting for equal rights for LGBTQ persons. American studies scholar Michael Denning writes that "out of these organized forms of struggle for cultural justice and the sometimes unorganized forms of popular culture resistance may come a third moment, or level, or cultural politics: the formation of a new culture, a new 'conception of the world,' as Gramsci put it, a cultural revolution."[97] Tyler's queer(ful) intersectional politics on behalf of LGBTQ communities include comic performances, national marches, supporting lesbian-owned businesses and artists, raising public awareness about sexism, homophobia, and religious and racial bigotry, boycotting products, producing women's festivals, spearheading successful online initiatives such as the StopDrLaura.com and DontAmend.com campaigns, developing organizations like the Equality Campaign, of which she is the executive director, and legislative reform for the marriage equality movement. She employs multiple tactics to optimize progress for the movement such as grooming a generation of twenty and thirty-somethings attending her festivals in the 1980s and 1990s to support and pursue the legal reforms necessary to change their status as second-class citizens; to become active in local and national politics; and to be ready to champion the constitutional reform Tyler herself would initiate in California in 2004. Combined, these tactics work to induct this "third moment" Denning writes about and may prove indispensable to a movement that still has much work to do when it comes to acquiring civil rights and liberties on par with their heterosexual counterparts.

There are many additional strategies for achieving social justice and equal rights for the LGBTQ community. Robin Tyler and Andy Thayer stress the importance of finding the linkages between various causes so people understand how these issues are related and how progress for one issue can positively impact other initiatives.[98] Further, along with Wanda Sykes and many others, they urge members of the LGBTQ community to become active in local and grassroots initiatives seeking legal reform to include LGBTQ persons. Writing a check to an organization and signing online petitions is not sufficient action for achieving the kinds of legislative reform and inclusion into the national polity that LGBTQ persons desire. Moreover, Tyler and Thayer write: "we need a radical reshaping of the terms of the debate. No legislative victories we might win will be secure until there is a wholesale shift in public opinion."[99] Using her own involvement in the financial fiasco at the MMOW as an example, she warns that while large-scale mobilizations are important for inspiring individuals to become active in their local communities, "if they are not combined with a savvy political strategy, the legislative result can be nil, the hopes of the affected community dashed, and a huge defeat reaped instead."[100]

The cultural practice of stand-up comedy, for Robin Tyler, offers a forum for producing charged humor specifically aimed at challenging homophobia and sexism and lobbying for civil rights and liberties. Fueled more by her activist sensibility than by dedication to the craft of comedy, Tyler's charged humor and personal politics are inextricable and at times her jokes lack punch lines. However, success in the industry requires laughter not ideological congruence. Signaling agreement with a statement is not the same as eliciting a laugh, and working comics quickly learn that it is far more savvy (by industry standards) to foreground the funny over the political. The comics desiring to build a repertoire of charged humor will have to consider that this choice will alienate a swath of potential viewers. Comics like Robin Tyler, whose commitment to producing charged humor prevails over any desire to be mainstreamed or widely syndicated, will in all likelihood not have broad visibility among the wider populous. Less visibility means fewer people granted access to her worldviews. There is something to be said for the comics who use charged humor, but also strive for balance in their material in order to achieve more fame and snag additional markets, thereby potentially influencing more people. Therein lays the limitations of charged humor. In an e-mail communication with me Tyler wrote:

> Had I not been so "radical" in my humor, I may have reached a larger audience. I think that when you are first to batter down the walls of prejudice, you have to be a sledgehammer. Then, others, (such as [Margaret] Cho, [Kate] Clinton, Ellen [DeGeneres], etc.) can follow. Birthing something is never easy. I have no regrets—not one.[101]

While I do not expect her brand of comedy to be on a network channel anytime soon, there is a spot at the table for rogue charged comics like Tyler. Consider the recent boon of gigs for comics willing to perform for nonprofit functions, pride festivals, and galas hosted by civil rights organizations, which has shaped and produced a small army of activist lesbian comics like Judy Gold, Kate Clinton, Marga Gomez, Suzanne Westenhoefer, Karen Williams, Lea DeLaria, René Hicks, Karen Ripley, and Julie Goldman. For human rights organizations, edgy progay liberal humor inspires and reinforces their agendas; however, when that comic material is an indictment of the movement—its narrow agenda, corporatist strategies, and disquieting dismissal of other needs for reform that seem unfundable—the comic runs the risk of losing paying jobs in this small but profitable market of entertainment. Robin Tyler uses stand-up comedy to vocalize discontent with the gay civil rights movement, not because she does not want to be a part of it, but ultimately because she wants it to be a better movement. A queer(ful) intersectional politics and practice like Robin Tyler's can help propel the gay movement toward increased inclusiveness, tackling a broad array of issues and representing the diversity of the queer community.

CHAPTER SIX

Micia Mosely
Humor out of the Mouths of Babes

As a former history teacher, I see what gets written in the history books, and if we don't document ourselves, there's no guarantee that someone else will. So, whether through art or, you know, in other ways, these characters I'm hoping are really documenting a—a group of people in the world right now. We might look different a hundred years from now, but there are people who are just like this right now.

Micia Mosely, personal interview

Most people, if asked to list mainstream representations of Black lesbians may haltingly cite the biracial character of Bette Porter played by Jennifer Beals on Showtime's *The L Word* or Wanda Sykes as an example of a Black lesbian comic.[1] We know Black lesbians exist in real life, and there are even some Black lesbian celebrities like Robin Roberts, Tracy Chapman, Raven-Symoné, and Wanda Sykes. But where do they show up as characters, protagonists, and heroines in television, film, theater, radio, or elsewhere? Creating representations that make Black lesbian subjectivities visible is a key goal in Micia Mosely's body of work as a comic performer. Her own social identities, background in education, and knowledge of history's occlusions fuel her desire to remedy Black lesbian invisibility. African American writer and activist Jewelle Gomez writes that "it is the *representation* of black lesbian lives, not simply its analysis and decon-struction that has the most immediate, broad-based and long-lasting cultural and historical impact."[2] Being represented—seeing someone like you—is itself powerful and creates opportunities for others (not like you) to consume varied and various representations of someone like you.

Mosely's stand-up comedy and one-woman show strive to address issues of race, gender, class, sexuality, and environmentalism. She describes her charged

humor as "funny to some and a little daggerish to others, but that's my comedy."[3] Born on April 2, 1973, in Charlotte, North Carolina, Micia Mosely was
raised by her mother and greatly influenced by her godfather, who has been a
strong presence in her life since the age of five.[4] She was raised and educated
in the public school system in New York City, going on to earn a bachelor's
degree in history at Brandeis University and a master's and doctorate in education at University of California, Berkeley. She has over a decade of experience
teaching social studies and history to young people, training teachers, coaching
administrators, and leading whole-school reform efforts. Her research areas—
urban education and equity-based school reform—inform her scholarship,
presentations, and now performances for professional organizations and academic
institutions.[5]

The city of San Francisco nurtures a thriving comedy scene and is well
known for producing comic talent of the likes of Mort Sahl, Robin Williams,
Richard Pryor, and George Carlin. Having welcomed queer migrants from all
over the country, the city is also home to a robust queer comedy scene. Founded
in 1982, the Valencia Rose Cabaret in San Francisco was the first gay comedy
club in the United States providing amateur and veteran performers alike a
safe space to perform to queer and queer-friendly audiences. Whoopi Goldberg
along with other comic notables like Karen Ripley, Monica Palacios, and Lea
DeLaria graced the stage at Valencia Rose. When the club shut its doors, the
still-thriving queer comedy scene found its way to Harvey's and Comedy Bo-
dega at Esta Noche where Mosely now performs regularly with Latina lesbian
comedy legend Marga Gomez. It is no surprise then that Mosely caught the
bug for performing comedy while earning her graduate degrees and living in
the Bay area in the late 1990s. Her first foray into comic theater began at Luna
Sea, a women's theater in San Francisco (no longer operating). There she was
exposed to a community of lesbian performers openly discussing issues of race
and sexuality.

> It blew my mind. I didn't realize my mind was getting blown at the time but I
> remember feeling so inspired and excited by it all. And that really opened me up
> to new possibilities of what I could do; that I didn't have to make fun of who I
> am for a community that was outside of my community. So, I didn't have to
> make fun of Black people for a White audience to get a laugh. I didn't have to
> make fun of gay and lesbian people in front of straight audiences to get a laugh.
> Instead I could talk to my communities and laugh, you know, sort of the intra-
> community jokes if you will.[6]

At Luna Sea Theater she hosted a show called *WET* (Women Expressing
Themselves), featuring women of color using all manner of creative means to
express their sexuality and race. During this time, she showcased a series of

sock puppets, all Black lesbian archetypes, some of which are early iterations of the five Black lesbians in her one-woman show *Where My Girls At? A Comedic Look at Black Lesbians* (2008–). Developed over a period of time, Mosely crafts these characters to address issues important to Black lesbians such as feeling like an outlier in the African American community or the LGBTQ community being generalized as White. In either situation, Black lesbians are ignored or go unnoticed. Because of this, Mosely makes providing representations of Black lesbians, where there are few, and documenting where Black lesbians are absent from history a central priority in her charged humor.

It is both common and natural to seek identification with the characters and identities represented in visual culture—you can see yourself in them: they are courageous like you are, they have character flaws and defects like you know you have, they are queer or Black or differently abled like you are, and so on. But what happens when identification is based upon false constructs such as stereotypes about marginalized groups or equally as troubling, when members of minority groups are not represented at all? How do we cope when we do not see ourselves represented anywhere? In *Where My Girls At? A Comedic Look at Black Lesbians*, Micia Mosely offers a counternarrative to the dearth of opportunities available to the public to identify with Black lesbian subjectivities. The show's interactive format encourages identification with any or all of the Black lesbians she portrays. Mosely invites audience members to coconstruct the performance by evaluating each character, and ultimately selecting one as the "winner" of the show.

This analysis begins with the crisis of the ideal or the problems arising when society's social ideal excludes gender nonconforming women and members of minority communities. When a community has little visibility and what little visibility we have is fraught with stereotypes, there are few alternatives: ignore or opt-out (read: stop consuming), accept the representation (read: continue consuming), or as performance studies scholar Jose Esteban Muñoz suggests, find a way to refigure such representations, what he calls disidentification (read: continue consuming but with a twist). There are many strategies useful for accomplishing the latter, or reading oneself back into a script in which one was never cast, a way of buying into the ideal (the images and identities upheld as most desirable) without conforming to that ideal. Examination of Mosely's performance texts and series of interviews reveal the objectives behind her production of charged humor (be it stand-up comedy or her one-woman show) and address the pressure and fluctuating desire she feels to represent the diversity of members in Black lesbian communities. The one-woman show, *Where My Girls At?* creates multiple transgressive representations of Black lesbians that prompt audiences to identify with the Other, expanding the ability of non-Black lesbians to identify with Black lesbian subjectivities and to establish important points of connection between communities and across categories of difference. For Black lesbian audience members, Mosely's one-woman show offers a rare occasion to see members of their communities represented, a chance to identify with representations that look and sound more like they do. In this way, Mosely's humor entices and solicits members of the dominant culture to learn to identify with the social, political, and cultural conditions of her life, offering opportunities to inform and mobilize constituents beyond their respective communities. Mosely's charged humor is a clarion call to connect across identity categories and to demonstrate the way identity for everyone is often a braided set of identifiers. We may not share all identity categories, but we do share the task of managing multiple categories of identity. Thus, it is humor production that shifts the dominant pattern (read: produced by men but meant for everyone) of humor consumption by forging a connection between the audience and the many Black lesbians she portrays in her show.

The Crisis of the Ideal

The history of audience reception to performance is full of solicitation, cues for applause, laugh tracks, and coercion, all aimed at training audiences to identify with a narrow, though dominant contingent of the public. Black stand-up comic and entrepreneur Darryl Littleton, also the author of *Black Comedians on Black Comedy: How African Americans Taught Us to Laugh*, reported in an interview on National Public Radio that his research unearthed evidence of such coercion when theaters became integrated in the early twentieth century. Performance venues allowed both Black and White patrons to frequent the same establishment at the same time though not in the same sections (Black folks were confined to theater balconies or back row equivalents). Black patrons watching vaudeville, minstrelsy, and musical comedies were laughing at different parts of the performance than White patrons. Whether a product of social discomfort or unease, an indication that Whites were not "getting it" or did not understand what was funny, or simply a matter of power, theater managers instructed Black patrons to wait to laugh until White patrons cued them to do so.[7] Cuing laughter and the need to do so assumes that the author and/or performer dictates the terms of what counts as humorous (read: I will tell you when it is time to laugh). Not laughing or laughing in moments not intended to be comical (though they are) are ways that audiences have historically asserted themselves, revealing comic frames particular to minority communities. The passage of time has not altogether outmoded social instruction aimed at dictating audience response. Live studio audience responses are still cued. Both comedy specials broadcast on television and traditional sitcoms include fake laugh tracks to indicate where home viewers can locate the funny.

In other ways too, we are still inundated with tacit (and sometimes not so tacit) social instruction, especially about which social identities are valuable in this society. The presence or absence of certain identities and certain world-views on stage and on screen is instructive. Over time, repeated exposure to the same kinds of representations convince the viewing public that they "know" about someone or an entire community without ever actually coming into contact with individuals or members of that group. A paucity of representations speaks just as loudly and can be equally informative about the value of certain identities relative to a white heterosexual ideal. In most of mainstream visual culture (e.g., film, television, theater) brown faces will watch white faces rule the roost, save the day, and bring home the bacon. When we do see representations of queer folks, people of color, and people who are differently abled, they become narrative device for evoking pity, hope, or triumph and few of these protagonists emerge with their humanity intact. Ubiquitous in visual culture, representations fostering a White, heterosexual, able-bodied, affluent, and male-centric ideal are meted generously to the public. Most would agree that life *is* better when you are White or male or rich or able-bodied or any combination of those dominant categories of identity. In more humorous terms, Louis C.K. jokes: "Seriously if you're not White you're missing out. Because this shit is thoroughly good [*laughter*]. Let me be clearly by the way. I'm not saying that White people are better. I'm saying that being White is clearly better [*laughter*]. Who could even argue [*laughter*]? If it was an option, I'd re-up every year [*laughter*]."[8] The overwhelming number of representations confirming White as ideal, heterosexual as ideal and so on implicitly asks audiences to admire, attain, and achieve that ideal. When categories of difference like being queer or a person of color obviate our ability to conform to that ideal, we are thrown into a crisis—the crisis of the ideal.

How do we make sense of our desire to be like someone that defies our own biology, phenotype, or ability, without negating our own self-worth?

> In a somewhat analogous fashion, queer desires, perhaps desires that negate self, desire for a white beauty ideal, are reconstituted by an ideological component that tells us that such modalities of desire and desiring are too self-compromising. *We thus disidentify with the white ideal. We desire it but desire it with a difference* [italics mine].[9]

One resolution, as Jose Esteban Muñoz points out, is to disidentify or "desire it [white ideal] with a difference," which foregoes wholesale adoption of the ideal. As we consume we also refigure the ideal, simultaneously understanding its cultural currency while making it meaningful and relevant to our own lives, identities, and worldviews. It becomes a way Others can reevaluate coded meanings that exclude them, recycling and reshaping those meanings in order to feel included. This strategy is neither assimilationist (desiring to be like) nor antiassimilationist (desiring to be different); rather, a buy-in strategy offering "the minoritarian subject a space to situate itself in history and thus seize social agency," a way in that makes use of dominant ideologies while maintaining a critical distance.[10] For example, I have always enjoyed rap music, a genre also having a reputation for being misogynist. When I hear the terms "bitch" and "ho" bandied about in the lyrics of a rap song, I know they are talking about me because I am a woman. However, I practice a kind of sex-blind application when it comes to using pejoratives like cunt, dick, bitch, slut, and so on. and I reserve those terms for anyone (male or female) acting in a manner deserving of such an epithet. So, when rap artist Ludacris, in his song "Move Bitch," repeatedly intones: "Move bitch, get out the way, get out the way bitch, get out the way," I do not imagine he is addressing me or women specifically, but any bitch (male or female) who is in his way. Perhaps it should matter to me whether Ludacris intends to disparage women, but if I only consumed visual and material culture created to empower women or queer folks, my options would be sorely lacking, especially since I can only take folk music for so long. Instead, I revise the substance of the text in ways that confer agency.

There are other strategies for coping with cultural invisibility or with a visibility that caricatures marginalized categories of identity. One such strategy includes harnessing popular cultural forms allowing for self-determination in creating better representations. Stand-up comics use charged humor to that effect—that is, communicating messages about their lives and beliefs in ways that dispel cultural myths and omissions. Comedy can explore experiences and points of view arising from a performer's sociological marginality, using the stage to call attention to the conditions of their otherness. Performance studies professor E. Patrick Johnson argues that "black performance provides a space for black culture to reveal itself to itself—to come to know itself, in the process of doing."[11] Johnson works to articulate Black performance as its own way(s) of knowing and just as usefully, as its own way of resisting mechanisms of oppression. Comedy also provides a space for identification between audience members and performers, making this kind of performance a useful one to combat the crisis of the ideal. There is power in this exchange between audience and performers and therein lies the potential to humanize, to educate, to instruct, and to laugh (sometimes about serious matters). In a filmed interview with Jennifer Corday at the Dinah Shore Classic in Palm Springs, California, Kate Clinton said, "I think people hear things that they might not ordinarily hear if they are laughing."[12] Micia Mosely agrees that comedy allows her a "smoother way in" and an inoffensive means of disseminating ideas and messages.

I use my comedy to open people, so that I can plant a seed. That's really it. It's like when you're laughing, there's a release. You don't have time to clam up because it's a natural physical thing. So you're open and releasing and laughing. I plant something so that when you draw that breath of air back in and when you take it all back up, part of what you're taking up is a message, is a consciousness, is a framework, is an awareness, is something that will stick with you longer than if I just preached and preached and preached. . . . To me, every opportunity I have to interact with someone outside myself is an opportunity to do my comedy and to do my political, social, intellectual work. It's all the same.[13]

Additionally, comic performances allow her "to speak openly about those things [sex and sexuality], not conflict them, but really tease out the issues, and help us understand who we are and how we can be in the world."[14] Charged humor like this works to unite minority audiences and expose audiences to alternative viewpoints and experiences. This kind of information affects core belief systems, which ultimately feed the way we participate in various systems (e.g., political, social, sexual, religious) and how we consume humor in the future.

Performing stand-up comedy for over twenty years, African American Melanie Comarcho arrived on the scene in the early 1990s along with hordes of other comic hopefuls. Although she maintains a professional career in comedy and opened for Martin Lawrence and Katt Williams on national tours, the content of her comedy—blue but charged prowoman humor—may explain why Comarcho opened for Williams who started performing nearly a decade after she began, instead of the other way around.

Where my independent women at? Make some noise independent women. [*Clapping and hooting*] . . . We representing in this new millennium. . . . Ain't nothing we can't do. Ain't nothing is a mission impossible for an independent woman, hello! [*clapping*]. Please. I done took a $1000, paid the rent, light, gas, phone bill, bought a bag of weed, half a tank of gas, AND still had $20 left [*laughter*]. You better ask some goddamn body. Still had twenty dollars left. You gotta ask somebody. Matter of fact, the only mission only came close to being impossible was finding a good man with some good credit, a good job, and some good dick. Hello? [*loud clapping and laughter*]. Now that's a damn mission impossible, shit.[15]

Situating herself as an independent woman, she invites women viewers to vocalize their support and identification with this identity: financially solvent, smart, and capable. Comarcho interrupts and dispels assumptions people have about Black women as gold diggers and welfare queens, and Micia Mosely does the same in her stand-up comedy with assumptions made about lesbians:

Dating is hard when you're a lesbian because people make assumptions. Some folks look at lesbians like me and think we want to be men and do traditional masculine things like carry stuff and fix stuff. Not true. We are sensible people, with sensible shoes. I myself am a lazy lesbian. I'm not interested in all of that active stuff. Like I wear pants almost every day and people confuse the wearing of slacks with some manly motions. So if I'm in the club people assume oh I'm wearing the pants, so I'm buying the drink. . . . No, I'm not. Ladies you will be very thirsty waiting for me to buy you a drink. I'm a 21st-century lesbian.[16]

Both of these jokes function to set the record straight. Not all women need nor want men to take care of them and butch lesbians are neither imitating men nor attempting to woo women using traditionally male methods. These jokes access a new reality, replace cultural fictions, and offer robust representations of formerly maligned or invisible communities.

Comics can use humor to explain the way they see the world, or how they un-see the world as the case may be. This might translate into a complete absence of rhetorical marginality as with Ellen DeGeneres or Bill Cosby, neither of whom use their marginalized subjectivity to inform the content and topics in their stand-up routines. It can also translate into a presentation of self playing into and on stereotypes circulating about that category of difference like Rita Rudner's (White) glorification of women as ditzy shopaholics dependent on men for survival or Ant's (White, gay) hyperbolic effeminacy on stage. Or this may come in the form of humor challenging erroneous and limiting depictions of certain social identities like the jokes by Mosely and Comarcho or in the form of humor that revises language, labels, and terms meant to disparage and subordinate. Chris Rock revises the word "faggot" in his concert film *Chris Rock: Kill the Messenger,* and much like I do with slurs aimed at women, argues that anyone can be a faggot. In other words, he contends that this appellation has little to do with queer identity and more to do with one's personal character or behaviors. Louis C.K. does something similar with the word "cunt":

A lot of words, they're not bad words. No words are bad but some people start using 'em a lot to hurt other people and then they become bad. . . . There's words that I love that I can't use because other people use them wrong to hurt other people. Like the word "cunt" is a beautiful word [*scattered laughter*]. To me, there's just beauty in that word. I mean aesthetically [*some clapping and cheers*]. It's like chocolaty and round on the ends [*laughter*]. Cunt. I just like the way it sounds. And I don't use it as an insult. . . . I would never call a woman a cunt, except my mom because she likes it for some weird reason [*laughter*]. But, it's a very misused word. It's supposed to mean vagina, which I don't think works at all because vaginas are so sweet. They're little pretty things with little flower petal lips [*laughter*]. I hear a piccolo in my head every time I see a vagina [*roaring laughter*].[17]

Whoopi Goldberg, along with many other comics, refigures the term "nigger," modeling her particular relationship to the term. While many people are decidedly opposed to saying "nigger" and consider it a "bad" word, Goldberg spins it this way in *The World According to Whoopi!*, a comedy special filmed at the The Rose Nagelberg Theatre and airing on Bravo in 2007:

> See it's not bad to me because I don't know any [niggers] and I've never been one [*sustained laughter, clapping, and cheers*]. So when I hear somebody say it, I don't turn around [*laughter*] because I know they're not talking to me. But apparently other people don't feel like that.[18]

At times, comedy offers rhetorical refutation of how we are represented in dominant culture, simultaneously suggesting alternatives for how viewers can remake meaning in the world around them.

The self-determination that comes of performing via a cultural form allowing for self-authorship like stand-up comedy can still be thwarted by promotional and marketing decisions that determine where and when comics can perform. Industry veteran Melanie Comarcho says, "As the black female comedian I can do the black night in any club in the country, but when it comes to a white night where there's a white audience, they're not putting us in those slots."[19] For Comarcho, this means that the audiences most likely to benefit are least likely to be exposed to her revisionist charged humor. Self-determination is even less available to women and minority actors in the film and television industry because they have little control over how they are represented to the viewing public. Minority performers face myriad obstacles when pursuing careers in acting. In theater and film, directors are more likely to cast White folks in the lead roles for fear of losing their mainly White patrons and if precious few meaty roles exist for White women, there are far fewer available allowing women of color to express the complexity of their identities and experiences. The roles that do exist for women of color are epitomized by the docile asexual Mammy, the hypersexualized gold digging Jezebel, or hypercritical overbearing Sapphire caricatures.[20] To combat these stock characters, Sabrina Lamb, a Black actress, turned to stand-up comedy and eventually to writing so she could exercise control over how she is portrayed—not an unusual trajectory for any performer, regardless of the categories of difference they occupy, seeking to exercise autonomy over their presentation of self.[21]

> After receiving offers for other roles where I was asked to be a Caucasian man's wet dream, and wondering who wrote this script, I began to ask myself, "How do I flip this script?" The answer came: "By writing the images myself." From

these pathetic experiences my writing career was fueled, and I joined the small cadre of black comedienne-writers. We as black women are still marginalized, fighting against Mammy, Sapphire, and Foxy Mama stereotypes. And in today's book market, where sitcom stardom is almost essential for a lucrative book deal, it is not surprising that African American comediennes, without sufficient opportunities in television, are also conspicuously absent in publishing. . . . Hopefully, more black comediennes will take the publishing plunge and put in print images created for us and by us.[22]

Micia Mosely echoes Lamb's frustration about the roles available to Black women when she says sadly: "I don't know what a Black comedic lead looks like in terms of someone who is also a comedienne."[23] Lamb, Mosely, and other Black women humorists are in quite a bind. They use comedy and writing in order to educate, endorse multiculturalism, and illumine shared human connections. But, even if this eventually yields name recognition or fame enough to place them in film or television, they are still most likely to be limited to the prevailing Black female stock characters.

This dilemma—that is, either a lack of roles altogether or only roles that advance negative or limiting perceptions about minority groups—affected Whoopi Goldberg, who has had a conflicting relationship with film. Enjoying newfound popularity after the success of *The Spook Show* (later titled *Whoopi Goldberg Live*)—a one-woman show that made it to Broadway (1984–1985) wherein Goldberg transformed into an array of characters to deliver politicized messages—film producers sought to place Goldberg in their films. Without a comic persona lending itself to any cinematic archetype (in main, because her comic persona does not replicate stock characters such as the lusty busty babe or overbearing mother-type), placement in traditional film roles became a difficult task. This made for an interesting film career wherein producers cast Goldberg as peripheral characters that both embodied and broke from stereotypical Black characters. As film and media studies scholar Bambi Haggins notes, Goldberg is someone "who occupies a space in the entertainment worlds that, as much as possible, she defines (or tries to define)."[24] Because Goldberg does not fit standard archetypes for Black women, she continues to have to carve out a niche for her comic persona using the stage, radio, film, and television (she is currently the moderator and cohost of the television talk show, *The View*) to champion human rights. Likewise, Mosely knows that there is no place (yet) for her to land as a funny Black woman in the mainstream. Aware of the difficult road that lies ahead, she continues to utilize comedy as a course of action in efforts aimed at social justice. While there is not a huge market for Black women's comedic nonfiction, Sabrina Lamb has managed to join a small number of Black women comedy writers able to publish such as Nikki Giovanni,

Mo'Nique Hicks, Bertrice Berry, Whoopi Goldberg, Kim Coles, René Hicks, and Jedda Jones.

Poet and civil rights activist Audre Lorde points out that stereotypes occur and are self-sustaining due to the process by which we learn to understand and read differences.

> Institutionalized rejection of difference is an absolute necessity in a profit economy which needs outsiders as surplus people. As members of such an economy, we have *all* been programmed to respond to human difference in one of three ways: ignore it, and if that is not possible, copy it if we think it is dominant, or destroy it if we think it is subordinate. But we have no patterns for relating across our human differences as equals. As a result, those differences have been misnamed and misused in the service of separation and confusion.[25]

Lorde's use of the verb "destroy" is more metaphorical than literal when it comes to responding to human difference, and in this case "destroy" can mean a willingness to "buy" into one's comic persona. In other words, as consumers we reject positions and worldviews that counter what we think we already know is true. Many individuals, regardless of their social positions, will opt to identify with and therefore ensure the success of comics representing the dominant culture and also mimic comic performers exhibiting the traits and characteristics of the social locations bearing dominance. Comics using charged humor or conscientious rhetorical marginality (comedy that draws from their sociological marginality) will have difficulty selling their comedy material because the general public has little incentive or prior experience in identifying with or understanding human difference. The public will consume what they understand, what looks familiar, and that which is closest in proximity to power and dominance. If the familiar includes stereotypical versions of an Other, then this is the image that will profit in this economy. It factors into the success (or lack thereof) of any comic using charged humor with regularity on stage, making it a difficult pursuit for Micia Mosely and the cadre of women of color and lesbians seeking to use the stage to establish a professional career *and* redress the balance.

To be accurate, the dominant culture does demonstrate a willingness to consume humor produced by racial/ethnic and sexual minorities; however, consumption of this humor tends to favor the comics who project and reify stereotypes (what I call modern-day minstrelsy). Entertainment, such as sketch comedy or stand-up comedy, can challenge bigotry as much as it can play a pivotal and lasting role in the maintenance of stereotypes and nativist sentiments. But, as I argue throughout, charged humor contesting social inequality is simply not, at least in the last thirty years, as commercially viable as the comedy reaffirming racist, ableist, sexist, and homophobic tropes. Televised comedy routinely depicts and audiences appear to enjoy humor that confirms our worst suspicions about Others, like this joke performed by White comic Daniel Tosh which delighted the audience:

> I have no problem with illegal immigration in this country except for the fact that they don't serve on jury duty [*laughter*]. That's horse shit. It should be the other way around: they should serve exclusively on jury duty [*laughter and clapping*]. Then it finally would be a jury of one's own peers [*laughter*]. It's not a stereotype if it's always true [*laughter*]. Yeah . . . then it becomes law. That joke is called Latinos are criminals [*laughter*]. [26]

Tosh perpetuates cultural beliefs about Latinos/as that when corroborated by multiple sources begins to inform social treatment and public policy, not to mention the impact this can have on individual self-efficacy and communal pride. People must enjoy this stuff for a variety of reasons, otherwise the jokes and the comics telling them would not be so successful. To counter such beliefs that circulate en masse, artists and entertainers will play with and combat the signifiers used to subordinate them (these could be words like "nigger" or "queer," or stereotypes like all Latinos/as are criminals and/or undocumented). However, a joke meant to challenge the veracity of stereotypes can be misread and instead function to confirm the stereotype. The dilemma of audience reception, rather, the inability to control how material is interpreted by consumers, poses a weighty concern to most comic performers who seek success but not at the expense of the community to which they belong. Dave Chappelle canceled the wildly popular *Chappelle's Show* that lampooned stereotypes about Black people because he was concerned that viewers were misinterpreting his efforts to subvert stereotypes and reading his comic material as a reinforcement of those stereotypes. Even if stereotypes are introduced as cultural myths we cannot say with certainty that viewers will not misinterpret performances to fulfill rather than challenge existing beliefs, to reinforce rather than raze stereotypes. It takes careful work to qualify and contextualize authorial intent to ensure that reception corresponds to intent and it is a difficult task for one person to undo years of cultural programming.

Stand-up comedy, performance art, and other forms of comic performance allow performance artists the opportunity to write and perform original material based on their personal experiences and lives. This holds great appeal given the limited roles available to women of any race or ethnicity. Comic performers, like Micia Mosely and other charged comics referenced can challenge the crisis of the ideal in two important ways. First, by using humor to mock the conventions of representation, that is, exposing negative representations as artifice. Comics have been doing this for decades. A stand-up comic who was just as well known for his role as Fred Sanford in *Sanford and Son* (1972–1977),

Redd Foxx jokes: "I carry a knife now because I read in a white magazine that all Black people carry knives [*laughter*]. So I rushed out and bought me one [*laughter*]."[27] Cleverly, Foxx turns this negative representation on its head, showing the influence the media has on shaping behavior and personal beliefs. Having no inclination to be violent or carry a weapon, Foxx internalizes this media message and strives to fulfill the magazine's dictums about Black people. He shows that he was not born but rather comes to embody White people's fears at their own behest.

A second way of challenging the crisis of the ideal comes of offering personal experiences and worldviews as counternarratives, that is, this is what a real Black lesbian thinks about, dreams about, laughs about, and so forth. Mosely addresses both strategies in her stand-up comedy:

> Now in my stand up I try to switch things around a bit. *I want to throw stuff back in people's faces and get the mainstream to laugh at their limits and problematize their reality, while still centering my experience* [italics mine]. For example, they may have no Black friends and that's o.k. I have no choice but to befriend White folks if I want social and economic capital. No White friends is like a tax. What's the penalty for Whites not having Black friends? Nothing.[28]

Here, she refers to one of her staple charged jokes, a variation of which is this:

> Let this be a call to the rest of you, if you only have one Black friend, I need you to add some. Not on facebook, on facetofacebook. It's a new network called *real life* and there is no app for it. I feel like if you are the only Black friend of a White person, you need to charge them. Because it's a lot of pressure and extra work.[29]

She entreats us to not only to think critically about institutional forces shape our social circles and networks, but to unpack the cultural and economic dimensions of interracial friendships. In doing so, she lays bare structures of power and privilege that will hit home for some and anger others. She concludes the bit by saying:

> If you're gonna ask me about Barack Obama, or Lebron James you need to buy me lunch. Wanna know what we really talk about when you're not around: put a couple of Benjamins on my student loans. Even that example! I gave you some 1990s Black slang. That's historical and Black; you should be paying double for that! I'm speaking for all the Black friends that you should have but don't. We are a whole race of people and we don't come cheap. Remember this is 2011 not 1811, so ain't no Black people working for free, you feel me. Matter of fact if you want another joke it will cost you beer and make it an import 'cause I'm educated and I have passport![30]

Charged performances serve as an open challenge to the negative representations manufactured and disseminated widely in mainstream media. Even
more importantly, though, charged comedy offers Others an opportunity to
identify with an experience of second-class citizenship and a representation
that looks familiar and dynamic. Just as in her stand-up comedy, this is what
Micia Mosely was up to when she wrote *Where My Girls At? A Comedic Look at
Black Lesbians*. When I asked her what kind of impact she hoped people got
from watching her perform, her face got serious as she replied: "I'm . . . really
trying to get them [characters in *Where My Girls At?*] to be seen by as many
different audiences, so that people can see themselves *in the characters* and see
people in the Black lesbian community that they may not really have a chance
to intimately interact with, because they either don't know the women in their
lives *are* lesbians, or they just don't know any at all."[31]

Where My Girls At?

Women use performance art and other kinds of solo performance like stand-
up comedy because it allows them the freedom to step outside the constraints
of formal theater, television, and film where they are largely undervalued and
underrepresented. With budgetary constraints and little funding for the performing arts in general, solo performance is also more financially feasible to
produce than other kinds of theatrical productions. Like Micia Mosely, Gloria
Bigelow, an African American lesbian comic, wants her comedy to offer representations where there are few to none. She says, "Growing up I didn't have,
I didn't see lesbians around that looked like me or that I could relate to or that
I knew. So I'd like for people to say like, 'That's a dyke we haven't seen before.' "[32]
Similarly, Sabrina Matthews, a White lesbian comic, expresses the desire to see
more diverse representations: "I have a vision of a nonpigeonholed show, like I
would love to be a character somewhat like myself in a show that represented
people that actually existed."[33] The opportunity to showcase their own marginalized identities becomes a means, albeit on a small scale, of offering a unique
representation to consumers.

The premise of Micia Mosely's one-woman show, *Where My Girls At? A Comedic Look at Black Lesbians*, is the creation of a new reality television series called
Black Beauty: America's Next Top Negress where a house full of Black women will
compete for this title. The show opens with Vanessa, the show's producer, introducing the concept and positioning the audience as casting directors assisting
the producer with selecting the winning contestant who will move on to live in
the mansion and compete for the title of America's Next Top Negress. To ensure
diversity, the show devotes its energies to securing at least one Black lesbian to
move into the house. The audience meets four Black lesbians, first viewing their
submission tapes and then seeing each one perform a monologue. In the iteration

I filmed in the Laboratory Theater at the Clarice Smith Performing Arts Center at the University of Maryland (UMD), the audience was divided into three sections, each one charged with the task of ranking each contestant on a scale of 1–10 (1=lowest; 10=highest) for one of three categories: blackness, woman-ness, and lesbian-ness. Other iterations of the performance have played with how these rankings occur sometimes having the entire audience as a whole rank for each category, other times dissecting the audience into three sections with each focusing on a specific category, and recent iterations have divided the audience into three sections while also electing a section leader who has a few moments to talk over the ranking with audience members in their group. Before the decision is made, the audience has an opportunity to ask the four contestants any questions that may help them determine their rankings and ultimately decide who is sent to the house. The contestant with the highest-ranking score over-all is determined by the strength of applause and audible feedback for each identity category.

While the show's producer, Vanessa, is also a lesbian and pivotal to the performance, her character is peripheral to the four contestants showcased throughout the performance. She functions more as narrator or interlocutor, instructing the audience, laying out the show's premise, leading the question and answer (Q&A) portion of the show at the end and determining the winner based on audience feedback. Each of the four contestants are tasked with answering the same series of questions, some of which are: "what makes you the woman that you are?"; "what makes my blackness beautiful?"; "what do you enjoy most about your lifestyle?"[34] They respond to the questions differently, some adhering to them with due diligence and others abandoning the questions and speaking candidly with the audience about some aspect of their life. The audience meets Playher first, a rowdy Casanova who interactively teaches the audience basic rules of "roll[ing] to the club" such as not going alone, not going with an ex-girlfriend, having gum on hand, and how to approach someone attractive or desirable.[35] Ziggy is the only character whose full name we are told—Zigawella Washington—which is emblematic of her precision and attention to details. Her response to how her blackness is beautiful begins:

> First, I want to acknowledge that the notion of blackness is a complicated one. It's important to recognize that race is a social construct with complicated histories as to its scientific and political formation. Whether you are talking about 18th century [Johann Friedrich] Blumenbach or 20th century [Karl Gunnar] Myrdal the whole notion of race wasn't even entirely based on color.[36]

This character, a popular one on college campuses, is highly analytical and self-reflexive. She is the mouthpiece for Black intelligentsia, incorporating key critical race theories, and exploring the dilemmas of interracial and intersexual coalition building.

Where Ziggy is the youngest of the contestants, Sistah is the oldest of the four as a youthful fifty-something who responds to potential surprise at her age saying, "Children, you see Black don't crack."[37] She uses her vibrant and charming personality to lead the audience in an abbreviated yoni (vulva) power workshop, drumming and coaxing the audience to find their own yoni power. The fourth and final contestant, Lady D, chooses to express an empowered femininity and uses her stage time to bring several volunteers forward in order to give them pointers on tapping into and "help[ing] them see their fabulousness."[38] Micia Mosely deftly moves from one character to another, and the most impressive feat is the Q & A portion when audience members pose questions to any of the four contestants. Mosely sits on a single chair in the middle of the stage and with no time lapses or signifying props, she slips in and out of characters answering the questions as different contestants, even having arguments, interruptions, and interactions between the various contestants. If you close your eyes, you could hardly guess that one woman generates this fiery and fast-paced repartee among four very different women.

In *Where My Girls At? A Comedic Look at Black Lesbians*, performer and audience coconstitute. Each iteration requires audience members to determine the show's outcome, thus the winning contestant varies from one performance to the next. Audience members are apprised of their role in this performance, a maneuver asking that they invest on some level in the performance. This participation in the outcome ensures that most audience members engage with the performance. Importantly, she hopes that throughout the show viewers will connect or identify with one or more of the Black lesbian contestants regardless of whether they occupy different or identical categories of difference. The audience at the performance held at UMD elected Sistah to win and move on to be in the faux reality television show. To date, every contestant has won at least once, but Playher and Sistah have the strongest record of wins, with Playher as the high-scorer. That more audiences can connect with Playher is interesting insofar that this character presents perhaps the most stereotypical portrayal of African Americans, complete with a sports jersey, Ebonics, and savvy sexual prowess. Do audiences find Playher the most recognizable of the four lesbian characters or do they simply enjoy her jive talk, party spirit, and relationship tips? Mosely reports that, based on the feedback she has received thus far, audience members vote in one of two ways: "who they think would actually be fun on the show, like, who they would want to watch if there was going to be a reality TV show, or it's who they feel the most comfortable with, and who they feel they've made a connection with. It's not always clear what that connection is."[39] Mosely does not presume the manifold ways viewers can connect to Playher, Ziggy, Lady D, and Sistah but does understand the importance that these connections have on the outcome (determining a winner) of the show.

On some level, Micia Mosely believes that her performance acumen for each character affects the outcome of the show; while the audience makes the decision, how she performs contributes to the final verdict delivered by viewers. When Lady D could not claim a single win after many performances, she focused on rewriting the character. Since Ziggy stopped winning the show (after a few wins during the first years of production) and Lady D, Playher, and Sistah repeatedly won audience affection, Mosely rescripted Ziggy to enhance her appeal. This refiguring of Ziggy is done in concert with the audience over time as she performs various versions of Ziggy to arrive at a winning persona, meaning Mosely and audience coconstruct and character revisions are coconstituted by Mosely and her audience. According to Mosely,

> It's the balance of staying true to their [each character] message and identity and "forcing" people to like them and see their reality. At the very least I want the audience to find the characters interesting regardless of difference. I also want each character to have an equal chance of winning. Personally I had a goal of affirming that my feminine expression "works" for an audience and since I'm so close to Ziggy I wanted to know that my past could be affirmed by mainstream audiences. I'm over that now, but five years ago it was really important to me.[40]

While I understand Mosely's vision that each character could be equally likeable, I do wonder why it is important for each Black lesbian to appeal to the audience and what the pedagogical and performance values are for creating characters that may not appeal to audience members. It could be equally instructive having a less popular character because this presents viewers with the opportunity to grapple with their dislike for the character. This may be particularly effective in this show where contestants are evaluated on their blackness, woman-ness and lesbian-ness because it would illumine where identification failed among specific categories of identity, forcing viewers to think more complexly about difference. While the show unapologetically celebrates Black lesbian identity, Mosely's reliance on audience feedback to revise the characters means that over time we might actually be celebrating other people's fantasies of Black lesbian subjectivity. When it comes to "getting it right," the question becomes whether you *can* get it right and whether or not you need to. Regardless of Mosely's intentions, her characters remain subject to interpretation, meaning they can still be read as recapitulating stereotypes. But if you know anything about her, you would know this is not her intention.

Black lesbian audience members attending *Where My Girls At?* indicate they are highly invested in any widely disseminated images of themselves. In turn, Micia Mosely conveys deference to the opinions and feedback from Black lesbian communities for whom she frequently performs. She is clear that the agenda here is "making fun of it [Black lesbians] in a way that's: 'Isn't life funny? Look at how much we're just like everybody else and look at how different we are, isn't life funny?' kind of a way."[41] Karen Williams, a Black lesbian comic performer, notes that the lesbian audiences she performs for "are knowledgeable, wise and informed, and you cannot put junk in front of them. They're not havin' it."[42] It is important to please your audience, but more than that Mosely has a sense of duty to represent Black lesbians fairly, respectfully, and accurately. They too are invested in her representations because members of other communities are attending her shows as well and making judgments and inferences based on her representations.

> I find that Black lesbians talk about these characters very different than anyone else because it's, it feels more like a "You got this right, you didn't get this right." It's a particular kind of investment. I'm going to go out on a limb and say that there aren't a whole lot of comedies about Black lesbians out there rolling around in theaters. You know, I don't know everything, but I'm guessing there aren't a whole lot. So, I think when people see this, internally I think people can get what we're up to in terms of documenting who we are, and they want to make sure we get it right. So when I say they talk about it in very different ways, the content isn't always different, but the way they talk about it . . . there is a sense of entitlement and you need to get this right.[43]

Some of their concerns are exaggerating stereotypes for a laugh, misrepresentations, and a lack of character complexity, all of which Mosely carefully attends to by soliciting feedback from her community via audience evaluations, talkbacks, and postshow discussions with audiences. Professor and cultural critic bell hooks notes that "attention to the politics of representation has been crucial for colonized groups globally in the struggle for self-determination" and encourages readers not to ignore the political power representations have to alter material circumstances.[44] This is a central concern for Mosely, and throughout the course of the show's tenure, she came to realize just how deeply invested fellow Black lesbians were in how they are represented, making it all the more imperative for Mosely to "get this right." Because she uses her own life to develop these characters and write this show, Mosely draws directly from her own Black lesbian subjectivity, a lived experience that informs the presentation of each character in her one-woman show.

Audience surveys collected include one open-ended question: "What did you enjoy about the show?" and space is reserved at the bottom for any additional comments audience respondents may have regarding the show, talkback, performer, and so forth. Common responses to the question generally express appreciation for the diversity and variety of characters portrayed: "I love the variety of people being represented"; I loved all the characters and how rich they were"; "They all represented very different black women"; "The wide

range of characters"; "The number of personalities and social issues she so skill-
fully displayed"; "Insightful characters." One respondent wrote "1 woman=all
women," which seems to indicate that Mosely's intentions to draw connections
among Black lesbians, between Black lesbians and other women, and between
Black lesbians and any person, were successfully conveyed to that individual.
Audience feedback from many shows indicates that she is offering well-conceived
depictions of Black lesbians.

Professor of gender studies L. H. Stallings states: "Black stand-up comedy . . . is an unacknowledged queer space that African American women have
been manipulating for their very own drag performances meant to annihilate
heteronormative prescriptions of gender and sexuality."[45] Mosely does this and
in the process expands what it means to be Black or gay or any other category
of difference. Because Mosely does not identify as exclusively Black or exclusively lesbian or exclusively woman, she uses charged humor to tease out a
braided set of identifiers, simultaneously acknowledging that these identifiers
are mutable. As part of her monologue, Ziggy interrogates the language of
sexuality in order to locate herself. Unhappy with the term "queer" because it
"means strange" and dissatisfied with the term "lesbian" because it is "derived
from women who lived on a Greek Island" and does not reflect her African
heritage, Ziggy prefers the term "woman-loving-woman, because it says who I
am and what I do."[46] Acknowledging the power of words to create, construct,
and confine, Ziggy defines herself and simultaneously offers the audience a
means of interpellating her—in and on her own terms. Ziggy's race and sexuality inform her preference for how she identifies. In this instance, audience
members are groomed to consider how her blackness and lesbian-ness intersect. Mosely works to complicate the intersection of these categories of difference and to train audience members to identify with queered *and* raced individuals. Each persona (e.g., Ziggy, Lady D, Playher, and Sistah) has qualities
making her relatable beyond the Black lesbian community. Identification with
one or all four of the main Black lesbian subjectivities portrayed expands, humanizes, and combats the flattening/reductionary work of stereotypes, which
helps to inform and mobilize (coalition building) constituents beyond their
respective communities.

Having filmed the show and spoken with Micia Mosely at length for many
years about her performance and career choices, it is clear that her objectives
remain consistent for *Where My Girls At?*, which are to insert voices and representations where there are few to none: "I think that what I seek to do in my
comedy whether it be my stand-up or in the show is to really create space for
myself and people like me. Because I feel like the more we do that for different
kinds of people then everyone gets to move through the world feeling normal,
feeling represented and being represented."[47] She works hard to make sure

these characters do not turn into caricatures, capitalizing on existing stereo-types about Black women or lesbians. As she typically does, during the talk-back at UMD, following the performance, she shares with the audience some of her goals for the show:

> I want people to have access to seeing variety in whatever way they can. When I make the choice to do that through comedy, when we look at most comedy you're automatically, you're kind of on that fine line whenever you decide to re-ally go there with comedy: Are you offending people? Is it political or is it just offensive? Is it a stereotype, is it a caricature? . . . For me, I'm much more inter-ested that people are able to have a conversation and look at the world differ-ently so the next time they see someone, who they may not have ever seen on the metro they can actually see that person. With Lady D, that people can see that there are femme Black women who are lesbians and are very excited about that and don't want to be ignored because they don't show up like Playher. And there's a whole bunch of people who embody Playher and are very proud of who they are and who want to be seen *as women* [emphasis hers] and everybody in between. So, for me, it's really just giving folks a little taste so that we can con-tinue the conversation and expand our notions.[48]

These characters are being consumed. As Mosely says, her characters give au-dience members a "little taste," a phrase that brings to mind bell hooks's essay "Eating the Other: Desire and Resistance," where she argues that commodifi-cation of the Other makes consumption of "difference" analogous to an exotic adventure or a spicy dish.[49] In this instance, though, Mosely gets to be author and producer of that "little taste," and while she cannot undo this tendency, this impulse to eat the Other, she can make sure that what is consumed is well-conceived and crafted with good intentions toward the communities she represents.

The show is purposefully tailored to prompt audience members to consider the intersecting and often-competing subject positions the characters face as Black lesbians. As she said in an interview: "it's not just the gay play, it's not just the Black play, it's, you know, a couple of things coming together. . . . I definitely think people's notions of African American-ness come into play rela-tive to sexuality."[50] The show intentionally introduces some interesting con-cerns about how we judge people based on social categories often treated as discreet such as race, sexuality, and gender. To that effect, the format forces viewers to question how and why they rank contestants according to black-ness, woman-ness, and lesbian-ness, a process Mosely knows will be uncom-fortable for most people and that functions to remind viewers that they live in a society where people do this informally on the daily. For example, Lady D, a highly feminized self-proclaimed diva, scores low for her lesbian-ness. Playher, a butchy heartthrob looking for Miss Right-Now, scores lower for her woman-ness. And Ziggy, a well-spoken, young civic-minded intellectual with a White girlfriend, receives low rankings for her blackness. These rankings reveal assumptions that people have about what it means to be lesbian, female, or Black.

> When one Black person says to another Black person, "you're not Black enough," there's an extra narrative at play that they're then using and internalizing and passing on. So to be able to have that exchange with folks and talk about what it means for them to be in a mostly White college, have people call them not Black enough, and then have them vote that Ziggy gets a "one" on her black-ness, is deep. It's deep and it's important for me that while we're laughing, we're also having those kinds of conversations. . . . And with that particular character [Ziggy], it was important for me for people to recognize the complexity of black-ness, and the complexity of lesbian-ness, and for us not to have to choose—I mean the whole show is definitely about that—but also for people to see differ-ent possibilities of who we are, and who we can be. And a lot of Black women my age in particular get written off depending on what category people put you in. So you're off in the kind of Afro-centric, only ever hang out with people of color, maybe only ever hang out with Black people, kinda Black lesbian. Or you have a White girlfriend and most of your friends are White, and you're very uncomfortable around Black people type of Black lesbian—and that's not lim-ited to lesbians, that's an experience that many Black people have faced. . . . For me, because there's so much marginalization in the larger society, when it comes to Black people and when it comes to gay people, when you're combining those two identities, I really wanted Ziggy to be able to tease out what happened within our community.[51]

These responses to various representations of Black lesbians reveal social limi-tations placed on various identity categories, particularly those grappling with competing and intersecting social identities. Ignoring the multiplicity of the minority subject "is not only theoretically and politically naïve, but also poten-tially dangerous," warns scholars E. Patrick Johnson and Mae Henderson.[52] It is prudent for advertisers, demographers, and politicians alike to understand the dynamism of the populous and the way identity categories intersect. Audi-ence members are challenged to consider how they compartmentalize various categories of difference neglecting to consider those that occupy multiple mar-ginalized subjectivities. Mosely asks her audience to confront their assump-tions about not one, but three intersecting categories of difference.

For Micia Mosely and other minority comic performers using charged hu-mor to enact cultural citizenship, achieving mainstream success *could* change the pattern of consumption of humor by transforming the kinds of humor valued and therefore consumed. In a social setting and cultural climate where

Black lesbians are seldom visible, Mosely's one-woman show gives viewers multiple parties with which to identify. In fact, she compels audience members who are themselves *not* Black lesbians to identify with one, several, or all of the personas developed. This may not be a difficult task, given the title of the performance, its billing, and the typical venues in which Mosely performs such as universities/colleges, performing arts festivals, and identity-based celebrations like gay pride. It is highly likely that those attending the show are willing or easily coaxed to identify with someone unlike them. Higher education and the arts in general boast an aptitude for and desire to promote diversity, so when Mosely performs in these spaces, she is often in good company with like-minded people. She may be preaching to the choir, but repeated exposure to charged comedy that resonates with viewers may render mainstream styles of comedy less satisfying and prompt folks to demand more opportunities to consume charged humor. With enough support from enough people, charged humor could certainly become a more viable commodity in the mainstream.

Post-show audience evaluations gathered from approximately half-a-dozen performances asks respondents to supply the following information: race, age, gender, sexual orientation, and zip code/region. An assessment of these evaluations, indicate that a little over half of the audience identify as members of the LGBTQ community. Even fewer identified themselves specifically as lesbians or dykes (their words). While this hetero-to-homo ratio will certainly vary depending on the performance, it is safe to assume that the majority of audience members will not identify as lesbians, thus are being placed in a position of identifying with someone unlike themselves in terms of sexual orientation. The same evaluations show that approximately forty percent of audience respondents identified as Black, African American, or biracial (with Black denoted as part of their racial makeup). Clearly Micia Mosely is presenting her work to audiences who are not all or even mostly Black lesbians, an aspect of the show that is very important to her.

And politically speaking, obviously, politically and socially and culturally, I want the audience to walk away with a deeper understanding of Black lesbians. Period. You know, I am who I am in the world, and I'm blessed to have so many friends and loved ones and family members who love me for all of who I am, and that is not true for everyone on this planet. There are women and men being beaten and raped and tortured every day because of who they are, because of their sexuality, because of their race, and I can't take my freedom for granted, and if doing this show allows some audience member a different insight into a human being that they may identify with or not identify with initially, then I feel like I'm helping us take a step in the right direction. And given where we are right now with race and sexuality on this planet, I feel like this particular project is very, very important for people to see no matter how you identify, and I want people to connect to the ways that feel appropriate for them and then push themselves a little bit further.[53]

The order of business here is to offer up a wide variety of Black lesbians demonstrating their complexity, dynamism, and diversity. As Jose Esteban Muñoz argues, performance can demonstrate "a politics of hybridity that works within and outside the dominant public sphere, and in doing so contests the ascendant racial, sexual, and class strictures."[54] What Mosely wants people to understand is that "it's *both/and* [italics mine]. It's not either/or."[55] Fellow Black lesbians are able to see parts of them and others in their community represented. Other audience members benefit from this rare access to so many different personalities and characters, all of whom are Black lesbians.

The uber feminine Lady D becomes mouthpiece for Micia Mosely's objectives for the show. Preening and strutting across the stage, she says: "America needs to see this fine example of Black beauty because too many images of the blackness is not beautiful. Or the beauty is not Black. I can give America a new vision of Black beauty à la lesbian-ness."[56] Lady D laments, along with the other characters, that she was not taught to embrace her beauty as Black or as a lesbian. Each of the characters reveals their own struggle to embrace their woman-ness, blackness, and lesbian-ness in a culture rendering Black lesbians invisible. Lady D reports that she had "to reprogram [her] brain" to become the sassy, self-loving woman you see confidently moving around the stage. She goes on: "I don't let anyone question my beauty. I don't let anyone question my intelligence because of my beauty and don't let people question my sexuality because some man may want to fuck me."[57] She shares her special talent—an ability to accessorize—with the audience by selecting several audience members who are then given individualized tips on coming into their own fabulousness. While this instruction is meant to be humorous, Micia Mosely also intends for it to be edifying and to flip the traditional script. How often does a Black lesbian get the chance to serve as role model, fashion expert, and motivational speaker to anyone, let alone members of the dominant culture? Where Lady D demonstrates that being a lesbian and being feminine are not mutually exclusive, Playher reminds the audience that androgynous self-expression does not obviate her woman-ness. She acknowledges that "some of ya'll may not be used to seeing a woman like [her]self" and suggests that the audience watch and learn from her; "I may not wear the heels and the makeup, but you know I *like* the heels and the makeup. But you gotta open your mind. Cause whether America is ready or not, this is a fine example of a Black beauty [indicating herself]."[58] Lady D challenges stereotypes about lesbian aesthetics and Playher challenges heteronormative constructions of femininity.

The performance also serves to temporarily place White and heterosexual patrons in positions similar to the daily experiences of the disenfranchised who are offered entertainment and information from a White straight male perspective. Micia Mosely's performance and presentation of multiple complex Black lesbian subjectivities challenges the crisis of the ideal. Instead, audience members belonging to the dominant culture or occupying positions of social privilege are placed in a position to identify with Black lesbians, temporarily making them cultural outsiders as the various personas draw from in-group humor and experiences. For the Black lesbian who gets to see four comedic representations of Black lesbians, she is (finally) offered an array of personas to identify with versus the typical experience of feeling excluded by virtue of gender, race, and sexuality. Simply by putting out their comedy for consumption, comics like Micia Mosely offer unapologetic performances that defend and celebrate their communities. They offer, to their own communities (and anyone else interested), thoughtful representations commenting on life, laughing at, and ultimately building their respective communities. These alternate representations confront the crisis of the ideal by calling it into question, particularly as they deviate so obviously from the narrow interpretations of gender, race, sexuality, and ability most commonly circulated. In doing so, charged humor and the folks that perform it incrementally challenge and reshape how and in what ways various communities figure into the national imagination.

"I don't want to fight you," says Micia Mosely, "I'm just going to show you something that I hope will turn your views upside down."[59] The conscientious work Micia Mosely does in crafting each character—Ziggy, Lady D, Playher, and Sistah—offers dynamic representations of Black lesbians with which one can identify—as women, as lesbians, and/or as African Americans. During an interview on the day after her performance at UMD, she said candidly:

> So for me it's about expanding those notions in multiple communities and pushing those boundaries so that what we think of as the norm we at least question because it might just simply be the norm that gets presented to us and I feel very, very strongly about the role of history and the media in all of this when it comes to representation. . . . What if Harriet Tubman were a lesbian? And what if she were an out lesbian? . . . Yes, there were lesbians who were enslaved and there were gay men who were enslaved. Like we didn't just pop up after emancipation like: "Oh I think I'll be gay, I'm free," you know [*laughing*]. So how do we change our notions of even our understanding of who we are and where we came from to include the truth of all of who we are and where we came from? So if the documentation has to start in the twenty-first century, fine. . . . But I don't want 200 years from now someone to simply look at whoever they would look at now and think that that's it.[60]

The predominant absence of women of color as leading protagonists in the entertainment industry prompted some women of color performers to develop theater collectives like Spiderwoman Theater Company and Rivers of Honey and create all-women performance spaces such as the WOW Café Theater in New York City. These collaborative ventures remain committed to illumining specific objectives deemed insignificant or radical by the dominant culture like attending to women's issues and perspectives, the political efficacy of anger and humor, and developing heterogeneous representations of women of color. Queer performance troupes like Split Britches, the Five Lesbian Brothers, the Nellie Olsens, the Mickee Faust Club, and the Gay Mafia confront similar issues of representation. Micia Mosely joins the company of the small but dedicated group of comedic performing artists working to develop rich and diverse representations of members of their respective communities. In doing so, she offers counternarrative to (the limited) circulated images of Black women that are devoid of Black lesbians. Like other comic performers described by English professor Carol Allen, Mosely uses her one-woman show and her stand-up comedy "to contend with life, for personal amusement, to entertain others, to educate, and to articulate social and political critique."[61] Her agenda for the show is clear, and audience evaluations indicate that viewers grasp the objectives for this performance; however, her work is limited by virtue of its relative lack of exposure nationally and globally.

Micia Mosely's ability to challenge the social invisibility of Black lesbians largely hinges on commercial success, which is already a struggle given her choice to create charged humor. Shalonda Ingram, herself a Black lesbian, is the cofounder of Queer Arts Impact and the founder of Nursha Project, which produces *Where My Girls At?* She sought to create a production company that, according to the Nursha Project mission statement, helps establish and represent performance artists in order to "elucidate sociopolitical activism through the incubation of sustainable ideas, strategic planning, collaborative project design, and product development."[62] It would seem obvious that Mosely's one-woman show would be popular and quite successful at gay pride events. But as Ingram explained to me during an interview at Café Sureia in Washington, DC, event planners are not willing "to make sure people learn about them [lesser-known performers]" or to "take the risk on our community, within our community at events that are specific to our community."[63] Thus, artists with less notoriety tend to get short shrifted and instead event producers hire celebrity entertainers to perform, who oftentimes are not members of the LGBTQ community and whose work does not necessarily advocate for gay civil rights or social acceptance. It is hard to reprimand mainstream theater productions for their lack of representations of difference when events expressly produced for queer communities ignore their own artists.

In spite of the difficulty she has placing the show at key national pride events, Ingram continues to promote Mosely's show, believing in its value and the message it imparts. For some years now, Mosely has been invited to perform at Black Pride in Washington, DC, though they are not offering compensation. After two years of struggling to subsist off of the show's revenue, Mosely began working full-time for the Posse Foundation, a nonprofit organization selecting and training young people to become student leaders on participating campuses across the nation. She used her vacation and personal days to continue performing the show as well as stand-up comedy, which she began performing in 2009. In winter 2012, she left the Posse Foundation to dedicate more time to her career as entertainer or what she has recently begun calling "comedy and commentary," a blend of stand-up comedy and commentary that often channels four of her best friends: Playher, Ziggy, Lady D, and Sistah.[64]

For African Americans, whose particular history of enslavement and exploitation in the United States shapes the production of cultural practices, humor functions as survival strategy, coping mechanism, a means to develop community, and an effective means of critique.[65] Truth couched in humor has a tendency to unmask and challenge racist, sexist, and homophobic cultural scripts, to offer a teachable moment that neither looks nor feels like "teaching." And while Micia Mosely continues to tour her show and has performed at colleges, arts festivals, and in theaters across the country, her work continues to play for audiences who, in main, are already receptive to examining differences in complex ways. The real boon will come when *Where My Girls At? A Comedic Look at Black Lesbians* achieves the same popularity enjoyed by Lily Tomlin's *Search for Signs of Intelligent Life in the Universe* or Whoopi Goldberg's *The Spook Show*, both of which became instantaneous hits on Broadway in the mid-1980s. Mosely's one-woman show undoubtedly has the same potential.

Each of the Black lesbians represented contain pieces of Mosely's identity: Ziggy's intellectualism, Sistah's earthiness, Playher's hip attitude, and Lady D's self-loving ethos. Regardless of whether you are a Black lesbian, she hopes that audience members will connect with some aspect of one or each character. Experiencing the pleasure of this connection may prompt viewers to change typical patterns of consumption that favor White heterosexual male performers, effectively altering the current economy of charged humor. Mosely's one-woman show evinces the need to look more complexly at difference, particularly among those occupying more than one subordinated category of difference. We, regardless of which minority community(ies) you identify with, are in desperate need of exposure to varying and complex representations of members in our own communities in order to rewrite racist, sexist, ableist, and homophobic scripts about our social, familial, and sexual proclivities; to gain social acceptance and respect; to offer members of the dominant culture opportunities to identify with diverse representations of members of society; to lend cultural currency to that identification and undermine the public's propensity to identify with men (often straight, often able-bodied); and to strengthen our respective communities so we can mobilize on behalf of social justice and to combat social inequities. Whether or not you believe something as seemingly innocuous as humor can adequately or effectively address so many important issues—Mosely's charged humor strives to do so. Intentionality yields possibility and that is where the work of charged humor begins—always with the possibility for change. While conventional news programming is on the decline, televised political satire is increasingly popular. One does not require an economist or market analyst to know that as demand for charged humor increases, so will opportunities to perform charged humor. Larger viewing audiences are tuning in to laugh and think simultaneously, a trend that could bode well for charged comics and even better for the nation at large.

CHAPTER SEVEN

Hari Kondabolu

Performing in the Age of Modern-Day Minstrelsy

There's a lot of things that people find funny that are really just bullying. When people get bullied, there are people that laugh. And I think that is a lot of comedy.

Hari Kondabolu, "The Feministing Five"

Monkey see, monkey do.

Anonymous

Currently following in the tradition of expert charged comics such as Richard Pryor, Paul Mooney, Margaret Cho, and Stewart Lee—all comics inspiring his work—Hari Kondabolu[1] was not always so conscientious about his production of humor. During his college years, much like any aspiring comic, he drew from the comic frames everyone could recognize: inaccurate generalizations about himself and other groups. Audiences loved it. Feeling disingenuous and recognizing the potential damage wreaked by perpetuating these untruths, he shifted to writing primarily charged humor, carefully crafting his jokes to present a point of view more reflective of his own. His is a story of dedication to the craft of comedy, which he commonly refers to as an "art form," alongside a commitment to writing charged comedy that targets bigots and oppression of all kinds. His comedy is not only about social justice issues though; he also talks about the *Back to the Future* trilogy, dinosaurs, vitamin water, and whatever else is on his mind. Drawing from various interviews with and stand-up performances by Hari Kondabolu, New York City native and South Asian American stand-up comic whose work is being compared to the likes of Lenny Bruce, I juxtapose Kondabolu's early reliance on modern-day minstrelsy with a subsequent self-imposed dictum to create humor that does not harm, that is, his current repertoire of charged humor. Charting the contemporary landscape of modern-day minstrelsy, I explore the nuances of minstrelsy, including identifying its many forms, how it can work in tandem with or even be charged humor, and the cultural and marketing pressures placed on comics to perform modern-day minstrelsy, caricaturing their own identities (and Others') for viewing pleasure.

In an age of globalization, where former stars of *Friends* are as widely recognized abroad as they are in the United States, the scope and impact of modern-day minstrelsy extends farther than national borders. What happens on stage does not stagnate; the values, ideologies, and personae of commercially successful comedians are mimicked and recreated all over the world. In other words, comics are selling personal points of view that influence and shape others' local, regional, national, and global worldviews. This can effect elections, consumption choices, attention given social issues (i.e., gay marriage, sanctioned racial profiling like New York City's Stop-and-Frisk Program), and even treatment of other people, groups, and nations. This is no small matter then, when Estonians, Norwegians, and Danes, among others, are consuming US comics peddling modern-day minstrelsy (and they are). Just as blackface minstrelsy was exported across oceans as early as 1852 direct to Japan courtesy of Commodore Matthew Perry, contemporary minstrelsy—raceface and queerface—is being exported abroad. Jeff Dunham, America's favorite (White) ventriloquist comic, ships "Achmed the dead terrorist" among other characters all around the world for his headlining performances at state fairs, casinos, and amphitheaters. Achmed's ineffectual reprise: "Silence! I kill you!" draws big laughs from the crowd who knows they are not actually in danger when Achmed fails repeatedly to instill fear as a "terrifying terrorist." Dunham's puppets' are ethnic stock characters—they *are* the jokes. But they also become mouthpiece for telling jokes that are racist and intolerant. Dunham does not have to lay claim to the jokes, the puppets do that for him and he absolves himself by gently rebuking and reprimanding Achmed when he quips things like: "Why don't we kill the Jews. No, I would not kill the Jews; I would toss a penny between them and watch them fight to the death [*huge laughter*]."[2] When greeted by Achmed the dead terrorist, the audience is offered limited options for expanding or refuting existing stock images of Muslim men as terrorists. After the massacre of sixty-nine people at a youth camp in Norway on the island of Utoeya on July 22, 2011 (bombs detonated in Oslo killing another eight people were a decoy for an attack on the camp) by the unremorseful self-appointed anti–Islamic crusader Anders Breivik, the bombings were originally believed and publicly declared to be the work of Muslim terrorists. These associations are strong and they have consequences for people.

Comedy as a cultural art form is a shaping tool as much as any popular cultural form like film, music, or fashion can be. That is to say, there are limitations to crediting or placing blame on any art for provoking actions, whether positive or negative by society's standards. And yet, we know society confers power to representations; otherwise, Eminem and Marilyn Manson would have spent more time making music and less time defending artistic choices in the courtrooms. Visual culture and representations can vindicate worldviews or challenge them, something that prompts Kondabolu to pose the following question as he writes comedy: Is this going to hurt someone else, will this harm in any way? This is a tricky question with many variables and no way to control for audience reception. Not all comics consider the question, and even some that do, will perform minstrelsy anyway for various reasons. Minstrelsy can earn an easy laugh or offer a way of building community or something else, depending on the setting, audience composition, the comic, and their intentions. Context is everything.

Sitting at the precipice of comedy stardom, Hari Kondabolu certainly has the potential to be the next Lenny Bruce, but these are different times and stand-up comedy has become a different kind of industry since Bruce waxed indignant to restless baby boomers in the 1950s and early 1960s. They do share similarities though. Lenny Bruce would use comedy to recount multiple arrests, the legal and public reaction to his comedy, and like Bruce, Kondabolu draws from audience backlash, making it part of his performance. Here is where they differ: Lenny Bruce may have been notorious but he was never mainstream (except perhaps posthumously) and would never have been as mainstream as Kondabolu professes he wants to be or is already. Having avoided being blacklisted from nearly every club as Bruce was, Kondabolu has the access and more importantly, the talent for making it big . . . another George Carlin. The real uncertainty lies in whether Kondabolu can continue in the mainstream while also maintaining the integrity of his performances, the content of which are primarily charged humor. So far, so good, but many comics have to make concessions along the way.

Ethnic Quotients

When you are just starting out, what matters is getting laughter, not so much how you achieve eliciting that laughter. Jokes written by Hari Kondabolu today may broach issues of racism, wealth disparity, ethnocentrism, privilege, Islamaphobia, and xenophobia, but this was not always the case. Like the professional evolution of most charged comics, attention to such issues developed over time for Kondabolu—sometimes reactively, sometimes as a means of grappling with diversity or difference, sometimes in outrage at proverbial arrows slung. Post 9/11 was one such turning point and he became more critical on stage and off when he witnessed the instantaneous fall from grace that racialized Arabs, Middle Eastern Americans, and Arab Americans overnight.

Tracking Kondabolu's transitions in content and style on stage reflects a journey unique to him, but interestingly, not one remarkably different from many comedy ingénues turned charged comics. This is also my story and the story of many comics, as much as it is his. Comic performer Micia Mosely, a Black lesbian fellow charged comic also earning her chops in New York City, confesses that writing charged humor, or humor that most effectively paints an accurate self-portrait is difficult, and she struggled throughout college "to find [her] comedic identity."[3] She says:

> But in my comedy what was really apparent when I was on stage with my troupe mates was our difference in race and so that's what I played on because you kind of would have to know me. So, when I look back on it I am very critical of that time because I feel like there were times when I did what I felt like I had to do for the joke but I was the joke. Like it got to the point where I was making fun of myself and that was a problem.[4]

Similarly for Kondabolu, initial impulses to secure laughs during his early stand-up comedy career gave way to commitment to addressing social issues in meaningful ways, in the hopes of sparking reflection and discussion beyond the performance.

Born in 1982 at Flushing Hospital in Queens, New York, where he also grew up, Hari Kondabolu began writing jokes at a young age. While in his teens, he watched Margaret Cho perform on Comedy Central; she was the first and only Asian American comic accessible to him during his youth. He also cites Stewart Lee, Paul Mooney, and Richard Pryor as comic legends making a lasting impact on the way he approaches the craft of comedy, all of whom, while different than the other, take a pointed and direct approach to writing comic material that leaves little room for ambiguity as to their level of commitment to confronting racism.

As a racial minority, comedy for Hari Kondabolu was a means of working through feelings of being an outsider and finding his voice, what is commonly referred to in stand-up comedy as one's unique point of view. He began his stand-up comedy career at Bowdoin College, performing for his peers there and at Wesleyan University where he spent his junior year in a domestic exchange program. Early comedy performed in college by Kondabolu offered up brownface minstrelsy, which he qualified in the following terms: "I made people laugh in my standup, but I wasn't saying much of anything. I used lots of stereotypes. I'm Indian-American. I used accents—stuff I wouldn't touch now. At the time, if I made them laugh, I made them laugh."[5]

Even as he drew inspiration from Cho, Mooney, Rock, and Pryor, he was not impervious to the common strategies and techniques, among them minstrelsy, employed by the endless parade of comics on television, fellow amateur college comics, and the comics he saw performing in New York City. Micia Mosely describes the comedy scene there in these terms:

> Most of the time when I'm performing in a mixed crowd, not in a specialized event like this, I feel actually assaulted in my person. . . . There's sexist, racist, homophobic jokes that are told. I'm just like, "wow!" I'm getting punched in the stomach for an hour to wait to get to do an eight-minute set. . . . And I think it's important that I'm there. And my job is to be funny. And the only way I could sort of shift that type of comedy is to be funnier in my comedy, so people want to see what I'm up to. So you know, it's not about insulting them, to get back at them making jokes about who I am, it's really like, I've got to show them that you can be funny without being those things. That you can, you know, really celebrate who people are and make them laugh.[6]

In local comedy scenes, cheap shots and poorly crafted jokes are de rigueur, the former because it is a lot of what we see in mainstream stand-up comedy and the latter because it takes time to learn how to write good material and find your own point of view on stage. The problem is that not all amateurs who become professionals learn to transcend the cheap shots—they just become better at writing them.

In part because Kondabolu modeled what he saw and in part because he understood what audiences were looking for—said differently: this is the kind of comedy having commercial appeal—Kondabolu fashioned his comedy to attract, to seduce audiences with stereotypical portrayals of a South Asian American young man. But the events on 9/11 and the discrimination experienced by Arabs and Muslims in America in the aftermath stoked the desire to write comedy differently.

> What I thought about the world and what I was writing comedically, it [wasn't] matching. It freaked me out and I knew I had to stop. . . . My writing up until that point either essentialized myself for laughs or said things that were racist, sexist, or homophobic. Early on I didn't see stand-up as anything more than making people laugh. . . . I didn't really have any real sense of "how am I affecting an audience other than laughter? What is it that I'm doing?" Which to be fair, every young comic has to figure that out for themselves to a certain extent.[7]

Comedy has a learning curve and it takes time to develop comic timing and strong point of view that translates to the masses. Most comics have early jokes that they would consider terrible in hindsight for different reasons, but exploring different comedic styles and strategies is just part of the process of becoming a professional. For Kondabolu, going to college, becoming active in organizing for immigrants' rights, attending graduate school, and the political and cultural landscape around him, all of these experiences informed and shaped his production of humor during his years as a twenty-something. Over time, old jokes were phased out or peppered throughout newer, mostly charged humor and jokes about Weezer.

In 2008, in a short mockumentary titled "Manoj" posted to YouTube, Kondabolu, who plays himself and an exaggerated minstrel character intended to be deliberately confusing, casts aspersion on modern-day minstrelsy by juxtaposing the minstrel (Manoj) with charged comic (himself). Writer for Racialicious.com, Caitlyn Boston, describes the film as "unpack[ing] this unfortunate comedic trend of hack-stereotype jokes by exploring the cyclically exploitative relationship between an audience and a Brown comedian who performs, in essence, a Brown minstrel show."[8] Manoj Krishnamurthy, a complete and utter fabrication, that is, not real (this will be important later), uses brownface minstrelsy by performing with an Indian accent, using humor that draws from cultural stereotypes about South Asians like making corny references to Hinduism, sacred cows, and eating monkey brains. Live comedy and interviews with Manoj and Hari are interspersed with commentary from audience members and comedy club managers who, much to Hari's dismay, all declare Manoj and his performance of brownface minstrelsy a singular stroke of comedy genius. We hear a comedy club manager tell him to "Indian it up tonight" because audiences "love that stuff" and audience interviews describe Manoj as "the best fucking comic" and excitedly report that "he's saying everything that you are thinking but don't want to say."[9] In a nutshell, the performance of modern-day minstrelsy often invites audiences to participate in racist, homophobic, or xenophobic thinking, which is made acceptable because the invitation commonly comes from someone belonging to that marginalized group or experiencing marginalization in similar ways as when Pablo Francisco (Latino comic) uses blackface minstrelsy to demonstrate that "Black people don't survive at Starbucks" because they lack the ability to order such fancy-sounding beverages. Finally defeated after three failed attempts to order a specialty coffee drink, he (playing the role of a Black man) orders an orange juice instead.[10]

"[*In an Indian accent*] I just flew in from India and, boy, are my eight arms tired [*laughter*]." It is hard to believe that this could be done: a hacky joke *and* an oblique reference to Hinduism. Get it? Lots of Hindu gods have eight arms—hilarious. And so begins this short cinematic romp following Manoj in America as he uses his otherness for comedic fodder (think: *Borat* as a one-man show):

[*In an Indian accent*] Let me go over some popular Hin-dos and Hin-don'ts. Eating a sandwich: Hin-do, Hin-do. Eating a *beef* sandwich: Hin-don't! [*laughter*]. Having sex after marriage: Hin-do! Eating beef: Hin-don't! [*laughter and clapping*]. Riding in a rickshaw: Hin-do. Riding a cow: Hin-don't! That's beef! [*laughter*]. Thank you![11]

Kondabolu never actually told these exact jokes in his real sets, but they are representative of the style and kind of jokes he sees as all too common on the comedy club circuit, a style tacitly encouraged by fellow comics, audience members, and comedy club managers alike. A savvy maneuver that anyone in public relations would admire, creating a fictional character like Manoj allows Kondabolu to critique the style of comedy without calling anyone out on their own use of minstrelsy. According to Kondabolu, Manoj is minimizing the experience of being South Asian, a problem he addresses in one of many interview-style shots in the short film when Kondabolu says of Manoj (read: says of modern-day minstrelsy):

> He's exploiting these stereotypes for his own gain, because he knows he's going to have a career out of it. People will pay to see this crap. People feel more comfortable laughing at something, I mean if there was a White guy saying racist jokes on stage, the club would get tons of angry responses, as they should. But when this guy does it, like, who's going to say anything? People are more comfortable with their racism, people are more comfortable laughing.[12]

In other words, consider those jokes that are "politically incorrect" but are still furtively and gleefully exchanged among members of the same racial and ethnic communities. Take all those jokes and put them in the mouth of the very race/ethnicity or sexuality targeted and suddenly the jokes become perfectly acceptable in public, if not desirable. People like those jokes; they also know they are not supposed to—like them or tell them. If someone else does, then great. If someone else does who also happens to belong to the group being made the butt of the joke (further confirming the joke as true), well . . . even better.

Rule number one in writing comedy: a joke is only funny when the listener shares the comic frame being created by the comic. This means that comics will be more successful if they draw from comic frames familiar to most or all of the audience. Many things unite a group of strangers assembled together like shared knowledge of current events, world history, politics, sports, popular culture, and geography. We also share knowledge of the specious stereotypes circulating about other groups or identities different than our own, making it more likely that audiences will recognize the comic frames in use. Resulting laughter could be explained as individuals delighting in discussion of a taboo topic, opening ourselves to urges we are trained to deny; it could be in response to amusing use of nonverbal communication and bodily gesture made by the performer; or it could be recognition of the comic frame alone or a combination of all those things and more things. Laughter is complicated but comics know they have multiple ways of getting it, and for some comics it is not the "why" that matters, but only that they get the laughter. Using profanity, making fun of women, gays, and racial Others or foreigners, and drawing from comic frames everyone will recognize, these are all elementary strategies for writing and performing live comedy. Combine them, give or take some cussing, and you have modern-day minstrelsy, a trusty comedy strategy for reeling in the laughs.

When asked if her comedy was always political, White lesbian comic and comedy writer for FX Network's *Totally Biased with W. Kamau Bell* (2012–2013), Janine Brito replied: "In the beginning, we all do the easy things to get a quick laugh because we're not quite comfortable on stage and we're kind of desperate to get a laugh. We're less likely to take risks and go for the more obvious jokes which aren't always the most respectable, good jokes—and not just in quality but the meaning behind it."[13] Unfazed by the knowledge that his success comes not from a natural comedic wit or physicality but from being "born with the ability to speak English with an accent," Manoj is blithely insouciant to the potential ramifications of such a performance. This is further evidenced by his final address to the camera: "I've headlined at a Ku Klux Klan convention. I got a standing ovation. That's how good I am. It's funny though, afterwards, everyone thought I was wearing paint."[14] By constructing Manoj as one-dimensional, Kondabolu connects the dots between the stand-up comedy of Manoj and history's tradition of minstrelsy, not to mention the quality of character of the audiences most appreciative of this style of performance. A rather important and telling aside: since this video is publicly available and posted on YouTube, to date, Kondabolu has received a couple inquiries, including from the University of Alaska, requesting a live performance from Manoj.

Interested in human rights and social justice, after college Kondabolu moved to Seattle to become an immigrant rights organizer where he also continued performing stand-up comedy from 2005 to 2007. A combination of personal growth and devotion to integrating comic and political sensibilities prompted Kondabolu to begin phasing out minstrelsy and hacky ethnic humor, which increasingly felt inconsistent with his own evolving world views. An HBO talent scout, much admired by Kondabolu, discovered him on the Internet in 2007 and invited him to join the HBO Comedy Festival, annually featuring up-and-coming young comics.[15] Seeing demo tapes from the comedy festival, producers from *Jimmy Kimmel Live* scheduled an appearance for Kondabolu, where he made his debut on national television. He performed charged humor as well as incorporating some of his older jokes, a strategy meant to draw laughter then, while appearing harmless, slip in something subversive. For example, opening with an older joke situating Kondabolu as a virgin and catering to a stereotype of Asian men as unable to "score," he follows with a joke that calls attention to the maltreatment of Arabs and Muslims or anyone looking the part following 9/11.

> All week my stomach's been acting up. My stomach has been a mess. And for a while there, I thought maybe I wasn't actually nervous—maybe I was pregnant [*laughter*]. That's of course not possible because I'm obviously, you know, a virgin [*laughter and clapping*]. That's the first joke I ever wrote when I was sixteen years old and it still very [*pause*] painful to me [*laughter*] and not that much fun to tell anymore. Anyway, my name is Hari. It's pronounced a few different ways in this country. It's pronounced HA-ri or Ha-RI or Harry. And since 9/11 I've been called sand nigger [*laughter and clapping*]. Multiple pronunciations of my name, apparently.[16]

Older jokes, remnants of his early work, were not minstrelsy per se but less representative of his point of view now when he performs. Later on in the set he jokes: "Politically, I am not a Republican, although I was at one point in my life when I was seven years old. Not my fault, symbol of the Republican Party is an elephant. I'm a Hindu. I got confused [*laughter and clapping*]." Kondabolu admits to being embarrassed by some of his older material, but argues that this is part of the process. When you perform your own material, you have the latitude to edit, revise, and develop as you deem necessary. Comics routinely develop new material, phasing out old jokes over time but not overnight.

Days after Kondabolu's debut on national television he received confirmation of his acceptance into the London School of Economics to pursue a master's degree in human rights. Opting to enroll in the program in 2007 and take a break from comedy, he left to begin his studies in London, though he did travel back to New York in the summer of 2008 to perform in Comedy Central's showcase *Live at Gotham*.[17] Remarkably, he landed his own half-hour special on Comedy Central a mere three years later in 2011 and a spot on *John Oliver's New York Stand-up Show* (season 3, 2012), where he told jokes like this:

> Just the other day I went to the supermarket to get some more cocoa butter when I noticed the cocoa butter had moved [*pause*] to the ethnic needs section of my supermarket [*laughter*]. And at first I was happy. I'm like ethnic needs: end of police brutality, more access to health care [*laughter*], more educational opportunities!! Finally! No. No. Just hair relaxers and cocoa butter [*laughter*].[18]

This and other jokes establish Hari Kondabolu as one of the most effective purveyors of charged humor in the contemporary comedy scene. He stands at a crossroads where substituting raceface minstrelsy for charged humor may prevent wider visibility and notoriety. Walking away from minstrelsy may appear a simple choice, but as a racial or sexual minority, it means potentially sacrificing favor with audiences and severely curtailing one's popularity. More likely, he will *not* compromise his point of view, continue to situate himself strategically for further mainstreaming, and hopefully find himself in a fecund moment when the public is hungry to hear charged humor, turning cultural and political critique into popular discourses.

The Market for Modern-Day Minstrelsy

Any comic will tell you that watching other comics helps to develop and hone one's craft. Comics follow a tradition, not only of format and structure, however loosely this might be based, but also a tradition of emulating and drawing from fellow comics, talented practitioners that influence the training and development of amateur stand-up comics. Samuel Clemens (a.k.a. Mark Twain) took notes from Charles Browne (a.k.a. Artemus Ward), Chris Rock learned from Richard Pryor, Joan Rivers influences Kathy Griffin, and Margaret Cho inspires Hari Kondabolu. If you are among those lucky enough to turn stand-up comedy into a full-time career, your agent will invariably ask that you develop some "shtick," in other words a marketable point of view. This requires crafting a memorable on-stage persona that is unique even as it models itself after commercially successful comics of yore. For the agent and mainstream comic alike, the objective lies in creating appeal among the largest consumer base possible. This often translates into doing what you know works, what sells, what has been deemed profitable by comedy fans.

Minstrelsy or mimicry of an Other for comedic purposes, be that queerface or raceface (more generally: minstrelsy), has historically proved to be a lucrative comedy style in the marketplace. Funny man Bo Burnham croons something to this effect into the microphone as he sings:

> Because stand-up comedy is actually pretty easy. If you're an Asian comic just get up and say "my mother's got the weirdest fuckin' accent." Then just do a Chinese accent because everybody laughs at the Chinese accent because they privately thought that your people were laughable and now you've given them the chance to express that in public.[19]

Burnham presents his audience with precisely this keen insight: minstrelsy sells. Whether blackface, yellowface, redface, Arabface, brownface, or queerface, mimicry of an Other has a long history of commercial appeal in the United States. Because of its popularity, emerging comics consume and mimic minstrelsy. Stereotypes, stock characters, and beliefs extolled do not necessarily reflect personal views of the performer though they certainly could for some comics, but they also could be a choice made to garner favor with audiences across America. Whether performing modern-day minstrelsy simply cashes in on a lucrative comedic style, creates community among minority audiences, exploits stereotypes to squeeze out the laughs, or at worst, works to confirm heinous suspicions about racial/ethnic and sexual stereotypes, it is important to note that most comics strive to produce comedy that sells. This means minstrelsy is in demand and begs the better question: why are so many people laughing and what are the implications of this laughter?

Bo Burnham, a young White man-boy of slender build, apprises us of many reasons people laugh in his short ditty called "What's Funny," which opens his comedy show *Words, Words, Words* (2010). Not (yet) a purveyor of charged humor, Burnham is young and still finding his point of view, which in this comedy special was hacky, ironic, and a cerebral that tries too hard. However, obliquely referencing a number of theories on laughter, specifically he points toward yellowface minstrelsy, wherein a person performs as an over-the-top Asian character, a performance tradition that gained commercial viability alongside the rise in Chinese immigrants brought into the United States as an immigrant workforce during the nineteenth century. Early yellowface performers used visual and linguistic signifiers, such as wearing a queue (a long braid usually attached to a skull cap) and speaking with an exaggerated Chinese accent, often depicting Chinese Americans as stealing work from White Americans. Yellowface continues to be quite marketable and performed by Asian and non-Asian comics alike. Lenny Bruce[20] performed yellowface minstrelsy to audiences in the early 1960s and Dat Phan, a Vietnamese American voted the winner of the first season of *Last Comic Standing* (2003), won viewers' adoration by performing mainly yellowface minstrelsy such as: "Parents, I think they go nuts after awhile. My mom says [*assumes Asian accent*], 'Dat Phan you don't watch cartoons anymore, they too violent. The cartoon is too violent.' [*Resumes normal voice*] This is the same woman who says, [*assumes Asian accent*], 'Dat Phan you don't take out the garbage, I will kill you' [*laughter*]."[21] Yellowface minstrelsy is perhaps the most common form of raceface minstrelsy performed right now; it would seem that every comic can pull off a generic Asian accent in order to invoke the same stereotypes referenced by Carlos Mencia in the following bit:

> Do you understand how easy it is to get a degree online? You can cheat on every test because nobody's watching [*laughter*]! Invite your Asian friend over [*laughter*]! Start taking the test and he'll be like [*in Asian accent*]: "Oh shit, I rove tests [*laughter*]! Let me take for you! This is the shit [*laughter*]! Oh, today you going to get a A Prus!" [*laughter and clapping*] . . . [*resumes normal voice*] He [God] gave you Asians great fucking minds and a hard work ethic. But you have little dicks. You see how that balances out? [*roaring laughter*].[22]

Assigning Asians innate intellectual superiority and suffering sexual prowess eliminates the threat of Asian men as sexual predators while cultivating Asian Americans as threatening in competitive professions like medicine, law, higher education, science, and engineering. Charged with taking the jobs of White women launderers in the nineteenth century, today Asian Americans purportedly pose a similar threat to middle-class professionals. Indeed, there has been a resurgence of anti-Asian sentiment and hostility citing this labor-thievery as a major grievance. Depending on the content of the joke and the comic performing yellowface, these jokes can either demonstrate this kind of thinking as problematic (as I will argue later that Margaret Cho does) or further corroborate and tacitly fuel misunderstanding and even antipathy toward Asian Americans.

Given our current efforts to be politically correct, it would seem that race-face minstrelsy would be an outmoded form of performance. In its original inception in the late eighteenth century on the streets of Catherine Market in New York City and later in other port cities along the Eastern seaboard, blackface minstrelsy drew from a working class ethos appealing to the economically downtrodden regardless of race or ethnicity. At the same time, in slave states in southern United States, those enslaved would parody White authority figures in ad hoc comedic performances. This veiled mockery, often performed before the watchful eye of the oppressors, ridiculed White upper-class pretensions. Misinterpreted as bona fide representations of African Americans, White performers fashioned stock characters from these representations, and thus Ethiopian delineators were born. From the early to mid-nineteenth century, Ethiopian delineators roamed the country performing in burnt cork. This was the antecedent to blackface minstrelsy, a loosely structured comedic performance tradition that became wildly popular and remained so for over a century. After being institutionalized as America's first original form of performance in the early 1840s, it became obvious for what it was: a hyperbolic mimicry of African American culture. Blackface minstrelsy offered a series of comic portrayals peddling stereotypes that coalesced into iconic stock characters like the Sambo, the Mammy, the Pickaninny, and the Zip Coon that survive to this day in various forms.[23] While it has moved from passé to downright unacceptable to perform in blackface, there exists in the slew of cultural effluvia all around us, contemporary vestiges of these stock images, remnants of a rather insidious and pervasive cultural strategy to maintain white supremacy.[24]

Performing raceface minstrelsy (encompassing blackface, brownface, redface, Arabface, yellowface, etc.) typically involves representation of a racialized Other via certain dialects, inflections, mannerisms and speech patterns. Anjelah Johnson, a young Latina professional cheerleader turned comic, quickly gained a following with her imitations of Tammy, a Vietnamese manicurist and Bon Qui Qui, a character she fashioned after a Black woman she met once at a fast-food restaurant. She amplifies the comedic effect of Bon Qui Qui, a modern-day Sapphire caricature, when she puts her "ghetto fabulous" character in unexpected places.

One day though I just wanna get on a plane and there be a real ghetto flight attendant on there. Just real ghetto [*laughter*]. That'd really make my day. [*Mimics patting her hair down and the crowd starts cheering. She proceeds to speak in a "ghetto" voice*] "Ay, ay. I say ay [*loud laughter*]. Wuzzup? [*laughter*]. My name's Bon Qui Qui [*laughter, whistles and applause*] and I'll be your flight attendant. So don't nobody axe me for nothing. Let's see, let's see. Ya'll on a plane flight. So don't get crazy [*laughter*]. Uhh, scuze me sir. Uh, sir. You don't see me going over my safe regamelations, sir? [*laughter*]. You just gonna go ahead and interrupt. You just gonna go ahead and interrupt. Gonna go ahead and interrupt [*laughter*]. Rude [*laughter and applause*]. I don't know, sir. Don't talk back sir. Sir, don't talk back to me, sir. Sir, you think you can talk back, sir? You think so, sir? Hell no. SACURITY [*laughter and applause*]. SACURITY! This dude need to go. Need to go. Bye bye. Anyway, don't nobody else get crazy, cuz I will cut you [*laughter and applause*]. I will cut you. Don't play. Don't play. And don't make me have to teach you how to put on your own seat belt.[25]

In this exchange, the audience gets to laugh at an outrageous caricature reinforcing notions of Black female dominance as well as Black inferiority and ineptitude. The laughter derives from superiority to Bon Qui Qui who is ill-equipped in this leadership role. Stump speeches, a staple performative trope in blackface minstrelsy, consisted of a man in blackface posing as authority figure or government official delivering an address full of malapropisms and mispronunciations. At that time, particularly during the Reconstruction Era, the message was clear. African Americans may have freedom but any efforts to achieve European (White) standards of civility, would be failed ones. Eerily, Bon Qui Qui also offers an address of sorts, invoking similar locutionary flaws as she bumbles over the word "regulation" and repeatedly mispronounces "security." Like most comics, Johnson has dozens of jokes in her repertoire, but the most successful and favorite among her fans are her performances of Tammy and Bon Qui Qui. The latter character has become so popular that Johnson created a music video called "Bon Qui Qui: I'm a Cut You," wherein Bon Qui Qui promises to "cut" all "haters" in her life. Not unimportantly, the music video has nearly a million hits on YouTube. In *That's How We Do It*, her first full-length comedy special, Anjelah has only to say the name Bon Qui Qui or utter a few words in Bon Qui Qui's "voice" and the audience roars in delighted anticipation, cheering for what they know will be an impression that pleases. And why should it not? It has for two centuries.

As Anjelah Johnson dons racialized caricatures of Vietnamese manicurists, Latina femme fatales, and Black service staff, she reminds audience members that all her imitations—whether Black, Asian, Hispanic, or queer—are constructed, that is, they are all performances. Facile with cultural dialects and behavior, she performs all manner of raceface and queerface minstrelsy, much to the enjoyment of her audience. Like Johnson, many modern-day minstrels are racial/ethnic minorities themselves because while it has become impolite and socially unacceptable to mock other race or ethnic groups, it is acceptable to mock the groups to which you belong or similarly marginalized social groups. The tacit rule for raceface minstrelsy includes that you can mock a subordinate category if you also share or experience some form of subordination; however, if you occupy a dominant category like being White, then it is not permissible to make fun of or denigrate communities made inferior by the same arbitrary standards that make White superior (unless you simultaneously occupy another subordinated category such as being queer, differently abled, or poor). Thus, you will not find copious numbers of White comics imitating a racial Other, though this does occasionally happen. Chris D'Elia performs blackface during a showcase on *Live Nude Comedy*, a flash in the pan show lasting six episodes. He opens his set:

> I feel kind of insecure, I've got this tie on, and uh, everyone backstage is like, "oh you're wearing a tie, huh? [*laughter*]. Fucking queer" [*laughter*]. Everyone always makes fun of what I wear. I think it's 'cause I'm White, you know what I mean? [*laughter*]. That's why I wish I were Black. Black people can wear anything and nobody says shit about it [*laughter*]. [26]

Going on to situate himself as physically inferior to Black men, D'Elia appears to be mocking himself as a weakling. An overt effort made to diminish his own power as White, helps prime the audience to accept his impression of a Black man wearing a *Dora the Explorer* t-shirt without compromising his masculinity. With this rhetorical maneuvering, this does not seem like a White man attacking a Black man, and yet the humor is derived from the hyperbolic impersonation of a Black man whose only intelligible words, which punctuate every sentence, are: "mothafucka." More often than not, however, comics performing raceface minstrelsy are also racial minorities (mocking their own race or that of other people of color), who are imitating what they know, or what they think everyone else believes about that Other. Discursive analyses of stand-up comedy reveals a widespread sensitivity (albeit sometimes reluctantly) toward issues of race/ethnicity that is not replicated when the subject matter turns queer.

When it comes to queerface minstrelsy, there seems to be an entirely different set of rules, wherein mocking LGBTQ persons is not the sole province of sexual minorities. Comics, heterosexuals, and queers alike, feel comfortable taking liberties in imitating a gay (usually male) affect. On television, in films, in stand-up comic performances of queerface minstrelsy . . . nearly every form of popular performance does make or has made its contribution to generating and perpetuating the continued circulation of the gay male stock character.

Patton Oswalt professes shock at an offer he got to audition for a ridiculously stereotypical role in a romantic comedy: "they wanted me to audition for the part of the gay best friend which [*he pauses and chuckles; audience starts to laugh and clap*]. It's 2011. It's 2011!! I might as well put on blackface and tap dance [*laughter and clapping*] that is how old that cliché is now."[27] There seems to be no end to the humor that the stock gay male character—effete, vain, witty, and sarcastic—provides.

It is neither uncommon nor irrational for cultures to create stock characters that unify a host of collected subjective observations about a group into a single comedic character that features character traits immediately recognizable to a wide audience. Called "representations," scholars conduct representational analyses to assess the kinds of representations being circulated by television, literature, film, and advertising. The comics—whether gay or straight—performing queerface minstrelsy often perform "gay" by donning a heightened hyperbolic gay affect for comedic effect. A high pitched lilting voice, an exaggerated lisp, and a hip jutting out to the side all characterize impressions of gay men, which is the most common impersonation in circulation. You can identify queerface minstrelsy when one does this not as a sustained comic persona but by inserting jokes that clearly contrast their normal voices with that of the gay character being assumed. Heterosexual comics performing queerface employ common strategies in order to soothe the sting of queerface minstrelsy, including citing affiliation with queers, for example, "my best friend is gay," or presenting oneself as sympathetic to gay civil rights before launching into an exaggerated and seemingly universal caricature of gayness. It is interesting that everyone's gay best friend is identical in comportment, diction, and affect. Similarly, by expressing admiration for Black men, Chris D'Elia employed this latter strategy, which helps audience members to lower their defenses. These tactics make it seem less like an attack and more like harmless ribbing. However, some comics make no effort to qualify or minimize the denigration of LGBTQ persons via queerface minstrelsy, for which there seems few social consequences and more likely some rewards (e.g., audience approval, increased following, or fan base).

Like raceface minstrelsy, queerface is not a recent phenomenon or some twenty-first-century ironic postmodern fad. Between gayness not being necessarily visible and America's English Puritan background, it took a while for the concept of homosexual or gay, as we know it, to emerge as a concept and an identity in public consciousness. Representations of gay men in popular culture turn up in films in the early twentieth century as gay-coded, sissy male characters exhibiting precisely the same qualities characterizing modern queerface minstrelsy. As for stand-up comedy, early comics such as Jonathan Winters[28] and Richard Pryor[29] used queerface minstrelsy to depict gay men as silly, queeny, and untrustworthy and Robin Williams, well known for assuming characters for comedic effect, has been impersonating queers since he began performing comedy in the mid '70s. Comic Ronnie Schell, in the *hungry i reunion* performance revue (1981), wonders aloud what it would be like if Chief Sitting Bull had been gay and "act[ed] the way he really was." The exchange between General Custard and the Chief, according to Schell, would have been much different, full of outbursts from the Chief like: "[*In a feminine voice*] General Custard screams for accessories [*laughter*]."[30] In his comedy special *Raw* (1987), seen by millions around the world, Eddie Murphy performs queerface minstrelsy:

> I did jokes about homosexuals a couple years ago, and faggots were mad. There's nothing like having a nation of fags looking for you. I'd be at parties, there's always two or three homosexuals at parties, and they'd be looking at me. [*Glares and speaks in an effeminate voice*] "He's an asshole!" [*laughter and applause*]. I can't travel the country anymore. I can't go to San Francisco. They got 24-hour homo watch waiting for me in the airport. Soon as I got off the plane, they'd be like, [*assumes gay voice*] "He's here, yes. It's him, yes it's him!" [*Resumes normal voice*] And the cars be rushing across town like, Woo woo woo woo! And it won't be no siren, it'll be a real fag sitting on the roof going, [*assumes gay voice*] "Woo woo woo woo! Wooooooo!! Pull over! Pull over! Pull over! I'm a read him his rights [*he snaps in the air to punctuate this statement*]. You have the right to remain silent, anything you say can and will be used against you in the court of law. You have the right to an attorney. Now turn around I'm gonna frisk you! [*mimes a pat-down with special attention on the buttocks*]. Are you carrying any concealed weapons? Are you carrying any?! [*Grabs his own crotch*] What is this? What is this?! [*Roaring laughter and applause*] Get down on the floor and spread 'em! [*laughter and applause*].[31]

These early examples invoke queerface using the same signifiers of gay affect: lisping, high-pitched voice, and feminizing gestures and mannerisms. Schell opens his joke by calling attention to discrimination against the LGBTQ community, distinguishing himself from Murphy by content but not by execution. Schell wants the laugh but does not want to appear homophobic, while it seems clear that this is less of a concern for Murphy. Regardless, they both perform queerface to similar ends. Persian American comic Max Amini offers a more contemporary example, using a rhetorical strategy similar to Schell. Like Schell and many others, Amini prefaces his performance of queerface minstrelsy with some version of the following sentiment: "I love the gays! Now I'm going to make a lot of jokes about them, but I'm only kidding."

My very good friend is gay and let me tell you he is the best wing man ever. You go out with a gay guy; girls are so friendly all of a sudden. You know what I mean? [*laughter*]. They don't get defensive at all. Gay guys, just let the gay guys start the conversation [*in an exaggerated fey voice*]: "Oh my God I love your shoes!" [*loud laughter; resumes normal voice*]. They get so excited! [*In a woman's voice not unlike the fey voice*] "Oh my God really? [*laughter*]. You like 'em? Oh my God!" [*Resumes normal voice*] And that's when you go on in and say the same shit: "Yea, I like your shirt, too. Ha ha." And then it just friggin' all happens from there. Best wing man ever.[32]

Amini goes on to describe his own reluctance to accompany his gay wingman to a gay club and after being goaded to go against his will, he proceeds to mock the various gay men he sees there, targeting their clothes (or lack thereof) and personal aesthetics and invoking the tired concern that he will be nothing short of molested upon walking inside the venue. In this exchange, the gay man serves as tool for facilitating heterosexual conjugal relations but placed in his "native" environment (a gay club) he becomes a hypersexualized deviant that threatens the masculinity of straight men who are presumed gay by association.

You have heard it before: "get yourself a gay" or "every girl needs a good gay." Sweeping the nation is a phenomenon that turns the gay man into a commodity. Everyone wants to be wanted, but being reduced to a tool to enhance your "cool," a mechanism for entertainment or eliciting laughter, an accessory for the straight girl, a direct conduit to fashion and popular culture, all of these render a gay man useful, but without his humanity intact. Sought to enhance status, his name is irrelevant as long as he performs gay, preferably mimicking Jack from *Will and Grace,* more sassy than anal retentive. On the comic stage, the notion of any man turned fey remains a constant source of humor and delight among audiences. It is funny because it defies expectations of performed masculinity. Comic Al Del Bene, new to fatherhood, jokes about the power that parents have to mold and shape children during infancy and early development, invoking queerface minstrelsy for a heightened comic effect:

I could spend the first two years of his life talking to him like this [*changes face, talks in a high, feminine voice with a lisp*], "Hello! Daddy's home! You like when Daddy's home, don't you? Yes. You. Do" [*laughter*]. [*Resumes normal voice*] See if you end up with a gay toddler. Have you ever seen a gay two-year-old? It would be fucking hysterical. [*Does feminine voice again, trotting around with hands on his hips, sticking out his tongue flirtatiously*] "Daddy! Daddy I have to go to potty [*laughter*]! [*Sticks out butt*] Wipe me Daddy, wipe me [*laughter and in an even more exaggerated sexual voice*], You have to wipe me 'cause you're my Daddy" [*laughter, clapping*]. [*Resumes normal voice*] Fucking hysterical. I would wake him up at parties like, "Come downstairs. Prance around for the people. Put on these funny hats. You're a riot" [*continuous laughter*].[33]

Despite being two years of age, Del Bene overlays elements of a gay stock character like hypersexuality and effeminacy onto his son. Potty-training becomes a flirtatious sexual overture and the joke turns the "gay" toddler into resident court jester, a source of amusement for himself and house guests. Many people assume causal links between sex (biological) and gender (social construction), where being male corresponds to performing a specific kind of masculinity and being female corresponds to performing a specific kind of femininity. We know that great variation exists among members of the same group, like men or women; in fact, there are greater differences within a group than there are between groups. Despite this, we seem hell-bent on reducing racial and sexual minorities (and other subordinated identity groups) to some stereotypical facsimile highlighting the ways they are different. Queerface and raceface minstrelsy both rely on adherence to a highly circulated and well-known set of qualities and traits ascribed (whether true or not) to a race, ethnicity, or sexuality. Represented on stage, the performer invites audience members to laugh at a shared perception or comic frame, to experience superiority in relation to that caricature, and to freely express impulses one must normally suppress. Its continued presence and flagrant usage by all comics, without the kind of hesitation being employed by raceface minstrelsy, signals (perhaps more ominously) a certain degree of comfort the public has to dismiss, ignore, or take less seriously the political concerns and social conditions of LGBTQ folk.

Minstrelsy is about the imitation of an Other, someone whose social identity makes them subordinate in the United States. Comics impersonate White people all the time and women imitate men, but this does not make what they are doing minstrelsy. Part humorist and part philosopher, Emily Levine addresses power dynamics between dominant and subordinate social groups and the implications of this for making jokes.

> I don't think a person of color making fun of White people is the same thing as a White person making fun of people of color; or a woman making fun of a man, the same as a man making fun of a woman; or poor people making fun of rich people, the same as rich people. I think you can make fun of the "haves," but not the "have- nots."[34]

Just as Levine argues that it is appropriate to joke "up" and not "down," for minstrelsy to take place, the target must be a marginalized identity in that social context. For instance, vaudevillians caricatured Italian, Irish, Eastern European Jews, and German immigrants on stage and for a period of time this would have been considered minstrelsy.[35] Strong nativist sentiments fueled a culture wherein immigrants, though White, were considered inferior. Italians, Irish, and European Jews were all "raced" in some way at the turn of the twentieth century, and there is a great deal of literature that explores this position as "not-quite-white" and "off-white."[36] Over time, these ethnic Whites assimilated, laying claim to their whiteness in various ways.[37] To impersonate an Italian now, despite deploying a stock character shaped from stereotypes drawn directly from *The Godfather* and *The Sopranos*, would not be considered minstrelsy. Italian Americans systematically benefit from our current racial order, where people of color do not; heterosexuals benefit from the present sexual order, where queer people do not. This does not mean that Italian stock characters or caricatures are not reductive and offensive. They may certainly be to some or many people. But since Italian Americans are not disadvantaged in the current racial order in the way that people of color are, these caricatures would not be considered minstrelsy.

To clarify further, modern-day minstrels reveal themselves via racialized or sexualized impersonation, so a gay comic like Ant, whose comic personae is reminiscent of anyone else's queerface, is not acting as minstrel throughout the whole show (though he may certainly be laying it on thick in order to garner laughs). Gary Owen, a White comic who appears to be acting Black but whose seemingly Black affect is consistent on and off-stage, is not a modern-day minstrel by virtue of adopting Black affectations. Former host for Black Entertainment Television (BET), he is married to a Black woman, has biracial children and comfortably situates himself within the Black community. He may offer up a comic persona but it also happens to be a fairly accurate representation of who he is in real life. He is not "acting" Black periodically throughout his sets—which is the calling card of the modern-day minstrels who command the focus of this investigation—he is instead crossing over racially or what some would call being a race traitor.[38] He does, however, perform yellowface minstrelsy when he, on several occasions, caricatures Asians as terrible drivers and brownface minstrelsy when he imagines what it would be like to have a Mexican Jesus who, of course, speaks in wheedling broken English and embodies other stereotypes about Mexicans. Modern-day minstrels are also easily distinguished from race, sex, or gender-neutral comics. The latter opt not to foreground or perform marginality even when and if they occupy a marginalized category of identity like being a woman, being a person of color, being queer, or differently abled. Wayne Brady and Ellen DeGeneres are perhaps the best known comics who have made successful careers out of comedy while seldom (if at all) drawing attention to their blackness or lesbian-ness (or woman-ness), respectively. For women comics, performing gender neutral has historically proven successful; audiences would rather not be reminded that this is a woman's point of view, making it harder for male audience members to identify. Women, on the other hand, are trained to identify with men early on and to see male struggle as human struggle. But for comics of color, performing race neutral can (though not always) yield the opposite result. Unlike comics like Kevin Hart, talented black male comics such as Wayne Brady, B.T., and Donald Glover work hard to achieve similar success with their race neutral comedy. One reason may be that the public wants them to call attention to their race and to perform in concert with their expectations about what being Black looks and sounds like (think: Bon Qui Qui). If performing race neutral does not sell, but "ghetto fabulous" does, it is more likely comics will opt for the latter style, which stand-up comic W. Kamau Bell describes as the "*Def-Jam school*" of comics.[39]

In defining what constitutes raceface and queerface minstrelsy, I am not proposing an essentialist understanding of any race, ethnicity, sexuality, or gender. Gender expressions vary greatly within sexes and there are certainly individuals who destabilize notions of an essentialist race or ethnicity (not to mention science) by crossing over and performing in ways that are not analogous to their perceived race or congruent with social expectations of how ethnicity should be performed. However, I am proposing that stereotypical deployment of certain identities marked by otherness finds favorable viewership among the American public, regardless of comic intent. There is always the danger that comedy will be misinterpreted and sometimes comedy meant to unpack racist stereotypes can function to reinforce those stereotypes; after all, comedy is subjective. For a long time, Kondabolu avoided drawing attention to his Indian-ness for fear of garnering laughs for the wrong reasons. Entertaining similar concerns, Dave Chappelle was extraordinarily successful with his sketch comedy that lampooned stereotypes about African Americans but was also aware that his work could and was being misread by the public, a misreading contributing to its popularity. Unwilling to continue taking the risk of misinterpretation, Chappelle canceled his show despite the millions being dangled as lure to keep him shucking and jiving for cable producers.

We know little about why individuals respond the way they do to humor or if they are laughing for the same reasons as their neighbor. Yes, there are theories of laughter but since multiple theories are in play at once (e.g., superiority theory, incongruity theory, repression theory) and individuals will interpret jokes differently, there is no single analysis that can divine why each person laughed at a particular joke. Audience reception is the big unknown in any study of performance, a problem discussed by UK comedy native Stewart Lee in his comedy special *41st Best Stand-Up Ever* (2008), performed live in Glasgow, Scotland:

> Now, one hesitates in the current climate to make a joke on the stage about the Muslims, right? Not for fear of religious reprisals—when has that ever hurt

anyone?—[*laughter*] but because of the slightly more slippery anxiety, which is like basically when you stand up in a small room it's like, we're all friends—hurray—and we can make a joke. But you don't really know how a joke is received or it could be that it's laughed at enthusiastically in a way that you don't understand. . . . The problem is 84 percent of people, apparently of the public, think that political correctness has gone mad. Now, um, I don't know if it has. People still get killed for being the wrong color or the wrong sexuality or whatever. And, what is political correctness? It's an often clumsy negotiation toward a kind of formally inclusive language and there's all sorts of problems with it but it's better than what we had before. But 84 percent of people think political correctness has gone mad. And you don't want one of those people coming up to you after the gig and going, "Well done mate, well done actually for having a go at the fucking Muslims [*laughter*]. Well done, mate. You know, you can't do anything in this country anymore mate, it's political correctness gone mad. You can't even write racial abuse in excrement on someone's car [*laughter*], without the politically correct brigade [*laughter*] jumping down your throat." And you don't want those people coming after you after gigs because that's Al Murray the pub landlord's audience [*laughter*], missing the point and laughing through bad teeth like the dogs they are [*laughter*].[40]

The inability to control why people laugh influences the production of humor. For some comics, being understood is essential to the process. Comedian and cast member of NBC's *Parks and Recreation*, Aziz Ansari intentionally chooses not to talk about or draw attention to his South Asian heritage: "I don't know. . . . I think it's too easy. Jokes about curry, oh, I just don't like to do that."[41] This candid statement, made prior to a performance on the televised comedy showcase, *Premium Blend*, assumes that any discussion about his ethnic or racial background would unquestionably draw interest and favor from audiences. Given the popularity of modern-day minstrelsy and the public's penchant for "eating the 'Other,'" Ansari is probably right. The point is he would never know why people were laughing if he were to draw attention to his Indian-ness, whether via minstrelsy or self-deprecating humor or other kind of technique, and that uncertainty is motivation enough to prevent him from joking about certain subjects.

Comic styles and techniques in stand-up comedy (i.e., from shock humor to the agitprop of Carrot Top) all function to enhance the comedic effect of the performer. This is also the case with modern-day minstrelsy. Since comedy always takes aim at something or someone, the target often falls to individuals and groups that stand out as different or inferior in some way, making minstrelsy most useful as comic strategy. The history of audience trends illustrate that this kind of comedy fares well among consumers. Vaudeville historians write of the glut of ethnic humor produced during swells of immigration at the turn of the twentieth century, remarking on its capacity to ease cultural tensions among disparate groups in urban centers, to aid immigrants in assimilating, and to teach various ethnic groups about one another. A more optimistic reading of early nineteenth blackface minstrelsy suggests that this performance genre offered means of coping with difference, but the question now becomes whether it is really a coping mechanism as much as it is simply a profitable maneuver for comics seeking fame and fortune. There will be some (or perhaps many) who wax the merits of such strategies, invoking a kind of Freudian rationale that turning our fears over to laughter provides psychic release or that in a world tacitly requiring political correctness, comedy offers a safe space to give voice to repressed desires. After all, it is not the audience acting profanely or in socially inappropriate ways; rather, the audience is merely responding to a single performer who gives voice to such inanities. And yet, showing appreciation for minstrelsy or bigoted world-views ensures that minstrelsy and ethnic/racial caricatures maintain themselves as a staple tradition among stand-up comics. White feature comic Kristen Key remands herself of any personal responsibility for telling a racist joke, instead shifting responsibility onto the audience when their laughter intensifies during a joke in which she alludes to Latinos/as as thieves and Asians as poor drivers:

> A gang war broke out in my refrigerator and the half-and-half didn't know which side it was on [*laughter*]. The salsa stole everything around it [*laughter*]. I had a bottle of soy sauce just crashing into shit [*loud laughter and clapping*]. You guys like that one didn't you [*loud laughter*]? You racist bastards. That's okay, we all know soy sauce can't drive [*laughter*]. If I saw soy sauce driving a Honda Civic on the highway I'd pull the fuck over [*laughter*].[42]

The audience delights in condiments anthropomorphized as the highly cultivated stereotypes about Asians and Latinos/as, but that delight is rendered suspect when Key reminds audience members that they are culpable in this exchange. In fact, the tension only subsides when she goes on to suggest ideological congruence by agreeing that indeed soy sauce (read: Asians) cannot drive. Importantly, Key would not keep telling this joke if it did not prove successful night after night in comedy clubs across the United States.

Laughter in response to minstrelsy could signal appreciation of the stereotypes or merely recognition of the stereotypes. One position agrees with the premise, and the other position simply recognizes the premise and perhaps appreciates its cleverness; both yield laughter. This is an important distinction, but one that is not easily discernible vis-à-vis audience reception. Someone can appreciate the structure of a joke without agreeing with its content, so you cannot assume causal lines between what you hear on stage and the politics or intentions of the minstrelsy performance. As audience member or consumer, we may be laughing alongside others who do agree with its content, but for completely different reasons. Neither are those performing minstrelsy simply unthinking or bigoted comics; rather, use of this comedic strategy may only be a marketing strategy, good natured fun, a way to build community, among other things. Comics may have no intention to harm or subordinate minorities, but we as audience members would not necessarily know that. Comics help clarify these intentions by contextualizing jokes, like when Louis C.K., just moments before performing queerface, does a whole bit that humorously dissects and summarily dismisses all the reasons supplied for outlawing gay marriage. C.K. situates himself firmly as LGBTQ ally, on one hand, minimizing the insult of queerface, but on the other hand, profiting from this strategy. Understanding a performer's intentions by being given additional context helps audience members in the process of interpretation. The sequence in which he tells these jokes allows the audience to have a sense of Louis C.K.'s position on gay civil rights indicating to the audience that it was fine to laugh when he later performed queerface minstrelsy. Comics can have a worldview that inspires them to write charged humor and minstrelsy jokes and place them side by side. This has been a useful strategy to employ for comics seeking wide commercial appeal. Performing minstrelsy will help secure fans and using charged humor alongside this lets viewers know that you do not actually believe what you are saying on stage.

One must also consider that minstrelsy, when performed in front of a racially homogenous audience—a Latino comic to a majority Latino/a audience or a queer comic in front of a queer audience—does not necessarily function in the same way as when a racial or sexual minority performs minstrelsy for a mainly White or mixed audience or a majority heterosexual audience. The latter is racialized/sexualized spectacle and the former can be a conduit for creating community in much the same way that charged humor builds cultural citizenship, a strategy for empowering marginalized social identities that move through the world as second-class citizens. Modern-day minstrelsy, when exchanged intraracially or sexually, has the capacity to make a mockery of the stock characters or stereotypes and explore common cultural practices, finding shared truths without being consigned the unidimensionality of a stock character. Depending on the joke and the context in which it is told and to whom, charged humor can look like modern-day minstrelsy as when Lea DeLaria performs in Los Angeles at the Outlaugh Festival, the first queer comedy festival.

We used to be queer. We were fuckin' queer. What are we now? Now we're middle-class mainstream assholes who sit around and talk about how we're just like straight people. . . . you go to the pride rallies and there's always some piss-ant mainstream faggot standing up there saying [*in a fey voice*], "We're just like everyone else." [*Resumes normal voice*] You know that asshole?! [*Assumes feminized voice again*] "We're like straight people, we're just like 'em. We are like straight people. We are like them and they are like us. We're like everyone else." [*Resumes normal voice*] Yeah and that's when the seven and a half foot tall drag queen walks by with three foot spangle platforms and opens his butterfly wings [*laughter and clapping*].[43]

Ranting about gay civil liberties while pacing the stage, DeLaria's point of view has trouble finding a home on televised comedy showcases or the like but among queer folks, she is well known and followed. She uses queerface minstrelsy to make a point about the shortcomings of assimilationist strategies for winning civil rights, but this bit would function differently if placed in another setting in front of a majority heterosexual audience. The punch line comes at the end when DeLaria, a White lesbian comic, describes a drag queen of epic proportions. Told to other queer people, the laughter appreciates both the critique of the marriage equality movement and the humorous description of a drag queen whose proxy we have all seen at one point during annual pride events. The laughter arises from affectionate familiarity with the scene described and we can comfortably laugh at her critique without compromising the integrity of the movement, that is, in all likelihood no queer person is going to abandon the movement because of her indictment of it. She critiques the movement to make it stronger and her queerface minstrelsy attacks the sentiment: "We're like everyone else," because DeLaria unapologetically demands access to civil liberties, not because queers can demonstrate how normal they are, but because civil rights are human rights that everyone deserves regardless of their differences. Queerface here is less about mocking a gay affect or reducing gay men to a one-dimensional caricature; rather, a way of illustrating a larger point. Every joke has its own life and should never be considered the sum total of a comic's abilities or point of view. Moreover, every joke can be interpreted differently by audience members whose social identities and experiences shape interpretation. What may feel empowering in a shared space of community members is subject to misinterpretation in a different, less homogenous setting. DeLaria's joke told to a straight audience may confirm their suspicions that queer folks are deviant or strange, perhaps even too abnormal to be allowed the right to adopt children, marry, become religious officials, or be in the Boy Scouts. Charged humor in one setting may read as modern-day minstrelsy in another, and in some instances comics use minstrelsy in order to perform charged humor, slipping in the critique but ensuring a laugh by using minstrelsy. Given the popularity of minstrelsy, comics like Margaret Cho learn to harness effective comedy strategies while developing a point of view that is clearly charged.

Margaret Cho has achieved and maintains a certain status as female comic icon because she appeals to several niche audiences like LGBTQ persons, feminists, liberals/leftists, Korean Americans, hipsters, Asian Americans, and intellectuals. Since 2000, Cho's comedy specials (all released as DVDs) push the envelope in ways that most televised female comics do not because by the turn of the twenty-first century she was established enough to produce comedy specials chock full of charged humor; in other words, she no longer had to pander to networks or network affiliates or middle America. Given this latitude, she overtly fights homophobia and gender and racist stereotypes and has used her comedy to expose Hollywood's preoccupation with beauty standards and white norms. She can do so because of her position *beyond* the night-club circuit; however, the material that made her famous and got her to this point in her career was not her more controversial charged humor employed now with more gusto and frequency but the ethnic humor she employed as a Korean American young woman impersonating her first-generation Korean immigrant mother in the 1990s.

> So hi, my name is Margaret Cho, and I'm Korean. SO Korean. I even have a Korean name. Muran. Which is a pretty name. But you have to understand, I've heard my mother scream it from across the hills: [*assumes Korean accent*] "Muran!!! [*laughter and applause*]. Muran!" [*resumes normal voice*]: WHAT???? I'm sure you can relate [*laughter and applause*]. My mother has a problem with blind intersections. She will sit there for a very long time and rant. [*assumes Korean accent*]: "They never give you chance" [*laughter and applause; resumes normal voice*]! I used to get so busted when I was a teenager because I was so into the film of *Flashdance* that I cut the neck out of all my sweat shirts. My mom was over it. [*assumes Korean accent*] "Why you cut the shirt?!? [*laughter and applause*]. Why cut—ooh, frashdance. Well I think you're the maniac" [*laughter and applause*].[44]

Notice that laughter and applause follows mimicry of her mother's Korean accent when speaking English; in fact, her jokes are set up such that the punch lines *are* this imitation. Early Cho material does include charged humor alongside yellowface minstrelsy. Since charged humor mainly flounders compared with other comic styles and techniques in mainstream markets, one explanation for Cho's meteoric rise to fame lies in frequent and profligate use of Korean mimicry, which on one hand confirms audience suspicions about immigrant outsider status and mocks acculturation struggles and on the other hand locates Cho as having in-group status, that is, sufficiently Americanized. Another comic deftly producing charged humor punctuated by minstrelsy, when Persian American comic Maz Jobrani invokes queerface minstrelsy he does so with the intention of bringing attention to unfair treatment of LGBTQ persons serving in the military. Before Don't Ask Don't Tell (DADT) was repealed, this joke was a favorite of Jobrani's and a standard in his act for some time:

> The U.S. military still has the rule, they're trying to change it, the Don't Ask Don't Tell rule. The U.S. military fired some Arabic translators who were American but they were doing Arabic translations; they fired them because they found out they were gay. Don't Ask Don't Tell. Translators! I was like, what are we afraid of? What are they gonna gay up the translation? Right? It'll be like, [*Puts finger to ear, with fingers out in an effeminate way, and with a feminized voice*] "Okay, I hear some chatter! They're gonna be a bombing at the embassy. [*Bites lip sexually*] And a sale at Prada, oh my God!" [*roaring laughter*].[45]

When I asked Jobrani to talk about whether or not his humor sought to educate or illuminate social issues important to him, he referenced this joke specifically, writing that he "had seen a *60 Minutes* episode where the US Navy had fired some Arabic translators who were American because they found out they were gay." He describes the rest of the joke and then says this of his intent: "The joke being that a gay man would be interested in the sale at Prada. But more importantly, I'm pointing out that the policy is ridiculous and that gay people should be allowed to serve in the military. I also make a point of stating at some point in that joke that gay people should be allowed to get married."[46] Cho couples her yellowface minstrelsy with charged humor; Jobrani does the same with queerface minstrelsy. Many comics take the time to contextualize their humor, earnestly indicating beliefs that may conflict with ensuing jokes. For example, K-Von, a Persian American comic, establishes himself as anti-racist up front, but whose jokes are (mostly Arabface) minstrelsy or maintain a steady stream of stereotypes about other groups:

> But honestly guys, because I am from a multicultural family, I like to promote peace. And I don't like racism. I just like to joke about our cultures and then let it go. Do you guys agree? We can be positive and support each other? [*clapping*]. And I realize even little things people miss. Like at my gym I play basketball with my Black friends. And sometimes they slam dunk the ball and they're like [*assumes a "Black" voice*], "Boom dog, in your face! Boo-ya!" [*Resumes normal voice*] Right to me. And I'm like dude, I'm White. I'm not supposed to be good at basketball [*laughter*]. I don't swim in front of my Black friends and be like [*in a triumphant voice repeated for each example given*] "In your face dog! Boo-ya, in

your face! [*laughter*] In your face!" [*laughter*]. That would be rude, and racist. Don't do that [*laughter*]. I don't parallel park in front of my Asian friends. Like: "Look in your face! [*laughter and clapping*]. No, I didn't hit it! In your face!" [*laughter and clapping continues*]. You wouldn't want to whip out your social security card in front of your Mexican friends, like: "In your face! In your face!" [*groaning mixed with laughter and clapping*].[47]

His comic narrative assures audience members that he does not intend to harm with his jokes and he even identifies these beliefs as racist stereotypes. The objective here is to laugh. He knows what it takes to secure those laughs, that cultural frames invoking common knowledges (erroneous or not) will fare well with most of his audience. By prefacing these particular jokes in this way, he avoids the negative audience responses (almost entirely) such as shaking the head, tsking, groaning, and booing and instead shifts those audible responses to favorable ones by assuaging audience concerns that he does not, in fact, actually agree with the stereotypes being cashed in for yucks. In the case of K-Von, he is careful when presenting jokes that build from racist cultural beliefs but takes more liberties when parodying his own Persian family members. He enacts modern-day minstrelsy because it draws from what he knows and because allusion to and mimicry of his Persian "otherness" makes him interesting (provides a point of view) and commercially viable in the current cultural economy of humor. Comics use minstrelsy as mainstay comic strategy or, like C.K., Cho, Jobrani, and K-Von, employ it as a means to an end, a comedic decoy that garners the laughs necessary to establish national notoriety even while exposing inequality, racial assumptions, and homophobia, in other words producing charged humor.

Mainstreaming Charged Humor

It's very strange to be an American in the UK because in America I'm not always an American. When people come up to me they normally say: "Hey man, where are you from?" and I tell them: "I'm from New York City." And then they're like "No, where are you *really* from?" [*laughter*]. Which, of course, is code for: "No, I mean why aren't you White?" [*laughter*]. Which is offensive right? I'm being judged based on the color of my skin, not by my most important qualities, which of course are the softness and smoothness of my skin [*laughter*].[48]

And so begins Hari Kondabolu's stand-up comedy performance on Russell Howard's *Good News*. Debuting on British television on April 4, 2011, and with several US television appearances under his belt since, Kondabolu is well situated for upward advancement in the comedy industry. Just months before he premiered on the BBC, he finished filming a half hour comedy special on Comedy Central, a monumental step toward becoming mainstream, or a hot-ticket item on the national comedy circuit. With precision timing in both performances, Kondabolu makes candid observations about irresponsible social behavior and drily recounts personal interactions that introduce issues of racism, homophobia, religious intolerance, health care, environmental consciousness, class inequality, and ignorance—these usually take place with someone who approaches him after a performance with a question or concern about a joke. In a sea of comics deploying modern-day minstrelsy or hacky stereotype jokes, Kondabolu stands out among his colleagues for his commitment to conscientious charged humor.

Because of his style of performance: aggressively progressive, on occasion he faces audience resistance, whether backlash from Islamophobic hecklers, people insisting Jesus is White, or individuals shouting: "Hey, why don't you tell some real jokes." While performing in Denmark he was told to go back to America, a directive Kondabolu found funny enough to include in future performances. He quips: "I've been told to go back to so many countries but never to America [*laughter*]. So, I've been told to go back to Iraq, Afghanistan, Libya. Whatever country we are bombing, I've been told to go back there at perhaps the least opportune time to go back [*laughter*]. It was nice to be told [to go back to] America, the country I was born and raised."[49] Thus, Kondabolu's charged humor becomes intricately layered. Audience members interrupt him during his sets just as often as they approach him following performances in order to challenge his beliefs and worldviews. Following this, there will be an exchange between this concerned citizen and Kondabolu, the substance of which he then incorporates into the joke in future performances. The original joke becomes a lead-in to a joke about audience response to the original joke. This strategy not only builds a longer repertoire of charged humor, but offers the audience insight into various human responses to controversial subject matters. For example, in his "white chocolate joke," it becomes a way to address and challenge racism and the numerous (and seemingly innocuous) ways it persists.

And I love chocolates [*pause*] for political reasons [*laughter*]. No, 'cause you see in America, Americans are assumed to be White unless otherwise specified. And that's why I like chocolates 'cause when you first think of chocolate you think of something brown [*laughter*]. And if you think of white chocolate first, well then, you're a fucking racist [*laughter*]. Honestly, who thinks of white chocolate in that situation? And that brings up the bigger issue. Why do we need white chocolate to begin with? [*laughter*]. What was wrong with chocolate exactly? It's chocolate. It's great. Why would you need to make white chocolate? You love the taste of chocolate but can't stand looking at it? [*laughter*]. Well, then try some white chocolate. It's from the people who brought you White Jesus [*laughter*]. Um, so I was telling that joke recently in the States, and some man came up to me after the show and told me he was really frustrated. He said, I don't really like that White Jesus joke. And I knew we had an issue because I've always considered that my white chocolate joke. So [*pause*] different perspectives. So, I ask him, what issues did you have with my joke? He's like, well I don't agree with you. I think Jesus was White. Well that's fine, you can believe whatever you want to believe. Look, I don't believe in gravity, but you don't see me flying [*laughter*]. You can believe what you want to believe, but the facts are the facts. Both of Jesus' parents are from the Middle East, for all intents and purposes they were brown, and two brown people cannot create a fucking Swedish tennis player [*laughter*]. He looks like Björn Borg for no reason. It's impossible! And then he said, look I'm not an idiot—which was debatable at that point in the conversation—I'm not an idiot I understand what you're saying. But here's the thing, his mom Mary, she was from the Middle East, she could be brown. But his father as we all know, God, was White [*laughter*]. Now, I really should have walked out of the room at that point, but I didn't. Because I wanted to know how this future joke was going to end [*laughter*]. What you're saying is crazy. You do realize this right? Mixing brown with white, does not create white. Any child or racist could tell you that [*laughter*].[50]

Kondabolu invites the audience to feel superior to and laugh at the man defending an Aryan Jesus. Laughter is aimed at those exhibiting ignorance, whose innocent questions reveal white supremacist attitudes that are challenged by Kondabolu and further condemned by an audience championing Kondabolu's indignation. To laugh at these jokes requires, on some level, knowledge of the comic frame, that is, the discourses that circulate about race, and agreement with the object or subject under derision. Part of the value of charged humor is its ability to offer solutions, and when Kondabolu recounts these interactions, he disseminates useful advice for engaging in similar discussions or debates. Provocative first-hand accounts such as these records a history of exchange between audience and performer, yields important data about audience response to charged humor, and illustrates precisely why charged humor is less marketable (i.e., it has the capacity to polarize) and why Kondabolu may be ghettoized as an activist comic.

Despite being a comic that undoubtedly writes and performs charged humor most of the time, Kondabolu shies away from the label "activist" and seeks to avoid being pigeonholed at this early stage in his professional career, saying: "When people call me an 'activist comedian' you marginalize me even though that's not your intent; I'm a mainstream comic."[51] Many comics in the mainstream incorporate some charged humor, but few use it to the exclusion of all other kinds of comedy writing, like Kondabolu does now. There are economic and professional consequences for being niched as an activist or political comic that Kondabolu would rather avoid. As opposed as he is to being called an activist comic, he is equally vehement that the mainstream comedy venues can and should include his charged points of view.

> Branding me as an activist makes me sound CORNY. It also marginalizes my comedy and the topics I like to discuss. These are not niche topics that are just relatable to a specific demographic. Racism, for example, is as real a thing as dogs and cats and Justin Beiber. It's part of my experience and the American experience. It affects my day-to-day. I want the mainstream American audience to hear it. Giving the topics I talk about a "special status" takes away the power of their existence in our day-to-day.[52]

Charged comedy arises from a comic intent to use comedy to edify and illumine social inequalities. Given the content of his comedy, Kondabolu could easily market himself exclusively to national nonprofit corporations, advocacy groups, and colleges and universities who routinely hire entertainment for fundraisers, award ceremonies, and student events. Human rights organizations supporting the marriage equality movement would love to have Kondabolu come and tell jokes like the one he delivers in a video blog for PBS:

> Marriage is just a big costume party, with health benefits and tax credits. If you're so concerned that the institution of marriage will be damaged and is so vulnerable shouldn't you try to ban celebrities from getting married? Those are the most public examples of failed marriages. . . . And you're worried about the sanctity of marriage? What is marriage, what has marriage been? I mean, it wasn't about love. It wasn't about romance. It was about property, it was about accumulating wealth. It was about producing boys to work on the farm. We've changed what marriage means. It's about love and partnership, companionship for the future. And if it's just about those things, well shouldn't gay people be allowed to have that as well? We all have the right to compromise our dreams for someone else and then die alone. That is a God given right![53]

But, he refuses to promote himself to these niche markets, claiming that his work is not esoteric. Indeed, bigotry is as American as apple pie. Everyone can understand the critiques couched in charged humor, but not everyone wants to hear those critiques, especially when the critiques leave little room for misinterpretation. Kondabolu works to ensure that, if possible, mainstream audiences do hear these critiques and that his performances do not run the risk of preaching to the converted.

Where minstrelsy leaves the performer uncertain as to why people are laughing—is it at the ridiculousness of stereotypes exploited or is it confirming existing beliefs about groups of people—audience response to Kondabolu's charged humor is a bit more transparent not only because he incorporates audience feedback into his comedy, but because he clearly situates himself as antibigoted, which helps communicate comic intent to his audience. He jokes:

> So I went to this party recently, people had been drinking, and you know when people get drunk they become a bit more honest and sometimes honesty sounds racist, sexist, homophobic, etc. So we're getting drunker and I hear this man say: "That ground zero mosque they're building is terrorizing Americans. It's just awful." So I go up to this man and I say, "Hey man. I just wanna say it's not a mosque; it's actually an Islamic community center. And even if it was a mosque, you know what? That'd be okay too." And he turned to me and he said, "you're just saying that because you're a Muslim." And I said: "Actually, I'm not a Muslim, I'm a Hindu." And he said, "Well that's like the same thing" [*laughter*]. And it's not the same thing. The first clue is that they are two different words [*laughter*]. Also, Hindus and Muslims have been killing each other for hundreds of years [*laughter*]. So I explained that to him. And he said: "Sorry, but you have to admit, you look like a Muslim" [*laughter*]. Fair enough. I was wearing a Weezer t-shirt and converse sneakers at the time [*laughter*], which all Muslims wear at all times regardless of our context [*laughter*]. What I actually told him was: "Here's the thing man, Islam is perhaps one of the most racially diverse religions of the world. So technically, White man, you also look a Muslim." I thought that was really clever. He did not [*laughter*]. 'Cause he said, "I'm a Christian, idiot." And I said, "Yes, you are a Christian idiot" [*laughter and clapping*]. And then he said: "What? What is that supposed to mean?" And that's when I lost my temper. Because the religious intolerance, I know how that works in the world but that was a basic grammar joke, man. I moved the comma to the right. If you do not understand a basic grammar joke then we have nothing in common [*laughter*].[54]

The following joke forces engagement with ways of thinking that call into question society's "natural" hierarchies of religion, race/ethnicity, and nationality. Clearly, he advocates religious tolerance, challenging Islamophobia, educating viewers about the racial diversity of Muslims, and offering a crash course in Hindu-Muslim relations. It is difficult to imagine someone misinterpreting Kondabolu's contempt for religious intolerance in this portion of his set on *Good News*, or that the ensuing laughter means much else other than audience affirmation of his point of view.

Every comic has a point of view. As many comics will attest, this evolves over time and new and revised jokes reflect this maturation process. Maz Jobrani reports that it took nearly thirteen years performing stand-up comedy before he found his point of view and started to feel more comfortable in his writing and performance style. Kondabolu crafted the jokes seen on television appearances over time, and years spent in the UK allowed him to broaden the scope of comics whose work he aspires to replicate. While Kondabolu confesses that it would be wonderful for people to be impacted by his comedy, he does not operate out of the belief that his comedy will necessarily change minds or beliefs.

> I don't see my comedy as a form of "activism." If others do, I really appreciate it, because it means that they value what I'm doing and perhaps my comedy resonates with the advocacy they are doing or with their beliefs. I love the idea that what I do can be cathartic for people, especially those working in the struggle for justice. However, my objective with standup is to create thoughtful laughter that is in line with my point of view [and] is from an honest place. That "place" happens to be one that is very sensitive and conscious about the world, the impact of words, and does not want to harm people.[55]

Whether or not Kondabolu's intends to change people's lives his commitment to producing charged humor that seeks not to harm means he will have an impact (positive or negative) on audiences.

Kondabolu knows his comedy reverberates beyond the performance venue. Tangible evidence of the impact of his comedy comes from viewers who offer feedback and sometimes criticism following performances. Kondabolu makes every effort to be conscientious, to craft thoughtful comedy that pays attention to words and their effects. Thus, he takes all feedback quite seriously. For instance, he has had conversations provoking consternation about word choices in his jokes such as "crazy," "dumb," and "bitch," all of which are loaded terms historically and been used to disempower and dismiss the concerns of women and the differently abled. He reflects on one such concern, saying:

> One time I was asked about the word "dumb." I used the word "dumb" in a joke—folks who are mute were called "dumb" historically as a slur—and I made the choice to keep a joke that used the word because I felt like that's what makes this point work. . . . I hate to make those choices because it pits one oppression over another but [as a comedian] you have to make choices and I decided, "this is a joke about immigration," so I went for it. If I took that word out it loses the power to push this immigrant's rights piece so I had to make a choice. I do the best I can to be deliberate with language and you know, I fail, but I try to acknowledge it.[56]

For every joke that contains terminology that may offend, you can be sure that Kondabolu has given great consideration to its inclusion and probably performed the bit in myriad ways with and without such terms. Most comics do this, make small adjustments to a joke to heighten its comedic effect or make clear their point of view or comic intent. Kondabolu distinguishes himself by making such adjustments because of the same impulse that initially moved him to write charged humor—namely, to cause as little harm as possible. And on that count, he does differ from other comics, who like him may analyze every word but not in order to ensure that they are being thoughtful or socially conscious.

Kondabolu wants his work to continue flourishing in the mainstream, for immigration reform to be as relatable and interesting to people as Katy Perry or Honey Boo Boo, and for charged humor to be as commonplace in the discussion as any other. For that to happen, charged comics require a consumer base large enough to give audience to their worldviews, meaning charged comedy would have widespread commercial appeal. Until charged comedy proves itself profitable, meaning the content will succeed with mainstream America (with special attention paid to men ages 18–36), advertisers will satisfy themselves to support programming that may appear edgy, but in main does not substantively critique social hierarchies or comment on privilege. Since the 1980s, when stand-up comedy centralized as a profitable form of entertainment, charged comedy became increasingly difficult to bring to wider audiences. Fearing that charged humor may polarize audiences and prevent commercial success, comics self-edited their material, agents encouraged comics to steer clear of sensitive matters on which audiences may be divided, and comedy club managers and bookers hiring comics, especially for television shows, simply did not hire comics whose material was primarily charged. Fast-forward thirty years to comedy whose content consists primarily of remonstrations against aging, the monotony of marriage, or struggles with dating, and the difficulties of parenting. Mainstream comedy that does deal with racial and sexual difference commonly invokes minstrelsy—a reification of otherness and inferiority—or uses shock humor to rail against the imposition of political correctness. Rebelling against social protocol, the shock comic establishes herself as irreverent, which becomes explanation and pardon for telling racist, sexist, ableist, and homophobic jokes. The success of shock humor relies on an audience willing, if not relieved, to divest themselves of the shackles of political correctness. In either scenario—minstrelsy or shock humor—issues of race, gender, sexuality, religion, or class are not substantively addressed nor exposed as they are with Kondabolu's charged humor.

Doing all the right things to be firmly situated in the mainstream, except changing the content of his jokes, at times Kondabolu gets frustrated. While he does not want to be a "road dog," consigned to traveling the comedy circuit, he does want to continue to see opportunities come up for him to write, perform, and make a living wage. While he may not be headlining for comedy clubs or sought after as much as he would like, Kondabolu has no shortage of opportunities to work. Fielding offers to perform at mainly liberal arts colleges, maintaining a video blog on PBS's website, and writing for W. Kamau Bell's show *Totally Biased with W. Kamau Bell*, which aired August 9, 2012, on the FX Network but was canceled after two seasons, he has steady work and makes a decent middle-class living, though he would like to have health insurance. He considers himself a mainstream comic, working mainstream gigs, and rightfully so; he wrote for a show on cable, he has his own half-hour special on Comedy Central, and mainstream television credits on his resume.

Though he certainly has good exposure, which bodes well for him, Kondabolu's take-no-prisoners-style of charged humor may limit where and to whom he can perform in the future unless he compromises the content of his stand-up material. He could scale back the charged humor, or perhaps market his comedy to specific racial/ethnic enclaves or political factions, or hope that shifts in consumer demand compel comedy club managers and advertisers to make different hiring and programming choices. The fact that Kondabolu's half-hour special on cable network's Comedy Central contains so many charged jokes does offer some hope for the future of charged humor in mainstream stand-up venues. In one such joke, he derides Arizona anti-immigration policies being passed that same year.

> There's still a lot of racism in this country, like what you're seeing in Arizona right now is remarkable. This anti-immigration legislation that they're trying to push that would allow police officers to racially profile undocumented immigrants, especially people in the Mexican community. I think that's horrendous. But what amazes me is that people support this law. I was watching the news, this woman in Arizona, looking at the camera, straight-faced, she says, "Hey! We're just trying to bring the country back to the way it used to be!" The way it used to be? Lady, you're in Arizona. It used to be Mexico. I mean what are you talking about? [*cheers, applause*].[57]

There are certainly possibilities for increased exposure to charged humor such as this in the mainstream; indeed, the last decade has given rise to many new ways—like the popularity of talent contests where a national viewership determines the winner—for consumers to talk back and influence programming and weigh in on determining the next big star. The onus, though, lies with viewers to demand and support charged comics. Caitlyn Boston, writes: "an audience who loves someone's art, no matter what it is, needs to be aware of the universe that the art exists in and the subsequent choices that an artist may be forced to make if they are to remain a viable and productive conduit of the medium."[58] The more audiences know about the current market for comedy and the concessions a comic must make, the better equipped they become to intervene and rally for substantive changes in which messages are broadcasted. Audiences should not only be aware of the choices the market may impose upon comics, but that they have the right to tune in or tune out, to purchase or not purchase certain points of view or comic strategies.

Most important to seeing a shift in public access to charged humor, emerging technologies offer new forums for virtual connections with people sharing recreational and intellectual interests and comics quickly learned to harness social media tools to leverage a wider following. Today comics have websites with the latest information on tour dates and clips of their comedy, accounts on Facebook and MySpace devoted specifically to updates about their professional and personal lives, and comedy blogs, an additional forum for comics waxing hilarious on topical issues. They create listservs comprised of fans and send biweekly or monthly updates, keeping interested parties aware of upcoming performances and professional activities and amusing them with humorous anecdotes or home-grown vodcasts. Rob Delaney, a virtual nobody in the comedy scene, skyrocketed to fame and got hired on the national comedy club circuit after thousands began following his tweets on Twitter. W. Kamau Bell, Janine Brito, and Nato Green raised over twenty thousand dollars on Kickstarter.com by reaching out to their respective fan bases to fund the making of *Laughter against the Machine Tour Documentary*, a film that follows the three of them as they tour the country performing in over a dozen major cities in the United States. Global communication networks offer access to charged humor unlike any time before, and depending on how these new technologies are used—by comedy fans, comics, and club managers/bookers—they may alter the landscape of comedy in the twenty-first century. These fruitful avenues for global self-promotion helped make Hari Kondabolu a part of the mainstream and could ensure that he remains there, exposing a wider audience to his unique point of view, which he describes in the following way:

> I talk about what I know. I love the first two Weezer albums, the *Back to the Future* trilogy, and the Ken Burns 10-part series on the history of baseball. I happen to also hate racism, sexism, colonialism, homophobia, classicism, etc.-ism. I'm not just one thing, so why should I be one thing on stage? I'm a full human being with a range of experiences. People are allowed to be contradictory and complicated and to be working through things. I think performers are too.[59]

From shelling out hacky ethnic humor to exposing cisgender privilege using charged humor, Kondabolu's humor, like every other comic, shifts and evolves and will continue to do so. Truly valuable for understanding any stand-up comic, he demonstrates the complexity of the comic soul and calls for audiences to accept his point of view, which is multidimensional, full of contradictions, surprises, and always capable of redemption . . . and that is just the next joke.

How to Avoid the Last Laugh

He [Mark Twain] saw that humorist and audience can enjoy
humor's transgressive pleasures only by treating humor as play, as
symbolic rather than instrumental activity. But when he added
that "it must do both if it would live forever" and then defined
forever as thirty years, he stressed the immediate social relevance
of comic play. In that sense, whether ridiculous or sublime,
American humor reveals the state of the nation.

> *Judith Yaross Lee,* Twain's Brand: Humor in
> Contemporary American Culture

On Friday July 6, 2012, two gals headed to the Laugh Factory in Hollywood to
enjoy the stand-up comedy stylings of Dane Cook and Daniel Tosh. They had
heard of Dane Cook but knew nothing of Daniel Tosh. To maintain the ano-
nymity of the women, the events of the evening were recounted in first person
on a friend's blog on Tumblr, a social media site hosting millions of bloggers.
According to that blog, during Tosh's set, he told rape jokes. In his concert
film special, *Happy Thoughts* (2010), he tells one about his sister getting raped
when as a practical joke he replaces her pepper spray with silly string. It is unclear whether he was telling that joke or a different one. One of the two young
women yelled out, "Actually, rape jokes are never funny." According to the
heckler, Tosh responded saying, "Wouldn't it be funny if that girl got raped by
like, 5 guys right now? Like right now? What if a bunch of guys just raped
her?" The audience laughed as the two women got up and left the club. In the
woman's own words:

> I should probably add that having to basically flee while Tosh was enthusing
> about how hilarious it would be if I was gang-raped in that small, claustrophobic

room was pretty viscerally terrifying and threatening all the same, even if the actual scenario was unlikely to take place. The suggestion of it is violent enough and was meant to put me in my place.[1]

The blogosphere, social media sites, and even news programming picked up the story and for days on the Web debate raged as to the limits of comedy, specifically the appropriateness of rape jokes. Feminists like media critic Jennifer Pozner, allow that rape jokes *can* be funny, just not when they reify and condone a culture of rape. Wanda Sykes tells a hilarious joke in which she wonders about the newfound freedoms women would have if "our pussies were detachable." In this scenario, women ward off sexual assault by telling the perpetrator: "Sorry I left it [pussy] at home. I have nothing of value on me."[2] Men and women alike enjoy that joke. The tenor and substance of a joke makes all the difference. Tosh's joke on his comedy special and no doubt the one told at the Laugh Factory that night comes from a different place, a place that trivializes while also sanctioning rape. Sykes's bit on rape is charged while Tosh's most decidedly is not. In the aftermath, many agreed—including those feminists renowned for not being able to take a joke—that anything goes in stand-up comedy. After all, the Constitution allows for freedom of speech. But, that does not mean we have to like it or that we will find it funny. With the advent of multiple online platforms allowing for direct communication and feedback between consumers and public figures, there are now places to lodge those complaints for everyone to see. As with the example of Tracy Morgan's tirade against gays in the introduction, Daniel Tosh may find that his worldviews endear him to some, while others may blacklist him.

Some comics narrate our nation in ways more palatable than others and some comics who perform charged humor may do so sparingly in order to enhance marketability. There are rewards for nonpoliticized content, such as increased economic viability, and there are consequences for pushing the envelope, like losing your audience or your sponsor. Lea DeLaria was dumped (if only temporarily) by leading organizations in the marriage equality movement, after a fundraising event in Palm Springs when she began criticizing former President George W. Bush. Foregoing any attempt at discretion, authorities silenced her microphone and summarily escorted her off stage. Following this censorship, Lea DeLaria used the experience in her stand-up as illustration of the ways certain opinions are stifled, even among seemingly progressive organizations.

Occupying a minority status and openly referencing that minority status does not charged humor make. Comics performing modern-day minstrelsy earn a living by caricaturing themselves and Others, capitalizing on recognizable stereotypes about minorities and corroborating gender norms. This humor not only lacks complexity and creativity but also tacitly functions to shore up heteronormativity and white supremacy. Reluctant to participate in such a system, comics use charged humor to comment on their and others' experiences as second-class citizens; they identify issues of inequality and offer possible solutions. For instance, on the Arab American comedy tour in 2006, Dean Obeidallah concluded his performance saying:

> You know we are all Palestinians. . . . we are all Egyptians and we are all Lebanese and we're all Iraqis and we're all every country in the Arab world and if we work together here we can do anything we want [*big applause*]. It's the truth. The more we get involved in politics and in the media, then we can do more to define who we are as opposed to letting others define us with their own agenda.[3]

Obeidallah casts a wide net and makes us all Arabs, charging all viewers to make it part of their task to challenge erroneous and harmful misrepresentations of Arabs. Charged humor locates structural and systemic inequality and presents options for retaliation and remediation, as with this joke by Margaret Cho:

> I think we should get really active [about gay marriage]. I think we should make all the wedding planners go on strike. [*In a mock "gay" voice*] "If I can't get married, you can't get married. Go ahead. Try to do your own makeup [*laughter*]. Oh boo hoo. Who need [*sic*] a floral arrangement now [*laughter*]?"[4]

This joke encourages activism, draws from the existing arsenal of oppositional tactics by alluding to a worker's strike, and reveals the irony of not being allowed to marry the person you love while working in the marriage industry. This encouragement to mobilize and how to do so is a central feature of charged humor. For Irish American comic Kathleen Madigan, voting in local and national elections is one way of ensuring that politicians are looking out for your interests. She reports on her voting strategy during a performance:

> I'm not even qualified to vote. Every time I vote, I think, okay I read the paper and stuff. [*She shakes head and laughs*] No. . . . The last time I voted there were four pages of judges. Well, the only judge I know anything about is Judy and she was *not* on the ballot [*laughter*]. But I didn't leave it blank. I just stood there and randomly hired and fired people for no good reason [*laughter*]. [*She mimes ticking off names on a ballot*] Like—well, all the women are stayin', I can tell you that [*cheers and laughter*]. There's a nice Irish name, one of my people. And I think I'll round it off with the Mexican fella' [*clapping and laughter*].[5]

Voting can be a daunting activity even for those well informed. Her voting strategy may appeal to others who share her frustration and sense of uncertainty and even encourage audience members opting out of this civic duty to give it another chance. Her message: you do not have to know everything about the candidate if you also know that women, LGBTQ folks, and racial/ethnic minorities are underrepresented politically. To suggest that changing the demographics of politicians will result in more inclusivity and social justice may seem an oversimplification or a myopic panacea. Indeed, there are women on the front lines of antifeminist efforts (pace: Ann Coulter), impoverished folks who support tax breaks for the rich, and LGBTQ people who ally with political and religious factions working against gay civil rights. Yet, for Madigan, participation in the process outweighs apathy and ambivalence and we the people can create a legislature that more accurately reflects the populous as a whole. It is a place to start.

Art can be beautiful (art for art's sake), but it can also be proactive—these qualities are not mutually exclusive. Not every artist compels viewers to action, but when they do they are undertaking a social compact with their audience. This relationship of mutual accountability between artist and audience helps buoy and sustain action even when that contact severs. Benedict Anderson says that the nation is an imagined political community. Though the ways we imagine communities (national and otherwise) may not be grounded in truth—that is, our personal (and sometimes limited) perceptions—following the performance, we can imagine that the social compact remains intact and we can also imagine that other individuals are united in the fight to achieve equality even if they are not. In this way, comic performance can instill and inspire a sense of community, of unity toward a common goal. It does not have to, which is something I often tell students whose hackles are raised in defense of the shock comedy and equal opportunity offending that is so popular right now. The point is that it can and there are many comics who opt to make their comic artistry meaningful, whatever that looks like for them. The essential considerations that remain are future scholarship, action, and possibilities able to foment the changes (legal, philosophical, political, and cultural) necessary so that all may have the experience of full citizenship—formal and substantive.

Future Scholarship

Micia Mosely's stand-up comedy and range of Black lesbian subjectivities expressed through her one-woman show, *Where My Girls At? A Comedic Look at Black Lesbians*, has the potential to engage members of the dominant culture to identify with minority subjects. Mosely spoke about a number of instances when White men, in particular, have approached her after she performs to express their delight with her comedy along with open surprise at that delight. These men report that they never thought they would have anything in common with a Black lesbian but were surprised at how they identified with her or the characters in her one-woman show. It must be a stunningly strange moment when the straight man realizes that he and the Black lesbian desire to bed the same women, when that becomes a way for him to relate. But this goes beyond pursuing similar sexual conquests. Though it may begin there, some-times all it takes is a foot in the door for that same viewer to identify with other qualities like Playher's street savvy sensibility, Sistah's altruism, Ziggy's hopefulness, and Lady D's confidence. Audience identification with Others humanizes individuals and demystifies their respective communities, but it is difficult to determine its long-term impact or effects. Performance artists concerned with audience reception should devise and distribute postshow surveys and evaluations assessing issues of identification and audience engage-ment. The resulting data can inform creative decisions and script revisions. Mosely uses this technique to workshop individual characters in the show when they repeatedly fail to gain the audience's favor. She wants all of her characters to have the chance to move on to the next round of *America's Next Top Negress* and audience surveys help her identify what worked and what did not in her presentation of the five Black lesbians featured in the show. She also wants to ensure that her objectives are coming through in the perfor-mance and that audience reception corresponds, at least in part, to authorial intentions.

In addition to performing her one-woman show and stand-up comedy, in January 2010 Micia Mosely began creating biweekly vodcasts called the "Prog-ress Report" in which she tackles various cultural and political issues with humor, verve, and critical dialogue either alone or sometimes with other Black intellectuals. In the inaugural vodcast, released in that post-new-year-fugue when goals are set and change is imminent (for at least two weeks), she tells you how to balance your budget, increase self-efficacy, and the key to taking good care of yourself. Subsequent vodcasts reflect on President Obama's ad-ministration and another released around Valentine's Day (2010) encourages viewers to find a Black person to love or to simply love yourself. Among the uploaded vodcasts is a two-part "Progress Report" on Black authenticity in which she interviews Dax-Devlon Ross, lawyer and author of *Beat of a Differ-ent Drum: The Untold Stories of African Americans Forging Their Own Paths in Work and Life* (Hyperion 2006). They amble through a residential neighbor-hood in Bedford-Stuyvesant, Brooklyn, discussing the value and function of Black-owned businesses, race loyalty, and the economy of cultural work. As cultural entrepreneurs themselves, when it comes to the folks consuming their work, they want members of their own community to benefit from work about, by, and for them but recognize the value of exposure beyond the African Amer-ican community. The market reduces the labor of cultural production to a value, regardless of the skin color, creed, or sexual orientation of those owning the means of production. Thus, according to Ross, responsibility lies with the producer—the writer, the performer, the musician, the craftsperson, the farmer—to exercise responsible production:

> To me, it really is about are you creating quality product and are you supporting the product. I'm not necessarily as concerned with who owns that means. . . . It's in the capitalist structure, which says that I as the owner am going to feel like I am more entitled to you as the worker. And that necessarily has nothing to do with race. Whether a Black person who owns it or a White person who owns it . . . I am going to enact pretty much the same means of co-opting your labor for a value that's less than probably what it's worth.[6]

For him, what is essential is the product itself. In this case, is the book, painting, or comic performance fair to the community it represents? Is it well intentioned, instructive, and meant to inspire rather than parody and mock? These are important questions for producers to ask of their work and for all consumers to ask of the products and entertainment they consume.

Humor continues to pervade nearly every facet of communication and form of entertainment, and over the course of the last forty years it has insinuated itself in news programming, resulting in the explosion of infotainment or "soft news." While scholars have mined the field of late-night television talk shows and adult cartoons like *South Park*, *Family Guy*, and *The Simpsons*, they have overlooked Chelsea Handler's work as host of *Chelsea Lately*, the way humor is used in daytime television talk shows like *The Ellen DeGeneres Show* and *The View*, and all-women prank and stunt shows like *Rad Girls* and *Girls Behaving Badly*. *Betty White's Off Their Rockers* is a prank show that offers rich terrain for examining intersections of age, race, sex, and class. I would encourage scholars examining stand-up comedy or other forms of comic performance to select comic practitioners or performances whose influence is broad but who have not *already* been the subjects of analysis; some suggestions are Wanda Sykes, Karen Williams, Paul Mooney, Maz Jobrani, Kate Rigg, Katt Williams, Louis C.K., Bobby Lee, Azhar Usman, Julie Goldman, or other charged comics included in the compendium. Relatedly, while there is scholarship documenting the cultural struggles, material conditions, and historical experiences of some minority communities, there is a paucity of literature on cultural practices emerging from social identities such as Arab, differently abled, Asian, Latino/a, and LGBTQ communities residing in the United States and its territories.

Furthermore, compared to other groups such as women and African Americans, there is a noticeable absence of scholarship on humorous cultural forms and practices such as comic performances arising from Latino/a Americans, Asian Americans, American Indians, Muslim and Middle Eastern Americans, young people, and persons who are differently abled. Years of research reveal an intellectual lacuna that I hope in some way to mitigate with this investigation; however, it is beyond the scope of this book to remedy all such absences or to do so thoroughly for each community. There is a need for additional scholarship about minority comics and performances (especially for those groups just mentioned) using humorous expression to illumine political, cultural, and historical coordinates specific to their experiences of occlusion, persecution, and forced assimilation.

Future investigations of charged humor would benefit from additional data on audience reception. This would help us to know how viewers interpret certain comic material and the impact and effects of charged humor on individuals. Follow-up surveys conducted months later can indicate the long-term impact humor can have. Audience members may not remember specific jokes, but what are the impressions that linger, what ideas, strategies, or instructions remain with them long after the curtain closes. Documentation of the strategies humor employs to curry favor and facilitate audience identification would be useful to members of social movements seeking to co-opt cultural practices such as entertainment and artistic production and to advance causes and initiatives more effectively. The International Ladies Garment Workers Union realized this and, in 1935, created Labor State Inc., an organ of the Union devoted to creating theater dealing with labor issues. The outcome, a Broadway hit called *Pins and Needles*, was the longest running show in the 1930s and undoubtedly helped to support and foster prounion sentiment among audience members. It is also important to gather information on as many of these comic voices on the fringe as possible, for their fringe status already obviates the likelihood that they will be documented and remembered. This was part of my project here, to document jokesters who produce charged humor and seek to use the domain of humor to enact cultural citizenship, but none of whom have been the subjects of study by performance or cultural studies scholars, Americanists, or humor studies scholars. It is certainly valuable, important, and helpful to direct readers toward the kinds of scholarship enhancing future analysis of performance; however, it takes both theory and praxis to invoke change. If you, curious reader, are not a scholar then the next sections offer additional inroads for change that can be employed by any and everyone.

Future Action

On November 5, 2008, the day after the passage of Proposition 8, Robin Tyler and Diane Olson were waiting when the courthouse opened at 9:00 a.m. They filed a petition to the California Supreme Court to overturn the proposition. Over the next five years, the case made its way to the United States Supreme Court where in June 2013 the governing body declined to rule, upholding a lower courts previous ruling, which ruled Proposition 8 unconstitutional.

Tyler had hoped the proposition would be overturned by the US Supreme Court, because in May 2008, when California's Supreme Court made its decision to legalize same-sex marriage, they also recognized LGBTQ persons as a "suspect class" or minority. Based on the earlier ruling that LGBTQ persons are a recognized minority, she was confident that Proposition 8 would be found unconstitutional. Things did not turn out exactly as she anticipated, but the lower court's ruling still makes same-sex marriage legal (again) in California.

Shane Phelan reminds us that "attempts to acquire citizenship without changing the construction of citizenship that prevails in the United States will fail, and they will harm our most vulnerable members in the process."[7] Accordingly, making legal changes to citizenship without changing public opinion or broadening who belongs in the national imagination may actually fail. Both forums—public opinion and policy/legislative changes—must be addressed when undertaking significant citizenship reforms (read: who is given full rights as a citizen). Shifts in public opinion require visibility, education, and acceptance, making performance a viable strategy for social justice efforts. Other strategies include marches, demonstrations, community outreach initiatives, and other means of generating public dialogue about the issues. Changes in the legal status and recognition of LGBTQ persons require federal protection against employment discrimination based on sexuality, the right for same-sex couples to marry anywhere in the United States and be afforded the 1,138 rights conferred upon heterosexual married couples, a reform of hate crime legislation, the right to foster and/or adopt, and the list goes on. Undocumented persons residing in the United States are part of this nation and contribute in manifold ways, regardless of legal status. We should treat them as citizen members and support legislative efforts that make them legal citizens. Passage of the DREAM Act at the federal level is one step in the right direction as is supporting public policy at the state level such as the recent passage of Colorado's Senate Bill 33, which grants undocumented Colorado residents in-state college tuition. These reforms require civic and legal actions like law suits, lobbying Congress, electing sympathizers to public office, and constitutional reform, to name a few.

An intersectional politics seeking to redress the balance must do so on cultural and legal fronts so that isolated tactics are not rendered impotent. Robin Tyler believes that "marches don't mean the politicians listen to you. But what it does, it motivates and activates youth."[8] Marches and protests that energize their activist base must combine these events with direction for future political intervention. The same is true of charged humor. How can audience members or sympathizers get involved beyond this gathering—in the street or in the theater? What tactics can be employed individually like letters, e-mails, and visits to local and national politicians and where can we direct interested parties to participate in future collective action be that a rally, a letter-writing campaign, or volunteering for a local nongovernment organization or nonprofit organization. The importance lies in offering critiques alongside possible solutions, instead of just the former.

Another necessary task is the de-stigmatization of civil protest and collective action; rather, strategically linking freedom and autonomy with those rights allowing us to make the political process meaningful. Neoliberalism continues to do its work to undermine the likelihood of positive reception to social movements and it is part of the neoliberal project to discredit and malign social movements aimed at "redistribution downwards."[9] We must start connecting ideal citizenry with active participation in the political process (regardless of how that manifests) that goes beyond voting every two or four years. Active participation in politics must be coupled with an inclusiveness that does not divest groups or individuals of their cultural differences. The image of the active constituent and the activities associated with cultural resistance and political activism is in dire need of a makeover, a new image if you will. Less patronizing responses to protests in the past few years indicate that a new positive image of the protestor may be taking hold. The rise in the number of protests alone and the different folks coming out to participate in them is also promising. The Occupy movement, Stomp and Holler rallies and immigration reform protests have all drawn thousands, even millions into the streets on behalf of social and economic equality. Recent historical events and shifts in cultural attitudes and political beliefs may present an opportunity to refigure the tenets of democracy and what it means to promote diversity and multiculturalism; to offer all constituents real freedom and equality. Cultural revolutions require numbers, legitimate grievances, and a receptive body politic. When it comes to gay civil rights, Kate Clinton believes that gay visibility is not enough, that we are "'in a particular historical moment when we need to come out again. It's a second outing. We need to come out and challenge people around us, or at least identify ourselves as gay in a world that is larger than a gay world."[10] This does not just apply to the LGBTQ community; all minorities need to enact their own form of "coming out" in order to change their material conditions and lived experiences.

Future Possibilities

Hari Kondabolu writes more comedy than he performs these days. He also devotes some of his spare time to creating podcasts with his brother Ashok Kondabolu, former member of the now defunct hip hop group Das Racist. Uncertain of what the future holds, Kondabolu enjoys current opportunities—whether penned or performed—to create thoughtful charged humor. From

2011 to 2013, his position as comedy writer for *Totally Biased with W. Kamau Bell* demanded his full attention. In *The New Yorker*, Emily Nussbaum writes that the show's "gimmick is intersectional progressivism: he [W. Kamau Bell] treats racial, gay, and women's issues as inseparable."[11] The gimmick proved successful though short-lived because the show was canceled in November 2013. In the first season, Kondabolu moved in front of the cameras of *Totally Biased . . .* for a brief cameo updating viewers on Indian American progress in the United States, similar to Micia Mosely's "Progress Report" vodcasts.

> Mindy Kaling has the first ever sitcom [*The Mindy Project*] starring an Indian American [*clapping*]. This is huge! We've had an amazing run the last few years with more Indians in the public eye than ever before. There's like, fourteen of us now [*laughter*] . . . There's now enough Indian people where I don't need to like you just because you're Indian [*laughter*]. Because growing up I had no choice but to like this [screen shows a picture of convenient store owner Apu from *The Simpsons*] Yeah [*loud clapping and laughter*]. Apu, a cartoon character voiced by Hank Azaria—a White guy. A White guy doing an impression of a White guy making fun of my father [*laughter*]. If I saw Hank Azaria do that voice at a party I would kick the shit out of him [*sustained laughter and clapping*]. Or I'd imagine kicking the shit out of him [*laughter and clapping*]. I mean we only put up with Apu for so long because he was still better than this [screen shows a picture from *Indiana Jones and the Temple of Doom* of an Indian man eating monkey brains] [*moaning and clapping*]. Yeah that's us eating monkey brains in *Indiana Jones*. Indians don't eat monkey brains [*laughter*]. I don't know how many times I have to make that clear [*laughter*]. You can't just make up random racist shit and pretend that it's true [*clapping and cheering*]. I mean, what if I said that White people's eyes turn red in photographs because they're part devil [*laughter and clapping*]. Alright, now I'll tell you something that is not true [*laughter and clapping*]. I'm joking. I'm joking [*pause*] kinda [*laughter*].[12]

In the last twenty years, successful high-profile Indian American doctors, politicians, and actors have begun to supplant harmful or disparaging representations of South Asian Indians and Indian Americans. Having more Indian Americans in the public eye (or at least fourteen, including Kondabolu) means Kondabolu can be honest about the ways some of them have disappointed him: Governor of Louisiana Bobby Jindal for not supporting abortion and gay marriage; and Dinesh D'Souza for creating the political film *2016: Obama's America*, which uses psychoanalysis to argue that President Obama secretly desires to undermine the United States as an imperial world power. The capacity for a show like *The Mindy Project* to succeed did not just happen overnight or because Mindy Kaling was discovered to be damn good at what she does, though she is. Margaret Cho's attempt at a sitcom in the 1990s tanked and yet she has been heralded as one of the funniest people alive. Members of minority communities have worked hard for decades on many fronts to garner cultural citizenship and a respectable place at the proverbial table. Recent strategies for challenging cultural invisibility and inaccurate caricatures include harnessing emergent technologies, particularly pertaining to the Internet. They may offer an explanation, at least in part, for why *The Mindy Project* succeeded when Cho's similar venture did not.

The ability to reach a wide viewing audience or readership, formerly the province of a select, carefully chosen few, has become available to anyone with Internet access and a yen for the creative. This does not mean that what you read is good or even true, but the democratizing aspects of the Internet have shifted or at least broadened the scope of worldviews and voices we can hear. The standards of propriety or decency upheld for film and television do not apply to the Internet, and home grown videos and blogs might get more "hits" than a state of the union address by the president. This bodes well for charged comics. Commercial success requires a supportive consumer base, and the Internet offers a platform for anyone to make their case to the public. Facebook, started in 2004 by Mark Zuckerberg as a social networking service for Ivy-Leaguers, has since been used by over a billion users who create personal profiles to communicate and connect with other users, called "friends." Comics direct fans to "friend" them and then use the site to provide updates about upcoming shows, tours, or stories of interest. Like Facebook, Flickr was launched in 2004 as a social media site allowing users to upload pictures and short video clips (ninety seconds). A year later, YouTube was born, an online platform allowing users to upload videos. Originally the site could only sustain clips up to ten minutes in length, but has since expanded this feature allowing comics to upload entire sixty to seventy minute sets. This means that a performance by a charged comic at a little-known venue across the world has, over time, the capacity to go viral and reach millions of viewers. Following on the heels of the success of YouTube, two New York University undergraduates developed Twitter, a social media site allowing users to "tweet" messages (of up to 140 characters) to other users. If you like someone and want to keep up with their tweets, you become a "follower." Comics utilize this service to test out new material and followers can chuckle at and even respond to their one-liners. Savvy programmers and entrepreneurs continue to develop other social media sites, including Tumblr, a microblogging platform where comics can post entire routines in text or video; Instagram, a social media interface that functions like Twitter but with images instead of text; Foursquare, a location-based social networking site linking users in close proximity with one another; and Pinterest, a site allowing users to collect and post anything of interest like recipes, favorite books, products they enjoy, and comics they think are funny.

These social media sites provide manifold possibilities for comics to generate interest and allegiance from consumers. Exchanges between comics and fans on social media sites can feel like a refreshing collapse of the traditional boundaries maintained between performers and their public. Sustained presence on any one or many of these sites makes the relationship between comic and fan feel more intimate, more like a friend versus a celebrity crush. The sites foster two-way communication, meaning fans get the added pleasure of immediacy and direct virtual contact. Unlike a typical web homepage containing a bio, tour dates, and merchandise, comics can use social media sites to promote their own work and direct users to other comics they admire, causes they support, and stories of interest. For instance: if you like my comedy, then go check out this comic; if you enjoyed this joke about Guantánamo Bay, then you should read this recent exposé on the same topic. The immediacy and intimacy of social networking sites may mean that messages spread by charged comics are taken more seriously and heard by more people. In turn, since the flow of information occurs both ways, fans can also place pressure on comics whose messages they do not appreciate or support, like when users on social media sites chided Daniel Tosh for his insensitivity toward rape.

Charged comics unable to get airtime now have alternatives. Getting a spot on a late-night television talkshow, reality show, or a televised showcase are no longer the stepping stones necessary or some of the few avenues available to garner national attention and admiration. Instead, comics unable to surmount industry hurdles can promote themselves on social media sites and let the fans place pressure on industry gatekeepers to offer them work. Just as the commercial success of Richard Pryor's comedy records, despite industry reticence, compelled film producers to hire Pryor for movie roles, if charged comics find ways of amassing a strong base, mainstream commercial opportunities will materialize. Luckily for charged comics these alternatives are not cost-prohibitive—social media sites are free and the price of cameras and other supporting technologies are more affordable than ever. Maria Bamford's Web series "The Maria Bamford Show" (2009) so far has reached over a half million viewers on YouTube and her more recent webisode series "Ask My Mom!" (2013) is quickly going viral. In 2012, she self-produced a full-length stand-up routine, *The Special Special Special!*, filming in her parent's living room, uploading the special to Chill.com and making it available to the public for a reasonable five bucks. This decision substantially lowered production costs while still making her comedy available to the public. New media and savvy comics able to capitalize on them is one critical piece necessary to enhance the economic viability of charged comedy. The other equally critical piece requires a consumer base seeking humor that impels laughter that simultaneously considers our discontents—political, social, and economic.

Buying into someone's worldview requires incentive. In the current economy of charged humor, comics whose identities represent dominant groups like being male, heterosexual, able-bodied have greater commercial viability. Comics not belonging to these dominant categories can secure success if they cater to well-established and entrenched stereotypes about their subordinate identity categories. While there may not be economic and cultural pay-offs to identify with LGBTQ folks, or women, or African Americans, there is, I believe, a moral incentive that has of late taken hold among some Americans. This sea change bodes well for charged comics in the future. It is unclear whether that moral incentive derives from individual desire to be politically correct, inclusive, or tolerant, the product of shifting racial/ethnic demographics in the United States, or a growing global awareness spurring individual and collective responsibility toward others. As legal and legislative triumphs bring LGBTQ persons into the fold by acknowledging their right to marry, raise families, be protected on the streets and on the job, and serve in the military, it will become increasingly unpopular and unacceptable to justify maltreatment. There is a moral incentive for supporting efforts aimed at conferring equal rights and civil liberties to everyone residing in the United States and its territories, a moral incentive that seeps into personal consumptive choices, like the way I can feel good about buying fair trade products. This could, over time, contribute to a shift in the economy of charged humor making charged comics a more profitable investment for industry gatekeepers.

In the meantime, comics producing charged humor pay a price. If their humor is consistently charged, it seems the best strategy to appeal to niche audiences with similar worldviews. Should national success and notoriety be the end goal, charged comics may consider tempering overt politicking and instead develop material that can play to a range of patrons. Success of this kind does not require abstaining entirely from employing charged humor; it just means comics may have to be more judicious about where and when they insert charged humor. Feigning ignorance or situating oneself as inferior to the audience are useful strategies to employ when desiring to deliver charged humor without appearing confrontational or intellectually superior. Jimmy Dore—author of the off-Broadway show *The Marijuana-logues* and an unassuming White male comic—takes this tack with audiences. Playing dumb allows him to introduce serious political and social critiques and explain difficult concepts like hegemony without alienating or incensing his audience.[13] Being male does not exactly hurt one's chances when it comes to breaking into the comedy industry and so men (if they so choose) can use their privileged status as cultural leverage to voice charged humor. The more (men) that do and the more audiences support charged humor, the more likely that industry gatekeepers will open their doors to charged comics. This requires devotion on the part of jokesters but responsibility also lies with consumers. Make a choice not to patronize comedy club national chains if they are only hiring one kind of voice, comic persona, or social identity. Contact booking agents at your local comedy club and tell them specifically who you would like to see perform and why. Buy the CDs and DVDs of charged comics you enjoy and share them with friends. Use social media sites to promote the comedy you find most hilarious and smart and tell your favorite comics how much you appreciate the work they are doing. We cast votes every day when we elect what television shows and films to watch, and we cast votes by purchasing tickets to see live performances. Increased consumption of charged humor will ensure that it remains available for consumption and force recognition of its viability as a sound economic investment, like when *The Queens of Comedy* (2001) was expected to generate modest sales and instead was wildly successful, spawning similar commercial ventures like *The Latin Divas of Comedy* (2007). Greater visibility of charged humor will also export important critiques, ideas, and worldviews to the very groups having the power to create the change you want to see in the world. Author Louise Bernikow said, "Humor tells you where the trouble is."[14] All you have to do is listen . . . oh yeah, and laugh.

Introduction

1. Gloria Bigelow in *Laughing Matters . . . Next Gen*, DVD, directed by Andrea Meyerson (US: All Out Films, 2009).

2. *Jake Johannsen: I Love You*, DVD, directed by Emery Emery and Patrick Rea (US: No Mold Productions, 2010).

3. *Michael McDonald: Model Citizen*, DVD, directed by Manny Rodriguez (US: Levity Productions, 2010).

4. Russell Peterson, *Strange Bedfellows: How Late-Night Comedy Turns Democracy into a Joke* (New Brunswick, NJ: Rutgers University Press, 2008), 149.

5. Bambi Haggins, *Laughing Mad: The Black Comic Persona in Post-Soul America* (New Brunswick, NJ: Rutgers University Press, 2007), 5.

6. *Comedy Central Presents: Kristen Schaal*, TV, produced by Paul Miller (California: Comedy Central, 2009).

7. *History of the Joke with Lewis Black*, DVD, directed by Dave Greene (New York: AETN, 2008).

8. Judy Gold in *Voices on Antisemitism—A Podcast Series*, United States Holocaust Memorial Museum, http://www.ushmm.org/museum/exhibit/focus/antisemitism/voices /transcript/?content=20100204 (accessed February 4, 2010).

9. Sean Zwagerman, *Wit's End: Women's Humor as Rhetorical and Performative Strategy* (Pittsburgh, PA: University of Pittsburgh Press, 2010).

10. Stuart Hall, "The Meaning of New Times," in *New Times: The Changing Face of Politics in the 1990s*, ed. Stuart Hall and Martin Jacques (London: Verso, 1990), 120.

11. As I use examples of comic material throughout, I intentionally include audience response in italics. In this way, readers have a window into the exchange of humor between performer and audience. I try to limit deriving any concrete conclusions from these exchanges unless I was present for the performance, acquired data from audience members via surveys or talk-backs, or the performer commented directly on the material in question.

12. "Emily Levine's Theory of Everything," Ted, www.ted.com/talks/emily_levine_s_ theory_of_everything.html (accessed August 18, 2011).

13. Stuart Hall, "Cultural Studies: Two Paradigms," in *Culture/Power/History: A Reader in Contemporary Social Theory*, ed. Nicholas B. Dirks, Geoff Eley, and Sherry B. Ortner (Princeton, NJ: Princeton University Press, 1994), 535.

14. In 1988, the Inter-University Program for Latino Research facilitated a working group resulting in a draft concept paper on cultural citizenship. Members of that working group included: Rina Benmayor, Richard Chabran, Richard Flores, William Flores, Ray Rocco, Renato Rosaldo, Pedro Pedraza, Blanca Silvestrini, and Rosa Torruellas. Copies of these draft concept papers are located in the archives at Hunter College.

15. IUP Cultural Studies Working Group, "Draft Concept Paper on Cultural Citizenship," unpublished working concept paper no. 2 (New York: Centro de Estudios Puertorriquenos, Hunter College, 1989), 9.

Chapter 1 · Making Connections

1. Stuart Hall and David Held, "Citizens and Citizenship," in *New Times: The Changing Face of Politics in the 1990s*, ed. Stuart Hall and Martin Jacques (London: Verso, 1990), 175.

2. I will draw from the second and arguably the most evolved version of the draft concept papers. Working group members generated this draft in 1988, though it was not complete until 1989. While Richard Flores did make revisions to this draft in 1991, the 1989 version reflects the latest collaborative effort to explore cultural citizenship by original working group members. IUP Cultural Studies Working Group, "Draft Concept Paper on Cultural Citizenship," Unpublished working concept paper no. 2 (New York: Centro de Estudios Puertorriquenos, Hunter College, 1989).

3. IUP, "Draft Concept Paper," 7.

4. Lauren Berlant, *The Queen of America Goes to Washington City: Essays on Sex and Citizenship* (Durham, NC: Duke University Press, 1997), 18–19.

5. Ibid.

6. William Rogers Brubaker, ed., "Introduction," in *Immigration and the Politics of Citizenship in Europe and North America* (Lanham, MD: University Press of America, 1989), 3.

7. Ibid.

8. W. Rogers Brubaker, *Citizenship and Nationhood in France and Germany* (Cambridge, MA: Harvard University Press, 1992), 40–41.

9. William V. Flores and Rina Benmayor, ed., "Introduction: Constructing Cultural Citizenship," in *Latino Cultural Citizenship: Claiming Identity, Space, and Rights* (Boston: Beacon Press, 1997), 12.

10. William V. Flores, "Citizens vs. Citizenry: Undocumented Immigrants and Latino Cultural Citizenship," in *Latino Cultural Citizenship: Claiming Identity, Space, and Rights*, eds. William V. Flores and Rina Benmayor (Boston: Beacon Press, 1997), 255.

11. Renato Rosaldo, "Cultural Citizenship, Inequality, and Multiculturalism," in *Latino Cultural Citizenship: Claiming Identity, Space, and Rights*, ed. William V. Flores and Rina Benmayor (Boston: Beacon Press, 1997), 37.

12. "Gay Marriage Poll: More Americans Support Marriage Equality," *Huffington Post* (December 9, 2012), www.huffingtonpost.com/2012/12/09/gay-marriage-poll_n_2267594 .html (accessed January 31, 2013).

13. *Maz Jobrani: Brown and Friendly*, DVD, directed by Brent Carpenter (US: Salient Media, 2009).

14. IUP, "Draft Concept Paper," 12.

15. *Live Nude Comedy*, Episode 4, TV, directed by Brent Carpenter (US: Showtime, 2009).

16. *George Lopez: America's Mexican*, DVD, directed by Marty Callner (US: HBO, 2007).

17. Engin F. Isin and Patricia K. Wood, *Citizenship and Identity* (Thousand Oaks, CA: Sage Publications, 1999), 152.

18. Blanca G. Silvestrini, "'The World We Enter When Claiming Rights': Latinos and Their Quest for Culture," in *Latino Cultural Citizenship: Claiming Identity, Space, and Rights*, ed. William V. Flores and Rina Benmayor (Boston: Beacon Press, 1997), 46.

19. IUP, "Draft Concept Paper," 1.

20. "LOL Lounge—2012—Hari Kondabolu—Female President," YouTube, www.you tube.com/watch?v=orq106sacxY (accessed July 30, 2012).

21. Richard Pryor and Todd Gold, *Pryor Convictions and Other Life Sentences* (New York: Pantheon, 1995), 137–38.

22. Hall and Held, "Citizens and Citizenship," 175.

23. *Louis C.K.: Hilarious*, DVD, directed by Louis C.K. (Milwaukee, WI: Comedy Central, 2010).

24. Judith Yaross Lee, *Twain's Brand: Humor in Contemporary American Culture* (Jackson: University Press of Mississippi, 2012), 6.

25. *Chris Rock: Kill the Messenger*, DVD, directed by Marty Callner (US: HBO, 2008).

26. "Nato Green, Live at the Purple Onion," YouTube, www.youtube.com/watch?v= DCeliH1SHXc (accessed July 16, 2012).

27. Russell Peterson, *Strange Bedfellows: How Late-Night Comedy Turns Democracy into a Joke* (New Brunswick, NJ: Rutgers University Press, 2008).

28. *The New Frontier*, LP, written by Mort Sahl (UK: Reprise Records, 1962).

29. Larry Getlen, "The Man's Man: Macho Laughman Adam Carolla Says Tom Cruise Is from Outer Space and Women Just Aren't Funny," *New York Post*, June 16, 2012, www.nypost.com/p/entertainment/the_man_man_NS5UgwY5j06KwJp4WYiOJL#ixz z1yLVJvloT (accessed June 25, 2012).

30. Linda Jean Kenix, *Alternative and Mainstream Media: The Converging Spectrum* (London: Bloomsbury, 2011), 10.

31. *Brown Is the New Green: George Lopez and the American Dream*, DVD, directed by Phillip Rodriguez (US: PBS Latino Public Broadcasting, 2007).

32. *Lily Tomlin: The Search for Signs of Intelligent Life in the Universe*, DVD, directed by John Bailey and written by Jane Wagner (US: Tomlin and Wagner Theatricalz, 1985).

33. Nachman, *Seriously Funny*, 29–30.

34. *Maria Bamford: Special, Special, Special*, online download (US: Chill.com, 2012).

35. *Brown Is the New Green*.

36. *Stand Up, Stand Out*, DVD, directed by David Pavlosky (US: DP Media Productions, 2013).

37. Janice Radway, "What's in a Name?," *AQ* 51, no. 1 (March 1999): 10.

38. Hall, "The Meaning of New Times," 133.

39. T. J. Jackson Lears, "The Concept of Cultural Hegemony: Problems and Possibilities," *American Historical Review* 90 (June 1985): 593.

Chapter 2 · Twentieth-Century Stand-Up

1. *In Living Black and White*, LP, written by Dick Gregory (NY: Colpix Records, 1961); Gregory, *What's Happening?* (NY: E. P. Dutton, 1965), 82–83.

2. Dick Gregory, *From the Back of the Bus*, ed. Bob Orben (New York: E. P. Dutton, 1962), 125.

3. *Dick Gregory: The Light Side: The Dark Side*, LP, produced by Kevin Eggers (US: Poppy Industries, 1969).

4. Alan Petigny, *The Permissive Society: America 1941–1965* (Cambridge: Cambridge University Press, 2009), 240.

5. Gerald Nachman, *Seriously Funny: The Rebel Comedians of the 1950s and 1960s* (New York: Pantheon Books, 2003), 25.

6. *hungry i reunion*, DVD, directed by Thomas A. Cohen (US: Hammermark Productions, 2005).

7. Nachman, *Seriously Funny*.

8. *hungry i reunion*.

9. Ibid.

10. *Dick Gregory: The Light Side: The Dark Side*.

11. *A Way of Life*, LP, written by Mort Sahl (US: Verve Records, 1960).

12. *The Future Lies Ahead*, LP, written by Mort Sahl (US: Verve Records, 1960).

13. Ibid.

14. *The New Frontier*, LP, written by Mort Sahl (UK: Reprise Records, 1962).

15. *The Carnegie Hall Concert*, CD, written by Lenny Bruce (Hollywood, CA: World Pacific, 1995 [1961]).

16. *I Am Not a Nut, Elect Me!*, LP, written by Lenny Bruce (US: Fantasy Records, 1960).

17. Ibid.

18. *Lenny Bruce—American*, LP, written by Lenny Bruce (US: Fantasy Records, 1961).

19. *I Am Not a Nut, Elect Me!*

20. *The Sick Humor of Lenny Bruce*, LP, written by Lenny Bruce (US: Fantasy Records, 1959).

21. *The Lenny Bruce Performance Film*, DVD, produced by John Magnuson (Port Washington, NY: KOCH Vision LLC, 2005 [1965]).

22. Nachman, *Seriously Funny*, 489.

23. *Dick Gregory: The Light Side: The Dark Side*.

24. *In Living Black and White*, LP, written by Dick Gregory (New York: Colpix Records, 1961).

25. Ibid.

26. *Dick Gregory: The Light Side: The Dark Side*.

27. Ibid.

28. Albert Rapp, *The Origins of Wit and Humor* (New York: Dutton, 1951).

29. Danielle Russell, "Self-Deprecatory Humor and the Female Comic: Self Destruction or Comedic Construction?," *thirdspace* 2, no. 1 (Nov. 2002): 1–16.

30. *Moms Mabley: Live at the Greek Theater*, LP, written by Moms Mabley (Chicago: Mercury Records, 1971).

31. *Lily Tomlin: The Search for Signs of Intelligent Life in the Universe*, DVD, directed by John Bailey, written by Jane Wagner (US: Tomlin and Wagner Theatricalz, 1991 [1985]).

32. Lily Tomlin, "Cast of One," VHS, interviewed by Jeffrey Lyons (US: Audio/Video Design Productions, 1985), Theatre on Film and Tape Archive, New York Public Library for the Performing Arts, New York, New York, 10023.

33. Jennifer Reed, "Lily Tomlin's *Appearing Nitely*: Performing Difference before Difference Was Cool," *Journal of Popular Culture* 37, no. 3 (2004): 437.

34. In a filmed interview with Lily Tomlin and Jane Wagner, someone noted that *The Search for Signs* was the first feminist comedy on Broadway and went on to inquire after the parameters of feminist comedy. This half hour interview is included as bonus material on *Lily Tomlin: The Search for Signs of Intelligent Life in the Universe.*

35. Ibid.

36. Ibid.

37. Ibid.

38. Sherry Glaser, *Family Secrets*, Theatre J in the Washington, DC, Jewish Community Center, April 15, 2007.

39. Richard Pryor and Todd Gold, *Pryor Convictions and Other Life Sentences* (New York: Pantheon Books, 1995).

40. *Richard Pryor*, LP, produced by Robert Marchese (US: Reprise Records, 1968).

41. Pryor and Gold, *Pryor Convictions*, 121.

42. *Richard Pryor: Live and Smokin'*, DVD, directed by Michael Blum (US: Weinstein, 2009 [1971]).

43. *Richard Pryor: Live and Smokin'.*

44. Ibid.

45. Pryor and Gold, *Pryor Convictions*, 128.

46. Ibid., 148.

47. *Richard Pryor: Bicentennial Nigger*, LP, produced by David Banks (Burbank, CA: Warner Bros. Records, 1976).

48. *Richard Pryor: Live in Concert*. DVD, directed by Jeff Margolis (US: HBO, 2006 [1979]).

49. *Richard Pryor: Live on the Sunset Strip*, DVD, directed by Joe Layton (US: Columbia Pictures, 2005 [1982]).

50. *Richard Pryor: I Ain't Dead Yet, #*%$#@!!*, DVD, directed by Billy Grundfest (US: Paramount Pictures, 2003).

51. *Richard Pryor . . . Here and Now*. DVD, directed by Richard Pryor (US: Columbia Pictures, 2005 [1983]).

52. *Richard Pryor: Live on the Sunset Strip.*

53. Pryor and Gold, *Pryor Convictions*, 177.

54. My longtime neighbor, talented pianist and dear friend, David Ylvisaker has been performing with the incomparable Julia Nixon for over thirty years. She brings the vocals (of the quality that will give you goose bumps) and he shines on the keyboard but has been known to pick up nearly any instrument and make it sound good. They performed at my wedding and every summer in August I meet Dave and Julia and a motley crew of musicians and artists at Lake Winnipesaukee in New Hampshire. In the evening, after ridiculously good food, if we are not jamming or talking politics then we are swapping stories outside by the campfire. Turns out that Dave and Julia, known in the early 1980s as Julia and Company, toured with Richard Pryor during the *Here and Now* Tour in 1983. They took turns talking about the experience sharing all kinds of anecdotes about that year. Most memorably, they talked about Pryor as a man who went after what he wanted, a man whose generosity knew no bounds. Within days of seeing them perform, Pryor arranged for them to come on tour with him. Julia gave up her role as understudy for a lead role in a Broadway production of *Dreamgirls*, and they took off on the road with Pryor (she was able to play that same lead role later and not as the understudy). They were moved time and

time again by his generosity—in payment for each show, but also for footing the bill for first-class travel accommodations across the country. Many headliners travel by plane, while a road crew and opening acts travel by bus, car, or train. While the main attraction sleeps in the lap of luxury, all other personnel sleep on lumpy beds and ward off cockroaches at nearby motels. This could not have been farther from the truth for Dave and Julia while traveling with Pryor. Insisting that they accompany him by plane, Julia and Dave and all others flew with him; he saw to it that staff booked rooms for them in the same hotels, and when they ran into financial problems with their recording studio—which early-on promised to chip in some money for the tour since they were singing tracks from, and thereby promoting, a recently released album—Pryor stepped in and paid the difference.

55. For a more detailed account of Carlin's arrest alongside Lenny Bruce, see Richard Zoglin's *Comedy at the Edge: How Stand-Up in the 1970s Changed America* (New York: Bloomsbury, 2008), 7–8.

56. *Bill Maher: . . . But I'm Not Wrong*, DVD, directed by John Moffitt (US: HBO, 2010).

57. Ibid.

58. George Carlin, *Class Clown*, CD (US: Little David Records / Eardrum Records, 2000).

59. *Maher . . . But I'm Not Wrong.*

60. Karen Stabiner, "The Belly Room Presented Comediennes," *Mother Jones* (July 1979): 45–49.

61. William Knoedelseder, *I'm Dying Up Here: Heartbreak and High Times in Stand-Up Comedy's Golden Era* (New York: Public Affairs, 2009); Zoglin, *Comedy at the Edge*.

62. T. H. Marshall, "Citizenship and Social Class," in *Citizenship and Social Class* (1950) (London: Pluto, 1992), 20–21.

63. Lisa Duggan, *The Twilight of Equality? Neoliberalism, Cultural Politics, and the Attack on Democracy* (Boston: Beacon Press, 2003), xi.

64. *Lily Tomlin: The Search for Signs of Intelligent Life in the Universe.*

65. *This Film Is Not Yet Rated*, DVD, directed by Kirby Dick (US: IFC Original Production, 2006).

66. *The Very Best of the Ed Sullivan Show*, 2 vols. DVD, directed by Andrew Solt (US: Sofa Home Entertainment, 1991).

67. Dick Gregory recounts these events in a personal interview filmed and included in: *Why We Laugh: Black Comedians on Black Comedy*, DVD, directed by Robert Townsend (US: Code Black Entertainment, 2009).

68. Peter M. Robinson, *The Dance of the Comedians: The People, the President, and the Performance of Political Standup Comedy in America* (Amherst and Boston: University of Massachusetts Press, 2010), 115, 140.

69. *Pryor: I Ain't Dead Yet, #*%$#@!!.*

70. *Dick Gregory: The Light Side; The Dark Side.*

71. Pryor and Gold, *Pryor Convictions*, 128.

72. Susan J. Douglas, *The Rise of Enlightened Sexism: How Pop Culture Took Us from Girl Power to Girls Gone Wild* (New York: St. Martin's Griffin, 2010).

73. Michael Kimmel, *Manhood in America* (New York: Oxford University Press, 2006).

Chapter 3 · Laughing into the New Millennium

1. *Patton Oswalt: My Weakness Is Strong*, DVD, directed by Jason Woliner (US: Generate Content, LLC, 2009).

2. Ibid.

3. *Kate Clinton: The 25th Anniversary Tour*, DVD, directed by Andrea Meyerson (US: All Out Films, 2007).

4. *Karen Williams: I Need a Snack!*, DVD, directed by Andrea Meyerson (US: All Out Films, 2008).

5. Kate Kendall, *Kate Clinton*.

6. Karen Williams, "Healing Humor," *Metroweekly*, April 24, 2008, 34.

7. René Hicks in *Laughing Matters . . . More!*, DVD, directed and produced by Andrea Meyerson (US: All Out Films, 2006).

8. Ibid.

9. I differentiate between Middle Eastern and Arab Americans because countries such as Turkey and Iran are not Arab, a cultural and geographic designation based on membership in the Arab League; yet, Iranians are subject to the same prejudices imposed on Arab Americans. Both Middle Eastern and Arab Americans are assumed to be Muslim, when this is not always the case, and people all over the world subscribe to the Islamic faith.

10. Nadine Naber investigates the sociocultural history of Arab Americans arguing convincingly that "state discourses have transformed 'the Arab' over time, from proximity to whiteness to a position of heightened Otherness" (39). Nadine Naber, "Arab Americans and U.S. Racial Formations," in *Race and Arab Americans before and after 9/11: From Invisible Citizens to Invisible Subjects*, ed. Amaney Jamal and Nadine Naber (Syracuse, NY: Syracuse University Press, 2008), 37.

11. "Mo" Amer in *Allah Made Me Funny: Live in Concert*, DVD, directed by Andrea Kalin (US: Unity Productions Foundations, 2008).

12. Maysoon Zayid in Richard Klin, *Something to Say: Thoughts on Art and Politics in America* (Teaticket, MA: Leapfrog, 2011), 81.

13. Ahmed Ahmed in *The Axis of Evil Comedy Tour*, DVD, directed by Michael Simon (US: Image Entertainment, 2007).

14. Dean Obeidallah in *The Arab American Comedy Tour*, DVD, videography by Oscar Films (Seattle and Dearborn, Michigan: Arab Film Distribution, 2006).

15. Usman in *Allah Made Me Funny*.

16. Cynthia Willet, *Irony in the Age of Empire: Comic Perspectives on Democracy and Freedom* (Bloomington: Indiana University Press, 2008), 13.

17. Preacher Moss in *Allah Made Me Funny*.

18. Maysoon Zayid in *The Arab American Comedy Tour*.

19. *Maz Jobrani: Brown and Friendly*, DVD, directed by Brent Carpenter (US: Salient Media, 2009).

20. Maz Jobrani, e-mail, July 14, 2011.

21. "Josh Blue at Last Comic Standing," YouTube, www.youtube.com/watch?v=qMSr pZi_6WM (accessed April 12, 2008).

22. Carrie Sandahl and Philip Auslander, eds., "Introduction: Disability Studies in Commotion with Performance Studies," in *Bodies in Commotion: Disability and Performance* (Ann Arbor: University of Michigan Press, 2005), 10.

23. Ibid., 3.

24. *Able to Laugh,* VHS, directed by Michael J. Dougan (Boston: Fanlight Productions, 1993).

25. Ibid.

26. Geri Jewell in *Look Who's Laughing,* VHS, directed by Salvatore Baldomar Jr. (Cicero, NY: Program Development Associates, 2004).

27. *Able to Laugh.*

28. *Look Who's Laughing.*

29. Maysoon Zayid in Richard Klin, *Something to Say: Thoughts on Art and Politics in America,* 85–86.

30. Alex Valdez in *Look Who's Laughing.*

31. Bridget McManus in *Laughing Matters . . . Next Gen,* DVD, directed by Andrea Meyerson (US: All Out Films, 2009).

32. Sabrina Matthews in *Laughing Matters . . . More!*

33. Edison Apple in *Laughing Matters . . . Next Gen.*

34. Janet Bing and Dana Heller, "How Many Lesbians Does It Take to Screw in a Light Bulb?," *Humor* 16, no. 2 (2003): 158.

35. DeAnne Smith, e-mail, September 15, 2011.

36. Margaret Cho in *The Outlaugh Festival on Wisecrack,* DVD, directed by Michael Dempsey (Hollywood: Logo Entertainment, Viacom International, 2006).

37. Suzanne Westenhoefer in *The Outlaugh Festival on Wisecrack.*

38. Elvira Kurt in *Laughing Matters . . . More!*

39. IUP Cultural Studies Working Group, "Draft Concept Paper on Cultural Citizenship," unpublished working concept paper no. 2 (New York: Centro de Estudios Puertorriquenos, Hunter College, 1989), 12.

40. *Wanda Sykes: I'ma Be Me,* DVD, directed by Beth McCarthy-Miller (US: HBO Home Video, 2010).

41. Rene Hicks in *Laughing Matters . . . More!.*

42. Gloria Bigelow in *Laughing Matters . . . Next Gen.*

43. Sabrina Matthews in *Laughing Matters . . . More!*

44. Ibid.

45. B-Phlat in *Comics without Borders,* DVD, directed by Scott Montoya (US: Salient Media, 2009).

46. *Dave Chappelle: For What It's Worth,* DVD, directed by Stan Lathan (US: Pilot Boy Productions, 2004).

47. Elsie Williams, *The Humor of Jackie Moms Mabley: An African Comedic Tradition* (New York: Garland, 1995), 3.

48. *The N Word: Divided We Stand,* DVD, directed by Todd Larkins (US: Post Consumer Media, 2004).

49. Williams, *The Humor of Jackie Moms Mabley,* 7.

50. Episode 146, King of Fruit with W. Kamau Bell, hosted by Jesse Thorn and Jordan Morris, "Jordan, Jesse GO!," *Public Radio International: The Sound of Young America,* September 23, 2010, www.maximumfun.org/shows/jordan-jesse-go?page=11 (accessed October 17, 2010).

51. *The Arab American Comedy Tour.*

52. Lanita Jacobs-Huey, "'The Arab Is the New Nigger': African American Comics Confront the Irony and Tragedy of September 11," *Transforming Anthropology* 14, no. 1 (April 2006): 60–64.

53. Episode 146, King of Fruit with W. Kamau Bell.

54. Micia Mosely, personal interview, May 15, 2011.

55. Paula Jai Parker in Darryl Littleton, *Black Comedians on Black Comedy: How African-Americans Taught Us to Laugh* (New York: Applause Theatre and Cinema Books, 2006), 292.

56. Carol Allen, "'Shaking That Thing' and All Its Wonders: African American Female Comedy," *Studies in American Humor* 3, no. 12 (2005): 99.

57. DoVeanna S. Fulton, "Comic Views and Metaphysical Dilemmas: Shattering Cultural Images through Self-Definition and Representation by Black Comediennes," *Journal of American Folklore* 117, no. 463 (2004): 82.

58. Ibid., 85.

59. Sue Ellen Case, "Women of Colour and Theatre," in *Feminism and Theatre* (New York: Methuen, 1988), 107.

60. *George Lopez: Tall, Dark and Chicano*, DVD, directed by Marty Callner (US: HBO, 2009).

61. *Brown Is the New Green: George Lopez and the American Dream*, DVD, directed by Phillip Rodriguez (US: PBS Latino Public Broadcasting, 2007).

62. Marilyn Martinez in "Latin Diva of Comedy Tribute," YouTube, www.youtube.com/watch?v=ViVgyyzBVhk (accessed January 10, 2010).

63. Lisa Alvarado in "America's Funniest Mom," YouTube, www.youtube.com/watch?v=5IzPCVocHFc (accessed February 2, 2010).

64. Felipe Esparza in *Comics without Borders*, DVD, directed by Scott Montoya (US: Salient Media, 2009).

65. Lisa Lowe, *Immigrant Acts: On Asian American Cultural Politics* (Durham, NC: Duke University Press, 1996), 22.

66. "Comedian Aparna Nancherla," YouTube, www.youtube.com/watch?v=Aq8m3ZcKd-s (accessed December 10, 2011).

67. Karen Shimakawa, *National Abjection: The Asian American Body Onstage* (Durham, NC: Duke University Press, 2002), 2.

68. Ibid., 3.

69. "Sheng Wang—New Stereotypes," Comedy Central, www.comedycentral.com/video-clips/ugaou4/john-oliver-s-new-york-stand-up-show-sheng-wang—new-stereotypes (accessed February 20, 2013).

70. Bobby Lee in *The Kims of Comedy*, DVD, directed by Chuck Vinson (US: Goldhill Entertainment, 2005).

71. Dr. Ken Jeong in *The Kims of Comedy*.

72. Kate Rigg quoted in Zeisler, "A Good Offense," 41; Kate Rigg, *Kate's Chink-O-Rama*, CD, 2002. [Promotional Copy]

73. "Kate Rigg," *The Naughty Show: Bad Girls of Comedy*, DVD, directed by Skye Blue (US: Eagle Rock Entertainment, 2004).

74. Ibid.

75. Gregory Mantsios, "Class in America: Myths and Realities," in *Privilege: A Reader*, ed. Michael S. Kimmel and Abby L. Ferber (Cambridge, MA: Perseus Books, 2003), 35.

76. *Comedy Central Presents: Hari Kondabolu*, TV, directed by Ryan Polito (California: Comedy Central, 2011).

77. Ibid.

78. Lynn Weber, *Understanding Race, Class, Gender and Sexuality: A Conceptual Framework* (New York: McGraw-Hill, 2001), 1.

79. "Gloria Bigelow Stand Up," YouTube, www.youtube.com/watch?v=eALtveYiz9A &feature=related (accessed October 10, 2011).

80. *Daniel Tosh: Happy Thoughts*, DVD, directed by Beth McCarthy (US: Black Heart Productions, 2010).

81. "Nikki Payne Performing in Montreal," YouTube, www.youtube.com/watch?v=Ei QCz2YXG3E (accessed March 22, 2012).

82. George Lipsitz investigates the myriad structural forces maintaining economic inequality and white supremacy in this nation in the past century. See *The Possessive Investment in Whiteness: How White People Profit from Identity Politics* (Philadelphia: Temple University Press, 1998).

83. *Maria Bamford: Unwanted Thought Syndrome*, CD (New York: Comedy Central Records, 2009).

84. "Jeff Caldwell Financial Woes," YouTube, www.youtube.com/watch?v=uXTvsb7 AV6Q&playnext=1&list=PL-Oii93ml4ohy4lKKOwR1SE6xbnxNkp9J&feature=results _main (accessed May 17, 2012).

85. "Hari Kondabolu—My Healthcare Proposal," YouTube, www.youtube.com/watch ?v=RTHXcRvxOTI (accessed July 10, 2012).

86. James Aston and John Wallis, "Doomsday America: The Pessimistic Turn of Post-9/11 Apocalyptic Cinema," *Journal of Religion and Popular Culture* 23, no. 1 (2011): 53–64.

87. Sommore in Littleton, *Black Comedians on Black Comedy*, 35; and Chris Rock in *Why We Laugh: Black Comedians on Black Comedy*, DVD, directed by Robert Townsend (US: Code Black Entertainment, 2009).

88. "Emily Levine's Theory of Everything," Ted, www.ted.com/talks/emily_levine_s_ theory_of_everything.html (accessed August 18, 2011).

Chapter 4 · When Women Perform Charged Humor

1. Christopher Hitchens, "Why Women Aren't Funny," *Vanity Fair*, no. 557 (January 2007), www.vanityfair.com/culture/features/2007/01/hitchens200701 (accessed February 2, 2007).

2. Lauren Berlant, *The Queen of America Goes to Washington City: Essays on Sex and Citizenship* (Durham, NC: Duke University Press, 1997), 17.

3. Stuart Hall, "The Meaning of New Times," in *New Times: The Changing Face of Politics in the 1990s*, ed. Stuart Hall and Martin Jacques (London: Verso, 1990), 131.

4. *Daniel Tosh: Happy Thoughts*, DVD, directed by Beth McCarthy (US: Black Heart Productions, 2010).

5. Engin F. Isin and Patricia K. Wood, *Citizenship and Identity* (London and Thousand Oaks, CA: SAGE, 1999), 123.

6. Maria Bamford in *The Comedians of Comedy: Live at the El Ray*, DVD, directed by Michael Blieden (US: Red Envelope Entertainment, Netflix Co., 2006).

7. Andi Zeisler quoted in Emily Wilson, "Are Men Threatened by Funny Women?," *Alternet* (September 4, 2007), www.alternet.org/story/61102/ (accessed September 28, 2007).

8. One comment referenced Christopher Hitchens's article in *Vanity Fair*, but did so disparagingly and a subsequent response pokes fun that Hitchens's argument was even offered as evidence in the discussion: "Did you honestly just try to make a point about female male relations by using Christopher Hitchens?" The comments are still available on a read-only basis. See Emily Wilson, "Are Men Threatened by Funny Women?," *Alternet* (September 4, 2007), www.alternet.org/story/61102#comments (accessed February 8, 2008).

9. Ibid.

10. Ibid.

11. Ibid.

12. Ibid.

13. Ibid.

14. *History of the Joke with Lewis Black*, DVD, directed by Dave Greene (New York: AETN, 2008).

15. Ibid.

16. *When Stand-Up Stood Out*, DVD, directed by Fran Solomita (US: Hieroglyphic Films, 2005).

17. *History of the Joke with Lewis Black*.

18. Sara Benincasa quoted in Danna Williams, "Ladies Are Funny Festival Interview: Sara Benincasa," *Austin AV Club* (May 6, 2009), www.avclub.com/austin/articles/ladies -are-funny-festival-interview-sara-benincasa,27555/ (accessed May 12, 2009).

19. *History of the Joke with Lewis Black*.

20. The comments made herein by Green do not in any way reflect the opinions or experience of the History Channel, AETN, or Triage Entertainment. Dave Greene, e-mail message to author, February 19, 2010.

21. Julie Goldman quoted in Andi Zeisler, "A Good Offense," *Bitch: Feminist Response to Pop Culture* 41 (Fall 2008): 39.

22. Robin Tyler, personal interview, May 11, 2008.

23. *Jen Kirkman: Hail to the Freaks*, CD (Hollywood: Aspecialthing Records, 2010).

24. Sommore quoted in Darryl Littleton, *Black Comedians on Black Comedy: How African-Americans Taught Us to Laugh* (New York: Applause Theatre and Cinema Books, 2006), 286.

25. Ibid., 284.

26. Comments to Wilson, "Are Men Threatened by Funny Women?"

27. Dave Greene, e-mail message to author, February 19, 2010.

28. Kenneth Winiecki Jr., e-mail message to author, May 9, 2008.

29. Ibid.

30. Joanne R. Gilbert, *Performing Marginality: Humor, Gender, and Cultural Critique* (Detroit: Wayne State University Press, 2004), 17.

31. Hall, "The Meaning of New Times," 130.

32. Pierre Bourdieu, *Distinction: A Social Critique of the Judgment of Taste*, trans. Richard Nice (London: Routledge and Kegan Paul, 1984), 66.

33. Norman N. Holland, "Unity Identity Text Self," in *Reader-Response Criticism: From Formalism to Post-Structuralism*, ed. Jane P. Tompkins (Baltimore: Johns Hopkins University Press, 1980), 123.

34. Shane Phelan, *Sexual Strangers: Gays, Lesbians and Dilemmas of Citizenship* (Philadelphia: Temple University Press, 2001), 149.

35. Kathleen Rowe, *The Unruly Woman: Gender and the Genres of Laughter* (Austin: University of Texas Press, 1995).

36. Audre Lorde, "Age, Race, Class, and Sex: Women Redefining Difference" (1980), in *Sister Outsider* (Freedom, CA: The Crossing Press, 1984), 114.

37. *History of the Joke with Lewis Black*.

38. "Men Aren't Funnier than Woman: Ridiculous Study Attempts to Answer Stupid Question," *Huffington Post*, November 17, 2011, www.huffingtonpost.com/carol-hartsell /men-arent-funnier-than-women-shut-up_b_1099805.html#s478346&title=Also_On_ Huffington (accessed December 2, 2011).

39. Many letters sent to *Vanity Fair* responding to Hitchens's article were published online. See Shaun Breidbart, "The Humor Gap" *Vanity Fair* (March 3, 2008), www.vanity fair.com/culture/features/2008/04/hitchens_letters200804 (accessed March 10, 2008).

40. Ibid.

41. Lawrence E. Mintz, "Standup Comedy as a Social and Cultural Mediation," *American Quarterly* 37, no. 1 (Spring 1985): 74.

42. L. H. Stallings, *Mutha' Is Half a Word: Intersections of Folklore, Vernacular, Myth, and Queerness in Black Female Culture* (Columbus: Ohio State University Press, 2007), 117.

43. May Joseph, "Bodies outside the State: Black British Women Playwrights and the Limits of Citizenship," in *The Ends of Performance*, ed. Peggy Phelan and Jill Lane (New York: New York University Press, 1998), 198.

44. Ibid., 197.

45. *Vince Vaughn's Wild West Comedy Show*, DVD, directed by Ari Sandel (US: MM-VII New Line Cinema Picturehouse Holdings, 2005).

46. Trevor Griffiths, *Comedians* (New York: Grove Press, 1976), 22.

47. Mary Crawford, "Just Kidding: Gender and Conversational Humor," in *Perspectives on Women and Comedy*, Series in Studies in Gender and Culture, Vol. 5, ed. Regina Barreca (Philadelphia: Gordon and Breach, 1992), 23–37.

48. Bonnie McFarlane in *Comedy Central Presents*, TV (California: Comedy Central, February 15, 2008).

49. Andy Medhurst, *A National Joke: Popular Comedy and English Cultural Identities* (New York: Routledge, 2007), 28–29.

50. Ellen Hopkins, "Who's Laughing Now? Women," *New York Times*, September 16, 1990, www.nytimes.com/1990/09/16/arts/who-s-laughing-now-women.html?src=pm (accessed October 4, 2010).

51. Kate Rigg quoted in Andi Zeisler, "A Good Offense," *Bitch: Feminist Response to Pop Culture* 41 (Fall 2008): 40.

52. Janet Bing and Dana Heller, "How Many Lesbians Does It Take to Screw in a Light Bulb?," *Humor* 16, no. 2 (2003): 158.

53. Kate Clinton (1987) quoted in Linda Pershing, "There's a Joker in the Menstrual Hut: A Performance Analysis of Comedian Kate Clinton," in *Women's Comic Visions*, ed. June Sochen (Detroit: Wayne State University Press, 1991), 222.

54. Rebecca Krefting, "Discharge," Original material written and first performed Spring 2002.

55. Gilbert, *Performing Marginality*, xviii.

56. "Woman's Sense of Humor: Mr. Depew, May Irwin and Other Discuss Its Existence," *The Washington Post*, June 23, 1901, 22.

57. This list draws from dozens and dozens of articles published in twentieth-century historical newspapers like *The New York Times, The Washington Post, Chicago Defender, Pittsburg Courier,* and *Los Angeles Times.* I would like to thank students enrolled in multiple sections of my course: *Introduction to American Studies: A Humorous (Dis)Course* for locating, analyzing, and discussing these articles and the evolution/cycles of this popular debate with me.

58. Hitchens, "Why Women Aren't Funny."

59. Dr. Allan Reiss quoted in Hitchens, "Why Women Aren't Funny."

60. Ibid.

61. Allan L. Reiss, "The Humor Gap." *Vanity Fair* (March 3, 2008), www.vanityfair .com/culture/features/2008/04/hitchens_letters200804 (accessed March 10, 2008).

62. Alessandra Stanley, "Who Says Women Aren't Funny?," *Vanity Fair,* no. 572 (April 2008), 185.

63. Christopher Hitchens, "Why Women Still Don't Get It," *Vanity Fair* (March 3, 2008), www.vanityfair.com/culture/features/2008/04/hitchens200804 (accessed March 10, 2008).

64. Ibid.

65. Abby Paige, "Laugh Trap," *Bitch: Feminist Response to Pop Culture* 41 (Fall 2008): 37.

66. Comments to "Are Men Threatened by Funny Women?"

67. Shaun Breidbart, "The Humor Gap."

Chapter 5 · Robin Tyler

1. Shane Phelan, *Sexual Strangers: Gays, Lesbians and Dilemmas of Citizenship* (Philadelphia: Temple University Press, 2001), 141.

2. Robin Tyler, personal interview, May 11, 2008.

3. Phelan, *Sexual Strangers.*

4. Michael Warner, *The Trouble with Normal: Sex, Politics, and the Ethics of Queer Life* (Cambridge, MA: Harvard University Press, 1999).

5. Tyler, personal interview, May 11, 2008.

6. Ibid., 8.

7. Robin Tyler and Andy Thayer, "The 'Gay Marriage' Struggle: What's at Stake and How Can We Win?," in *Defending Same-Sex Marriage* Vol. 3, ed. Martin Dupuis and William A. Thompson (Westport, CT: Praeger, 2007), 21.

8. Jane Ward, *Respectably Queer: Diversity Culture in LGBT Activist Organizations* (Nashville, TN: Vanderbilt University Press, 2008), 136.

9. There are a number of articles ranging in length and detail about the life and career of Robin Tyler, which include Betsy Borns, *Comic Lives: Inside the World of American Stand-Up Comedy* (New York: Simon and Schuster, 1987), 303; Ed Karvoski Jr., *A Funny Time to Be Gay* (New York: Simon and Schuster, 1997), 23–28; Barbara J. Love, ed., *Feminists Who Changed America: 1963–1975* (Champaign: University of Illinois Press, 2006); Linda Martin and Kerry Segrave, *Women in Comedy: The Funny Ladies from the Turn of the Century to the Present* (Secaucus, NJ: Citadel Press, 1986), 419–423; an interview with Robin Tyler by Laura Post, "Robin Tyler," in *Revolutionary Laughter: The World of Women Comics,* ed. Roz Warren (Freedom, CA: Crossing Press, 1995), 247–253. For the most comprehensive biographies of Robin Tyler, see Paul D. Cain, *Leading the Parade: Conversations with America's Most Influential Lesbians and Gay Men* (Maryland: Scarecrow Press, 2002),

131–41, and Val Edwards, "Robin Tyler: Comic in Contradiction," *Body Politic* (1979): 21–23. Details about her life were corroborated via personal interview, autobiographical solo performances, her resumes for activism and performance, as well as primary documents and sources such as newspaper and magazine articles referencing her activities and career, original recordings of performances, speeches, and workshops.

10. I obtained a copy of this article from Robin Tyler, and noted that in this particular passage she had the word "not" crossed out and replaced with "and" so the quote would read as it does above. It is unclear whether she was misquoted or whether it was a mistake made by Robin Tyler when being asked to comment for this piece. Her performances and engagement with the public indicate that she does seek to *educate and entertain*. The quote was taken from a magazine article whose author is unknown: "Gay Lib Blues for College Prexy," *The Advocate,* December 20, 1972. Part of Robin Tyler's personal memorabilia.

11. "Robin Tyler in Phyllis Diller's First Annual Funny Women's Show on Showtime," YouTube, www.youtube.com/watch?v=BUB5w5anVLc&feature=youtu.be (accessed July 10, 2011).

12. Tyler, personal interview, May 11, 2008.

13. *Always a Bridesmaid, Never a Groom*, DVD (Los Angeles: ACME Comedy Theatre, February 10, 2007). [Work Film]

14. Ibid.

15. Tyler, personal interview, May 11, 2008.

16. Del Martin and Phyllis Lyon met and began dating in 1952. Together, they founded the Daughters of Bilitis (DOB) and remained active in the fight for gay rights. Del Martin passed away August 27, 2008. She and Phyllis were together over 56 years. DOB published *The Ladder: A Lesbian Review* from 1956–1972. The exact issue that Tyler is referring to is unknown though it is most likely an issue published in the years 1960–1962.

17. Cain, *Leading the Parade*, 132.

18. Tyler, personal interview, May 11, 2008.

19. Ibid.

20. Alfred T. Hendricks, "Cops Grab 44 in Dresses—and a Real Girl in Slacks," *New York Post*, Sunday October 28, 1962.

21. Tyler, personal interview, May 11, 2008.

22. Robin Tyler quoted in Val Edwards, "Robin Tyler: Comic in Contradiction," *Body Politic* (1979): 22.

23. Tyler, personal interview, May 11, 2008.

24. Robin Tyler in Pat Harrison and Tyler, personal interview, May 11, 2008

25. *Always a Bridesmaid, Never a Groom* (2007).

26. Pat Harrison and Robin Tyler, *Try It You'll Like It*, LP (US: Dore Records, 1971).

27. Pat Harrison and Robin Tyler, *Wonder Women*, LP (US: 20th Century, 1973).

28. Ibid.

29. *Always a Bridesmaid, Never a Groom* (2007).

30. Ibid.

31. Tyler gave me a copy of her personal resumes: activism and performance, which in many instances contain descriptions of events and activities. Here I have taken direct passages from her biographical sketches.

32. *Always a Bridesmaid, Never a Groom* (1979).

33. Ibid.

34. Robin Tyler, *Just Kidding*, LP (Southern Women's Music and Comedy Festival, Camp Coleman (Cleveland, GA: Harrison and Tyler Productions, 1985). Original LP available at the June Mazer Lesbian Archives.

35. This quote is taken from a promotional flyer for Robin Tyler's performance in St. Paul, Minnesota. This document is part of the collection of memorabilia saved and stored in Tyler's personal library.

36. Information about the Gay Freedom Train was taken primarily from Robin Tyler's resume, her autobiographical performances, and the LP documenting the event: *The National March on Washington for Lesbian and Gay Rights* (US: Magnus Records in association with Alternate Publishing, 1979). The LP can be found at June Mazer Lesbian Archives.

37. Tyler, personal interview, May 11, 2008.

38. *Always a Bridesmaid, Never a Groom* (1979).

39. Ibid.

40. Lisa Duggan, *The Twilight of Equality? Neoliberalism, Cultural Politics, and the Attack on Democracy* (Boston: Beacon Press, 2003), 50.

41. Robin Tyler in *Annul Victory*, DVD, directed by Cheryl Riley (California: Manmade Multimedia, 2009).

42. Phelan, *Sexual Strangers*.

43. Ibid., 5.

44. Ibid., 12.

45. Ibid., 148.

46. May Joseph, *Nomadic Identities: The Performance of Citizenship* (Minneapolis: University of Minnesota Press, 1999), 153.

47. Brochure for the first National March on Washington for Lesbian and Gay Rights held in conjunction with the National Third World Lesbian/Gay Conference (October 12–15, 1970; March held on Oct. 14). Part of Robin Tyler's personal memorabilia.

48. MMOW ended up being a financial disaster with millions in revenue missing after the march. Robin Tyler delivered a speech to the Board of Directors warning of impending disaster if they allowed a member of the board's business to sponsor and profit from the march. In an article written by Michelangelo Signorile and published online in the news section of http://gay.com, "Ex-MMOW Executive Producer Prophesied Financial Disaster," Robin Tyler is quoted as informing the board well before the march that "unless the gate is tightly controlled by bonded people, there is no way to insure the cash not being stolen." This article was accessed online May 26, 2000, and is part of Robin Tyler's personal memorabilia. For further information on the MMOW debacle, see Michelangelo Signorile's "Collapse of MMOW's House of Cards Reveals Flawed Strategy" and "MMOW Committee Fumbles Its Way Deep into Debt." Both were published in the news section of http://gay.com, accessed online May 26, 2000, by Robin Tyler and part of Tyler's personal memorabilia.

49. Robin Tyler, "What Are We Marching For?," June 8, 1999. Part of Robin Tyler's personal memorabilia. Based on e-mail correspondence with Tyler, the manifesto was published but she does not recall where.

50. Claire Cox, "Prejudice Is Not Funny: Noted Humorist Analyzes No. 1 Problem," *Chicago Defender*, November 12, 1959, 13.

51. Robin Tyler quoted in Leah Hendry, "Gay Comic Comes Home: Tyler to Emcee Rainbow Resource Centre's 30th Anniversary," *Winnipeg Free Press*, Saturday, November 3, 2001, local section.

52. Edwards, "Robin Tyler," 23.

53. *Wonder Women.*

54. "Women Sit-In at Football Game," *Los Angeles Times,* Sunday August 23, 1970. Part of Robin Tyler's personal memorabilia.

55. Steve Bisheff, "Ram-Raiders Game Women's Lib Target," *Los Angeles Herald Examiner*, Sunday, August 23, 1970, Sports section.

56. Robin Tyler, "Letter to the Editor," *The Hollywood Reporter*, Thursday, March 11, 1971.

57. Susan Stocking, "Feminist Forum Duo Loved, Hated," *Los Angeles Times*, Thursday, April 27, 1972.

58. Ibid.

59. "Gay Lib Blues for College Prexy."

60. *Always a Bridesmaid, Never a Groom* (1979).

61. *The Axis of Evil Comedy Tour*, DVD, directed by Michael Simon (US: Image Entertainment, 2007).

62. Robin Tyler, *Always a Bridesmaid, Never a Groom.* (University of New Mexico, Albuquerque: Olivia Records, 1979). An original LP recording is available at the June Mazer Lesbian Archives.

63. Ibid.

64. Robin Tyler, "Robin Tyler," in *Eden Built by Eves: The Culture of Women's Music Festivals*, ed. Bonnie J. Morris (US: Alyson Publications, 1999), 39.

65. Ibid.

66. Duggan, *The Twilight of Equality?*, xi.

67. *Just Kidding.*

68. Duggan, *The Twilight of Equality?*, xii.

69. Ibid.

70. Jodi Melamed, "The Spirit of Neoliberalism: From Racial Liberalism to Neoliberal Multiculturalism," *Social Text* 89 (Winter 2006): 2.

71. "Chris Matthews on Obama SOTU: 'You know I forgot he was black tonight for an hour,'" *Think Progress*, http://thinkprogress.org/2010/01/27/matthews-obama-black/ (accessed January 29, 2010).

72. Melamed, "The Spirit of Neoliberalism," 3.

73. Her stance on victimage is taken from a workshop she conducted at the 1987 Women's Music and Comedy Festival in Yosemite, CA. A VHS of that workshop is available at the Mazer Lesbian Archives in Los Angeles, CA.

74. Tyler, *Eden Built by Eves*, 40.

75. Ibid., 41

76. Tyler, *Just Kidding.*

77. Having listened to nearly all of her performance work, I conclude that she was setting up for a joke that she's been doing for years without negative responses and which is merely an introduction to talking about her work as a female impersonator.

78. Tyler, *Eden Built by Eves*, 43.

79. Lauren Berlant, *The Queen of America Goes to Washington City: Essays on Sex and Citizenship* (Durham, NC: Duke University Press, 1997), 4.

80. Duggan, *The Twilight of Equality?*, 14.

81. This campaign used the following website: www.stopdrlaura.com/ to educate, inform, and coordinate opposition to Dr. Laura Schlesinger's programming.

82. Tyler and Thayer, "The 'Gay Marriage' Struggle," 24.

83. While the online campaign is no longer active, you can view original web pages for www.dontamend.com via the Internet archive: Way Back Machine. See http://web.archive .org/web/20031029163941/www.dontamend.com/subpages/aboutus.html.

84. Berlant, *The Queen of American Goes to Washington City*, 7.

85. Tyler, personal interview, May 11, 2008.

86. Ibid.

87. Phelan, *Sexual Strangers*, 103.

88. Tyler, personal interview, May 11, 2008.

89. Duggan, *The Twilight of Equality?*, 45.

90. Tyler and Thayer, "The 'Gay Marriage' Struggle," 12.

91. Ibid., 4.

92. Ibid., 11.

93. Teresa Wright represented San Francisco couples in Tyler's case. Now she represents the City of San Francisco in the case filed in response to Proposition 8. Tyler, personal interview, May 11, 2008.

94. Tyler and Thayer, "The 'Gay Marriage' Struggle," 27.

95. "Wanda Sykes' Speech (Original)," YouTube, www.youtube.com/watch?v=RRyVH -1zadg (accessed November 18, 2008).

96. While Wanda Sykes's friends and family were aware that she is a lesbian, it was not something she shared with her public until a recent decision to use her recognition and status to enlist support for gay civil rights. She now incorporates her lesbian identity into her comedy.

97. Michael Denning, *Culture in the Age of Three Worlds* (London: Verso, 2004), 165.

98. Tyler and Thayer, "The 'Gay Marriage' Struggle," 15.

99. Ibid., 20.

100. Ibid., 22.

101. Robin Tyler, e-mail message to author, July 15, 2011.

Chapter 6 · *Micia Mosely*

1. Following the passage of Proposition 8 in California, Wanda Sykes officially "came out" to the public on November 15, 2008, at a rally in Las Vegas, Nevada. The comedy that made her popular did foreground race and gender, but her more recent comedy also draws from her identity as a lesbian.

2. Jewelle Gomez, "But Some of Us Are Brave Lesbians: The Absence of Black Lesbian Fiction," in *Black Queer Studies: A Critical Anthology*, ed. E. Patrick Johnson and Mae G. Henderson (Durham, NC: Duke University Press, 2005), 290.

3. Micia Mosely, personal interview, May 15, 2011.

4. Micia Mosely, personal interview, May 23, 2008.

5. She is the recipient of numerous awards and fellowships, including Louise Patterson Award for Academic Achievement (1999–2000), Spencer Foundation Research Training Fellowship (2000–2001), Facing History and Ourselves Fellow for Northern California (1997–1998), National Endowment for the Humanities Teaching Fellow (1997), and Diane

A. Rottenberg Davis Memorial Endowment Prize for Excellence in Education (1994–1995). This information was taken from Micia Mosely's CV mailed to me in April 2008.

6. Micia Mosely, personal interview, May 23, 2008.

7. Tony Cox, 2007, "A Short History of Black Comedy," *News & Notes*, radio program. Guest speaker Darryl Littleton. US: NPR Radio, February 26. See also Darryl Littleton, *Black Comedians on Black Comedy: How African-Americans Taught Us to Laugh* (New York: Applause Theatre and Cinema Books, 2006).

8. *Louis C.K.: Chewed Up*, DVD, directed by Shannon Hartman (US: Image Entertainment, 2008).

9. Jose Esteban Muñoz, *Disidentifications: Queers of Color and the Performance of Politics* (Minneapolis: University of Minnesota Press, 1999), 15.

10. Ibid., 1.

11. E. Patrick Johnson, "Black Performance Studies: Genealogies, Politics, Futures," in *The SAGE Handbook of Performance Studies*, ed. D. Soyini Madison and Judith Hamera (California: Sage Publications, 2006), 449.

12. *Kate Clinton: The 25th Anniversary Tour*, DVD, directed by Andrea Meyerson (US: All Out Films, 2007).

13. Micia Mosely, personal interview, May 15, 2011.

14. Mosely, personal interview, December 27, 2008.

15. *Melanie Comarcho: Independent Woman*, DVD, directed by Melanie Comarcho (US: Uproar Entertainment, 2010).

16. Micia Mosely, e-mail, July 31, 2011. Upon request, Mosely sent me a document containing the text of some jokes she uses when performing stand-up comedy.

17. *Louis C.K.: Hilarious*, DVD, directed by Louis C.K. (Milwaukee: Comedy Central, 2010).

18. *The World According to Whoopi*, TV, directed by Paul Miller (US: Bravo, 2007).

19. Melanie Comarcho in Darryl Littleton, *Black Comedians on Black Comedy: How African-Americans Taught Us to Laugh* (New York: Applause Theatre and Cinema Books, 2006), 292.

20. Sue Ellen Case, "Women of Colour and Theatre," in *Feminism and Theatre* (New York: Methuen, 1988), 95–111.

21. Jewelle Gomez examines the relative absence of Black lesbian fiction in "But Some of Us Are Brave Lesbians: The Absence of Black Lesbian Fiction," arguing that this genre has been marginalized in part due to the rise in popularity of nonfiction. More likely though, Black lesbian nonfiction will suffer the same publishing and marketing difficulties with major presses because "with the narrowing of the market it has become more difficult for independent publishers to maintain themselves" (295). See *Black Queer Studies: A Critical Anthology*, ed. E. Patrick Johnson and Mae G. Henderson (Durham, NC: Duke University Press, 2005), 289–97.

22. Sabrina Lamb is the author of *Keepin' It Real: The Rise of Bullshit in the Black Community* (Cambridge House Books, 2006) and *Come Meet Miss Jones* (Random House, 2007). She also developed and produced the docu-comedy *Unbeweavable: Woman, What Did You Do to Your Hair?* See also Sabrina Lamb, "Laughing, Lying and Writing: Black Comediennes Turned Authors!," *Black Issues Book Review* 1, no. 5 (Sept./Oct. 1999): 29–30.

23. Mosely, personal interview, May 15, 2011.

24. Bambi Haggins, "Crossover Diva: Whoopi Goldberg and Persona Politics," in *Laughing Mad: The Black Comic Persona in Post-Soul America* (New Brunswick, NJ: Rutgers University Press, 2007), 134.

25. Audre Lorde, "Age, Race, Class, and Sex: Women Redefining Difference," (1980) *Sister Outsider* (Freedom, CA: The Crossing Press, 1984), 115.

26. *Daniel Tosh: Happy Thoughts*, DVD, directed by Beth McCarthy (US: Black Heart Productions, 2010).

27. *Why We Laugh: Black Comedians on Black Comedy*, DVD, directed by Robert Townsend (US: Code Black Entertainment, 2009).

28. Mosely, e-mail, January 26, 2012.

29. Mosely, e-mail, July 31, 2011.

30. Ibid.

31. Mosely, personal interview, December 27, 2008.

32. Gloria Bigelow lives and performs in Los Angeles, California. Gloria Bigelow in *Laughing Matters . . . Next Gen*, DVD, directed by Andrea Meyerson (US: All Out Films, 2009).

33. Sabrina Matthews in *Laughing Matters . . . More!*, DVD, directed and produced by Andrea Meyerson (US: All Out Films. 2006).

34. *Where My Girls At? A Comedic Look at Black Lesbians*, by Micia Mosely, directed by Tamilla Woodard, Laboratory Theatre, Clarice Smith Performing Arts Center, University of Maryland, College Park, MD, November 20, 2008.

35. Ibid.

36. Ibid.

37. Ibid.

38. Ibid.

39. Mosely, personal interview, December 27, 2008.

40. Mosely, e-mail message to author, January 26, 2012.

41. Ibid.

42. Karen Williams, "Healing Humor," *Metroweekly* 14, no. 50 (April 24, 2008): 36.

43. Mosely, personal interview, December 27, 2008.

44. bell hooks, *Yearning: Race, Gender, and Cultural Politics* (Boston: South End Press, 1990), 72.

45. L. H. Stallings, *Mutha' Is Half a Word: Intersections of Folklore, Vernacular, Myth, and Queerness in Black Female Culture* (Columbus: Ohio State University Press, 2007), 115.

46. *Where My Girls At?*

47. Mosely, personal interview, November 21, 2008.

48. Mosely, "Talk-Back," *Where My Girls At? A Comedic Look at Black Lesbians*, by Micia Mosely, directed by Tamilla Woodard, Laboratory Theatre, Clarice Smith Performing Arts Center, University of Maryland, College Park, MD, November 20, 2008.

49. bell hooks, "Eating the Other: Desire and Resistance," in *Eating Culture*, ed. Ronn Scapp and Brian Seitz (Albany: State University of New York, 1998), 181–200.

50. Mosely, personal interview, December 27, 2008.

51. Ibid.

52. E. Patrick Johnson and Mae Henderson, eds., "Introduction: Queering Black Studies / 'Quaring' Queer Studies," in *Black Queer Studies: A Critical Anthology* (Durham, NC: Duke University Press, 2005), 5.

53. Mosely, personal interview, December 27, 2008.

54. Muñoz, *Disidentifications*, 141.

55. Mosely, personal interview, December 27, 2008.

56. *Where My Girls At?*

57. Ibid.

58. Ibid.

59. Mosely, personal interview, February 15, 2010.

60. Mosely, personal interview, December 21, 2008.

61. Carol Allen, "'Shaking That Thing' and All Its Wonders: African American Female Comedy," *Studies in American Humor* 3, no. 12 (2005): 97.

62. Direct quotes are taken from the mission statement for Nursha Project, which is available at http://nurshaproject.com/about-us/missionvision.

63. Shalonda Ingram, personal interview, February 21, 2009.

64. Mosely, personal interview, May 15, 2011.

65. For a lengthy discussion of the roots of African American humor, see Elsie Williams, *The Humor of Jackie Moms Mabley: An African Comedic Tradition* (New York: Garland, 1995).

Chapter 7 · Hari Kondabolu

1. I have spoken with Hari Kondabolu on several occasions regarding his career choices as a writer and a comic. These conversations have helped to provide valuable background biographical information, ensure that I understand motivation and intention behind his comedy, and supply feedback on the chapter as it developed. However, the terminology, arguments and analysis in the chapter do not necessarily reflect Kondabolu's personal views or opinions.

2. *Jeff Dunham: Spark of Insanity*, DVD, directed by Michael Simon (US: Image Entertainment, 2007).

3. Micia Mosely, personal interview, May 23, 2008.

4. Ibid.

5. Hari Kondabolu in Anna Sterling, "The Feministing Five: Hari Kondabolu and Janine Brito," *Feministing*, July 7, 2012, http://feministing.com/2012/07/07/the-feministing-five -hari-kondabolu-and-janine-brito/ (accessed July 11, 2012).

6. "Micia Mosely," Vimeo, http://vimeo.com/10534442 (accessed January 9, 2012).

7. Caitlin Boston, "Race+Comedy: Hari Kondabolu Balances His Conscience with His Craft," *Racialicious*, July 6, 2012, www.racialicious.com/2012/07/06/race-comedy-hari -kondabolu-balances-his-conscience-with-his-craft/ (accessed July 9, 2012).

8. Ibid.

9. "Manoj," YouTube, www.youtube.com/watch?v=uNeyWm64kGo (accessed March 9, 2011).

10. "Pablo Francisco—Black People at Starbucks," YouTube, www.youtube.com/watch ?v=u3y5WSH_u1A (accessed February 12, 2012).

11. "Manoj."

12. Ibid.

13. Janine Brito in Anna Sterling, "The Feministing Five: Hari Kondabolu and Janine Brito."

14. "Manoj."

15. The HBO Comedy Festival began in 1985 and on average features eighty comics over a four-day period. While this annual comedy festival continues, it is no longer an HBO enterprise and has been produced by TBS since 2008.

16. Hari Kondabolu on *Jimmy Kimmel Live*, February 19, 2007, YouTube, www.youtube .com/watch?v=9TerRcWDdsc (accessed July 9, 2012).

17. *Live at Gotham*'s weekly show featured comic talent from around the country and ran from 2006 to 2009, averaging eight showcases per season, each featuring a host and six comics. Hari Kondabolu was cast in Season 3, Episode 6, which aired on July 18, 2008.

18. "Hari Kondabolu at John Oliver's NY Stand Up," YouTube, www.youtube.com/ watch?v=pv7AELM1e-E (accessed June 2, 2011).

19. *Bo Burnham: Words Words Words*, DVD, directed by Shannon Hartman (US: Comedy Partners, 2010).

20. Lenny Bruce performs yellowface in his album: *Lenny Bruce—American* (1961). Interestingly, the performance seems to laugh at the joke's content and not simply at the impersonation. More commonly, an audience will discernibly appreciate the impression and laugh at anything said in that voice. Bruce's audience did not laugh at the impression until he got to a punch line.

21. "Dat Phan *Last Comic Standing*," YouTube, www.youtube.com/watch?v=QeEr TVCqV6I (accessed July 7, 2012).

22. "Carlos Mencia on Asians," YouTube, www.youtube.com/watch?v=esKwU3BrUfM (accessed February 22, 2012).

23. For a detailed filmic exploration of this history of Black stock characters circulating in popular culture, watch *Ethnic Notions: Black People in White Minds*, DVD, directed by Marlon Riggs (US: California Newsreel, 2004).

24. For useful sources on the history of blackface minstrelsy, see: W. T. Lhamon Jr., *Raising Cain: Blackface Performance from Jim Crow to Hip Hop* (Cambridge, MA: Harvard University Press, 1998); Elsie Williams, *The Humor of Jackie Moms Mabley: An African American Comedic Tradition* (New York: Garland, 1995); Alexander Saxton, "Blackface Minstrelsy and Jacksonian Ideology," in *Locating American Studies: The Evolution of a Discipline*, ed. Lucy Maddox, 114–142 (Baltimore: Johns Hopkins University Press, 1999); Eric Lott, *Love and Theft: Blackface Minstrelsy and the American Working Class* (New York: Oxford University Press, 1993).

25. *Anjelah Johnson: That's How We Do It*, DVD, directed by Bobcat Goldthwait and Anjelah Johnson (US: Warner Bros., 2010).

26. *Live Nude Comedy*, Season 1, Episode 4, TV, directed by Brent Carpenter (US: Salient Media, August 6, 2009).

27. *Patton Oswalt: Finest Hour*, CD (New York: Comedy Central Records, 2011).

28. Jonathan Winters performed several queerface minstrelsy jokes that remained recurring jokes on his albums, including *Down to Earth* (1960); *Humor through the Eyes of Jonathan Winters* (1962); *Movies are Better than Ever* (1967); and *Jonathan Winters Wings It* (1968). Bob Newhart also performs using queerface (though minimally) for a joke about a gay man and his pussycat that can be heard on his album *Bob Newhart: This Is It!* (1967).

29. *Richard Pryor: Live and Smokin'*, DVD, directed by Michael Blum (US: Weinstein Co, 2009).

30. *hungry i reunion*, DVD, directed by Thomas A. Cohen (US: Hammermark Productions, 2005).

31. *Eddie Murphy: RAW*, DVD, directed by Robert Townsend (US: Paramount, 1987).

32. "Max Amini—Gay Wingman," YouTube, www.youtube.com/watch?v=dJ7jkuRvDVY (accessed July 24, 2011).

33. "Al Del Bene—Gay Toddler," YouTube, www.youtube.com/watch?v=5BFCpOXJ8io (accessed February 15, 2012).

34. "Emily Levine's Theory of Everything," Ted, www.ted.com/talks/emily_levine_s_theory_of_everything.html (accessed August 18, 2011).

35. John Strausbaugh, *Black Like You: Blackface, Whiteface, Insult and Imitation in American Popular Culture* (New York: Penguin, 2006); Lawrence J. Epstein, *The Haunted Smile: The Story of Jewish Comedians in America* (Cambridge, MA: Perseus, 2001).

36. For detailed exploration of the racialization of early twentieth-century ethnic Whites, see David R. Roediger, *Working toward Whiteness: How America's Immigrants Became White* (New York: Basic Books, 2005); Jennifer Guglielmo, *Are Italians White? How Race Is Made in America* (New York: Routledge, 2003); and Noel Ignatiev, *How the Irish Became White* (New York: Routledge, 2005).

37. This was a main argument made in Eric L. Goldstein's *The Price of Whiteness: Jews, Race, and American Identity* (Princeton, NJ: Princeton University Press, 2006).

38. Noel Ignatiev encourages people to become race traitors so as to belie racial/racist assumptions and defy essentialist arguments connecting culture and intelligence to race. He was founder and editor of the short-lived *Race Traitor: Journal of the New Abolitionism*.

39. Episode 146: King of Fruit with W. Kamau Bell, hosted by Jesse Thorn and Jordan Morris, "Jordan, Jesse GO!," *Public Radio International: The Sound of Young America*, September 23, 2010, www.maximumfun.org/shows/jordan-jesse-go?page=11.

40. *Stewart Lee: 41st Best Stand Up Ever*, DVD, directed by Michael Cumming (UK: Real Talent, 2008).

41. Aziz Ansari said this directly to the camera prior to entering the stage for his performance. *Premium Blend*, Season 9, Episode 3 (Comedy Central, February 3, 2006).

42. "Kristin Key on Pot and Food Wars," YouTube, www.youtube.com/watch?v=7OfvZX3pfi4 (accessed July 19, 2011).

43. *Outlaugh: The Best of Queer Comedy*, DVD, directed by Gene Merker (US: Edit This Productions, 2007).

44. "Margaret's Mom," Comedy Central, http://comedians.jokes.com/margaret-cho/videos/margaret-cho—margaret-s-mom (accessed September 30, 2011).

45. I saw him perform this joke at the 2011 Just for Laughs Festival in Montreal, Quebec, Canada. DADT was repealed a few months later.

46. Maz Jobrani, e-mail, July 14, 2011.

47. K-Von in *Comics without Borders*, Season 1, Episode 3, Showtime TV, directed by Scott Montoya (US: Salient Media, 2008).

48. "Hari Kondabolu on Russell Howard's *Good News*," YouTube, www.youtube.com/watch?v=W-KSI5ZoI9o (accessed June 2, 2011).

49. "LOL Lounge 2012—Hari Kondabolu," YouTube, www.youtube.com/watch ?v=H4Ij86UJwck&feature=related, November 3, 2012, Youtube (accessed August 12, 2012).

50. "Hari Kondabolu on Russell Howard's *Good News*."

51. Boston, "Race+Comedy."

52. Coco Papyon, "Persephone Pioneers: Hari Kondabolu," *Persephone Magazine*, July 15, 2011, http://persephonemagazine.com/2011/07/15/persephone-pioneers-hari-kondabolu/ (accessed July 9, 2012).

53. "Hari Kondabolu on 'The Sanctity of Marriage,'" YouTube, www.youtube.com /watch?v=WYPmJIosddw (accessed September 12, 2011).

54. "Hari Kondabolu on Russell Howard's *Good News*."

55. Papyon, "Persephone Pioneers: Hari Kondabolu."

56. Boston, "Race+Comedy."

57. *Comedy Central Presents: Hari Kondabolu*, TV, directed by Ryan Polito (California: Comedy Central, 2011).

58. Ibid.

59. Papyon, "Persephone Pioneers: Hari Kondabolu."

Conclusion

1. "So a Girl Walks into a Comedy Club," Tumblr, http://breakfastcookie.tumblr.com /post/26879625651/so-a-girl-walks-into-a-comedy-club (accessed August 2, 2012).

2. *Wanda Sykes: Sick and Tired*, DVD, directed by Michael Drumm (US: Image Entertainment, 2006).

3. Dean Obeidallah in *The Arab American Comedy Tour*, DVD, videography by Oscar Films (Seattle and Dearborn: Arab Film Distribution, 2006).

4. *Annul Victory*, DVD, directed by Cheryl Riley (California: Manmade Multimedia, 2009).

5. *Kathleen Madigan: In Other Words*, DVD, directed by Michael Drumm (US: Warner Bros., 2006).

6. Dax-Devlon Ross in "Progress Report #5: Black Authenticity Part B," YouTube, www.youtube.com/watch?v=Y8fKV2w5dyo&feature=channel (accessed March 2, 2010).

7. Shane Phelan, *Sexual Strangers: Gays, Lesbians and Dilemmas of Citizenship* (Philadelphia: Temple University Press, 2001), 152.

8. *Annul Victory*.

9. Lisa Duggan, *The Twilight of Equality? Neoliberalism, Cultural Politics, and the Attack on Democracy* (Boston: Beacon Press, 2003), x.

10. Aimee Dowl, "L in a Handbasket: Kate Clinton's Politics of Funny," *Bitch: Feminist Response to Pop Culture* 30 (Fall 2005): 39.

11. Emily Nussbaum, "Small Wonders: Comedy Off the Radar," *The New Yorker*, December 24, 2012, www.newyorker.com/arts/critics/television/2012/12/24/121224crte_television _nussbaum (accessed January 2, 2013).

12. "Hari Kondabolu Explains Why *The Mindy Project* Is Good for Indian-Americans on 'Totally Biased,'" Huffington Post, September 24, 2012, www.huffingtonpost.com/2012/09 /24/hari-kondabolu-the-mindy-project-totally-biased_n_1910310.html (accessed November 2, 2012).

13. *Jimmy Dore: Citizen Jimmy*, DVD, directed by Michael Drumm (US: Image Entertainment, 2008).

14. Louise Bernikow, "Humor," in *The New Beacon Book of Quotations by Women*, ed. Rosalie Maggio (Boston: Beacon Press, 1996), 330.

Ahmed Ahmed: An Egyptian American actor and comedian, Ahmed moved to Hollywood at nineteen years old to pursue his career. He was the winner of the first annual Richard Pryor Award for ethnic comedy at the Edinburgh Festival, Scotland, in 2004.

Comedy Filmography

Tough Crowd with Colin Quinn, Comedy Central, Episode 2 (June 12, 2003)

Casting Calls, TV Documentary (2003)

National Lampoon Live: The International Show, TV Movie (2004)

Last Call with Carson Daly, NBC, Episode 323 (February 6, 2006)

Wild West Comedy Show: 30 Days and 30 Nights—Hollywood to the Heartland, Documentary (2006)

Armstrong and Getty: Radio on TV, KKSF, Episode 1 (June 15, 2007)

HBO Fist Look, HBO, Episode 261 (January 25, 2008)

The Tonight Show with Jay Leno, NBC, 2 Episodes (February, 2008)

Gab's Blabs, Current TV, Episode 19 (August 25, 2008)

Comics without Borders, Showtime, Episode 9 (October 16, 2008)

History of a Joke, TV Documentary (2008)

Ahmed, Say Something Funny . . . , Documentary (2008)

The Axis of Evil Comedy Tour, Video (2008)

1st Amendment Stand Up, Starz, Episode 54 (October 1, 2010)

I Am Comic, Documentary (2010)

Just Like Us, Documentary (2010)

Bridging the Gap: A Middle East Comedy Conference, TV Movie (2010)

Laugh Out Loud Comedy Festival, Syndicated, Episode 12 (February 17, 2011)

Valentino's Ghost, Documentary (2012)

Sunset Strip, Documentary (2012)

Lisa Alvarado: Born in Chicago, Illinois, to Peruvian parents, Alvarado wanted to be a comedian her entire life. She currently tours at national comedy clubs, college campuses, and for corporate shows.

Comedy Filmography

Inside Joke, TV Series (2004)

Comedy.TV, Comedy Central, Season 1 Episode 4 (2009)

Live! From the Future, thestream.tv, Episode 3 (February 24, 2009)
Comics Unleashed, Comedy Central, Episode 98 (April 26, 2010)
Latino 101, SiTV, 7 Episodes (2010–2011)
The Real LA, Video (2011)
Ladies Night Out, TV Series (2011)

Mohammed "Mo" Amer: Born July 24, 1981, in Kuwait, Amer was raised in Houston, Texas, after his family left Kuwait during the Persian Gulf War. He is a Sunni Muslim. He started doing stand-up as a teenager by impersonating family members, and has now toured almost thirty countries around the world. Amer is part of the touring stand-up show *Allah Made Me Funny*. His one-man show *Legally Homeless* is in production for a premium cable television special.

Comedy Filmography
Allah Made Me Funny: Live in Concert, Showcase (2008)

Max Amini: A comedian of American Iranian descent, Amini regularly performs at The Comedy Store and the Laugh Factory in Los Angeles. His comedy focuses on general topics as well as his ethnicity. In 2012, he was chosen for the CBS Diversity Comedy Showcase.

Comedy Filmography
ADHDtv: With Lew Marklin, TV Guide, Episode 50 (August 5, 2009)
Bridging the Gap: A Middle East Comedy Conference, TV Movie (2010)
Funny: The Documentary, Documentary (2012)

Edison Apple: Born on the Tohono O'odam Indian Reservation and raised in San Diego, Apple graduated from the American Academy of Dramatic Arts and is an openly gay comic who often performs in queer comedy showcases around the country.

Comedy Filmography
Laughing Matters . . . Next Gen, Showcase (2009)

Sarah Arafat: Arafat is a Muslim comedian from New Jersey who maintains the blog *Mind of a Muslimah* and performs sporadically.

David Arnold: Based out of Los Angeles, Arnold performs at comedy clubs across the country. He is a writer for Tyler Perry's *Meet the Browns* and the host of *Black Men Revealed*.

Comedy Filmography
Before They Were Stars! 2001, TV Movie (2001)
Raymann Is Laat, Syndicated, Season 7 Episode 9 (April 15, 2005)
Just Jokes: Comedy DVD Tour Vol. 1, Video (2005)
The Tonight Show with Jay Leno, NBC, Season 14 Episode 218 (November 30, 2006)
Black Men Revealed, TVONE.TV, 8 Episodes (2006)
BET's Comicview, BET, 2 Episodes (2006–2008)
1st Amendment Stand Up, Starz, Season 2 Episode 22 (June 13, 2007)
The Funny Spot, Syndicated, Episode 4 (February 15, 2008)
Def Comedy Jam, HBO, Season 8 Episode 7 (February 17, 2008)

Next Up, Video (2008)
After Hours Comedy, Vol. 2, Video (2010)
Spirit of Comedy Vol. 2, Video (2010)
Funny: The Documentary, Documentary (2012)
Russell Simons Presents: The Ruckus, TV Series (2012)

Aundre the Wonderwoman: Aundre is a political and racial up-lift satirist who has made her name in the Bay Area of California. She performs stand-up sporadically and won first place at the 1999 Russian River Resort Comedy Competition, was a semifinalist in the 2005 San Francisco International Comedy Competition, and the recipient of the 2008 Stand Up for Justice Award from Death Penalty Focus.

Michele Balan: A Brooklyn native, Balan tours regularly doing her stand-up and often does events that are specifically gay or Jewish focused. She was a finalist on *Last Comic Standing*, among other film and television credits and writes for several different magazines. Balan was voted one of the "Top 10 Comics" by *Backstage*, a magazine geared toward professionals in the theater arts. She left a high-paying executive job at a computer company in order to pursue comedy.

Discography

Neurotic by Nature (1999)

Comedy Filmography

Wisecrack: Outlaugh Festival Part 4, MTV, Season 2 Episode 4 (2005)
Last Comic Standing, Season 4, NBC (2006)
Live! (Just Barely), Comedy Special (2006)
Stand-Up 360: Edition 2, Showcase (2009)
Stand-Up: Inside Out, Showcase (2009)
Comedy.TV, Season 1 Episode 22 (2011)
From Ecstasy to Vitamin C!, Comedy Special (2011)
Funny: The Documentary, Documentary (2012)

Maria Bamford: A stand-up comedian hailing from Duluth, Minnesota, Bamford is best known for performing a host of wacky characters that include some loosely based on her own family and friends. Open about her struggle with bipolar disorder, Bamford uses comedy to work through related issues as well as writing and performing poignant comedy that addresses a variety of social and political issues.

Discography

The Burning Bridges Tour (2005)
How to Win! (2007)
Unwanted Thoughts Syndrome (2009)
Ask Me About My New God! (2013)

Comedy Filmography

The Martin Short Show, SCTV, Episode 25 (October 15, 1999)
Late Night with Conan O'Brien, NBC, 2 Episodes (1999–2000)
Comedy Central Presents, Comedy Central, Episode 47 (July 2, 2001)

The Tonight Show with Jay Leno, NBC, 2 Episodes (2001)
Late Friday, NBC, 2 Episodes (2001–2002)
Premium Blend, Comedy Central, Episode 31 (July 19, 2002)
Comic Remix, Series (2002)
Funny Money, GSN, Episode 1 (July 13, 2003)
Heroes of Comedy: Women on Top, TV Mini-series Documentary (2003)
The World Comedy: Women on Top, TV Special (2003)
The Glass House, ABC, Episode 80 (April 2, 2004)
Stand Up!, ABC, Episode 7 (April 8, 2004)
Jimmy Kimmel Live!, ABC, Episode 411 (September 16, 2004)
The Comedy Factory, ABC, Episode 2 (February 11, 2005)
The Glass House, ABC, Episode 123 (April 20, 2005)
The Comedians of Comedy, Documentary (2005)
Just for Laughs, BBC, Episode 47 (November 20, 2005)
The Late Late Show with Craig Ferguson, CBS, 2 Episodes (2005–2010)
Comics Unleashed, Syndicated, Episode 5 (September 29, 2006)
The Comedians of Comedy: Live at the El Ray, Video (2006)
Comedy Central Presents, Comedy Central, Episode 186 (February 16, 2007)
Comedians of Comedy: Live at the Troubadour, Video (2007)
The Comedy Can Television Series, TV Movie (2007)
Heckler, Documentary (2007)
Stand Up Face the Fear, Documentary (2008)
Plan B (2010)
Global Comedians, Global, Episode 1 (2010)
New York Stand-Up Show, BBC, 3 Episodes (2010–2011)
Comedy.TV, Comedy Central, Episode 15 (2011)
From Nothing, Something: A Documentary on the Creative Process, Documentary (2012)
Maria Bamford: The Special Special Special! (2012)

Web Series

The Maria Bamford Show (2007–2008)
Ask My Mom (2013)

Roseanne Barr: Born November 3, 1952, in Salt Lake City, Utah, Barr ran away from home to Colorado at age 18 and began working as a stand-up comedian there. She worked at The Comedy Store in Los Angeles and her first television appearance was in 1985 on *The Tonight Show. Roseanne,* a television sitcom based on her comic persona, premiered in 1988. She has won an Emmy and a Golden Globe, among several comedy awards, and tried to run for president as a Green Party candidate in 2012, but lost the nomination.

Nonfiction Writing

Roseanne: My Life As a Woman (1989)
My Lives (1994)
Roseannearchy: Dispatches from the Nut Farm (2011)

Discography

I Enjoy Being A Girl (1990)

Comedy Filmography

The Tonight Show with Johnny Carson, NBC, Episode 2040 (August 23, 1985)

Rodney Dangerfield: It's Not Easy Being Me, Showcase (1986)

Late Night with David Letterman, CBS, 10 Episodes (1986–2011)

On Location: The Roseanne Barr Show, HBO (1987)

Roseanne Barr Live from Trump Castle (1991)

Saturday Night Live, NBC, Host, 3 Episodes (1991–1994)

The Tonight Show with Johnny Carson, NBC, Episode 0678 (May 20, 1992)

Comic Relief V, HBO (1992)

Roseanne and Tom: Getting Away with It (1992)

Roseanne Arnold (1992)

The Tonight Show with Jay Leno, NBC, 12 Episodes (1993–2011)

Saturday Night Special, Fox, 4 Episodes (1996)

The Roseanne Show (1997–1999)

The Ms. Foundation's Women of Comedy (1998)

Comic Relifer VIII, HBO (1998)

Get Bruce, Documentary (1999)

The Daily Show with Jon Stewart, Comedy Central (June 30, 1999)

Sandra Bernhard: Giving Them Lip, Documentary (2001)

Inside the Actor's Studio, HBO, Season 7 Episode 18 (August 19, 2001)

Late Night with Conan O'Brien, NBC (February 5, 2003)

Heroes of Comedy: Women on Top (2003)

The Real Roseanne Show, ABC, reality show (2003)

The Late Late Show with Craig Kilborn, CBS, 2 Episodes (2003–2004)

Jimmy Kimmel Live!, ABC, 7 Episodes (2003–2011)

Funny Already: A History of Jewish Comedy, Documentary (2004)

Roseanne Barr: Blonde and Bitchin' (2006)

Rockin' with Roseanne (2006)

Comic Relief 2006, HBO (2006)

Real Time with Bill Maher, HBO, 3 Episodes (2006–2008)

The Late Late Show with Craig Ferguson, CBS, 3 Episodes (2006–2011)

Sit Down Comedy with David Steinberg, TV Land, Season 2 Episode 3 (March 7, 2007)

Alexis Arquette: She's My Brother (2007)

Slacker Uprising, Documentary (2007)

Make 'Em Laugh: The Funny Business in America, Documentary (2009)

Tavis Smiley, PBS, 2 Episodes (2009–2011)

I Am Comic, Documentary (2010)

Lopez Tonight, ABC (January 12, 2011)

Chelsea Lately, E! (January 13, 2011)

Looking for Lenny, Documentary (2011)

Roseanne's Nuts, Lifetime (2011)

Conan, Season 1, Episode 139 (September 13, 2011)

W. Kamau Bell: One of the fastest rising sociopolitical comics in the United States, Bell is the founding member of the stand-up comedy collective Laughter against the Machine. He is also the cohost of "The Field Negro Guide to Arts and Culture" podcast.

He currently stars in his own comedy series, *Totally Biased with W. Kamau Bell*, on the FX Network, for which Chris Rock is the executive producer.

Discography

One Night Only (2007)
Face Full of Flour (2010)

Comedy Filmography

Imagine, BBC, Episode 96 (December 20, 2011)
Laughter against the Machine, Tour Documentary (2012)
Totally Biased with W. Kamau Bell, FX (2012–2013)
The Comedy Club, Documentary (2013)

Sara Benincasa: As a comedian and political journalist, Benincasa is best known for her imitations of Sarah Palin and Michele Bachmann. She is a comedic blogger, has a YouTube channel, and a popular podcast called *Sex and Other Human Activities*, but no discography, filmography, or television appearances to speak of. She has also done comedic work about agoraphobia and anxiety disorders. Different newspapers have praised her for her innovative comedic journalism.

Nonfiction Writing

Agorafabulous! (2011)

Gloria Bigelow: Born and raised in Pittsburgh, Pennsylvania, Bigelow attended Spelman College where she majored in drama. She began performing comedy after moving to New York City and has since relocated to the West Coast to continue her professional career. She can be seen at countless comedy clubs like New York Comedy Club, the Laugh Factory, and the Outlaugh Comedy Festival.

Comedy Filmography

Hot Gay Comics, Here! TV, Season 1 Episode 6 (January 23, 2009)
Out in the City, Documentary Short (2009)
Laughing Matters . . . Next Gen, Showcase (2009)
One Night Stand Up, Logo TV, Episode 108 (May 6, 2010)
Fierce Funny Women, Showtime (March 10, 2011)

Lewis Black: Black is a stand-up comedian, author, playwright, social critic, and actor. His comedic style includes ranting and ridiculing history. He went to the University of North Carolina at Chapel Hill where he studied playwriting. He has been performing stand-up comedy since the 1980s and can be seen periodically on *The Daily Show*.

Nonfiction Writing

Nothing Sacred (2006)
Me of Little Faith (2009)
I'm Dreaming of a Black Christmas (2011)

Discography

The White Album (2000)
The End of the Universe (2002)

Rules of Enragement (2003)
Lewis Black: Luther Burbank Performance (2005)
Lewis Black: The Carnegie Hall Performance (2006)
Anticipation (2008)
Stark Raving Black (2010)
The Prophet (2011)
In God We Rust (2012)
Old Yeller (Live at the Borgata) (2013)

Comedy Filmography

Stand-Up Spotlight, VH1 (1988)
Politically Incorrect, Comedy Central, Episode 5 (July 18, 1995)
HBO Comedy Showcase, HBO (1995)
The Daily Show with Jon Stewart, Comedy Central, 320 Episodes (1996–2012)
Comic Cabana, Comedy Central (1997)
The Daily Show Andy Williams Christmas Special, TV Movie (1997)
Late Night with Conan O'Brien, NBC, 15 Episodes (1997–2008)
Comedy Central Presents, Comedy Central, Episode 4 (December 22, 1998)
Monday Night Clive, BBC, Episode 1 (May 17, 1999)
The Daily Show Third Anniversary Special, TV Movie (1999)
The Great Millennium, TV Movie (1999)
Comedy Central Presents, Comedy Central, Episode 22 (June 7, 2000)
Just for Laughs: Montreal Comedy Festival, TV Movie (2001)
Comedy Central Presents, Comedy Central, Episode 62 (April 22, 2002)
Lewis Black: Taxed Beyond Belief, TV Documentary Short (2002)
Tough Crowd with Colin Quinn, Comedy Central (2002)
60 Spins around the Sun, Documentary (2003)
Lewis Black Unleashed, Video (2003)
Uncensored Comedy: That's Not Funny!, TV Documentary (2003)
The World Comedy Tour: Melbourne 2003, TV Special (2003)
Heroes of Jewish Comedy, TV miniseries Documentary (2003)
Comedy Central Presents the Commies, TV Documentary (2003)
Just for Laughs, BBC, 3 Episodes (2003–2006)
Bar Mitzvah Bash!, TV Movie (2004)
Shorties Watchin' Shorties, Comedy Central, Episode 8 (September 15, 2004)
Last Call with Carson Daly, NBC, Episode 194 (September 30, 2004)
Lewis Black: Black on Broadway, TV Movie (2004)
Funny Already: A History of Jewish Comedy, TV Documentary (2004)
Weekends at the DL, Comedy Central, Episode 2 (July 30, 2005)
Last Laugh '05, TV Movie (2005)
The Aristocrats, Documentary (2005)
Red State Diaries, TV Movie (2005)
Dean's List, WGN, Episode 38 (February 20, 2006)
Lewis Black: Red, White and Screwed, TV Movie (2006)
Screenwipe, TV Documentary (2006)
Comic Relief 2006, TV Movie (2006)
Last Laugh '06, TV Movie (2006)

Live at Gotham, Comedy Central, Episode 8 (May 25, 2007)

20 on 20, TV Movie (2007)

Heckler, Documentary (2007)

Last Laugh '07, TV Movie (2007)

Late Show with David Letterman, CBS, Episode 216 (March 12, 2008)

George Carlin: Mark Twain Prize, TV Movie (2008)

History of the Joke, TV Documentary (2008)

Comedy Central Roast of Bob Saget, TV Movie (2008)

Root of All Evil, Comedy Central (2008)

Just for Laughs, CTV, Episode 2 (October 5, 2009)

Stark Raving Black (2009)

Surviving the Holidays with Lewis Black, TV Movie (2009)

Late Night with Jimmy Fallon, NBC, 2 Episodes (2009–2010)

The Late Late Show with Craig Ferguson, CBS, 5 Episodes (2009–2011)

Just for Laughs, CTV, Episode 1 (October 11, 2010)

Teenage Paparazzo, Documentary (2010)

I Am Comic, Documentary (2010)

The Battle for Late Night, TV Documentary (2010)

Basic Black: The Lewis Black Story, Video Documentary (2010)

A Night of Too Many Stars: An Overbooked Concert for Autism Education, TV Movie (2010)

The Green Room with Paul Provenza, Showtime, Season 2 Episode 4 (August 4, 2011)

Caris' Peace, Documentary (2011)

Let Fury Have the Hour, Documentary (2011)

Ron White's Comedy Salute to the Troops, TV Movie (2011)

Looking for Lenny, Documentary (2011)

The Pig Roast with Otto and George, Bash Box TV (2011)

In God We Rust, TV Movie (2012)

Josh Blue: Voted the winner of *Last Comic Standing* during its fourth season, Blue is a comedian with cerebral palsy. His routine focuses on his disability, showing audiences that people with disabilities can make an impact. He was voted the 11th best comedian by viewers in Comedy Central's Stand-Up Comedy Showdown in 2011.

Discography

Good Josh, Bad Arm (2008)

Comedy Filmography

Mind of Mencia, Comedy Central, Episode 8 (August 24, 2005)

Kathy Griffin: My Life on the D-List, Bravo, Episode 11 (July 11, 2006)

LIVE! With Kelly, ABC, Episode 779 (August 10, 2006)

Ellen: The Ellen DeGeneres Show, NBC, Episode 479 (September 21, 2006)

7 More Days in the Tank, Video (2006)

Last Comic Standing, NBC (2006–2007)

Accidently Famous, TV Movie (2007)

NESN Comedy All-Stars, Episode 10 (September 26, 2008)

Comedy.TV, Comedy Central, Episode 10 (September 28, 2008)

Comedy Central Presents, Comedy Central, Episode 241 (March 27, 2009)

(Sex)Abled: Disability Uncensored, Documentary Short (2009)
Hemispheres: A Documentary on Cerebral Palsy, Documentary (2009)
The Cohesion Project, Documentary (2011)
Josh Blue: *A Sticky Change*, TV Movie (2012)

Elayne Boosler: Boosler was born and raised in Brooklyn, New York. She started out doing stand-up comedy in the late 1970s and became the first female to get her own hour comedy special on cable TV. Today she still performs comedy and is dedicated to political activism.

Comedy Filmography

The Dean Martin Comedy World, NBC, Episode 6 (August 15, 1974)
Rock Concert, ABC, Episode 53 (October 7, 1975)
On Location: Freddie Prinze and Friends, TV Movie (1976)
Rock Concert, ABC, 2 Episodes (1976–1977)
The Alan Hamel Show, CTV, 3 Episodes (1978–1980)
Late Night with David Letterman, NBC, 2 Episodes (March 2, 1982, 1989)
The Shape of Things, NBC, 3 Episodes (April 1982)
The Andy Kaufman Show, TV Movie (1983)
Comedy from Here, TV Movie (1984)
Elayne Boosler: Party of One, TV Movie (1985)
Comic Relief '87, TV Movie (1987)
All-Star Party for Joan Collins, TV Movie (1987)
The Arsenio Hall Show, CBS, Episode 134 (November 7, 1989)
Comic Relief III, TV Special Documentary (1989)
Jerry Lewis MDA Labor Day Telethon, FOX, Episode 6 (September 1, 1990)
The Arsenio Hall Show, CBS, Episode 232 (November 6, 1990)
Comic Relief IV, TV Movie (1991)
Live Nude Girls, TV Movie (1991)
A Party for Richard Pryor, TV Special (1991)
In A New Light: A Call to Action in the War against AIDS, TV Documentary (1992)
Broadway Baby, TV Movie (June 2, 1993)
In a New Light, TV Special (1994)
The Daily Show with Jon Stewart, Comedy Central, 3 Episodes (1996–1999)
Politically Incorrect, Comedy Central, 2 Episodes (1999–2001)
When Stand-Up Comics Ruled the World, TV Documentary (2004)
45th Annual Los Angeles County Holiday Celebration, TV Movie (2004)
LA Holiday Celebration, TV Movie (2005)

B-Phlat: Born Beverly Nelson in St. Louis, Missouri, her comedy career started while attending graduate school in 1995 when her friends signed her up for a talent show in Philadelphia without her knowing. She has toured extensively, especially with the Urban Comedy Cabaret Tour and has made appearances on several television programs as well. She also has a one-woman show called *St. Philly: My Black Utopia*.

Comedy Filmography

Park City: Where Music Meets Film, WETV (2007)
Def Comedy Jam, HBO, Season 8 Episode 9 (March 2, 2008)

1st Amendment Stand Up, Starz, Season 3 Episode 7 (August 20, 2008)
BET's Comicview, BET, Season 17 Episode 6 (September 25, 2008)
Comics without Borders, Showtime, Season 1 Episode 5 (October 9, 2008)
Comics Unleashed, Comedy Central (July 8, 2009)
Sex, Drugs, and Comedy, Documentary (2011)

Janine Brito: Winner of the 2009 SF Women's comedy competition, Brito is an out lesbian who has been doing stand-up comedy in St. Louis, Missouri, and beyond for years and was a member of the Laughter against the Machine tour. She is currently a writer for FX's late-night show *Totally Biased with W. Kamau Bell.*

Comedy Filmography
Laughter against the Machine, Tour Documentary (2012)
Totally Biased with W. Kamau Bell, FX (2012–2013)

Dylan Brody: Born April 24, 1964, Brody is a humorist, playwright, and comic. He has written two novels, and one of his plays won the Stanley Drama Award. He lives in Los Angeles and is an expert and teacher in East Asian martial arts. He also writes stories for young adults.

Discography
Brevity (2009)
A Twist of Wit (2009)
True Enough (2011)
Chronological Disorder (2012)

Comedy Filmography
Live from the NYPL: A Tribute to George Carlin (2010)

Lenny Bruce: Born in Mineola, New York, Bruce was a comedian, social critic, and satirist. He was renowned for his open, improvisational, honest, and critical form of comedy that integrated politics, religion, and sex. He is regarded as one of the best comedians of the twenty-first century.

Discography
Interviews of Our Times (1958)
The Sick Humor of Lenny Bruce (1959)
I am Not A Nut, Elect Me! (1960)
American (1961)
Why Did Lenny Bruce Die (1966)
Is Out Again (1966)
Lenny Bruce (1967)
The Berkeley Concert (1969)
To Is a Preposition; Come Is a Verb (1970)
Carnegie Hall (1972)
The Law, Language and Lenny Bruce (1974)
The Real Lenny Bruce (1975)
Lenny Bruce Originals Vol. 1 (1991)

Lenny Bruce Originals Vol. 2 (1991)
The Trials of Lenny Bruce (The Fall and Rise of an American Idol) (2002)
Let the Buyer Beware (2004)

Comedy Filmography

Talent Scouts, CBS, Episode 1 (April 18, 1949)
Broadway Open House, NBC, Episode 1 (May 1950)
The Steve Allen Plymouth Show, NBC, 2 Episodes (1959)
One Night Stand: The World of Lenny Bruce, TV Movie (1959)
The Pierre Berton Show, CTV, Episode 1 (February, 1966)
Lenny Bruce in "Lenny Bruce," Documentary (1967)
Dynamite Chicken, Movie (1971)
The Actor, Documentary (2013)

B.T.: Originally from Muskogee, Oklahoma, B.T. lives in Los Angeles and regularly tours the country with his stand-up comedy.

Comedy Filmography

B.T.: I'm Not Black Enough, Comedy Special (2007)

Kathy Buckley: Buckley is the first hearing-impaired comedian and a five-time American Comedy Award nominee. She entered a comedy contest as a dare in 1988 and has been making people laugh ever since. She has authored countless books, appears at comedy clubs and on television, speaks publicly, and teaches at camps for children and teens.

Nonfiction Writing

If You Could Hear What I See: Lessons about Life, Luck and the Choices We Make (2001)

Comedy Filmography

The Chuck Woolery Show, ABC, Season 1 Episode 53 (November 27, 1991)
The Tonight Show with Jay Leno, NBC, Episode 2.106 (June 17, 1993)
Look Who's Laughing, TV Movie (1994)
Howard Stern, FOX, Episode 149 (June 26, 1995)
The Rosie O'Donnell Show, NBC, Episode 149 (June 26, 1995)
The Howard Stern Radio Show, FOX, Episode 49 (February 5, 2000)
Hear This! Turning a Deaf Hear to Negativity, TV Movie (2000)
Kathy Buckley—No Labels, No Limits: A Command Performance by America's First Hearing-Impaired Comedian, VHS Tape (October 9, 2001)
CBC Winnipeg Comedy Festival, CBC, Episode 14 (February 17, 2007)

Jerry Calumn: Calumn is a contemporary comic and producer who works with humor to open minds on both gay and lesbian issues as well as HIV/AIDS. Calumn has been performing comedy since 2002 and prior to that worked for the AIDS Resource Center and the Gay and Lesbian Community Center in Dallas, Texas for sixteen years. He is a regular performer at The Comedy Store, Hollywood Improv, and a member of the Gay Mafia improv group.

Comedy Filmography

Outlaugh!, Documentary (2006)

George Carlin: Carlin was an American comedian and film actor born in the Bronx, New York. He started his career as a radio talk host and grabbed the attention of television producers who helped him start up his stand-up comedy career. In 2004, Comedy Central named him the second greatest stand-up. His routines centered on life's idiosyncrasies and sociopolitical critique.

Nonfiction Writing

Sometimes a Little Brain Damage Can Help (1984)
Brain Droppings (1997)
Napalm and Silly Putty (2001)
When Will Jesus Bring the Pork Chops (2004)
Three Times Carlin: An Orgy of George (2004)
Watch My Language (2009)
Last Words (2009)

Discography

Burns and Carlin at the Playboy Club Tonight (1963)
Take-Off and Put-Ons (1967)
FM & AM (1972)
Class Clown (1972)
7 Words You Can't Say on T.V. or the Radio (1972)
Occupation: Foole (1973)
Toledo Window Box (1974)
An Evening with Wally Londo Featuring Bill Slaszo (1975)
On the Road (1977)
A Place for My Stuff (1981)
Carlin on Campus (1984)
Playin' with Your Head (1986)
What Am I Doing in New Jersey (1988)
Doin' It Again (1990)
Jammin' in New York (1992)
Back in Town (1996)
You Are All Diseased (1999)
Complaints and Grievances (2001)
Life Is Worth Losing (2006)
It's Bad for Ya (2008)

Comedy Filmography

The Merv Griffin Show, CBS, 9 Episodes (July 20, 1965–1970)
The Mike Douglas Show, KYW, 5 Episodes (1965–1976)
The Hollywood Palace, ABC, 4 Episodes (1966–1967)
The Tonight Show Starring Johnny Carson, NBC, 31 Episodes (September 9, 1966–1986)
The Ed Sullivan Show, CBS, 9 Episodes (1967–1971)
The Joey Bishop Show, ABC, Season 2 Episode 223 (July 30, 1968)

Operation: Entertainment, ABC, Season 1, Episode 2 (January 12, 1968)
The Smothers Brothers Comedy Hour, CBS, Season 2 Episode 223 (January 5, 1969)
This Is Tom Jones, ABC, 2 Episodes (1969)
The Jimmie Rogers Show, NBC, Season 10 (July 14, 1969)
The David Frost Show, BBC, 4 Episodes (1970–1972)
The Flip Wilson Show, NBC, 6 Episodes (February 4, 1971–1973)
The Midnight Special, NBC, Season 1 Episode 1 (February 2, 1973)
The Helen Reddy Show, NBC, Season 1 Episode 2 (July 5, 1973)
The Burns and Schreiber Comedy Hour, ABC, Episode 3 (July 28, 1973)
Dinah!, CBS, 2 Episodes (1974–1975)
Saturday Night Live, NBC, 2 Episodes (1975–1984)
The Arsenio Hall Show, CBS, 3 Episodes (November 30, 1989–1991)
The Tonight Show with Jay Leno, NBC, 12 Episodes (1992–2006)
Late Night with David Letterman, CBS, 3 Episodes (1994–2001)
The Chris Rock Show, HBO, Season 2 Episode 10 (November 28, 1997)
Dennis Miller Live, HBO, 2 Episodes (1997–2004)
The Daily Show with Jon Stewart, Comedy Central, 3 Episodes (1999–2004)
Uncomfortably Close with Michael McKean, Comedy Central, Season 1 Episode 6 (April 21, 2001)
Make 'Em Laugh: The Funny Business of America, PBS, 4 Episodes (January 2009)

Compilations
Indecent Exposure: Some of the Best of George Carlin (1978)
The George Carlin Collection (1984)
Classic Gold (1992)
The Little David Years (1971–1977) (1999)
Georg Carlin on Comedy (2002)

Dave Chappelle: Chappelle is a comedian, screenwriter, television/film producer, actor, and artist. He is widely known for his sketch comedy show, *Chappelle's Show*, which aired from 2003 to 2005 on Comedy Central. His work infuses pop culture references and satire, mimicking Richard Pryor, one of his greatest influences.

Discography
Killin' Them Softly (2003)
For What It's Worth (2005)

Comedy Filmography
½ Hour Comedy Hour, ABC, Episode 1.76 (1990)
Evening at the Improv, A & E (January 1991)
The Word, Channel 4, Season 4 Episode 1 (November 19, 1993)
Comic Justice, Comedy Central (1993)
Def Comedy Jam, HBO (1993)
Comedy: Coast to Coast, TV Movie (1994)
Apollo Theater Hall of Fame, TV Documentary (1994)
Comic Relief VI, TV Special Documentary (1995)
1995 Young Comedians Special, TV Movie (1995)

Late Show with David Letterman, CBS, 3 Episodes (1995–2004)

The Rosie O'Donnell Show, NBC, Episode 18 (July 2, 1996)

Biography, A & E, Episode 850 (July 8, 1996)

Comics Come Home 2, TV Movie (1996)

HBO Comedy Half-Hour, HBO, 6 Episodes (1997–1998)

The Larry Sanders Show, HBO, Episode 82 (April 5, 1998)

The Rosie O'Donnell Show, NBC, Episode 419 (June 4, 1998)

The Dave Chappelle Project, TV Movie (1998)

Comic Relief VIII, TV Special Documentary (1998)

Late Night with Conan O'Brien, NBC, 15 Episodes (1998–2008)

MTV Jams, MTV (1999)

The Daily Show with Jon Stewart, Comedy Central, 3 Episodes (1999–2004)

Dave Chappelle: Killin' Them Softly, TV Documentary (2000)

Howard Stern, FOX, Episode 990 (June 18, 2001)

Open Mic, Documentary (2001)

Howard Stern, FOX, Episode 1174 (December 3, 2002)

Heroes of Black Comedy, TV Miniseries Documentary (2002)

Russell Simmons Presents Def Poetry, Episode 4 (2002)

The Tonight Show with Jay Leno, NBC, 2 Episodes (2002–2004)

Jimmy Kimmel Live!, ABC, Episode 100 (June 5, 2003)

Uncensored Comedy: That's Not Funny!, TV Documentary (2003)

VH1 Big in 03, TV Special (2003)

Richard Pryor: I Ain't Dead Yet, #*%$#@!!, TV Documentary (2003)

Comedy Central Presents: The Commies, TV Documentary (2003)

Chappelle's Show, Comedy Central (2003–2004)

60 Minutes, CBS, Episode 59 (December 29, 2004)

Bar Mitzvah Bash!, TV Movie (2004)

Dave Chappelle: For What It's Worth, TV Movie (2004)

Just for Laughs, BBC, Episode 23 (February 16, 2005)

Russell Simmons Presents Def Poetry, Episode 29 (June 10, 2005)

Block Party, Documentary (2005)

Richard Pryor: The Funniest Man Dead or Alive, TV Special Documentary (2005)

Inside the Actors Studio, A & E, Episode 179 (February 12, 2006)

Biography, A & E, Episode 247 (July 31, 2006)

Ohio Players, Video Documentary Short (2006)

Inside the Actors Studio, A & E, Episode 208 (November 10, 2008)

Margaret Cho: Cho is a comedian, fashion designer, actress, author, and singer-songwriter. She incorporates her Korean national heritage into comedy and her routines focus on politics and social issues particularly related to issues of race, gender, and sexuality.

Nonfiction Writing

I'm the One That I Want (2000)

I Have Chosen to Stay and Fight (2005)

Discography

Drunk with Power (1996)
I'm the One That I Want (2001)
Notorious C.H.O (2002)
Revolution (2003)
Margaret Cho: Beautiful (2009)
Cho Dependent (2010)
Mother! (2014)

Comedy Filmography

Stand-Up Spotlight, VH1 (1988)
1/2 Hour Comedy Hour, ABC, Season 1 Episode 76 (1990)
Bob Hope Presents the Ladies of Laughter, TV Movie (1992)
HBO Comedy Half-Hour, HBO, Episode 26 (July 28, 1994)
Late Show with David Letterman, CBS, Episode 1140 (September 27, 1994)
All-American Girl, ABC (1994)
The Tonight Show with Jay Leno, NBC, Episode 1759 (April 10, 1995)
Out There in Hollywood, TV Movie (1995)
Comic Relief VII, TV Movie (1995)
State of the Union: Undressed, TV Movie (1996)
Comics Come Home 3, TV Movie (1997)
Pulp Comics: Margaret Cho, TV Movie (1998)
Comedy Central Presents: The NY Friars Club Roast of Drew Carey, TV Movie (1998)
The Daily Show with Jon Stewart, Comedy Central, 2 Episodes (1998–1999)
The Rosie O'Donnell Show, NBC, Episode 617 (June 16, 1999)
Celebrity Profile, E!, Episode 29 (October 1, 1999)
Get Bruce, Documentary (1999)
The Remarkable Journey, TV Series (2000)
I'm the One That I Want, Documentary (2000)
The Rosie O'Donnell Show, NBC, Episode 994 (June 6, 2001)
The Best of Colin's Sleazy Friends, Video Documentary (2001)
Life 360, TV Series (2001)
The American Experience, PBS, Episode 166 (January 27, 2002)
Notorious C.H.O, Documentary (2002)
Real Time with Bill Maher, HBO, Episode 15 (August 22, 2003)
Art in the Twenty-First Century, PBS, Episode 8 (September 2003)
Richard Pryor: I Ain't Dead Yet, #*%$#@!!, TV Documentary (2003)
CHO Revolution, Video (2004)
Just for Laughs, BBC, Episode 21 (February 14, 2005)
Freedom to Marry, Documentary (2005)
Margaret Cho: Assassin, Documentary (2005)
Girls Who Do: Comedy, BBC, Episode 1 (August 13, 2006)
Spread TV, ManiaTV!, Episode 15 (August 23, 2007)
Wisecrack, Logo TV, Outlaugh Festival on Wisecrack Part 1–8 (2007)
The Tyra Banks Show, the CW, Episode 200 (March 7, 2007)
Shining Through: Behind the Scenes at True Colors, TV Documentary (2007)

Wamego Strikes Back, Documentary (2007)
SexTV, CTV, Episode 209 (January 21, 2008)
Spread TV, ManiaTV, Episode 44 (March 13, 2008)
Up Close with Carrie Keagan, NGTV, 2 Episodes (August 2008)
Underbelly, Documentary (2008)
11th Annual the Kennedy Center Mark Twain Prize for American Humor: George Carlin, TV
    Movie (2008)
The Best Comics Unleashed with Byron Allen, Video (2008)
Bump and Grind: The Making of a Burlesque Diva, TV Documentary (2008)
The Cho Show, VH1 (2008)
Allez a L.A., Documentary (2008)
The Late Late Show with Craig Ferguson, CBS, 7 Episodes (2008–2012)
Annul Victory, Documentary (2009)
The Wanda Sykes Show, FOX, Episode 3 (November 21, 2009)
How Bruce Lee Changed the World, TV Documentary (2009)
America: The Story of Us, The History Channel, 2 Episodes (May 2010)
Late Night with Jimmy Fallon, NBC, Episode 303 (September 7, 2010)
I Am Comic, Documentary (2010)
Comic Unleashed, CBS, 2 Episodes (2010)
Chelsea Lately, E!, Episode 354 (January 3, 2011)
This Week in Comedy, Comedy Central, Episode 25 (January 9, 2011)
Breakfast, BBC, Episode 1794 (August 5, 2011)
The Green Room with Paul Provenza, Showtime, Season 2 Episode 5 (August 11, 2011)
Dave's Old Porn, Showtime, Episode 7 (December 1, 2011)
Miss Representation, Documentary (2011)
Conan O'Brien Can't Stop, Documentary (2011)
Sexing the Transman, Documentary (2011)
Cho Dependent, Movie (2011)
AKA Blondie, Documentary (2012)

Louis C.K.: Born Louis Szekely on September 12, 1967, in Washington, DC, C.K.'s first language is Spanish. He first tried doing stand-up at an open mike in 1984 and it went so badly that he did not try again for two years. He moved to Manhattan in 1989 and opened for the likes of Jerry Seinfeld. Since then, he has performed many feature-length comedy specials, written movies, starred in TV shows, and won an Emmy.

Discography

Live in Houston (2001)
Chewed Up (2008)
Hilarious (2011)
Live at the Beacon Theater (2011)
WORD: Live at Carnegie Hall (2012)

Comedy Filmography

1995 Young Comedians Special, HBO (1995)
HBO Comedy Showcase, HBO (September 1995)
HBO Comedy Half-Hour, HBO (September 27, 1996)

Comics Come Home 2, Comedy Central (1996)
Kicking Aspen: Extreme Comedy, New Line (1996)
Late Night with Conan O'Brien, 10 Episodes (1998–2009)
Pulp Comics: Louis C.K.'s Filthy Stupid Talent Show, Comedy Central (1999)
Late Friday, NBC, Season 1 Episode 8 (March 9, 2001)
Comedy Central Presents, Comedy Central, Season 5 Episode 10 (September 3, 2001)
The Tonight Show with Jay Leno, NBC, 8 Episodes (2001–2011)
Dinner for Five, IFC, Season 2 Episode 6 (February 24, 2003)
Jimmy Kimmel Live!, ABC, 5 Episodes (2003–2011)
Weekends at the DL, Comedy Central, Season 1 Episode 9 (August 19, 2005)
One Night Stand, HBO, Season 1 Episode 1 (August 19, 2005)
The Late Late Show with Craig Ferguson, 2 Episodes (2005–2007)
The View, ABC (June 19, 2006)
Comic Relief 2006, Comedy Central (2006)
Maxed Out, Documentary (2006)
The Daily Show with Jon Stewart, Comedy Central, 4 Episodes (2006–2011)
Talk Show with Spike Feresten, Fox, Season 2 Episode 4 (October 6, 2007)
Louis C.K.: Shameless (2007)
Lucky Louis: A Week in the Life (2007)
Largo (2008)
Louis C.K.: Chewed Up (2008)
Tavis Smiley, PBS (September 25, 2009)
Just for Laughs, CBC, Season 1 Episode 1 (September 28, 2009)
Live from the NYPL: A Tribute to George Carlin (2010)
Lopez Tonight, TBS (June 24, 2010)
Louis C.K.: Hilarious (2010)
I Am Comic, Documentary (2010)
Late Show with David Letterman, CBS, Season 18 Episode 172 (July 28, 2011)
Real Time with Bill Maher, HBO, Season 9 Episode 27 (September 16, 2011)
Late Night with Jimmy Fallon, NBC, Season 1 Episode 572 (December 21, 2011)
Louis C.K.: Live at the Beacon Theater (2011)
Talking Funny, HBO (2011)
Louis C.K.: Oh My God, HBO (2013)

Kate Clinton: Clinton is a political humorist and entertainer. Originally a teacher, she began performing in her thirties and has been ever since. She uses her feminist comedy to challenge sexism, homophobia, racism, and advance LGBTQ rights.

Nonfiction Writing

Don't Get Me Started (2000)
What the L (2005)
I Told You So (2010)

Comedy Filmography

Out There 2, TV Movie (1994)
Pride Divide, Documentary (1997)
We're Funny That Way, Documentary (1998)

My Coolest Years, VH1, Episode 5 (December 21, 2004)
Laughing Matters, Documentary (2004)
Here Comedy Presents Kate Clinton, TV Movie (2005)
The Evolution Will Be Televised, TV Documentary (2005)
Kate Clinton: 25th Anniversary Tour (2007)
The Big Gay Sketch Show, LOGO TV, Episode 11 (February 26, 2008)
Out in America, TV Documentary (2011)

Sarah Colonna: Born December 29, 1974, in Wiesbaden, Germany, Colonna moved to the United States and was raised in Farmington, Arkansas. She is an actress and a comedian, and her first televised comedy performance was on *Premium Blend*. She is a friend of Chelsea Handler's and was hired as a head writer for *Chelsea Lately* and is a regular guest on the show. She was a semifinalist on NBC's *Last Comic Standing*.

Comedy Filmography

Premium Blend, Comedy Central (January 15, 2001)
Comics Unleashed (2006)
Stand Up or Sit Down Comedy Challenge, TBS (2006)
The World Stands Up, Comedy Central (April 1, 2007)
Last Comic Standing, NBC (2007)
Chelsea Lately, E!, 165 Episodes (2007–2013)
Comedians of Chelsea Lately, E! (2009)
The Tonight Show with Jay Leno, NBC, 2 Episodes (2010–2012)
After Lately, E!, 24 Episodes (2011–2013)
The Jeff Probst Show, CBS, 1 Episode (2012)
Gotham Comedy Live, AXS TV (2013)
AXS Live, AXS Live, 1 Episode (2013)

Melanie Comarcho: Born in Chicago, Illinois, and raised in Inglewood, California, Comarcho entered comedy on a dare and was spotted by *Def Comedy Jam* producers. She won favorite female stand-up at the Soul Train Comedy Awards in 1993. She has been on tour with a number of talented comics including Katt Williams and Martin Lawrence.

Discography

Independent Woman (2010)
Melanie Comarcho: Hello! (2012)

Comedy Filmography

Showtime at the Apollo, US, Episode 35 (May 1, 1993)
Comic Groove, Comedy Central, Episode 4 (September 23, 2002)
Def Comedy Jam, HBO, Season 7 Episode 4 (October 1, 2006)
1st Amendment Stand-up, Starz, Season 2 Episode 8 (June 6, 2007)
Funny Spot, TV One, Episode 1 (January 19, 2008)
Katt Williams Presents: Katthouse Comedy, Showcase (2009)
Katt Williams: 9 Lives, Documentary (2010)
I Am Comic, Documentary (2010)
Phunny Business: A Black Comedy, Documentary (2010)

Stand Up in Stilettos, TV Guide Network, Season 2, Episode 6 (2012)
BET's Comicview, BET (2012)
The Arsenio Hall Show, CBS, Season 1, Episode 45 (2013)

Sara Contreras: Contreras is a Latina stand-up comedian, writer, and actor. She is a regular performer on the NY tri-state comedy club/college circuit. She has been the featured comedian on Wendy Williams' radio show.

Comedy Filmography
The Latin Divas of Comedy, Documentary (2007)
Stand-Up 360: Muy Caliente Edition 2 (2009)
The Wendy Williams Show, BET, Episode 730 (2012)

Rebecca Corry: Born March 23, 1971, in Kent, Washington, Corry has had roles in some major comedy films, including *Yes Man* and *Big Fat Liar*. She spent nine years in Chicago and studied at Second City before moving to Los Angeles. In her spare time she is an activist for animal rescue. She has had two one-woman theatrical shows and was a finalist on *Last Comic Standing*.

Comedy Filmography
Late Friday, NBC, Season 1 Episode 26 (November 9, 2001)
Premium Blend, Comedy Central (August 25, 2005)
Last Comic Standing, NBC (2006)
Comedy Central Presents, Comedy Central, Season 13 Episode 12 (February 13, 2009)
Who Wants to Date a Comedian?, Entertainment Studios, Season 1 Episode 8 (September 28, 2011)
Comedy.TV, Season 1 Episode 23 (2012)
Funny: The Documentary, Documentary (2012)

Lavell Crawford: Crawford is an American stand-up comedian and actor. He got his big break in comedy during the 1980s. He has struggled with his weight and uses this as comic material.

Discography
Can A Brother Get Some Love? (2011)

Comedy Filmography
Showtime at the Apollo, NBC, Season 4 Episode 1 (September 15, 1990)
BET's Comicview, BET, Episode 4 (1992–2004)
Def Comedy Jam, HBO, Season 5 Episode 8 (April 21, 1995)
Motown Live, BET, Episode 6 (1998)
Jamie Foxx Presents Laffapalooza, BET, Season 1 Episode 3 (May 9, 2003)
Premium Blend, Comedy Central, Season 7 Episode 7 (January 2, 2004)
Jamie Foxx Presentes Laffapalooza, BET, Season 2 Episode 1 (February 25, 2006)
Jamie Foxx's Laffapalooza, TV Movie (2006)
Last Comic Standing, NBC, 10 Episodes (2007)
1st Amendment Stand-Up, Starz, 4 Episodes (2007–2008)
Comedy Central Presents, Comedy Central, Season 12 Episode 13 (February 22, 2008)

Reality Bites Back, Comedy Central, 6 Episodes (2008)
Laffapalooza, TV Movie (2008)
Comics Unleashed, Syndicated, 4 Episodes (2008–2010)
Black to the Future, TV Series (2009)
All Star Comedy Jam: Live from South Beach, TV Movie (2009)
Chelsea Lately, E!, 19 Episodes (2009–2013)
Phunny Business: A Black Comedy, Documentary (2010)
Just for Laughs, CTV, Episode 10 (October 4, 2010)
C'Mon Man, Movie (2012)

Lea DeLaria: DeLaria is a comedian, actress, and jazz musician from Illinois. She was the first openly gay comic to break the late-night talk-show barrier, on the *Arsenio Hall Show*. She is known for her scathing cultural critiques and integrating jazz into her stand-up comedy.

Discography

Bulldyke in China Shop (1996)
Box Lunch (1997)
Play It Cool (2001)
Double Standards (2005)
The Very Best of Lea DeLaria (2006)
Live Smoke Sessions (2008)
Be a Santa (2010)

Comedy Filmography

The Word, Channel 4, Season 4 Episode 3 (December 3, 1993)
Out There, TV Movie (1993)
Camp Christmas, TV Movie (1993)
Out There in Hollywood, TV Movie (1995)
The Rosie O'Donnell Show, NBC, 3 Episodes (November 10, 1998)
We're Funny That Way, Documentary (1998)
Just for Laughs, TV Documentary (2002)
Outlaugh!, Documentary (2006)
Ptown Diaries, Documentary (2009)

Demetria Dixon: Dixon is a stand-up comic, writer, and actress who is located in Texas. She started stand-up rather late at the age of 43. She now works for DemDix Comedy Productions in Houston, Texas.

Laurie Elliott: She is a comedian actress and stand-up comic. She was nominated for the Best Female Stand-up Canadian Comedy Award in 2006. She is a member of the sketch comedy group Kevlor-2000 with Kevin MacDonald.

Comedy Filmography

Cream of Comedy, CTV (2000)
Just for Laughs, CBC, Episode 3 (April 6, 2002)
The Halifax Comedy Fest, Mini Series (2002)
New Year's Resolutions, CTV (2002)

The Next Big Thing, TV Mini-Series (2003)
Comedy Now!, CTV (2004)
PopCultured, The Comedy Network (2005)
Video on Trail, CTV (2006–2009)
The Naughty Show, TV Special (2007)
Just for Laughs, BBC, Episode 31 (February 14, 2007)
Canadian Comedy, CTV (2009)
Great Canadian Laugh Off, CTV (2010)

J. D. England: In 1985, J. D. was paralyzed from the neck down, making him the first "sit down" comedian ever. His comedy was about his life, wheels and all. He performed in New York at Dangerfield's and the Comic Strip and in Los Angeles at Igbys, The Comedy Store, and the Improv.

Comedy Filmography

Evening at the Improv, A & E (January 1990)
Look Who's Laughing, TV Movie (1994)

Felipe Esparza: Born and raised in East Los Angeles, Esparza is a comedian and actor. His material centers on the struggles of everyday life. He was the winner of NBC's *Last Comic Standing* in 2010.

Discography

Rebound Material (2010)
What's Up Fool? (2010)
Felipe Esparza: They're Not Gonna Laugh at You (2012)

Comedy Filmography

Inside Joke, TV Series (2004)
Premium Blend, Comedy Central, Episode 47 (December 9, 2005)
Cheech Marin and Friends: Live from South Beach, TV Movie (2006)
Comics Unleashed, Syndicated, 2 Episodes (2007–2012)
Comics without Borders, Showtime, Episode 12 (October 30, 2008)
Man Up, Stand-Up, Comedy Time, Season 1 Episode 7 (August 26, 2009)
Comedy.TV, Comedy Central, Episode 12 (2009)
Russell Simmons Presents: Stand-Up at the El Ray, Comedy Central, Episode 5 (August 1, 2010)
Rageous, TV Movie (2010)
Last Comic Standing, NBC, 14 Episodes (2010)
Latino 101, SiTV, 18 Episodes (2010–2011)
The Wedding Zinger, TV Movie (2012)
BET's Comicview, BET (2012)
The Arsenio Hall Show, CBS, Episode 43 (2013)

Chris Fonseca: Known as Chris "Crazy Legs," Fonseca is one the first comedians to have cerebral palsy. He has performed on numerous television shows and even for President George W. Bush at the anniversary of the Americans with Disabilities Act.

Discography

Not Tonight, I Have Cerebral Palsy (1997)
Get in the Van (2001)

Comedy Filmography

Looking Who's Laughing, TV Movie (1994)
Loco Slam, TV Series (1994)
Latino Laugh Festival, TV Movie (1996)
Christopher Reeve: A Celebration of Hope, TV Documentary (1998)
Inside Joke, Si TV (2004)
CBC Winnipeg Comedy Festival, CBC, Episode 14 (February 17, 2007)

Adele Givens: Hailing from Chicago, Illinois, Givens is an African American actress and comedian. She was the 1989 Grand Prize Winner of the Crown Royal Comedy.

Comedy Filmography

Def Comedy Jam, HBO, 5 Episodes (1995–2006)
Comedy Half-Hour, HBO, Episode 1 (October 4, 1996)
The Queens of Comedy, Video Documentary (2001)
Comedy Central Presents, Comedy Central, Episode 67 (May 27, 2002)
Heroes of Comedy: Women on Top, TV Miniseries Documentary (2003)
1st Amendment Stand Up, Starz, Episode 54 (October 1, 2010)
Phunny Business: A Black Comedy, Movie (2010)

Judy Gold: Gold was dared to do stand-up during her undergraduate time at Rutgers University. Since then she has won two daytime Emmys for work as a writer and producer on *The Rosie O'Donnell Show*. She has performed several one-woman shows including: *25 Questions for a Jewish Mother* and *Mommy Queerest*. She is openly gay and lives with her girlfriend and two sons in New York City.

Nonfiction Writing

25 Questions for a Jewish Mother (New York: Voice, 2007)

Discography

Judith's Roommate Had a Baby (2004)

Comedy Filmography

Laughing Back: Comedy Takes a Stand, TV Movie (1992)
Girls' Night Out, TV Movie (1994)
The Tonight Show with Jay Leno, NBC, Episode 1776 (August 9, 1995)
HBO Comedy Half-Hour, HBO, Episode 20 (August 24, 1995)
Comic Relief VII, TV Special Documentary (1995)
Comedy Central Presents, Comedy Central, Episode 36 (September 13, 2000)
The Rosie O'Donnell Show, NBC, Episode 998 (June 12, 2001)
Tough Crowd with Colin Quinn, Comedy Central (2002)
I Love the '80s, TV Series Documentary (2002)
Bar Mitzvah Bash!, TV Movie (2002)
Heroes of Jewish Comedy, TV Miniseries Documentary (2003)

Comedy Central Presents: 100 Greatest Stand-ups of All Time, TV Miniseries (2004)
Funny Already: A History of Jewish Comedy, TV Documentary (2004)
Wisecrack, Logo TV, Episode 4 (August 18, 2005)
The Aristocrats, Documentary (2005)
A Comic's Climb at the USCAF, TV Documentary (2005)
Inside TV Land: Tickled Pink, TV Documentary (2005)
TV Land's Top Ten, TV Series Documentary (2005–2006)
All Aboard! Rosie's Family Cruise, TV Documentary (2006)
Fired!, Documentary (2007)
Judy Troll: The Funniest Woman You've Never Heard Of, Documentary (2007)
Making Trouble, Documentary (2007)
Relative Madness, TV Series Documentary (2008)
Stand-Up 360: Edition 4, Movie (2009)
Stand-Up 360: Inside Out, Movie (2009)
Surviving the Holidays with Lewis Black, TV Movie (2009)
This Week in Comedy, Comedy Central, Episode 13 (September 20, 2010)
I Am Comic, Documentary (2010)
The Wendy Williams Show, FOX, 2 Episodes (2010)
The Wendy Williams Show, BET, 4 Episodes (2010–2013)
The Joy Behar Show, HLN, Episode 124 (July 26, 2011)
The Late Late Show with Craig Ferguson, CBS, Episode 1454 (October 28, 2011)
The Smoking Gun Presents: World's Dumbest, TruTV (2012–2013)
Why We Laugh: Funny Women, TV Movie Documentary (2013)
When Jews Were Funny, Documentary (2013)
The Last Laugh, Documentary (2015)

Whoopi Goldberg: Born Caryn Elaine Johnson on November 13, 1955, in New York City, Goldberg debuted on Broadway with her one-woman show, *The Spook Show* (1984) and was cast in *The Color Purple* in 1985. She has an Academy Award, two Emmys, two Golden Globes, and several awards for her work as an activist. In addition to her extensive work in film, she has been a long-standing host of *The View.*

Nonfiction Writing
Book (1999)
Is It Just Me or Is It Nuts out There? (2010)

Discography
Whoopi: Original Broadway Recording (1985)
Whoopi Goldberg: Fontaine. . . . Why Am I Straight? (1988)
Whoopi: The 20th Anniversary Show (2005)

Comedy Filmography
Late Night with David Letterman, CBS (November 7, 1984)
Whoopi Goldberg: Direct From Broadway (1985)
Comic Relief, HBO (1986)
The Arsenio Hall Show, CBS, 6 Episodes (1986–1994)
Ebony/Jet Showcase, 3 Episodes (1986–1994)

The Tonight Show with Johnny Carson, NBC (February 27, 1987)

The Late Show, FOX (March 4, 1987)

Dolly, ABC, Season 1 Episode 2 (October 4, 1987)

Comic Relief '87, HBO (1987)

The Pointer Sisters: Up All Nite (1987)

Carol, Carl, Whoopi, and Robin, ABC (1987)

The D.C. Follies, Season 2 Episode 6 (October 20, 1988)

Comic Relief III, HBO (1989)

The Debbie Allen Special (March 5, 1989)

Tales from the Whoop, MTV (1990)

The Marsha Warfield Show, Season 1 Episode 5 (March 30, 1990)

CBS This Morning, CBS (March 30, 1990)

Donahue, ABC (May 9, 1990)

Wogan, BBC (October 8, 1990)

Comic Relief IV, HBO (1991)

Chez Whoopi (1991)

Comic Relief V, HBO (1992)

The 34th Annual Grammy Awards, Host (1992)

Wisecracks, Documentary (1992)

The Whoopi Goldberg Show (1992–1993)

Late Show with David Letterman, CBS, 5 Episodes (1993–2010)

The 66th Annual Academy Awards Show, Host (March 21, 1994)

Comic Relief VI, HBO (1994)

The Tonight Show with Jay Leno, NBC, 9 Episodes (1994–2009)

The Celluloid Closet, Documentary (1995)

Comic Relief VII, HBO (1995)

Comic Relief's American Comedy Festival, HBO (1996)

The 68th Annual Academy Awards, Host (1996)

The Rosie O'Donnell Show, 12 Episodes (1996–2002)

The Chris Rock Show, HBO, Season 2 Episode 3 (September 26, 1997)

Comic Relief VIII, HBO (1998)

The Roseanne Show, Season 1 Episode 1 (September 14, 1998)

Inside the Actor's Studio, HBO (October 18, 1998)

Get Bruce, Documentary (1999)

The 71st Annual Academy Awards, Host (1999)

The Martin Short Show, Season 1 Episode 40 (November 5, 1999)

Heroes of Black Comedy, Comedy Central, Season 1 Episode 3 (February 18, 2002)

The 74th Annual Academy Awards, Host (2002)

Searching for Debra Winger, Documentary (2002)

Marshall's Women in Comedy Festival (2002)

Heroes of Comedy: Women on Top, Comedy Central, Season 1 Episode 3 (March 5, 2003)

Late Night with Conan O'Brien, 2 Episodes (2003–2004)

The N Word, Documentary (2004)

The Aristocrats, Documentary (2005)

Real Time with Bill Maher, HBO, 2 Episodes (2005)

The View, Co-Host (2005–2013)

Girls Who Do: Comedy, BBC, Season 1 Episode 1 (2006)
Comic Relief 2006, HBO (2006)
The World According to Whoopi!, Bravo (April 5, 2007)
Jimmy Kimmel Live!, ABC, Season 6 Episode 95 (June 16, 2008)
Comic Relief: The Greatest . . . and the Latest, HBO (2008)
The 62nd Annual Tony Awards, Host (2008)
Just For Laughs (September 28, 2009)
Make 'Em Laugh: The Funny Business of America, Documentary (2009)
Late Night with Jimmy Fallon, 3 Episodes (2009–2011)
Live from the NYPL: A Tribute to George Carlin (2010)
The Black List: Volume Three, Documentary (2010)
The Wendy Williams Show, BET, 4 Episodes (2010–2013)
The Daily Show with Jon Stewart, Comedy Central, Season 17 Episode 52 (January 30, 2012)
The Colbert Report, Comedy Central, Season 8 Episode 52 (January 30, 2012)
Why We Laugh: Funny Women, TV Movie Documentary (2013)
Moms Mabley: I Got Somethin' To Tell You, Documentary (2013)
Richard Pryor: Omit the Logic, Documentary (2013)
Misery Loves Comedy, Documentary (2014)

Julie Goldman: Born in Boston, Massachusetts, but currently living in Los Angeles, Goldman is a comedian, actress, and musician. She starred in the first three seasons of the *Big Gay Sketch Show* and performs across the country. She currently cohosts *Julie and Brandy in Your Box Office* and writes for Joan Rivers on Fashion Police.

Comedy Filmography
Imx Show, FUSE-TV, Gay for a day special (February 26, 2004)
My Coolest Years, TV Miniseries Documentary, Season 1 Episode 4 (December 21, 2004)
The Big Gay Sketch Show, LOGO TV (2006–2010)
Lesbian Sex and Sexuality, TV Miniseries Documentary, Season 1 Episode 4 (February 2, 2007)
Live at Gotham, Comedy Central, Season 2 Episode 5 (June 22, 2007)
One Night Stand Up, Logo TV, Episode 103 (February 3, 2009)
Julie and Brandy: In Your Box Office, Web series (2010)
Pride Comedy Jam, TV Movie (2011)
The People's Couch, TV Mini-Series (2013)

Marga Gomez: Born to a Cuban comedian and Puerto Rican dancer, Gomez was raised in New York. She now identifies as a bicoastal Gemini. She made her stage debut at the age of 7. She has many accomplishments in comedy, theater, film, and television.

Discography
Hung Like a Fly (1997)

Comedy Filmography
Latino Laugh Festival, TV special (1997)
Desi's Looking for a New Girl (2000)
Laughing Matters, Documentary (2005)
One Night Stand Up, Logo TV, Episode 104 (January 23, 2009)

Nato Green: Named SF Weekly's best comedian of 2012, Green was a member of the Laughter against the Machine tour. He is currently a writer for FX's late-night show *Totally Biased with W. Kamau Bell.*

Discography

That Nato Green Party (2012)

Comedy Filmography

Laughter against the Machine, Tour Documentary (2012)
Totally Biased with W. Kamau Bell, FX (2012–2013)

Dick Gregory: Born in St. Louis, Missouri, Gregory is a comedian, social activist, social critic, writer, and entrepreneur. His work has influenced the way both White and Black people view civil rights. On Comedy Central's list of 100 greatest standups, he is number 82.

Discography

In Living Black and White (1961)
East and West (1961)
So You See . . . We All Have Problems (1964)
Dick Gregory's Frankenstein (1969)
Dick Gregory On (1969)
Dick Gregory Live at the Village Gate (1970)
At Kent State (1971)
Caught in the Act (1973)
Running for President (1964)

Comedy Filmography

ABC Close-Up!, ABC, Episode 43 (June 12, 1962)
The Merv Griffin Show, NBC, 4 Episodes (1962–1967)
World in Action, BBC, Episode 22 (September 29, 1963)
Freedom Spectacular, TV Movie (1964)
The Regis Philbin Show, ABC, 2 Episodes (1964–1965)
The Eamonn Andrews Show, BBC, 3 Episodes (1965–1966)
Tempo, ABTV, Episode 11 (February 21, 1966)
The Mike Douglas Show, NBC, Episode 116 (December 26, 1966)
Dee Time, BBC, Episode 3 (April 18, 1967)
BBC Show of the Week, BBC, Episode 11 (June 10, 1967)
Rowan and Martin's Laugh-in, NBC, Season 2 Episode 8 (November 11, 1968)
Baldwin's Nigger, Documentary (1968)
It's a Revolution Mother, Documentary (1968)
American Revolution, Documentary (1969)
The David Frost Show, Episode 7 (1969–1972)
The Ed Sullivan Show, CBS, Season 24 Episode 9 (June 15, 1970)
Prologue, Movie (1970)
The Tonight Show with Johnny Carson, NBC, 5 Episodes (1970–1972)
The Mike Douglas Show, NBC, Episode 321 (February 14, 1971)
The Helen Reddy Show, NBC, Season 1 Episode 7 (August 9, 1973)

Black Journal, Net-TV, 2 Episodes (1974–1975)
Good Night America, ABC, Episode 3 (March 6, 1975)
Black Journal, Net-TV, Episode 27 (April 4, 1976)
Soul Train, TV Series Documentary (1980)
Donahue, ABC, Episode 53 (May 2, 1986)
In Remembrance of Martin, Documentary (1986)
Comic Relief, TV Special (1986)
Ebony/Jet Showcase, BET, Episode 28 (September 25, 1987)
A Party for Richard Pryor, TV Special (1991)
The Real Malcolm X, TV Documentary (1992)
Apollo Theatre Hall of Fame, TV Documentary (1994)
Headliners and Legends: Chris Rock, TV Movie (2001)
Inside TV Land: African Americans in Television, TV Documentary (2002)
The N-Word, Documentary (2004)
Letter to the President, Video Documentary (2005)
The Bright Shining Moment, Documentary (2005)
Richard Pryor: The Funniest Man Dead or Alive, TV Special Documentary (2005)
100 Greatest Stand-Ups, TV Documentary (2007)
Comics Unleashed, Syndicated, 2 Episodes (July, 2008)
When Comedy Went to School, Video Documentary (2008)
Clean Mic: Laughing until It Hurts, Documentary (2008)
Why We Laugh: Black Comedians on Black Comedy, Documentary (2009)
Make 'Em Laugh: The Funny Business of America, TV Series Documentary (2009)
Stand, Documentary (2009)
1st Amendment Stand-Up, Starz, 2 Episodes (2009)
Way Black When: Primetime, TV Series (2011)
Bowl of Dreams, Documentary (2011)
My Brother Marvin, Documentary (2012)
Irwin and Fran, Documentary (2012)
Diary of a Decade: The Story of a Movement, Documentary (2012)
When Comedy went to School, Documentary (2013)
The Journey Part 1, Documentary (2013)
Citizen Lane, Documentary (2013)

Kathy Griffin: Griffin is an Irish American actress, comedian, model, writer, and producer. She was born in Oak Park, Illinois, but now resides in Los Angeles. Her work centers on popular culture, using observational comedy. She starred in her own reality show, *My Life on the D-List*, and currently hosts the talk show *Kathy*.

Nonfiction Writing
Official Book Club Selection: A Memoir According to Kathy Griffin (2010)

Comedy Filmography
The More You Know, NBC (1989)
It's Pat, Movie (1994)
HBO Comedy Half-Hour, HBO, Episode 22 (October 18, 1996)
Viva Variety, Comedy Central, Episode 13 (June 24, 1997)

Oddville, MTV, Episode 13 (June 24, 1997)

Un-Cabaret, TV Movie (1997)

Premium Blend, Comedy Central, 9 Episodes (1997–1998)

The Daily Show with Jon Stewart, Comedy Central, 3 Episodes (1997–1999)

The Rosie O'Donnell Show, NBC, 7 Episodes (1997–2001)

Dennis Miller Live, HBO, Episode 98 (April 28, 1998)

The Roseanne Show, ABC, Episode 9 (September 24, 1998)

Instant Comedy with the Groundlings, FX, Episode 1 (1998)

Kathy Griffin: Hot Cup of Talk, TV Movie (1998)

Comic Relief VIII, TV Special Documentary (1998)

The Daily Show Second Anniversary Special, TV Movie (1998)

Late Night with Conan O'Brien, NBC, 3 Episodes (1998–2009)

The Martin Short Show, SCTV, Episode 2 (September 14, 1999)

Jackie's Back!, TV Movie (1999)

The Howard Stern Radio Show, FOX, 3 Episodes (1999–2001)

Howard Stern, FOX, 2 Episodes (1999–2003)

Howard Stern, FOX, Episode 879 (October 5, 2000)

The Late Late Show with Craig Kilborn, CBS, 3 Episodes (2000–2001)

Weakest Link, BCC, Comedians Special (May 20, 2001)

The Andy Dick Show, MTV, Episode 13 (September 9, 2001)

Kathy's So-Called Reality, MTV (2001)

Headliners and Legends: Brooke Shields, TV Documentary (2001)

The Laugh Factor, TV Documentary (2001)

The Chris Isaak Show, CTV, Episode 34 (July 9, 2002)

Run Ronnie Run, Movie (2002)

Whose Line Is It Anyway?, ABC, 4 Episodes (2002–2003)

MADtv, FOX, Episode 199 (November 22, 2003)

Comedy Central Presents: The Commies, TV Documentary (2003)

Heroes of Comedy: Women on Top, TV Miniseries Documentary (2003)

The Wayne Brady Show, ABC, 2 Episodes (2003–2004)

The Sharon Osbourne Show, Syndicated, 3 Episodes (2003–2004)

The Jay Leno Show, NBC, 12 Episodes (2003–2010)

The Yesterday Show with John Kerwin, JLTV, Episode 1 (2004)

Kathy Griffin: The D-List, TV Movie (2004)

Super Secret Movie Rules, TV Series Documentary (2004)

50 Most Wicked Women of Primetime, TV Documentary (2004)

Kathy Griffin: Allegedly, Video (2004)

VH1 Big in the 04, TV Documentary (2004)

VH1 Big in the 06, TV Documentary (2004)

Last Laugh '04, TV Movie (2004)

Last Call with Carson Daly, NBC, 8 Episodes (2004–2008)

The Surreal Life, VH1, Episode 27 (January 9, 2005)

Weekends at the DL, Comedy Central, Episode 14 (September 10, 2005)

MADtv, FOX, Episode 241 (September 24, 2005)

Kathy Griffin Is . . . Not Nicole Kidman, TV Movie (2005)

VH1 Big in the 05, TV Documentary (2005)

Kathy Griffin: My Life on the D List, Bravo (2005–2010)
Kathy Griffin: Strong Black Woman, TV Movie (2006)
Loose Women, ITV, Episode 540 (May 2, 2007)
Ellen: The Ellen DeGeneres Show, NBC, Episode 626 (September 11, 2007)
E! True Hollywood Story, E!, Episode 273 (October 20, 2007)
MADtv, FOX, Episode 291 (November 24, 2007)
Kathy Griffin: Straight to Hell, TV Movie (2007)
Judy Troll: The Funniest Woman You've Never Heard Of, Documentary (2007)
Kathy Griffin: Everybody Can Suck It, TV Movie (2007)
In Search of Puppy Love, Documentary (2007)
Mr. Warmth: The Don Rickles Project, Documentary (2007)
Heckler, Documentary (2007)
History of the Joke, TV Documentary (2008)
Rosie Live, TV Movie (2008)
Just for Laughs, BBC, Episode 25 (February 21, 2009)
MADtv, FOX, Episode 312 (March 21, 2009)
A-List Awards, TV Movie (2009)
Kathy Griffin: She'll Cut a Bitch, TV Movie (2009)
Kathy Griffin: Balls of Steel, TV Movie (2009)
The Tyra Banks Show, the CW, Episode 402 (May 14, 2009)
Comedy Central Roast of Joan Rivers, TV Special (2009)
The Wendy Williams Show, FOX, 4 Episodes (2009–2012)
Chelsea Lately, E!, 4 Episodes (2009–2012)
Joan Rivers: A Piece of Work, Documentary (2010)
I Am Comic, Documentary (2010)
Kathy Griffin Does the Bible Belt, TV Movie (2010)
Larry King Live, CNN, 2 Episodes (2010)
Kathy Griffin: Whores on Crutches, TV Movie (2010)
A Bundle of Sticks, Documentary (2010)
The Green Room with Paul Provenza, Showtime, Season 2 Episode 2 (July 21, 2011)
Kathy Griffin: Pants Off, TV Movie (2011)
Kathy Griffin: Gurrl Down, TV Movie (2011)
Kathy Griffin: 50 and Not Pregnant, TV Movie (2011)
Conan, TBS, 2 Episodes (2011–2012)
Kathy, Bravo (2012)
Kathy Griffin: Pants Off / Tired Hooker, Video (2012)
Kathy Griffin: Seaman 1st Class, TV Movie (2012)
Love You, Mean It with Whitney Cummings, E!, Episode 7 (2013)
Why We Laugh: Funny Women, TV Movie Documentary (2013)
Kathy Griffin: Kennedie Center On-Hers, TV Movie (2013)
Kathy Griffin: Calm Down Gurrl, TV Movie (2013)

Tissa Hami: An Iranian American Muslim stand-up comic who grew up in a suburb of Boston, Hami does comedy that attempts to break down stereotypes of Muslim Americans. She has been recognized for her potential by various popular media and was named one of the *San Francisco Chronicle's* Top 11 female comedians in the country.

Comedy Filmography

The Coexist Comedy Tour (2012)
Stand Up: Muslim American Comics Come of Age (2009)

Laura Hayes: Laura Hayes is from the Bay Area in California. She began her career when taking improv classes at the local college. She began performing at the Oakland Ensemble Theater and went on to pursue a career in television. She gathered a large following when cohosting BET's *Comicview.* She then turned her attention to film and filmmaking. She describes herself as a "Hip-Hop Baby-Boomer."

Comedy Filmography

Sinbad and Friends: All the Way Live . . . Almost!, TV Documentary (1991)
BET's ComicView, TV Series (1992)
Def Comedy Jam, TV Series (1993)
The Queens of Comedy, Video Documentary (2001)
Heroes of Comedy: Women on Top, TV Miniseries Documentary (2003)
Weekends at the DL, Comedy Central, Episode 14 (September 10, 2005)
Phunny Business: A Black Comedy, Documentary (2010)

Sherif Hedayat: Hedayat is an Egyptian American comedian who started performing in 1996 while obtaining his undergraduate degree from Wright State University. His comedy centers on Middle Eastern culture and identity. He has a blog, an active Twitter account, and videos on YouTube but no official website and no television or film appearances.

René Hicks: Hicks is an African American comedian who was named NACA Comedy Entertainer of the year in 1995 and 1997. An openly lesbian comic, she uses comedy to comment on racial and sexual social identities, especially where they intersect.

Nonfiction Writing

Renee Hicks (2012)

Comedy Filmography

Stand-Up Spotlight, VH1 (1988)
½ Hour Comedy Hour, ABC, Season 1 Episode 76 (1990)
The Daily Show with Jon Stewart, Comedy Central, Episode 52 (September 14, 1998)
Comedy Central Presents, Comedy Central, Episode 40 (December 18, 2000)
The World Comedy Tour: Melbourne 2002, TV Special (2002)
Coming Out Party, Video (2003)
Out on the Edge, TV Special (2004)
Laughing Matters . . . More!, Showcase (2006)

Steve Hofstetter: Born September 11, 1979, in Queens, New York, Hofstetter's early material focused on college life. Though he still tours colleges around the country, much of his comedy is now about sports and general social commentary. He hosts a couple of different radio shows and writes for various sports magazines.

Discography

Tastes Like Bliss (2004)
Curse For the Cable Guy (2006)
Dark Side of the Room (2008)
Steve Hofsetter's Day Off (2009)
Pick Your Battles (2011)

Comedy Filmography

Profile: A Documentary about Steve Hofstetter, Documentary (2006)
Whiteboyz in the Hood, Showtime, Episodes 5 and 8 (2006)
Whiteboyz in the Hood (2007)
The Late Late Show with Craig Ferguson, CBS, Season 5 Episode 14 (September 18, 2008)
NESN Comedy All-Stars (2008)
High Hopes (2008)
Attack of the Show!, G4, Episode 922 (February 18, 2009)

Stephanie Howard: Howard began her comedy career in 1999 at Los Angeles Improv. She has starred in *Premium Blend, Giggles, Still Standing*, and was featured in the first annual gay comedy festival: Outlaugh, 2006.

Comedy Filmography

Premium Blend, Comedy Central, Season 6 Episode 9 (December 28, 2002)
Giggles, LOGO TV (2004)
Outlaugh!, Showcase (2006)
Wisecrack, Logo TV, Episode 9 (February 20, 2007)

D. L. Hughley: Born in Los Angeles, Hughley is best known for his work as a stand-up comic and as the creator of the sitcom *The Hughleys*. He is also an actor, political commentator, and a radio personality in New York City.

Comedy Filmography

One Night Stand, HBO, Season 4 Episode 12 (October 11, 1992)
HBO Comedy Half-Hour, HBO, Episode 6 (1994)
Def Comedy Jam, 12 Episodes (1995–2008)
The Chris Rock Show, Season 3 Episode 14 (October 9, 1998)
The Hughleys, TV Series, 4 Seasons (1998–2002)
Late Night with Conan O'Brian, 5 Episodes (1998–2005)
The Tonight Show with Jay Leno, 19 Episodes (1998–2013)
D. L. Hughley: Goin' Home, HBO (August 7, 1999)
The Daily Show with Jon Stewart, 4 Episodes (1999–2012)
The Howard Stern Radio Show (March 11, 2000)
The Rosie O'Donnell Show, Season 5 Episode 44 (March 15, 2000)
The Original Kings of Comedy, Documentary (2000)
Richard Pryor: I Ain't Dead Yet, #%$#@!!*, TV Documentary (2003)
The Late Late Show with Craig Kilborn, 9 Episodes (2003–2004)
Premium Blend, 7 Episodes (2003–2004)
Jimmy Kimmel Live!, 8 Episodes (2003–2005)

Real Time with Bill Maher, 13 Episodes (2003–2012)
Before They Were Kings: Vol. 1, Video Documentary (2005)
Weekends at the DL, TV Series, Season 1 28 Episodes (2005)
S.O.B.: Socially Offensive Behavior, BET, 5 Episodes (2007)
D. L. Hughley: Unapologetic, TV Documentary (2007)
Ellen: The Ellen DeGeneres Show, 2 Episodes (2007–2008)
Larry King Live, 6 Episodes (2007–2009)
The Late Late Show with Craig Ferguson, 2 Episodes (2007–2011)
Live at Gotham, Comedy Central, Season 3 Episode 7 (June 20, 2008)
Shaken Not Stirred, IGN, 3 Episodes (2008)
The Jay Leno Show, 3 Episodes (2008)
D. L. Hughley Breaks the News, 2 Seasons 16 Episodes (2008–2009)
All Star Comedy Jam: Live from South Beach, TV Movie (2009)
Why We Laugh: Black Comedians on Black Comedy, Documentary (2009)
D. L. Hughley: The Endangered List, TV Documentary (2012)
D. L. Hughley: Reset, TV Documentary (2012)
Phunny Business: A Black Comedy, Documentary (2012)
Who Gets the Last Laugh?, TBS, Season 1, Episode 2 (2013)
Gotham Comedy Live, Comedy Central (2013)

Page Hurwitz: Hurwitz was born in New York and moved to the West Coast where she first tried stand-up. She fell in love with stand-up and has since pursued it. She is an out lesbian and has recently moved toward working as a producer.

Comedy Filmography

Wisecrack, Logo TV, Episode 1 (January 1, 2005)
Outlaugh!, Showcase (2006)

Gabriel Iglesias: Iglesias is an American stand-up comedian and actor. He employs storytelling, effected voices, and sound effects in his act. Much of his comedy relies on poking fun at his weight.

Discography

Gabriel Iglesias: Hot and Fluffy (2007)
Gabriel Iglesias: I'm Not Fat . . . I'm Fluffy (2009)

Comedy Filmography

Make Me Laugh, TV series (1997)
The Clint Howard Variety Show, TV Miniseries (2002)
The Tonight Show with Jay Leno, NBC, 2 Episodes (2002–2006)
Comedy Central Presents, Comedy Central, Episode 73 (February 7, 2003)
The Drop, SiTV, Episode 22 (April 15, 2004)
Inside Joke, TV Series (2004)
Last Comic Standing, NBC, Season 4 Episode 5 (June 27, 2006)
The Late Late Show with Craig Ferguson, CBS, Season 3 Episode 47 (November 22, 2006)
Live at Gotham, Comedy Central, Season 2 Episode 4 (June 8, 2007)

Loco Comedy Jam Volume 1, Video (2008)
The Tonight Show with Conan O'Brien, NBC, Season 1 Episode 115 (December 2, 2009)
Gabriel Iglesias Presents Stand-Up Revolution, Comedy Central, 13 Episodes (2011–2012)
Made In Hollywood, USA, Season 8, Episode 38 (2013)
Gabriel Iglesias: Aloha Fluffy (2013)

Erin Jackson: Jackson is a Washington, DC, native who first performed comedy at colleges and small venues on the east coast. Since then, she has brought her conversational style of comedy to television (*The Ellen DeGeneres Show*, for example) and on tour with the Pumps and Punchlines tour. She was a semifinalist on NBC's *Last Comic Standing*.

Comedy Filmography
Live at Gotham, Comedy Central, Season 3 Episode 3 (June 13, 2008)
Last Comic Standing, NBC (2008)
Ellen: The Ellen Degeneres Show, NBC (September 16, 2008)
Comedy.TV, Entertainment Studios, Season 1 Episode 24 (2012)

Elham Jazab: Born in Shiraz, Iran, but now living in the United States, Jazab graduated with a degree in theater from Northwestern University and obtained a master's degree from Columbia College Chicago. She is an actress/comedian and has several videos on YouTube but no television or film appearances. She performs regularly in Los Angeles, where she now lives.

Dr. Ken Jeong: Born July 13, 1969, in Detroit, Michigan, and also known as Doctor Ken, he graduated from Duke University and then earned a medical degree from the University of North Carolina. While completing his residency in New Orleans, Jeong developed his stand-up comedy and won the Big Easy Laff-Off competition. Judges at that competition urged him to move to Los Angeles. Since doing so, he has had roles in television and film, most recognizably in *The Hangover* movies and NBC's *Community*.

Comedy Filmography
Comic Groove, Comedy Central, Season 1 Episode 1 (September 2, 2002)
Funny Munny, GSN (2003)
Live In Hollywood, Season 1 Episode 2 (2003)
Latino Laugh Festival: The Show, SiTV (February 16, 2004)
Asia Street Comedy, InternationalTV, Episode 10 (December 8, 2004)
1st Amendment Stand-Up, Starz, Season 1 Episode 6 (November 16, 2005)
Kims of Comedy (2005)
Comedy Zen, ImaginAsian TV, Season 1 Episode 6 (2006)
Last Call with Carson Daly, NBC (March 12, 2009)
Jimmy Kimmel Live!, ABC, Season 7 Episode 87 (June 12, 2009)
The Tonight Show with Conan O'Brien, NBC, Season 1 Episode 89 (October 14, 2009)
Late Night with Jimmy Fallon, NBC, 2 Episodes (2009–2013)
The Tonight Show with Jay Leno, NBC, 4 Episodes (2010–2013)
Conan, TBS, Season 1 Episode 95 (May 23, 2011)
Late Show with David Letterman, NBC, 1 Episode (June 19, 2013)
The Hour, CTV, Season 9, Episode 156 (2013)

Made In Hollywood, USA, Season 8, Episode 26 (2013)
The Late Late Show with Craig Ferguson, CBS, Season 10, Episode 29 (2013)
The Arsenio Hall Show, BET, Season 1, Episode 20 (2013)

Geri Jewell: Originally from Buffalo, New York, Jewell is most famous for her role in the television program *The Facts of Life*. She began doing comedy in 1978. She has cerebral palsy and is a lesbian.

Nonfiction Writing

Geri (1984)
I'm Walking as Straight as I Can (2011)

Comedy Filmography

I Love Liberty, TV Special (1982)
Inside America, Episode 1 (April 4, 1982)
Wisecracks, Documentary (1992)
Looking Who's Laughing, TV Movie (1994)
E! True Hollywood Story, Episode 404 (November 28, 1999)
Biography, TV Series Documentary (2005)
Arts: A Film about Possibilities, Disabilities and the Arts, Documentary (2009)
Hemispheres: A Documentary on Cerebral Palsy, Documentary (2009)
Imaginary Circumstances, Documentary Short (2010)
CinemAbilitiy, Documentary (2012)

Maz Jobrani: Jobrani is an Iranian-born American comedian who is part of the Axis of Evil comedy group. He was born in Tehran, Iran, and raised in the San Francisco Bay area of California. His jokes focus on social issues and identity, especially that of Middle Easterners.

Comedy Filmography

The Late Late Show with Craig Kilborn, CBS, 2 Episodes (September 28, 2004)
The World Stands Up, BBC (2004)
The Late Late Show with Craig Ferguson, CBS, Episode 186 (November 18, 2005)
The Colbert Report, Comedy Central, Episode 158 (October 5, 2006)
The Tonight Show with Jay Leno, NBC, Episode 539 (June 25, 2007)
The Watch List, TV Movie (2007)
Gab's Blabs, Current TV, Episode 20 (August 26, 2008)
Talkshow with Spike Feresten, FOX, Episode 50 (November 1, 2008)
ADHDtv: With Lew Marklin, TV Guide, Episode 39 (2008)
The Axis of Evil Comedy Tour, Video (2008)
Just for Laughs, BBC, Episode 24 (February 14, 2009)
The 7PM Project, Network Ten, Episode 68 (October 22, 2009)
Chelsea Lately, E!, Episode 232 (November 10, 2009)
Comedy.TV, Comedy Central, Episode 11 (2009)
Maz Jobrani: Brown and Friendly, TV Movie (2009)
Robins, Episode 55 (November 13, 2010)
MaDiWoDoVrijdagShow, Episode 49 (November 17, 2010)

Just Like Us, Documentary (2010)
Lopez Tonight, TBS, Episode 155 (January 11, 2011)
Gabriel Iglesias Presents Stand-Up Revolution, Comedy Central, Episode 6 (November 10, 2011)
Looking for Lenny, Documentary (2011)
Pauly Shore's Vegas Is My Oyster, TV Movie (2011)
Comics Unleashed, Syndicated, Episode 263 (January 30, 2012)
Valentino's Ghost, Documentary (2012)
Sunset Strip, Documentary (2012)
Funny: The Documentary, Documentary (2012)
Maz Jobrani: I Come In Peace, TV Movie (2013)
Gotham Comedy Live, Comedy Central (2013)
Shame on Shelley Bennett, Documentary (2013)

Aron Kader: Kander is a comedian based in Hollywood at The Comedy Store. He is a founding member of the Axis of Evil Comedy Tour and trained with the Groundlings Theatre in Los Angeles. He is the first person to formally teach comedy in the Middle East.

Comedy Filmography
Premium Blend, Comedy Central, Season 6 Episode 9 (December 28, 2002)
Whiteboyz in the Hood, Showtime, Episode 10 (November 23, 2006)
10 Ways to Become America's Sweetheart, TV Movie (2006)
The Watch List, TV Movie (2007)
The Axis of Evil Comedy Tour, Video (2008)
Last Call with Carson Daly, NBC, Season 9 Episode 26 (November 4, 2009)
Who Wants to Date a Comedian, Comedy TV, Episode 31 (November 14, 2011)
Valentino's Ghost, Documentary (2012)
The Muslims Are Coming!, Documentary (2012)

Jen Kirkman: Born August 28, 1974, in Needham, Massachusetts, Kirkman performs stand-up in Los Angeles and is best known for her performances in HBO's short series *Drunk History* and for being a regular guest on the *Chelsea Lately Show*. In 2009, *Entertainment Weekly* named her one of the top 12 rising stars of comedy.

Discography
Self Help (2006)
Hail to the Freaks (2011)

Comedy Filmography
Late Friday, NBC, Season 1 Episode 29 (December 14, 2001)
The Comedians of Comedy: Live at the El Rey (2006)
The Late Late Show with Craig Ferguson, CBS, Season 5 Episode 62 (November 26, 2008)
Drunk History, HBO, Volumes 3 and 5 (2008)
Chelsea Lately, E!, 108 Episodes (2009–2013)
New York Stand-Up Show, Comedy Central, Season 2 Episode 6 (April 28, 2011)
Conan, TBS 2 Episodes (2011–2013)

After Lately, E!, 16 Episodes (2011–2013)
Stand Down: True Tales From Stand-Up Comedy, Comedy Central (2012)

Samson Koletkar: Born in Mumbai, raised Jewish, and now living in San Francisco, Koletkar is a first generation immigrant in America. His comedy addresses religious and political hypocrisies, social issues, immigrant rights, and day-to-day absurdities winning him access to many comedy tours including: Make Chai not War, Pundits with Punchlines, and Slumdog Comedy Tour.

Hari Kondabolu: Born in 1982 in Queens, New York, Kondabolu has a BA in comparative politics and a master's in human rights. He began performing stand-up in college and his first comedic television appearance was on the *Jimmy Kimmel Show*. He is currently a writer for *Totally Biased with W. Kamau Bell*.

Comedy Filmography
Jimmy Kimmel Live!, ABC, Season 4 Episode 401 (February 19, 2007)
Live at Gotham, Comedy Central, Season 3 Episode 6 (July 18, 2008)
Seattle Komedy Dokumentary, Documentary (2010)
New York Stand-Up Show, Comedy Central, 3 Episodes (2010–2012)
Comedy Central Presents, Comedy Central, Season 15 Episode 7 (February 11, 2011)
Live at the Electric, BBC, Season 1 Episode 1 (May 31, 2012)
Totally Biased with W. Kamau Bell, FX (2012–2013)
Bridgetown Documentary, Documentary (2014)

Elvira Kurt: Kurt is a Canadian comedian and the host of *PopCultured* with Elvira Kurt. Openly lesbian, she has established the term "fellgirly" to describe her and other queer females who dress as both butch and femme. She was voted the Funniest Female Comic at the Canadian Comedy Awards and received a Gemini-nomination for her one-hour comedy special.

Discography
Kitten with a Wit (1999)

Comedy Filmography
Comedy Now!, The Comedy Network, Episode 102 (July 12, 1998)
We're Funny that Way, Documentary (1998)
Comedy Central Presents, Comedy Central, Episode 2.11 (May 28, 1999)
Just for Laughs, BBC, Episode 17 (March 28, 2004)
Out on the Edge, TV Special (2004)
PopCultured, the Comedy Network (2005)
Laughing Matters . . . More!, Documentary (2006)
CBC Winnipeg Comedy Festival, CBC, Episode 18 (January 8, 2008)
HypaSpace, TV Series Documentary, Season 7 Episode 14 (April 4, 2008)
One Night Stand Up, Logo TV, Episode 102 (October 14, 2008)
The Hour, CBC, Season 8 Episode 15 (October 10, 2011)
The Gayest Show Ever, TV Series Documentary (2011)
The Debaters, CBC, 3 Episodes (2011)
The Hour, CTV, 3 Episodes (2011–2013)

Brett Leake: Leake is a stand-up sit-down comic with multiple sclerosis. He defines himself as a motivational comedian.

Comedy Filmography
The Tonight Show with Jay Leno, NBC, 4 Episodes (1992–1994)
Knuckleball: The Documentary, Documentary (2007)

Bobby Lee: Born September 17, 1972, in San Diego, California, Lee decided to try stand-up in 1995 after working odd jobs for The Comedy Store in San Diego. After becoming a regular presence on stage there, he joined the *MADtv* cast in 2001, has been in several films, and works regularly at The Comedy Store in Los Angeles.

Comedy Filmography
Late Friday, NBC, Season 1 Episode 19 (July 27, 2001)
MADtv (2001–2009)
The Tonight Show with Jay Leno, NBC (April 26, 2002)
Asia Street Comedy, International Channel (October 6, 2004)
Minding the Store, TBS, 2 Episodes (2005)
Kims of Comedy (2005)
Comedy Zen, ImaginAsian TV, Season 1 Episode 4 (2006)
The Slanted Screen, Documentary (2006)
Heckler, Documentary (2007)
The Bobby Lee Project (2008)
2008 Asian Excellence Awards, Host (2008)
Live at Gotham, Season 4 Episode 2, Host (October 23, 2009)
Snorfin with Bobby Lee, ManiaTV (2010)
Chelsea Lately, E!, 49 Episodes (2010–2013)
After Lately, E! (2011)
Who Gets the Last Laugh?, TBS (2013)
Gotham Comedy Live, Comedy Central (2013)
Funny: The Documentary, Documentary (2013)

George Lopez: Born April 23, 1961, in Los Angeles, California, he started doing comedy in the 1980s. Before becoming famous with his ABC sitcom, which Sandra Bullock produced after approaching him because she liked his stand-up comedy so much, he worked as the host of a radio show in California. He has also won humanitarian awards for his work as an activist.

Nonfiction Writing
Why You Crying? (2005)

Discography
Right Now Right Now (2001)
Team Leader (2003)
Alien Nation (2005)
El Mas Chingon (2006)
America's Mexican (2007)
Tall Dark and Chicano (2009)

Comedy Filmography

Comedy Club, ABC (September 12, 1987)

The Arsenio Hall Show, Paramount (August 3, 1989)

Latino Laugh Festival, Si TV (1997)

Second Annual Latino Laugh Festival, Si TV (May 3, 1998)

The Tonight Show with Jay Leno, NBC, 2 Episodes (2002–2005)

The Original Latin Kings of Comedy (2002)

The Late Late Show with Craig Kilborn, CBS (March 10, 2003)

The 55th Annual Primetime Emmy Awards, Host (September 21, 2003)

Richard Pryor: I Ain't Dead Yet, #*%$#@!!, Documentary (2003)

Jimmy Kimmel Live!, ABC, 12 Episodes (2003–2007)

Why You Crying? (2004)

The 5th Annual Latin Grammy Awards, Host (September 1, 2004)

Late Night with Conan O'Brien, 3 Episodes (2003–2005)

Sit Down Comedy with David Steinberg, TV Land, Season 1 Episode 6 (January 18, 2006)

Last Call with Carson Daly, NBC, 3 Episodes (2005–2006)

Stand Up or Sit Down Comedy Challenge, TBS (November 17, 2006)

Comic Relief 2006, HBO (November 18, 2006)

George Lopez: America's Mexican (2007)

Brown Is the New Green: George Lopez and the American Dream, Documentary (2007)

Mr. Warmth: The Don Rickles Project, Documentary (2007)

Tavis Smiley, PBS (August 13, 2008)

Just for Laughs: Best of 2007, 25th Edition, RTE (2008)

Loco Comedy Jam Vol. 1 (2008)

The Late Late Show with Craig Ferguson, CBS, Season 6 Episode 57 (December 3, 2009)

Make 'Em Laugh: The Funny Business of America, Documentary (2009)

George Lopez: Tall, Dark, and Chicano (2009)

Lopez Tonight, TBS (2009–2011)

Conan, TBS, 2 Episodes (2010–2012)

Late Show with David Letterman, CBS (July 11, 2011)

Vocas Vivas, Documentary (2011)

Hollywood Uncensored with Sam Rubin, Season 1, Episode 98 (2012)

George Lopez: It's Not Me, It's You, TV Movie (2012)

The Latino List: Volume 2, Documentary (2012)

Richard Pryor: Omit the Logic, Documentary (2013)

The Arsenio Hall Show, BET, 2 Episodes (2013)

Loni Love: Born on July 12, 1971, Love is an American comedian and actress. In 2003 she was the runner-up in *Star Search* and was named a top comic to watch. She performs observational comedy that often focuses on relationships and current events.

Comedy Filmography

Hot Tamales Live: Spicy, Hot and Hilarious, Video (2003)

Premium Blend, Comedy Central, *Premium Blend* (2004)

Redlight Greenlight, TV Series (2004)

The Tonight Show with Jay Leno, NBC, Season 13 Episode 132 (July 26, 2005)

1st Amendment Stand Up, Starz, Season 1 Episode 5 (November 11, 2005)
Weekends at the DL, Comedy Central, 4 Episodes (2005)
Comedy Central Presents, Comedy Central, Season 11 Episode 12 (February 23, 2007)
Comics Unleashed, Syndicated, Season 2 Episode 11 (July 23, 2008)
Chelsea Lately, E!, 95 Episodes (2008–2013)
D. L. Hughley Breaks the News, CNN, 2 Episodes (2009)
Surviving the Holidays with Lewis Black, TV Movie (2009)
Comedy.TV, Comedy Central, 6 Episodes (2009–2012)
Comics Unleashed, Syndicated, Episode 87 (January 27, 2010)
Loni Love: America's Sister, TV Movie (2010)
After Lately, E!, 4 Episodes (2011–2013)
Gotham Comedy Live, Comedy Central (2013)
The Real, FOX, 20 Episodes (2013)

Luenell: Born Luenell Campbell, on March 12, 1959, in Tollette, Arkansas, she is one of eight children. Luenell got her start on an Oakland, California, cable show in the 1990s and her first film role was in *So I Married an Axe Murderer*. She has since had small roles in many films and was one of the only actors in the film *Borat*, in which she played a prostitute.

Comedy Filmography

BET's Comicview, BET, Season 14 Episode 2 (2005)
Paul Mooney: Know Your History—Jesus Is Black . . . So Was Cleopatra (2007)
Reflections on Paul Mooney, Documentary (2007)
Comics Unleashed, Entertainment Studios, February 23 Episode (2007)
The John Kerwin Show, Briarwood Productions, February 28 Episode (2007)
Comedy Central Roast of Flavor Flav, Comedy Central (2007)
Katt Williams: American Hustle (2007)
I Love the New Millennium, VH1 (2008)
Reality Bites Back, Comedy Central, "Shock of Love" Episode (2008)
1st Amendment Stand Up, Starz, Angelo Lozada Episode (2008)
Katt Williams Presents: Katthouse Comedy (2009)
Katt Williams: 9 Lives (2010)
Latino 101, SiTV, 10 Episodes (2010–2011)
Way Black When: Primetime, TV One, Season 1 Episode 4 (February 3, 2011)
In the Flow with Affion Crockett, FOX, Season 1 Episode 5 (September 4, 2011)
Reel Black Love, Documentary (2012)
Snoop Dogg Presents: The Bad Girls of Comedy, TV Movie (2012)
StandUp in Stilettos, TV Guide, 2 Episodes (2012)
Backstage at Budz House, Video Documentary (2012)
Comedy Underground, 1 Episode (2012)
Who Gets The Last Laugh?, Comedy Central (2013)

Bill Maher: Born January 20, 1956, in New York, Maher first started doing stand-up during his undergraduate years at Cornell. His first act was at a Chinese Restaurant. Best known for his comedic political commentary, Maher has had two of his own shows, *Politically Incorrect* and *Real Time with Bill Maher*. He is an advocate for same-sex marriage, the legalization of marijuana, animal rights, and separation of church and state. He owns part of the New York Mets. He has been nominated for 26 Emmys.

Nonfiction Writing

True Story: A Novel (1994)
When You Ride Alone with Bin Laden (2003)
Keep the Statue of Liberty Closed: The New Rules (2004)
New Rules: Polite Musings from a Timid Observer (2005)
The New New Rules: A Funny Look at How Everybody but Me Has Their Head Up Their Ass (2011)

Discography

New Rules: Polite Musings from a Timid Observer (2006)

Comedy Filmography

The 8th Annual Young Comedians Show, HBO (1983)
The Tonight Show with Johnny Carson, NBC, 4 Episodes (1986–1991)
Funny, You Don't Look 200: A Constitutional Vaudeville, ABC (October 12, 1987)
One Night Stand, HBO, 2 Episodes (1989–1991)
The Tonight Show with Jay Leno, NBC, 45 Episodes (1993–2013)
Comic Relief VI, HBO (January 15, 1994)
Politically Incorrect, ABC (1994–2002)
Bill Maher: Stuff That Struck Me Funny, Comedy Showcase (1995)
Dennis Miller Live, HBO, 3 Episodes (1995–2002)
Comedy Club Superstars, Comedy Showcase (1996)
Bill Maher: The Golden Goose Special, Comedy Showcase (1997)
Great Performances, PBS, 2 Episodes (1997–2001)
The Daily Show with Jon Stewart, Comedy Central, 3 Episodes (1998–2008)
Late Night with Conan O'Brien, NBC, 5 Episodes (1999–2008)
The Chris Rock Show, HBO (October 13, 2000)
Bill Maher: Be More Cynical, Comedy Showcase (2000)
See How They Run, Documentary (2001)
Smothered: The Censorship Struggles of the Smothers Brothers Comedy Hour, Documentary (2002)
Stupidity, Documentary (2003)
Uncensored Comedy: That's Not Funny!, HBO (2003)
Bill Maher: Victory Begins at Home, Comedy Showcase (2003)
Real Time with Bill Maher, HBO (2003–2013)
Last Call with Carson Daly, NBC (September 16, 2004)
The Late Late Show with Craig Kilborn, CBS (September 23, 2004)
Comedy Central's Bar Mitzvah Bash!, Comedy Central (2004)
There's Something about W, Comedy Showcase (2004)
Tavis Smiley, PBS, 4 Episodes (2004–2009)
Earth to America, TBS, HBO (November 20, 2005)
Inside Deep Throat, Documentary (2005)
Escape to Canada, Documentary (2005)
The Aristocrats, Documentary (2005)

Bill Maher: I'm Swiss, Comedy Showcase (2005)

Fuck, Documentary (2005)

The Late Late Show with Craig Ferguson, CBS, 6 Episodes (2005–2013)

Late Show with David Letterman, CBS, 7 Episodes (2005–2013)

A/k/a Tommy Chong, Documentary (2006)

Comic Relief 2006, HBO (2006)

Bill Maher: The Decider, Comedy Showcase (2007)

Heckler, Documentary (2007)

Religulous, Documentary (2008)

Iconoclasts, Sundance Channel, Season 4 Episode 4 (November 6, 2008)

Make 'Em Laugh: The Funny Business of America, Documentary (2009)

Bill Maher: Monologues from Around the World (2009)

The Tonight Show with Conan O'Brien, NBC, Season 1 Episode 51 (2009)

The Jay Leno Show, NBC, 3 Episodes (2009–2010)

Sex, Drugs, and Religion, Documentary (2010)

Bright Day!, Documentary (2010)

Bill Maher:. . . But I'm Not Wrong, Showcase (2010)

Jimmy Kimmel Live!, ABC, 2 Episodes (2010–2011)

Late Night with Jimmy Fallon, NBC (November 17, 2011)

Bill Maher: CrazyStupid Politics (2012)

Owned and Operated, Documentary (2012)

Occupy L.A., Documentary (2012)

Chelsea Lately, E!, 2 Episodes (2012–2013)

Conan, TBS, 2 Episodes (2012–2013)

Inside Comedy, Showtime, Season 2, Episode 9 (April 8, 2013)

The Arsenio Hall, BET, Episode 23 (2013)

Marilyn Martinez: Martinez was a Hispanic American stand-up comedian and actress. She was a regular performer at The Comedy Store in Hollywood.

Comedy Filmography

Hot Tamales Live: Spicy, Hot and Hilarious, Video (2003)

Urban Jungle, SiTV Episode 9 (2004)

1st Amendment Stand Up, Starz, Episode 16 (May 2, 2007)

The Latin Divas of Comedy, Documentary (2007)

Monique Marvez: Marvez is a radio and television personality, writer, and comedian. She first gained popularity on the Miami comedy scene and ever since then she has appeared on HBO, Comedy Central, and ABC.

Nonfiction Writing

Not Skinny, Not Blonde (2009)

Discography

Built for Comfort (1999)

The Reality Chick (2003)

Comedy Filmography

Urban Jungle 2, SiTV (2005)
Comedy Zen, ImaginAsian TV, Episode 6 (2006)
The Latin Divas of Comedy, Documentary (2007)
Comedy.TV, Comedy Central, Episode 5 (2009)
Snoop Dogg Presents, TV Movie (2012)
Monique Marvez: Not Skinny, Not Blonde, TV Movie (2013)

Sabrina Matthews: Matthews began her comedy career in San Francisco, California, although she now resides on the East Coast. She appears regularly at clubs, colleges, cruises, and festivals around the world. She is openly lesbian who relates the absurdities of the everyday in a witty anecdotal style.

Comedy Filmography

Premium Blend, Comedy Central, Episode 17 (December 27, 1997)
Comedy Central Presents, Comedy Central, Episode 45 (January 22, 2001)
Coming Out Party, Video (2003)
Queer Edge with Jack E. Jett, Q Television Network, Season 1 Episode 6 (October 3, 2005)
Laughing Matters . . . More!, Documentary (2006)
Outlaugh!, Documentary (2006)
Comedy.TV, Comedy Central, Episode 27 (2012)

Alexis McGuire: McGuire is a dyslexic teacher and comic who combines the two professions, using humor to teach and the comedy stage to promote understanding of disabilities and differently abled persons.

Comedy Filmography

Able to Laugh, Documentary (1993)

Bridget McManus: A graduate of New York University's Tisch School of the Arts and Los Angeles' Second City Conservatory Program, McManus has headlined many festivals from the Sweet's Cozumel Palace Resort and the 8th International Gay Games. By national poll, she was ranked third funniest lesbian in the lesbian magazine *Curve*.

Comedy Filmography

Cherry Bomb, LOGO TV, Episode 15 (September 5, 2008)
Laughing Matters . . . Next Gen, Video (2009)
Brunch with Bridget, LOGO TV (2009)
One Night Stand Up, Logo TV, Episode 108 (May 6, 2010)
Trip Out TV, LOGO (2013)

Eugene Mirman: Born July 24, 1974, in Russia, Mirman emigrated to the United States when he was four years old. His stand-up albums have made several best-of lists. He often plays music venues and has toured with rock bands such as The Shins, Modest Mouse, and Cake. Mirman also had a recurring role on HBO's *Flight of the Conchords*.

Nonfiction Writing

The Will to Whatevs (2009)

Discography

The Absurd Nightclub Comedy of Eugene Mirman (2004)
Invite Them Up (2005)
En Garde, Society! (2006)
Comedians of Comedy 3" Tour CD (2006)
God Is a Twelve-Year-Old Boy with Asperger's (2009)

Comedy Filmography

Late Night with Conan O'Brien, NBC, 4 Episodes (2000–2008)
New York Noise, NYC TV, Season 4 Episode 3 (October 4, 2005)
Last Call with Carson Daly, NBC (August 4, 2006)
The Comedians of Comedy: Live at the Troubadour (2007)
Heckler, Documentary (2007)
Comedy Central Presents, Comedy Central, Season 12 Episode 7 (February 1, 2008)
New York Stand-Up Show, Comedy Central, Season 1 Episode 1 (January 8, 2010)
The Benson Interruption, Comedy Central, Season 1 Episode 2 (November 12, 2010)
The Green Room with Paul Provenza, Showtime, 2 Episodes (2011)
Funny As Hell, CTV, Season 2, Episode 7 (2012)
G4 Presents Comic Con 2012 Live, TV Movie (2012)
Eugene Mirman: A Evening of Comedy in a Fake Underground Laboratory, TV Movie (2012)
Comedy Gives Back, TV Movie (2013)
When Jews Were Funny, Documentary (2013)

Mo'Nique: Born Monique Angela Hicks, she started performing comedy at an early age in the downtown Baltimore Comedy Factory Outlet. She reached fame once she starred in *The Parkers* and has maintained a strong presence as a comic and actress.

Nonfiction Writing

Skinny Women Are Evil: Notes of a Big Girl in a Small-Minded World (2004)
Beacon Hills High (2008)

Discography

Uptown Comedy Club (1993)
The Queens of Comedy (2002)
Platinum Comedy Series: Mo'Nique—One Night Stand (2004)
Mo'Nique: I Coulda Been Your Cellmate (2007)

Comedy Filmography

Sin City Spectacular, FX, Season 1 Episode 7 (September 7, 1998)
Def Comedy Jam, TV Series (1998)
The Tonight Show with Conan O'Brien, NBC, Episode 672 (August 17, 2000)
The Rosie O'Donnell Show, NBC, Episode 964 (April 19, 2001)
The Queens of Comedy, Video Documentary (2001)
Showtime at the Apollo, TV Series (2002)
Intimate Portrait, Lifetime, Episode 199 (November 17, 2003)
Last Comic Standing, NBC, TV Series (2003)
Heroes of Comedy: Women on Top, TV Miniseries Documentary (2003)
Ellen: The Ellen DeGeneres Show, NBC, 3 Episodes (2003–2008)

Pryor Offenses, TV Movie (2004)
TV in Black: The First Fifty Years, Video Documentary (2004)
The Big Black Comedy Show, Vol. 1, Video (2004)
Apollo at 70: A Hot Night in Harlem, TV Documentary (2004)
Tavis Smiley, PBS, 3 Episodes (2004–2007)
The Big Black Comedy Show, Vol. 2, Video (2005)
Mo'Nique's Fat Chance, TV Movie (2005)
Made You Look: Top 25 Moments of BET History, TV Special Documentary (2005)
Richard Pryor: The Funniest Man Dead or Alive, TV Special Documentary (2005)
The Late Late Show with Craig Ferguson, CBS, 6 Episodes (2005–2009)
Thank God You're Here, NBC, Episode 2 (April 9, 2007)
Mo'Nique: I Coulda Been Your Cellmate, Video (2007)
Mo'Nique's F.A.T. Chance: The Road to Paris, TV Movie (2007)
Mo'Nique: Behind Bars, TV Documentary (2007)
TV One on One, NBC, Episode 14 (May 18, 2008)
Up Close with Carrie Keagan, NGTV, 2 Episodes (2008)
Why We Laugh: Black Comedians on Black Comedy, Documentary (2009)
Starz Inside: Comics on Screen, TV Documentary (2009)
The Mo'Nique Show, TV Series, 309 Episodes (2009–2012)
The Precious Ensemble, Video Documentary Short (2010)

Paul Mooney: Born Paul Gladney on August 4, 1941, in Shreveport, Louisiana, he began his comedy career by writing jokes while he worked at a circus. Mooney cowrote material with Richard Pryor and Redd Foxx in addition to being the head writer of *In Loving Color* for a time. He gave Robin Williams and Sandra Bernhard their big breaks.

Nonfiction Writing
Black Is the New White (2009)

Discography
Race (1993)
Master Piece (1994)

Comedy Filmography
Black Omnibus, Season 1 Episode 5 (1973)
The Richard Pryor Show, NBC, Season 1 Episode 4 (1977)
Late Night with David Letterman, 2 Episodes (1982–2008)
The Debbie Allen Special, TV (1989)
Mo' Funny: Black Comedy in America, Documentary (1993)
Andrew Dice Clay and His Gang Live!: The Valentine's Day Massacre, TV (1993)
Comic Justice, Comedy Central (1993)
The Legend of Dolemite, Documentary (1994)
The South Bank Show: Darker Than Me, ITV, Season 17 Episode 15 (1994)
Def Comedy Jam, HBO, Season 5 Episode 7 (1995)
The Sandra Bernhard Experience, A&E, August 31 Episode (2001)
Paul Mooney: Analyzing White America (2002)
Heroes of Black Comedy, Comedy Central (2002)

Tough Crowd with Colin Quinn, Comedy Central (2002)
Donahue, MSNBC, December 11 Episode (2002)
Bitter Jester, Documentary (2003)
Uncensored Comedy: That's Not Funny! (2003)
The N Word, Documentary (2004)
BET Comedy Awards, TV (2004–2005)
Queer Edge with Jack E. Jett, Season 3 Episode 7 (2006)
That's What I'm Talking About, TV Land, "Greats, Dates, and Debates" Episode (2006)
Howard Stern on Demand, HBO, Episode 626 (2006, 2007)
Paul Mooney: Know Your History—Jesus Is Black . . . and So Was Cleopatra (2007)
Reflections on Paul Mooney, Documentary (2007)
Clean Mic: Laughing until It Hurts, Documentary (2008)
Why We Laugh: Black Comedians on Black Comedy, Documentary (2009)
Good Hair, Documentary (2009)
Make 'Em Laugh: The Funny Business of America, PBS, 2 Episodes (2009)
TV One's Roast and Toast: John Witherspoon, TV One (2009)
Tavis Smiley, PBS, November 18 Episode (2009)
Blacking Up: Hip Hop's Remix of Race and Identity, Documentary (2010)
Paul Mooney: It's the End of the World (2010)
The Mo'Nique Show, BET, March 4 Episode (2010)
The Green Room with Paul Provenza, Showtime, Season 1 Episode 4 (2010)
Supreme Court of Comedy, DirecTV, "Aries Spears vs. Paul Mooney" (2010)
Looking for Lenny, Documentary (2011)
The Godfather of Comedy (2012)
Paul Mooney: The Godfather of Comedy, TV Movie (2012)
Sunset Strip, Documentary (2012)
Richard Pryor: Omit the Light, Documentary (2013)

Eman Morgan: Morgan is an Egyptian American stand-up comic born in Los Angeles. He has performed all across the country and is a regular at the world famous Laugh Factory in Hollywood. He has also done numerous shorts for www.funnyordie.com.

Comedy Filmography
Just Like Us, Documentary (2010)
Bridging the Gap: A Middle East Comedy Conference, Showtime, Comedy Showcase (2010)

Micia Mosely: Since earning her PhD from University of California, Berkeley, Mosely has turned to the stage as a comedian, actress, and educational speaker. In 2009 her one woman show, *Where My Girls At? A Comedic Look at Black Lesbians* was nominated for a New York Innovative Theater Award. She is the founding artist with the Nursha Project, a group committed to supporting artists and projects rooted in sociopolitical offerings.

Filmography
How to Make Movies at Home, Documentary (2013)

Preacher Moss: Moss is a comedian and writer from Washington, DC, where he earned his nickname "Preacher" for his imitations of the pastor of his family's church. He wrote his own show *The End of Racism* and now travels promoting the ideas of multiculturalism and critical race theory.

Comedy Filmography

Allah Made Me Funny: Live in Concert (2008)
The Muslims Are Coming!, Documentary (2012)

Morgan Murphy: Born October 23, 1981, in Portland, Oregon, Murphy has toured as a comic and was a writer for both Jimmy Fallon and Jimmy Kimmel. She has also toured with Aimee Mann and been in a couple of films by Bobcat Goldthwait.

Comedy Filmography

Funny Munny, GSN (August 4, 2003)
Premium Blend, Comedy Central, 2 Episodes (2004–2005)
Jimmy Kimmel Live!, ABC, 7 Episodes (2004–2007)
Last Call with Carson Daly, NBC (April 7, 2006)
The Comedians of Comedy: Live at the Troubadour (2007)
Late Night with Jimmy Fallon, NBC, 7 Episodes (2010–2011)
Chelsea Lately, E!, 8 Episodes (2012–2013)
New York Stand-Up Show, Comedy Central, Season 4, Episode 4 (2013)

Aparna Nancherla: Nancherla was born in Washington, DC, although she now lives a bicoastal life style. She currently writes for and sometimes appears in *Totally Biased with W. Kamau Bell*.

Comedy Filmography

Totally Biased with W. Kamau Bell, FX (2012–2013)
Conan, TBS, 1 Episode (2013)

Vijai Nathan: Nathan is one of the leading Indian American female comedians. She was featured at the Montreal International Comedy Festival and has performed at the Kennedy Center. Her material comes from her experience as an Indian girl growing up in America.

Comedy Filmography

Indian Invasion Comedy, Movie (2007)
Indian Comedy Tour, Movie (2010)

Tig Notaro: Born in Mississippi and raised in Texas, Tig dropped out of school to pursue a career as a band manager. In Los Angeles she tried stand-up comedy for the first time. She was on the show *Last Comic Standing* in 2006 although she did not make it into the house. She is now featured on *Comedy Central Presents* and the *Sarah Silverman Program*. She frequently writes with Kyle Dunnigan.

Discography

Good One (2011)
Tig Notaro: Live (2012)

Comedy Filmography

Premium Blend, Comedy Central, Season 4 Episode 7 (January 19, 2001)
Movies at Our House, AMC (2002–2004)
Comedy Central Presents, Comedy Central, Episode 125 (May 14, 2004)
Jimmy Kimmel Live!, ABC, Episode 845 (October 6, 2006)
Comedy Colosseum, TV Movie (2006)
Comic Unleashed, CBS, Episode 100 (June 1, 2007)
Last Call with Carson Daly, NBC, Episode 558 (October 11, 2007)
Have Tig at Your Party, Video (2008)
Biography, TV Series Documentary (2008)
Live Nude Comedy, Showtime, Episode 3 (July 30, 2009)
The Tig Series, Short (2009)
The Late Late Show with Craig Ferguson, CBS, Episode 1158 (June 15, 2010)
The Benson Interruption, Comedy Central, Episode 5 (December 10, 2010)
Late Night with Jimmy Fallon, NBC, Episode 489 (August 10, 2011)
The Daily Habit, Fuel TV, Episode 882 (September 12, 2011)
Conan, TBS, 3 Episodes (2011–2013)
This American Life Live!, TV Series (2012)
Why We Laugh: Funny Women, TV Movie Documentary (2013)
Take Part Live, YouTube (2013)

Dean Obeidallah: Obeidallah is a Palestinian American/Italian American comedian who was born and raised in New Jersey. He has been compared to the groundbreaking minority comedians of the 1960s and the 1970s who used comedy to raise political and social issues in an effort to facilitate change.

Comedy Filmography

Man Is a Bridge, Short video (2005)
Arab-American Comedy Tour, Movie (2005)
Comics Unleashed, Syndicated, Episode 20 (February 2, 2007)
The Watch List, TV Movie (2007)
The View, ABC, 2 Episodes (2007–2008)
Dan Rather Reports, HDNet, Season 3 Episode 5 (February 5, 2008)
Gab's Blabs, Current TV, Episode 19 (August 25, 2008)
Warai de Tatakae: Amerika Arabukei Comedian no Chousen, TV Documentary (2008)
The Axis of Evil Comedy Tour, Video (2008)
What the Week, CNN (2010)
Geraldo at Large, FOX, Episode 43 (April 25, 2010)
The Joy Behar Show, HLN, 4 Episodes (2010–2011)
Geraldo at Large, FOX, Episode 51 (March 5, 2011)
Rock Center with Brian Williams, NBC, Episode 6 (December 5, 2011)
The Muslims Are Coming!, Documentary (2012)
The Arab Americans, Documentary (2013)
A Thousand and One Journeys: The Arab Americans, Documentary (2013)

Rosie O'Donnell: O'Donnell is a comedian, actress, author, and TV personality. She was raised in Commack, New York, where she went to high school before attending Boston University. After doing stand-up in clubs on Long Island in the 1970s, she was on *Star Search* where she gained national exposure. In the years following, she had her own talk show and cohosted *The View*. She now lives in New York City with her girlfriend and four children.

Nonfiction Writing

Kids are Punny: More Jokes sent by Kids to the Rosie O'Donnell Show (1997)
Kids are Punny 2: More Jokes sent by Kids to the Rosie O'Donnell Show (1998)
Find Me (2002)
Celebrity Detox: (The Fame Game) (2007)

Comedy Filmography

Star Search, CBS, 6 Episodes (1984)
Showtime Comedy Club Network, Showtime (1987)
Stand-Up Spotlight, VH1 (1988)
Pair of Jokers with Rosie O'Donnell and Bill Engvall, TV Documentary (1989)
LIVE! With Kelly, ABC, Episode 152 (January 15, 1990)
The Marsha Warfield Show, NBC, Episode 8 (July 19, 1990)
Saturday Night Live, NBC, 2 Episodes (1993–1996)
Larry King Live, CNN, 3 Episodes (1993–2005)
The Tonight Show with Jay Leno, NBC, 6 Episodes (1993–2006)
In a New Light, TV Special (1994)
Late Show with David Letterman, CBS, 5 Episodes (1994–2006)
The Larry Sanders Show, HBO, Episode 64 (November 15, 1995)
Rosie O'Donnell, TV Movie (1995)
The Most Fascinating Women of 1996, TV Documentary (1996)
The Good, the Band and the Beautiful, TV Special Documentary (1996)
Very Personal with Naomi Judd, TV Special (1996)
The Rosie O'Donnell Show, TV Series (1996–2002)
Say It, Fight It, Cure It, TV Movie (1997)
Dennis Miller Life, HBO, 2 Episodes (1997–1998)
The Today Show, NBC, Episode 487 (September 7, 1998)
Comic Relief VIII, TV Special (1998)
Bravo Profiles: The Entertainment Business, TV Miniseries Documentary (1998)
Kids Are Punny, TV Movie (1998)
The Martin Short Show, SCTV, Episode 56 (December 6, 1999)
Discovering Bedrock, Video Documentary Short (1999)
Jackie's Back!, TV Movie (1999)
Late Night with Conan O'Brien, NBC, 5 Episodes (1999–2008)
Secrets Through the Smoke, Documentary (2001)
Primetime Glick, Comedy Central, Episode 14 (March 16, 2002)
The Colin Quinn Show, Comedy Central, Episode 2 (March 18, 2002)
E! True Hollywood Story, TV Series Documentary (March 2, 2003)
Living It Up! with Ali and Jack, CTV, Episode 6 (December 3, 2003)
Intimate Portrait, TV Documentary (2003)

The Tony Danza Show, 2 Episodes (2004–2005)
20/20, ABC, Episode 144 (April 8, 2005)
Inside the Actors Studio, Episode 166 (June 19, 2005)
Pursuit of Equality, Documentary (2005)
I'm Going to Tell You a Secret, Documentary (2005)
The View, ABC (2005–2007)
The Late Late Show with Craig Ferguson, CBS, 3 Episodes (2005–2010)
That's Kentertainment!, Time Warner, Season 5 Episode 4 (May 4, 2006)
All Aboard! Rosie's Family Cruise, TV Documentary (2006)
Deep Inside the Kid's Choice Awards, TV Movie (2007)
Shining Through: Behind the Scenes at True Colors, TV Documentary (2007)
A Night of Too Many Stars: An Overbooked Concert for Autism Education, TV Movie (2008)
Rosie Live, TV Movie (2008)
The Big Gay Sketch Show, LOGO TV (2008–2010)
The Tyra Banks Show, The CW, Episode 93 (February 26, 2009)
The Bonnie Hunt Show, Episode 134 (February 27, 2009)
The Rosie O'Donnell Show: Season One—Rosie Reminisces, Video Documentary (2009)
Late Night with Jimmy Fallon, NBC, 2 Episodes (2009–2012)
Starz Inside: Comics on Screen, TV Documentary (2010)
Teenage Paparazzo, Documentary (2010)
A Family Is a Family Is a Family: A Rosie O'Donnell Celebration, TV Documentary (2010)
The Doc Club with Rosie O'Donnell, TV Movie (2011)
Wish Me Away, Documentary (2011)
The Rosie Show, OWN (2011–2012)
Watch What Happens: Live, Bravo, Episode 63 (January 12, 2012)
The Club, Documentary (2012)
Outlook TV, CTV, Season 3, Episode 6 (2013)
The Business of Charity, Documentary (2014)

Patton Oswalt: Oswalt is a stand-up comedian, writer, actor, and voice actor. His stand-up comedy covers topics ranging from pop culture to foreign policy and religion.

Discography

Feelin' Kinda Patton (2004)
Werewolves and Lollipops (2007)
My Weakness Is Strong (2009)
Patton Oswalt: 222 (2010)
Finest Hour (2011)

Comedy Filmography

HBO Showcase, HBO (1995)
Make Me Laugh, TV Series (1997)
Comics Come Home 3, TV Movie (1997)
HBO Comedy Half-Hour, 6 Episodes (1997–1998)
Late Night with Conan O'Brien, NBC, 14 Episodes (1998–2010)
Comedy Central Presents, Comedy Central, Episode 19 (May 10, 1999)

Tough Crowd with Colin Quinn, TV Series (2002)
Jimmy Kimmel Live!, ABC, 12 Episodes (2003–2013)
Patton Oswalt: No Reason to Complain, Comedy Showcase (2004)
Dennis Miller Live, HBO, Episode 54 (March 30, 2005)
Too Late with Adam Carolla, Comedy Central, Episode 13 (October 26, 2005)
Happy Game Fun Bomb, TV Movie (2005)
The Comedians of Comedy, Documentary (2005)
The Comedians of Comedy, TV Series Documentary (2005)
Last Laugh '05, TV Movie (2005)
The Henry Rollins Show, IFC, Episode 10 (June 3, 2006)
Live at Gotham, Comedy Central, Season 1 Episode 3 (August 4, 2006)
Last Laugh '06, TV Movie (2006)
The Comedians of Comedy: Live at the El Ray, Comedy Showcase (2006)
The Sophisticated Misfit, Documentary (2007)
An Evening with P. Oswalt, Comedy Showcase (2007)
The Comedians of Comedy: Live at the Troubadour, Comedy Showcase (2007)
The Comedy Can Television Series, TV Movie (2007)
Heckler, Documentary (2007)
The Tonight Show with Jay Leno, NBC, 2 Episodes (2007–2008)
History of the Joke, TV Documentary (2008)
Largo, Comedy Showcase (2008)
G4 Presents Comic-Con '08 Live, TV Movie (2008)
Root of All Evil, Comedy Central, 6 Episodes (2008)
Late Show with David Letterman, CBS, Season 16 Episode 192 (August 21, 2009)
Patton Oswalt: My Weakness Is Strong, Comedy Showcase (2009)
Up Close with Carrie Keagan, NGTV, 2 Episodes (2009–2012)
Blood into Wine, Documentary (2010)
Real Time with Bill Maher, HBO, Season 8 Episode 13 (May 21, 2010)
Seattle Komedy Dokumentary, Documentary (2010)
The Daily Show with Jon Stewart, Comedy Central, Episode 2136 (January 6, 2011)
Patton Oswalt: Finest Hour, Comedy Showcase (2011)
Who the F#ck Is Chip Seinfeld (2011)
Made in Hollywood, STARS, Season 7 Episode 10 (November 26, 2011)
Sidewalks Entertainment, Syndicated, Season 22 Episode 12 (December 8, 2011)
The Late Late Show with Craig Ferguson, CBS, 4 Episodes (2011–2012)
Late Night with Jimmy Fallon, NBC, 3 Episodes (2011–2013)
Conan, TBS, 6 Episodes (2011–2013)
The Bitter Buddha, Documentary (2012)
Stand Down: True Tales from Stand-Up Comedy, Comedy Central (2012)
Comedy Bang! Bang!, Comedy Central (2012)
The American Cinematheque Tribute to Ben Stiller, TV Movie (2012)
The Brotherhood of the Traveling Rants, Documentary (2013)
Patton Oswalt—To Be Loved and Understood, Documentary (2013)
Bridgetown Documentary, Documentary (2014)
Out of Print, Documentary (2014)

Paula Jai Parker: Born in Cleveland, Ohio, Parker graduated from Howard University. She is best known for her role as Lexus in *Hustle and Flow* and as the voice of Trudy Proud on the *Proud Family*.

Comedy Filmography

The Apollo Comedy Hour, TV Series (1992–1993)
Soul Train, WCUI-TV, Season 23 Episode 22 (March 19, 1994)
Express Yourself, TV Series (2001)
My Coolest Years, TV Miniseries Documentary (2004)
Angels Can't Help but Laugh, Documentary (2007)
So You Want Michael Madesen?, Documentary (2008)
Mama and Me, Documentary (2011)
Kiss and Tell: The History of Black Romance in Movie (2011)
Reel Black Love, Documentary (2012)

Nikki Payne: Payne is a comedian and actress from Canada. She has won three Canadian Comedy Awards for Best Stand-up Newcomer and Best Female Stand-Up.

Comedy Filmography

The Halifax Comedy Fest, CBC, 2 Episodes (2002–2004)
Comedy Now!, The Comedy Network, Episode 129 (September 13, 2003)
The Next Big Thing, TV Miniseries Documentary (2003)
Video on Trial, MuchVideo, 11 Episodes (2005–2008)
The Naughty Show, TV Special (2007)
Hot Tamales Live Kiki Melendez Presents, TV Movie (2009)
The Hour, CBC, Episode 450 (April 28, 2010)
The Debaters, CBS, Episode 20 (2011)

Richard Pryor: Pryor was a stand-up comedian, actor, social critic, and writer. He was one of the first comedians to examine race and topical contemporary issues in his routines. He is regarded as one of the most important and influential stand-up comedians ever.

Nonfiction Writing

Pryor Convictions: And Other Life Sentences (1997)

Discography

Richard Pryor (1968)
CRAPS—After Hours (1971)
Pryor Goes Foxx Hunting (1971)
That Nigger's Crazy (1974)
. . . Is It Something I Said? (1975)
Bicentennial Nigger (1976)
Richard Pryor Meets . . . Richard and Willie and SLA!! (1976)
Insane (1976)
L.A. Jail (1976)
Holy Smoke (1976)
Are You Serious??? (1976)

Who Me, I'm Not Him (1977)
Black Ben the Blacksmith (1978)
The Wizard of Comedy (1978)
Wanted: Live in Concert (1978)
Outrageous (1979)
Rev. Du Rite (1981)
Live on Sunset Strip (1982)
Richard Pryor Live! (1982)
Supernigger (1982)
Here and Now (1983)
Richard Pryor . . . And It's Deep Too! (2000)
Anthology: 1968–1992 CDs (2002)
Evolution/Revolution: The Early Years (1966–1974) (2005)

Comedy Filmography

One Broadway Tonight, CBS, Episode 1 (August 31, 1964)
The Merv Griffin Show, NBC, 11 Episodes (1965)
The Kraft Summer Music Hall, TV Movie (1965)
The Ed Sullivan Show, CBS, 13 Episodes (1965–1970)
The Mike Douglas Show, Syndicated, 10 Episodes (1965–1975)
The Joey Bishop Show, ABC, 14 Episodes (1967–1969)
Operation: Entertainment, Episode 3 (January 19, 1968)
The Steve Allen Show, NBC, Episode 7 (April 9, 1968)
The Pat Boone Show, ABC, 5 Episodes (1968)
Operation: Entertainment, 2 Episodes (1968)
This Is Tom Jones, TV Series Documentary (1969)
The David Frost Show, Episode 294 (August 25, 1970)
The Phynx, Movie (1970)
Dynamite Chicken, Movie (1971)
Richard Pryor: Live and Smokin', Documentary (1971)
Wattstax, *Documentary* (1973)
Soul Train, TV Series Documentary (1973–1977)
The Tonight Show Starring Johnny Carson, NBC, 8 Episodes (1973–1984)
The Midnight Special, NBC, Episode 23 (May 24, 1974)
Saturday Night Live, NBC, Episode 7 (December 13, 1975)
The Richard Pryor Special?, TV Movie (1977)
The Richard Pryor Show, NBC, 4 Episodes (1977)
Richard Pryor Live in Concert, Documentary (1979)
Richard Pryor Live on the Sunset Strip, Documentary (1982)
Hollywood: The Gift of Laughter, TV Documentary (1982)
On Location: The Comedy Store's 11th Anniversary Show, TV Movie (1983)
Richard Pryor . . . Here and Now, Documentary (1983)
Pryor's Place, CBS, 10 Episodes (1984)
A Party for Richard Pryor, TV Special (1991)
The Comedy Store's 20th Birthday, TV Movie (1992)
Apollo Theatre Hall of Fame, TV Special Documentary (1993)

A Century of Cinema, Documentary (1994)
Apollo Theatre Hall of Fame, TV Special Documentary (1994)
Who Makes You Laugh?, TV Special (1995)
Biography, A&E, Episode 850 (July 8, 1996)
27th NAACP Image Awards, TV Special (1996)
The Blackberry Inn, TV Series (1996)
Sam Kinison: Why Did We Laugh?, TV Documentary (1998)
The Mark Twain Prize: Richard Pryor, TV Movie (2003)
Bitter Jester, Documentary (2003)

Jasper Redd: Born June 9, 1979, in Knoxville, Tennessee, Redd first became unique as a comedian because he performed his jokes with polyrhythmic timing. Since then, however, he uses more traditional performance techniques. He has appeared on several late night shows and is touring with Daniel Tosh.

Comedy Filmography

Premium Blend, Comedy Central, Season 8 Episode 6 (January 21, 2005)
Def Comedy Jam, HBO, Season 7 Episode 9 (October 29, 2006)
Last Call with Carson Daly, NBC, 2 Episodes (2006)
Late Night with Conan O'Brien, NBC (April 30, 2007)
The Comedians of Comedy: Live at the Troubadour (2007)
Comedy Central Presents, Comedy Central, Season 13 Episode 5 (January 23, 2009)
Tosh.0, Comedy Central, Season 2 Episode 5 (February 10, 2010)
Comics Unleashed (March 25, 2010)
Lopez Tonight, TBS (February 2, 2011)
Daniel Tosh: Happy Thoughts, Warm-up comic (2011)
BET's Comicview, BET, 1 Episode (2013)

Kate Rigg: Originally from Canada and Australia, Rigg moved to New York City and graduated from the Julliard School. She is a stand-up comedian who has appeared on NBC's *Late Friday* and National Lampoon's International Comedy DVD. She was a 2004 New York Foundation of the Arts fellow. She is a member of the Nuyorasian hip-hop band called Slanty Eyed Mama.

Comedy Filmography

Late Friday, NBC, Episode 27 (November 16, 2001)
Heroes of Comedy: Women on Top, TV Miniseries Documentary (2003)
SexTV, TV Series Documentary (September 11, 2004)
Queer Edge with Jack E. Jett, Q Television Network, Season 2 Episode 23 (December 13, 2005)
The Naughty Show, Video (2005)
Independent Lens, TV Series Documentary (2005)
Crossing the Line: Multiracial Comedians, Documentary (2008)
One Night Stand Up, Logo TV, Episode 6 (October 3, 2009)
Brunch with Bridget, LOGO TV (2009)
Kiki Melendez' Hot Tamales Live, TV Movie (2012)

Karen Ripley: Ripley is an American-born lesbian comic, songwriter, and actor. She has been performing stand-up for over twenty years. She spends her time teaching improv at the Harvey Milk Institute in San Francisco, California, and performing stand-up.

Comedy Filmography

Outlaugh!, Showcase (2006)
Wisecrack, Logo TV, Episode 8 (February 13, 2007)

Chris Rock: Born February 7, 1965, in Andrews, South Carolina, Rock grew up in Brooklyn. Rock began doing stand-up in 1984 in New York City and worked his way through the comedy scene there until getting noticed by Eddie Murphy, who then befriended him and gave him his first major film role. Since then, Rock has been a *Saturday Night Live* cast member, appeared in countless films, and has hosted the Oscars.

Nonfiction Writing

Rock This! (1997)

Discography

Born Suspect (1991)
Roll with the New (1997)
Bigger and Blacker (1999)
Never Scared (2005)

Comedy Filmography

Uptown Comedy Express (1987)
Showtime at the Apollo, NBC, 3 Episodes (1987–1989)
Comedy's Dirtiest Dozen (1988)
Who Is Chris Rock? (1989)
Ebony/Jet Showcase, BET (March 19, 1993)
HBO Comedy Half Hour, HBO (June 16, 1994)
Def Comedy Jam: Primetime, HBO (1994)
Chris Rock: Big Ass Jokes (1994)
Comic Relief VII, HBO (1995)
Def Comedy Jam, HBO (March 24, 1996)
Saturday Night Live, NBC, Season 22 Episode 5 (November 2, 1996)
State of the Union: Undressed (1996)
Chris Rock: Bring the Pain (1996)
The Tonight Show with Jay Leno, NBC, 9 Episodes (1996–2010)
The Chris Rock Show, HBO (1997–2000)
Comic Relief VIII, HBO (1998)
Best of the Chris Rock Show (1999)
Chris Rock: Bigger and Blacker (1999)
Late Night with Conan O'Brien, NBC, 8 Episodes (1999–2007)
The Daily Show with Jon Stewart, Comedy Central, 3 Episodes (2001–2010)
Heroes of Back Comedy, Comedy Central, Season 1 Episode 1 (February 4, 2002)
Last Call with Carson Daly, NBC (June 7, 2002)
Comedian, Documentary (2002)
MTV Video Music Awards, MTV, Host (2003)

Richard Pryor: I Ain't Dead Yet, #*&%$@!, Documentary (2003)
Real Time with Bill Maher, HBO, 6 Episodes (2003–2010)
Before They Were Kings, Vol. 1 (2004)
Chris Rock: Never Scared (2004)
The N Word, Documentary (2004)
Late Show with David Letterman, CBS, 8 Episodes (2004–2011)
The Aristocrats, Documentary (2005)
The 77th Annual Academy Awards, Host (2005)
Legends: Rodney Dangerfield, Documentary (2006)
Inside the Actor's Studio, Bravo, Season 13 Episode 5 (March 13, 2007)
Black Men: The Truth, Documentary (2007)
Tavis Smiley, PBS, 2 Episodes (2007–2010)
Chris Rock: Kill the Messenger (2008)
Why We Laugh: Black Comedians on Black Comedy, Documentary (2009)
Good Hair, Documentary (2009)
Make 'Em Laugh: The Funny Business in America, Documentary (2009)
Jimmy Kimmel Live!, ABC, 3 Episodes (2010–2012)
Late Night with Jimmy Fallon, NBC, 2 Episodes (2010–2012)
I Ain't Scared of You: A Tribute to Bernie Mac, Documentary (2011)
Talking Funny, Documentary (2011)
Inside Comedy, Showtime, Season 1 Episode 2 (February 2, 2012)
The Announcement, TV Movie Documentary (2012)
Woody Allen: A Documentary, Documentary (2012)
Eddie Murphy: One Night Only, TV Movie (2012)
Totally Biased with W. Kamau Bell, FX, 6 Episodes (2012–2013)
Comedians in Cars Getting Coffee, YouTube (2013)
12-12-12, Documentary (2013)
Tumor, It's in the System, Documentary (2013)
Todd vs. High School, Documentary (2013)

Mort Sahl: Sahl is a Canadian-born American comedian and actor. He was the first comedian to record a live album and the first to perform on college campuses. He was labeled the "Patriarch of new school of comedians." He is rated one of the best stand-up comedians of all time.

Nonfiction Writing

Heartland (1977)

Discography

Mort Sahl at Sunset (1955)
The Future Lies Ahead (1958)
1960, or Look Forward in Anger (1960)
A Way of Life (1960)
At the hungry i (1960)
The Next President (1960)
The New Frontier (1961)
On Relationships (1961)

Anyway . . . Onward (1967)
Sing a Song of Watergate (1973)
Mort Sahl's America (1997)

Edwin San Juan: Juan is a Filipino American actor and comedian. His routines focus on sharing his multicultural life experiences, using observational humor, world play, and poking fun at ethnic stereotypes. He is the creator of SlantED Comedy.

Discography

Edwin San Juan's Pacific Rim Comedy aka Slant Ed Comedy (2011)

Comedy Filmography

Latin Comedy Fiesta Vol. 1, Video (2003)

Inside Joke, TV Series (2004)

Comedy Zen, ImaginAsian TV, Season 1 Episode 5 (2006)

The Payaso Comedy Slam, TV Movie (2007)

Comics without Borders, Showtime, Episode 7 (October 23, 2008)

The Best Comics Unleashed with Byron Allen, Video (2008)

Rageous, TV Movie (2010)

Latino 101, NuvoTV, 3 Episodes (2010)

Gabriel Iglesias Presents Stand-Up Revolution, Comedy Central, Episode 5 (November 3, 2011)

Comedy.TV, Comedy Central, Season 1 Episode 28 (2012)

Vickie Shaw: Shaw is a Texas native and a preeminent lesbian comic. She grew up in a very conservative family, and when she came out first tried stand-up. She performs in stand-up venues, women's festivals, and Olivia cruises. Her comedic focus is on coming out, marriage, and motherhood.

Comedy Filmography

Wisecrack, Logo TV, Episode 5 (August 25, 2005)

Laughing Matters . . . More!, Showcase (2006)

Vickie Shaw: You Can Take the Girl Outta Texas, Comedy Special (2008)

Maria Shehata: Shehata is an Egyptian American comedian and actress born and raised in Columbus, Ohio. She blends Midwest with the Middle East, giving her a point of view that is hilarious and unique. She can be seen Comedy Central's *The Watch List* and at numerous comedy festivals.

Comedy Filmography

Just Like Us, Documentary (2010)

Bridging the Gap: A Middle East Comedy Conference, TV Movie (2010)

The Cradle of Comedy, Australia TV Show (2012)

100 Jokes, Documentary (2013)

Jen Slusser: A native Chicagoan, Slusser is a stand-up comic as well as a teacher, counselor, and artist. She has been featured on *Last Comic Standing, Upright Citizen's Brigade*, and NBC's *Starting Over* among other specials. She was also the vocal producer for the Los Angeles radio program *The Link* and is often on the Chicago radio program *Mancow's Morning Madhouse*.

Comedy Filmography

Wisecrack, Logo TV, Episode 13 (2005)
Outlaugh!, Documentary (2006)

DeAnne Smith: She is an award-winning Canadian-American comedian, writer, and columnist. In 2008, she won the Best Newcomer Award in Sydney Comedy Festival's Time Out. She continues to tour internationally.

Comedy Filmography

Last Comic Standing, NBC, Season 5 (2007)
The Comedy Network, Canada (2009)
Good News Week, Network Ten, 4 Episodes (2010–2011)
Funny as Hell, CTV (2011)
Melbourne International Comedy Festival, Channel Ten (2012)
Comedy Up Late, Comedy Central, Season 1, Episode 2 (2013)
The Late Late Show with Craig Ferguson, CBS, Season 9, Episode 105 (2013)
The Montreal Experience, TV Movie (2013)

JB Smoove: Smoove is an American actor and writer, who began his TV career on *Russell Simmons' Def Comedy Jam*. He is known for his recurring role as Leon on *Curb Your Enthusiasm.*

Discography

That's How I Dooz It (2012)

Comedy Filmography

Def Comedy Jam, Comedy Central, Season 5 Episode 11 (May 12, 1995)
Jimmy Kimmel Live!, ABC, 12 Episodes (2004–2010)
Ego Trip's Race-o-Rama, TV Documentary (2005)
Great Things about the Holidays, TV Movie (2005)
Talkshow with Spike Feresten, FOX, Season 3 Episode 10 (December 13, 2008)
The Tonight Show with Jay Leno, NBC, 6 Episodes (2008–2013)
Rise of the Radio Show, TV Series (2009)
Late Night with Jimmy Fallon, NBC, Season 1 Episode 292 (August 6, 2010)
Russell Simmons Presents: Stand-Up at the El Ray, Comedy Central, 6 Episodes (2010)
Cedric the Entertainer's Urban Circus, TV Movie (2010)
Comics Unleashed, Syndicated, 2 Episodes (2010–2011)
Funny as Hell, CTV (2011–2013)
Watch What Happens: Live, Bravo, Season 6 Episode 52 (March 29, 2012)
JB Smoove: That's How I Dooz It, TV Movie (2012)
Russell Simons Presents: The Ruckus, TV Series (2012)
Phunny Business: A Black Comedy, Documentary (2012)
Quality Balls, Documentary (2013)
Four Course with JB Smoove, MSG, Host (2013)
Gotham Comedy Live, Comedy Central (2013)

The Arsenio Hall Show, BET, Season 1, Episode 18 (2013)
Delivery, Documentary (2014)

Sommore: Sommore reigns as the undisputed "Queen of Comedy." Born in Trenton, New Jersey, she has been performing for years. She is a writer, producer, and entrepreneur. She can be seen on the stage internationally.

Discography

The Queens of Comedy (2001)

Comedy Filmography

BET's Comicview, BET (1994–1995)
Def Comedy Jam: All Stars Vol. 11, TV Special (1999)
The Queens of Comedy, Video Documentary (2001)
The Amanda Lewis Show, CBS, Episode 7 (September 8, 2001)
Latham Entertainment Presents, Video (2003)
Heroes of Comedy: Women on Top, TV Miniseries Documentary (2003)
The Late Late Show with Craig Kilborn, CBS, Episode 564 (November 15, 2004)
Weekends at the DL, Comedy Central, Season 1 Episode 18 (September 24, 2005)
Richard Pryor: The Funniest Man Dead or Alive, TV Special Documentary (2005)
The Tom Joyner Show, Syndicated, Episode 15 (January 21, 2006)
Live at Gotham, Comedy Central, Season 1 Episode 6 (September 1, 2006)
Def Comedy Jam, HBO, Episode 14 (September 10, 2006)
Something New, Video (2006)
Comedy Central Roast of Flavor Flav, TV Movie (2007)
Comics Unleashed, Syndicated, 3 Episodes (2007–2009)
Comics Unleashed, Syndicated, Episode 70 (January 30, 2008)
Sommore: The Queen Stands Alone, TV Movie (2008)
Why We Laugh: Black Comedians on Black Comedy, Documentary (2009)
Cedric the Entertainer's Urban Circus, Video (2012)
Sommore: Chandelier Status, TV Movie (2012)

Wanda Sykes: Sykes is an American writer, stand-up comedian, actress, and voice artist. In 2004 she was named one of the funniest people in America. She is openly gay.

Nonfiction Writing

Yeah, I Said It (2005)

Comedy Filmography

Stand-Up Spotlight, VH1 (1988)
HBO Comedy Showcase, HBO (1995)
Comedy Central Presents, Comedy Central, Episode 1 (December 1, 1998)
Late Night with Conan O'Brien, NBC, 6 Episodes (1999–2008)
The Tonight Show with Jay Leno, NBC, 41 Episodes (2001–2013)
100 Sexiest Artists, TV Documentary (2002)
Premium Blend, Comedy Central, 4 Episodes (2002–2003)
Heroes of Comedy: Women on Top, TV Miniseries, Episode 3 (March 5, 2003)

Chappelle's Show, Comedy Central, Episode 14 (July 16, 2003)

MADtv, FOX, Episode 194 (September 27, 2003)

Wanda Sykes: Tongue Untied, Documentary (2003)

Richard Pryor: I Ain't Dead Yet, #*%$#@!!, TV Documentary (2003)

The Daily Show with Jon Stewart, Comedy Central, 4 Episodes (2003–2011)

Bar Mitzvah Bash!, TV Movie (2004)

Wanda Does It, Comedy Central (2004)

Last Call with Carson Daly, NBC, 2 Episodes (2004–2006)

Ellen: The Ellen DeGeneres Show, NBC, 10 Episodes (2004–2013)

Richard Pryor: The Funniest Man Dead or Alive, TV Special Documentary (2005)

The Late Late Show with Craig Ferguson, CBS, 6 Episodes (2005–2011)

That's What I Am Talking About, CBS (February 2006)

Girls Who Do: Comedy, BBC, Episode 1 (August 13, 2006)

Train Wreck!, Video Documentary (2006)

Wanda Sykes: Sick and Tired, TV Documentary (2006)

The Cho Show, VH1 (2008)

Wanda Sykes: I'ma Be Me, TV Movie (2008)

Late Night with Jimmy Fallon, NBC, Episode 139 (October 30, 2009)

The Tonight Show with Conan O'Brien, NBC, Episode 125 (December 16, 2009)

The Jay Leno Show, NBC, 3 Episodes (2009–2010)

Close Up, TV Guide Network, Episode 99 (February 27, 2010)

The Wanda Sykes Show, FOX, 20 Episodes (2010)

Larry King Live, CNN, 2 Episodes (2010)

The Rosie Show, Episode 2, OWN (October 11, 2011)

Chelsea Lately, E!, 2 Episodes (2012)

NewNowNext Vote with Wanda Sykes, TV Movie (2012)

Totally Biased with W. Kamau Bell, FX, Season 1, Episode 12 (2012)

The Out List, Documentary (2013)

Wanda Sykes Presents Herlarious, TV Movie (2013)

Wil Sylvince: Born and raised in Brooklyn, New York, Sylvince's comedy gives a fresh outlook on political and social issues. He has performed at New York's comedy clubs and colleges across the country.

Comedy Filmography

The Big Black Comedy Show, Vol. 3, Video (2005)

Def Comedy Jam, HBO, Season 8 Episode 5 (February 3, 2008)

Live at Gotham, Comedy Central, Episode 23 (October 16, 2009)

Russell Simmons Presents: The Ruckus, Comedy Central, Episode 4 (February 9, 2012)

Amy Tee: Deemed a rising star by the *Boston Globe*, Tee performs in world famous clubs, theaters, and colleges across the country. She is a regular performer at the Boston Comedy Festival and featured on Satellite Radio and the Lesbian Lounge.

Comedy Filmography

Laughing Matters . . . Next Gen, Video (2009)

Baratunde Thurston: Born in Washington, DC, Thurston attended Harvard University and graduated with a degree in philosophy. He has authored four books and contributes to the *Huffington Post*, *Weekly Dig*, and was the director of digital at *The Onion* until 2012. Thurston is also the cofounder of the African American political blog *jackandjillpolitics.com*. He currently lives and performs stand-up comedy in New York City.

Nonfiction Writing

Better than Crying: Poking Fun at Politics, the Press and Pop Culture (2004)
Keep Jerry Falwell Away from My Oreo Cookies (2005)
Thank You Congressional Pages (For Being So Damn Sexy!) (2006)
How to Be Black (2012)

Comedy Filmography

Life In Perpetual Beta, Documentary (2010)
Totally Biased with W. Kamau Bell, FX (2013)

Lily Tomlin: Tomlin is an American actress, comedian, writer, and producer. She has been a major force in American comedy since the 1960s when she began performing stand-up. She has won many awards ranging from a Tony to a Grammy. Her humor is sharp and insightful, but also wacky.

Discography

The Best of Lily Tomlin (2003)
This Is a Recording (2011)
And That's the Truth (2011)
Modern Scream (2011)

Comedy Filmography

The Garry Moore Show, CBS, Episode 217 (September 11, 1966)
The Glen Campbell Goodtime Hour, CBS, 2 Episodes (March, 1970)
The Best on Record, TV Special (1970)
The Tonight Show Starring Johnny Carson, NBC, 18 Episodes (1970–1991)
The David Frost Show, 2 Episodes (1971–1972)
A Royal Gala Variety Performance, TV Movie (1972)
The New Bill Cosby Show, CBS, Episode 2 (September 18, 1972)
The Carol Burnett Show, CBS, Episode 143 (November 8, 1972)
The Lily Tomlin Show, TV Movie (1973)
Dinah's Place, NBC, Episode 66 (October 29, 1973)
Lily, TV Movie (1974)
Saturday Night Live, NBC, 2 Episodes (1975–1983)
The American Film Institute's 10 Anniversary Special, TV Movie (1977)
Disco Fever: "Saturday Night Fever" Premiere Party, TV Movie (1977)
The Midnight Special, NBC, Episode 151 (January 30, 1981)
Lily: Sold Out, TV Movie (1981)
Lily for President?, TV Special (1982)
Saturday Night Life, TV Movie (1984)
Late Show with David Letterman, CBS, 3 Episodes (1985–1999)
Waiting Tables, Video Documentary Short (1986)

Lily Tomlin, Documentary (1986)

The First Annual American Comedy Awards, TV Movie (1987)

A Show of Concern: The Heart of America Responds, TV Movie (1987)

Funny, You Don't Look 200: A Constitutional Vaudeville, TV Documentary (1987)

Free to Be . . . a Family, TV Movie (1988)

Appearing Nightly, TV Movie (1990)

An Evening with . . . TV Movie (1990)

American Masters, PBS, Episode 37 (July 1, 1991)

One on One with Josh Tesh, NBC, Episode 51 (November 17, 1991)

A Party for Richard Pryor, TV Special (1991)

The Player, Movie (1992)

The Tonight Show with Jay Leno, NBC, 6 Episodes (1992–1996)

Free to Laugh: A Comedy and Music Special for Amnesty International, TV Special (1992)

In A New Light: A Call to Action in the War against AIDS, TV Documentary (1992)

A Comedy Salute to Andy Kaufman, TV Documentary (1995)

Who Makes You Laugh?, TV Special (1995)

The Celluloid Closet, Documentary (1995)

The Roseanne Show, ABC, Episode 8 (September 23, 1998)

Reno Finds Her Mom, Documentary (1998)

Get Bruce, Documentary (1999)

AFI's 100 Years . . . 100 Stars: America's Greatest Screen Legends, TV Special Documentary (1999)

Saturday Night Live 25, TV Special Documentary (1999)

The Rosie O'Donnell Show, NBC, 2 Episodes (1999–2000)

Heroes of Black Comedy, TV Miniseries Documentary (2002)

A Salute to Robert Altman, an American Maverick, TV Movie (2002)

Gilda Radner's Greatest Moments, TV Special (2002)

Great Women of Television Comedy, TV Movie (2003)

Women on Top: Hollywood and Power, TV Documentary (2003)

The Mark Twain Prize: Lily Tomlin, TV Movie (2003)

Lily's Detroit, Documentary Short (2004)

Superstar in a Housedress, Documentary (2004)

Goodnight, We Love You, Documentary (2004)

Inside TV Land: Primetime Politics, TV Special Documentary (2004)

Happy Birthday Oscar Wilde, TV Documentary (2004)

The Late Late Show with Craig Ferguson, CBS, 3 Episodes (2004–2011)

The Gym, TBD, Episode 5 (October 10, 2005)

Live from New York: The First 5 Years of Saturday Night Live, TV Documentary (2005)

The Daily Show with Jon Stewart, Comedy Central, Episode 1288 (June 8, 2006)

Enough Rope with Andrew Denton, ABC1, Episode 116 (August 28, 2006)

The Kennedy Center Honors: A Celebration of the Performing Arts, TV Movie (2008)

Make 'Em Laugh: The Funny Business of America, PBS, Episode 1 (January 14, 2009)

Kathy Griffin: My Life on the D List, Bravo, Episode 32 (June 15, 2009)

Comedy Central Roast of Joan Rivers, TV Special (2009)

A Bundle of Sticks, Documentary (2010)

The 7PM Project, Network Ten, Episode 339 (February 25, 2011)

Saturday Night Live Backstage, TV Documentary (2011)
Vito, Documentary (2011)
Carol Channing: Larger than Life, Documentary (2012)
Betty White's 2nd Annual 90th Birthday, TV Movie (2013)
Inside Comedy, Comedy Central (2013)
Why We Laugh: Funny Women, TV Movie Documentary (2013)
One for Ten, Documentary (2013)
Richard Pryor: Omit the Logic, Documentary (2013)

Tapan Trivedi: Born in India, Trivedi moved to the United States at the age of 22 and began doing stand-up comedy at open mike nights in Houston. After some struggle, he became a finalist in the Funniest Person in Houston competition. Trivedi has toured with comedy festivals around the country and gone to Japan and Korea to perform for the US military.

Aisha Tyler: Tyler is an American actress, stand-up comedian, and author. She attended Dartmouth College where she earned a degree in environmental policy and founded the Dartmouth Rockapellas, a group devoted to spreading social awareness through song.

Discography
Aisha Tyler: Is Lit; Live at the Fillmore (2009)

Comedy Filmography
Politically Incorrect, Comedy Central, Season 9 Episode 3 (March 22, 2000)
Talk Soup, E!, 3 Episodes (2001–2002)
The Tonight Show with Jay Leno, NBC, 4 Episodes (2001–2013)
Player$, G4, Season 1 Episode 6 (2002)
Last Comic Standing, TV Series, NBC (2003)
Heroes of Comedy: Women on Top, TV Miniseries Documentary (2003)
Tavis Smiley, PBS, Season 1 Episode 16 (January 26, 2004)
On-Air with Ryan Seacrest, E!, Episode 17 (January 30, 2004)
The Late Late Show with Craig Kilborn, CBS, Episode 540 (October 4, 2004)
G-Phoria 2004, TV Documentary (2004)
Ellen: The Ellen DeGeneres Show, NBC, Episode 230 (February 2, 2005)
Comic's Climb at USCAF, TV Documentary (2005)
The Late, Late Show with Craig Ferguson (2005)
LIVE! with Kelly, ABC, 2 Episodes (2005–2007)
Siskel and Ebert, ABC, 3 Episodes (2006)
Up Close with Carrie Keagan, NGTV, Episode 110 (August 29, 2007)
Under the Balls: The Life of Bill Wrangler, Video Documentary Short (2007)
Yes We Can, Video Short (2008)
History of a Joke, TV Documentary (2008)
Just for Laughs, BBC, Episode 5 (October 26, 2009)
Aisha Tyler Is It: Live at the Fillmore, TV Documentary (2009)
The Hour, CBC, Season 7 Episode 158 (June 7, 2011)
The Talk, CBS, 174 Episodes (2011–2012)
Late Show with David Letterman, CBS (July 22, 2013)
Funny: The Documentary, Documentary (2013)

Why We Laugh: Funny Women, TV Documentary (2013)
Totally Biased with W. Kamau Bell, FX, Season 1 Episode 21 (2013)
Late Night with Jimmy Fallon, NBC (2013)
Whose Line Is It Anyway?, CW, 9 Episodes (2013)

Robin Tyler: Tyler is a comedian and one of the first original plaintiffs in the California Supreme Court lawsuit *Tyler v. County of LA*. She has produced over twenty-five major Women's Music and Comedy Festivals and is a pioneer of the gay liberation and civil rights movements.

Discography

Try It—You'll Like It (1972)
Wonder Women (1973)
Always a Bridesmaid, Never a Groom (1979)
Just Kidding (1985)

Comedy Filmography

The NBC Comedy Hour, NBC, Episode 15 (May 13, 1956)
Wide Wide World, NBC, Episode 1 (June 25, 1958)
The George Gobel Show, NBC, Episode 115 (February 3, 1959)
The Steve Allen Plymouth Show, NBC, Episode 154 (March 14, 1960)
The Ed Sullivan Show, CBS, 4 Episodes (1960–1965)
ABC Close-Up!, ABC, Episode 43 (June 12, 1962)
Howard K. Smith, ABC, Episode 56 (March 24, 1963)
The Jerry Lewis Show, NBC, Episode 2 (September 28, 1963)
The Week that Was, BBC (1964)
The Joey Bishop Show, NBC, Episode 312 (July 17, 1968)
The Smothers Brothers Comedy Hour, CBS, Episode 68 (March 23, 1969)
The Merv Griffin Show, NBC, 3 Episodes (1970–1977)
Rowan and Martin's Laugh-In, NBC, Episode 109 (January 10, 1972)
The Krofft Comedy Hour, TV Series (1978)
hungry i Reunion, Documentary (1981)
American Masters, TV Documentary (1989)
The World of Jewish Humor, Documentary (1990)
Wisecracks, Documentary (1992)
A Stand Up Life, TV Movie (1993)
When Comedy Went to School, Video Documentary (2008)
Make 'Em Laugh: The Funny Business of America, TV Series Documentary (2009)
Looking for Lenny, Documentary (2011)

Sheryl Underwood: Underwood first gained public notice as the first female finalist in the Miller Lite Comedy Search in 1989. She is currently a cohost on *The Talk* on CBS.

Discography
Sheryl Underwood: Too Much Information (2005)
Comedy Filmography
Def Comedy Jam, STARZ (1993)

Make Me Laugh, TV Series (1997)
Oh Drama!, TV Series (2000)
Tough Crowd with Colin Quinn, TV Series (2002)
Jamie Foxx Presents Laffapalooza, BET, Season 1 Episode 2 (May 2, 2003)
Heroes of Comedy: Women on Top, TV Miniseries Documentary (2003)
Comedy Central Presents, Comedy Central, Episode 96 (July 27, 2003)
Weekends at the DL, Comedy Central, Episode 19 (September 30, 2005)
Just for Laughs, BBC, Episode 46 (November 13, 2005)
A Comic's Climb at the USCAF, TV Documentary (2005)
Made You Look: Top 25 Moments of BET History, TV Special Documentary (2005)
BET's Comicview, TV Series, 16 Episodes (2005–2006)
Getting Played, TV Movie (2006)
Bring That Year Back 2006: Laugh Now, Cry Later, TV Movie (2006)
Comics Unleashed, CBS, 4 Episodes (2007–2010)
1st Amendment Stand Up, Starz, 4 Episodes (2007–2010)
The Best of Comics Unleashed with Byron Allen, Video (2008)
Laffapalooza, TV Movie (2009)
The Talk, CBS, 492 Episodes (2011–2013)
Phunny Business: A Black Comedy, Documentary (2012)
Why We Laugh: Funny Women, TV Movie Documentary (2013)
The Arsenio Hall Show, BET, Episode 39 (2013)

Azhar Usman: Usman was born on December 23, 1975, in Skokie, Illinois, and now lives in Chicago. He has a law degree from the University of Minnesota. He practiced law for some time before performing comedy, starting in 2001. Much of his comedy surrounds issues of Muslim identity and culture. Georgetown University listed Azhar as one of the world's 500 Most Influential Muslims. His *Allah Made Me Funny—Official Muslim Comedy Tour* has toured over twenty countries around the world.

Comedy Filmography
Me and the Mosque, Comedy Showcase (2005)
Allah Made Me Funny: Live in Concert, Comedy Showcase (2008)
Stand Up: Muslim-American Comics Come of Age, PBS (2009)

Alex Valdez: Valdez grew up in Santa Ana, California, where he still resides. He lost his eyesight at the age of 7. He emceed at the Newport Beach where he met Jim O'Brien—his partner in comedic routines.

Comedy Filmography
Look Who's Laughing, Documentary (1994)

Sandra Valls: Valls is a human rights activist, writer, and comedian. GLAAD has honored her with a Recognition Award for her groundbreaking achievements in production.

Nonfiction Writing
Out on the Edge: America's Rebel Comics (2008)

Comedy Filmography

Habla Again, TV Documentary (2004)
Inside Joke, TV Series (2004)
1st Amendment Stand Up, Starz, Episode 2 (October 21, 2005)
The Latin Divas of Comedy, Documentary (2007)
I Love "Shanghai Surprise"!, Video Short (2007)
One Night Stand Up, Logo TV, Episode 1 (January 29, 2008)
Jill-Michele Meleàn: Guys Have It Easy, TV Movie (2008)
Latino 101, NuvoTV, 4 Episodes (2010)
Pride: The Gay and Lesbian Comedy Slam, TV Movie (2010)

Greg Walloch: Walloch uses humor to expose cultural and social fault lines. He stars in the concert film, *Fuck the Disabled* along with a cast that included Stephen Baldwin and Jerry Stiller. He tours all around the world. Walloch has cerebral palsy.

Comedy Filmography

The Howard Stern Radio Show, FOX, Episode 1 (June 17, 1998)
Howard Stern, FOX, 2 Episodes (August, 1998)
Keeping It Real: The Adventures of Greg Walloch, Documentary (2001)
The Moth, TV Series (2002)
Fuck the Disabled, Documentary (2002)

Sheng Wang: Wang is a Taiwanese-American stand-up comic who began performing in the San Francisco Bay area in 1998. His routines are based on personal stories, experiences, and humorous observations. Wang currently lives and performs in New York City.

Comedy Filmography

Live at Gotham, Comedy Central, Season 2 Episode 4 (June 8, 2007)
Comedy Central Presents (January 28, 2011)
John Oliver's New York Stand Up Show, Episode 306 (August 3, 2012)
Totally Biased with W. Kamau Bell, FX, Season 2, Episode 37 (2013)

Suzanne Westenhoefer: Westenhoefer is an out lesbian stand-up comedian. After accepting a dare, she began her career delivering gay-themed material to straight audiences. Her comedy centers on her life as a lesbian.

Discography

Nothing in My Closet but My Clothes (1997)
I'm Not Cindy Brady (2000)
Guaranteed Fresh (2003)

Comedy Filmography

Out There, TV Movie (1993)
HBO Comedy Half-Hour, HBO, Episode 34 (July 14, 1994)
Comic Relief VII, TV Special Documentary (1995)
Lauren Hutton and . . . CBS**,** Episode 115 (February 27, 1996)
Politically Incorrect, Comedy Central, Episode 93 (April 10, 2002)
Late Show with David Letterman, CBS, Episode 1597 (March 18, 2003)

Where the Girls Are, Documentary (2003)
Suzanne Westenhoefer: Live at the Village, TV Movie (2004)
Wisecrack, Logo TV, Episode 1 (January 1, 2005)
Laughing Matters, Documentary (2005)
I've Got a Secret, CBS, 7 Episodes (2006)
Suzanne Westenhoefer: A Bottom on Top, TV Movie (2007)
Pride Comedy Jam, TV Movie (2011)
Out in the Desert, Documentary (2013)

Karen Williams: Williams started doing comedy because it didn't cost anything. Quickly, she realized that she could use comedy to promote self-awareness and self-confidence. Presently, she performs nationally and teaches stand-up comedy at her alma mater, Cleveland State University.

Discography
Human Beings: What a Concept (1999)

Comedy Filmography
We're Funny That Way, Documentary (1998)
I Need a Snack, Comedy Special (2009)

Katt Williams: Williams was born on September 2, 1973, in Cincinnati, Ohio. In 1999, Williams became a presence at The Improv, The Comedy Club, and The Icehouse as well as had his own room at The Hollywood Park Casino. His goal is to build a comedy empire and restore dignity to the profession of stand-up comedy.

Discography
Katt Williams Live: Let a Playa Play (2006)
Katt Williams: It's Pimpin' Pimpin' (2009)
Katt Williams: Katt Box (3 CD set) (2009)
Katt Williams: American Hustle (2010)
Katt Williams: Pimp Chronicles, Pt. 1 (2010)
Katt Williams: Pimpadelic (2012)

Comedy Filmography
BET Comicview, BET, 2 Episodes (2005)
Def Comedy Jam, HBO, Season 7 Episode 4 (October 1, 2006)
Katt Williams: The Pimp Chronicles Pt. 1 (2006)
Katt Williams Live (2006)
Comic Relief: Hurricane Katrina, Showcase (2006)
Comedy Central Roast of Flavor Flav, Roastmaster (2007)
Katt Williams: American Hustle (2007)
Katt Williams: It's Pimpin' Pimpin' (2008)
Why We Laugh: Black Comedians on Black Comedy, Documentary (2009)
Katt Williams Presents: Katthouse Comedy, Emcee in Comedy Showcase (2009)
All Star Comedy Jam, Showcase (2009)
Katt Williams: Pimpadelic (2009)
The Katt Phenomenon, Short Documentary (2009)

Katt Williams: 9 Lives, Documentary (2010)
Comics Unleashed, CBS, Season 7 Episode 5 (February 6, 2012)
Katt Williams: Kattpacalypse, TV Movie (2012)
Iceberg Slim: Portrait of a Pimp, Documentary (2012)

Ali Wong: Wong was born in San Francisco, where she was selected as the best comedian of 2009. She has since moved to Los Angeles, California. In 2010 she was named one of seven comics to watch. She has performed at the Just for Laughs Comedy Festival and will be in the new NBC series, *Are You There Vodka? It's Me Chelsea.*

Comedy Filmography
The Tonight Show with Jay Leno, NBC, Episode 1221 (July 15, 2011)
Chelsea Lately, E!, 5 Episodes (2011–2012)
Controversial Racist, Funny or Die Sketch Video (2012)
Funny As Hell, CTV, Season 3, Episode 2 (2013)
Hey Girl, MTV, 5 Episodes (2013)
@midnight, Comedy Central, Season 1, Episode 9 (2013)

Alysia Wood: Born in Louisiana, Wood started doing comedy during her tenure in Seattle but has now relocated to Los Angeles. Several different radio shows and magazines have recognized her as an up-and-coming new comedian. She was a finalist in California's Funniest Female Competition. While she has not had any television appearances yet, she does have several videos on YouTube.

Discography
Princess (2012)

Nick Youssef: A stand-up comic from Los Angeles, California, Youssef performs regularly at the World Famous Comedy Store, Hollywood Improv, and Laugh Factory.

Maysoon Zayid: Zayid is a New Jersey born actress, comedian, and activist. Labeling herself as a Palestinian Muslim virgin with cerebral palsy, she performs self-deprecating routines. She is considered one of America's first Muslim women comedians and the first person ever to perform stand-up in Palestine and Jordan.

Comedy Filmography
Arab-American Comedy Tour, Movie (2005)
Stand Up: Muslim-American Comics Come of Age, Movie (2009)
The Muslims Are Coming!, Documentary (2012)
The Arab Americans, Documentary (2013)
A Thousand and One Journeys: The Arab Americans, Documentary (2013)